CASE CLOSED

VOLUME 2

Gosho Aoyama

Case Briefing:

Subject: **Jimmy Kudo**
Occupation: **High School Student/Detective**
Special Skills: **Analytical thinking and deductive reasoning**

The subject is hot on the trail of a pair of suspicious men in black when he is attacked from behind and is administered a strange substance which physically transforms him into a first grader. Realizing that he is a hunted man, the subject takes on the new identity of first grader Conan Edogawa and stays with his friend and neighbor Rachel Moore. When the subject confides in the eccentric inventor Dr. Agasa about his troubles, they decide to keep his true identity a secret for the safety of those around him. As the subject desperately seeks a cure for his condition, he continues to assist the police force with their most baffling cases. The only problem is that nobody takes him seriously anymore. Will the subject ever get back to his old self again?

Table of Contents

CASE CLOSED

CONFIDEN

ZZZ ZZZ

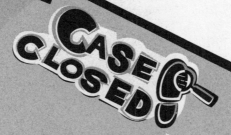

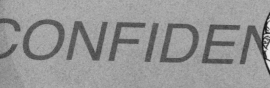

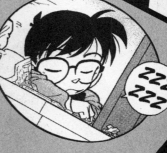

CASE CLOSED

Volume 2 • Action Edition

GOSHO AOYAMA

English Adaptation
Naoko Amemiya

Translation
Joe Yamazaki

Touch-up & Lettering
Walden Wong

Cover & Graphics Design
Veronica Casson

Editor
Andy Nakatani

Managing Editor **Annette Roman**

Director of Production **Noboru Watanabe**

Editorial Director **Alvin Lu**

Sr. Director of Licensing & Acquisitions **Rika Inouye**

Vice President of Sales **Joe Morici**

Vice President of Marketing **Liza Coppola**

Executive Vice President **Hyoe Narita**

Publisher **Seiji Horibuchi**

© 1994 Gosho Aoyama/Shogakukan, Inc.
First published by Shogakukan, Inc. in Japan as "Meitantei Conan"
New and adapted artwork and text © 2004 VIZ, LLC.
All rights reserved.

Printed in the U.S.A.
Published by VIZ, LLC
P.O. Box 77010
San Francisco, CA 94107

Action Edition
10 9 8 7 6 5 4 3 2 1
First printing, October 2004

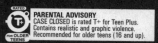

FILE 1:
A LUCRATIVE TAILING JOB

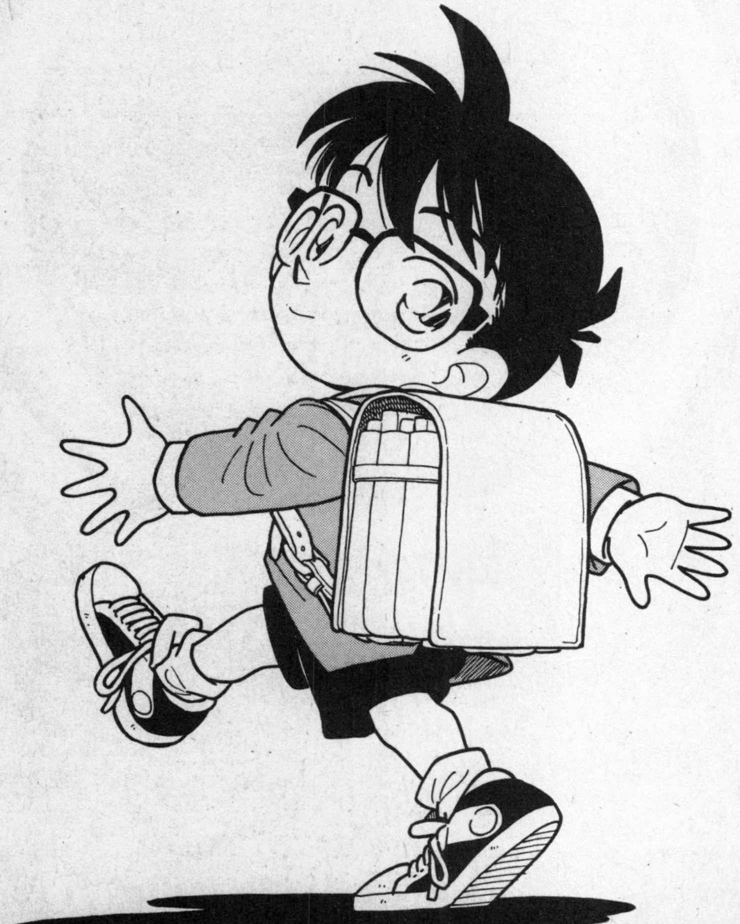

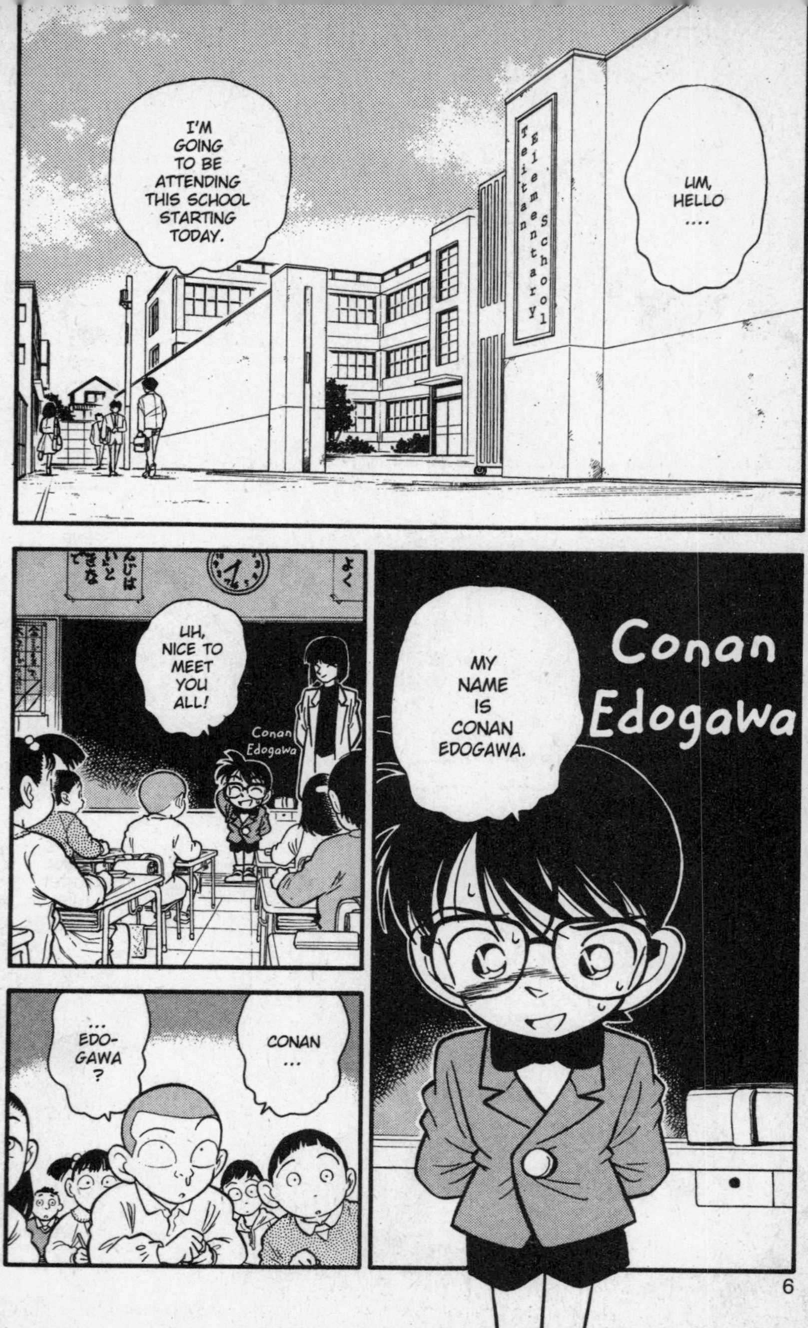
UM, HELLO ....
Teitan Elementary School
I'M GOING TO BE ATTENDING THIS SCHOOL STARTING TODAY.
MY NAME IS CONAN EDOGAWA.
Conan Edogawa
UH, NICE TO MEET YOU ALL!
Conan Edogawa
CONAN ...
... EDO-GAWA ?

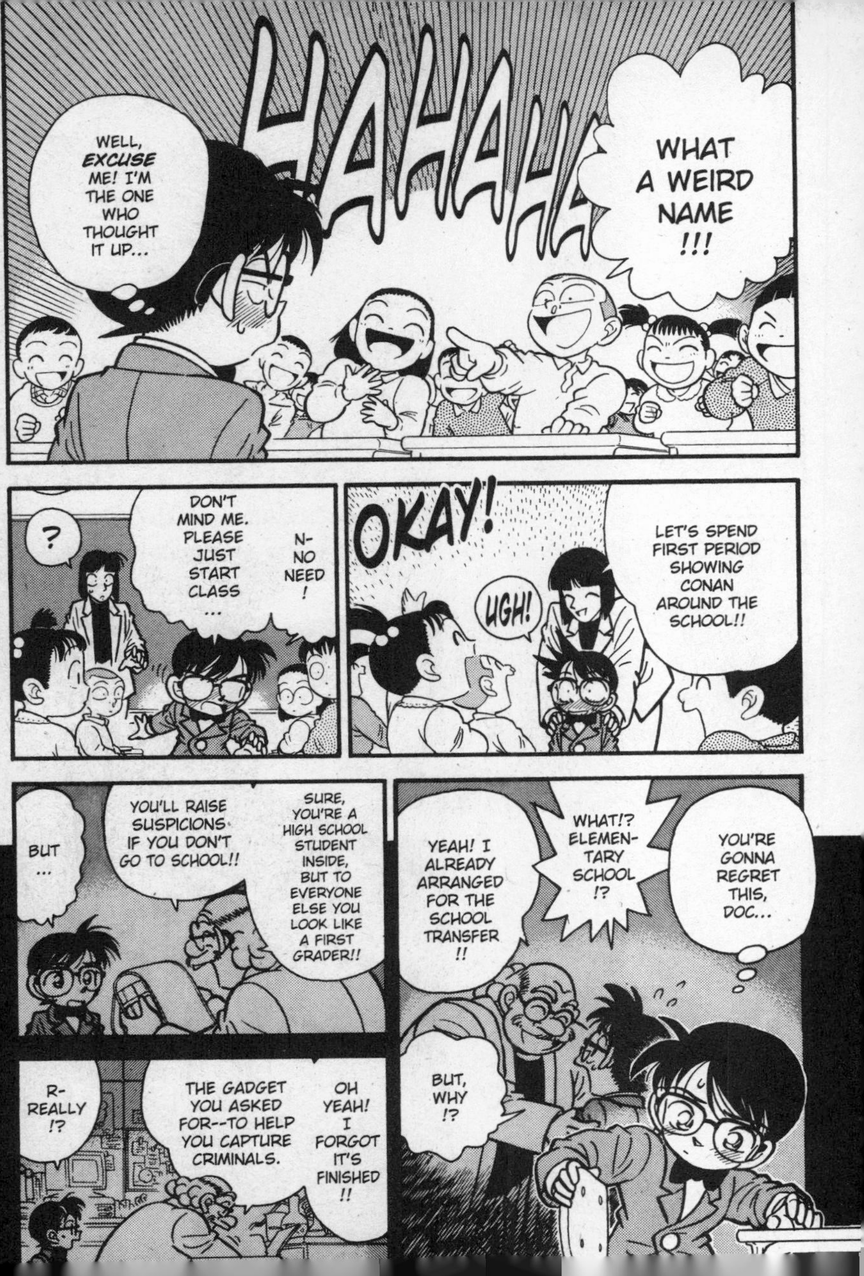

WHAT A WEIRD NAME!!!
HAHAHA
WELL, *EXCUSE* ME! I'M THE ONE WHO THOUGHT IT UP...
LET'S SPEND FIRST PERIOD SHOWING CONAN AROUND THE SCHOOL!!
OKAY!
UGH!
N-NO NEED!
DON'T MIND ME. PLEASE JUST START CLASS...
?
YOU'RE GONNA REGRET THIS, DOC...
WHAT!? ELEMENTARY SCHOOL!?
YEAH! I ALREADY ARRANGED FOR THE SCHOOL TRANSFER!!
BUT, WHY!?
SURE, YOU'RE A HIGH SCHOOL STUDENT INSIDE, BUT TO EVERYONE ELSE YOU LOOK LIKE A FIRST GRADER!!
YOU'LL RAISE SUSPICIONS IF YOU DON'T GO TO SCHOOL!!
BUT...
OH YEAH! I FORGOT IT'S FINISHED!!
THE GADGET YOU ASKED FOR--TO HELP YOU CAPTURE CRIMINALS.
R-REALLY!?

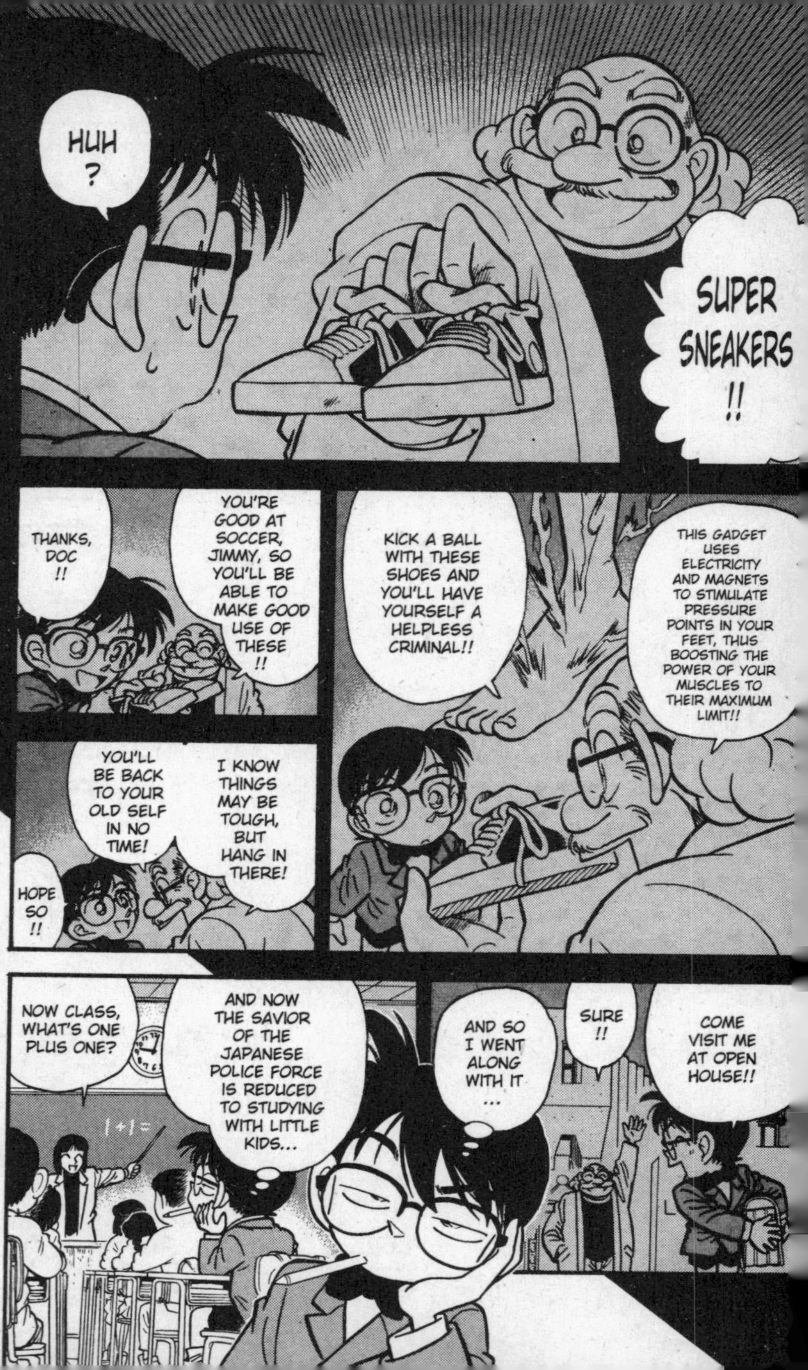

SUPER SNEAKERS !!
HUH ?
THIS GADGET USES ELECTRICITY AND MAGNETS TO STIMULATE PRESSURE POINTS IN YOUR FEET, THUS BOOSTING THE POWER OF YOUR MUSCLES TO THEIR MAXIMUM LIMIT!!
KICK A BALL WITH THESE SHOES AND YOU'LL HAVE YOURSELF A HELPLESS CRIMINAL!!
YOU'RE GOOD AT SOCCER, JIMMY, SO YOU'LL BE ABLE TO MAKE GOOD USE OF THESE !!
THANKS, DOC !!
I KNOW THINGS MAY BE TOUGH, BUT HANG IN THERE!
YOU'LL BE BACK TO YOUR OLD SELF IN NO TIME!
HOPE SO !!
COME VISIT ME AT OPEN HOUSE!!
SURE !!
AND SO I WENT ALONG WITH IT ...
AND NOW THE SAVIOR OF THE JAPANESE POLICE FORCE IS REDUCED TO STUDYING WITH LITTLE KIDS...
NOW CLASS, WHAT'S ONE PLUS ONE?
1+1=

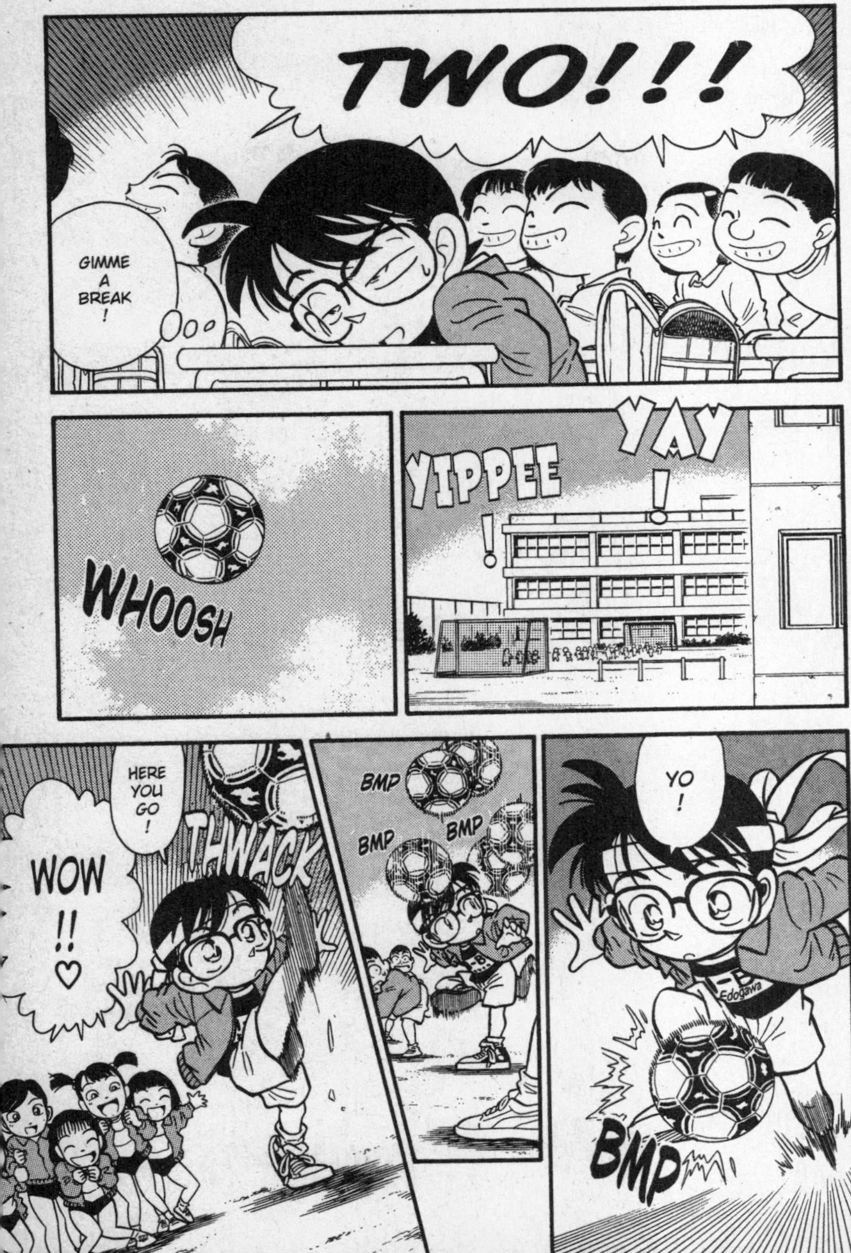
TWO!!!
GIMME A BREAK!
YAY!
YIPPEE!
WHOOSH
YO!
BMP
BMP
BMP
BMP
HERE YOU GO!
THWACK
WOW!! ♥

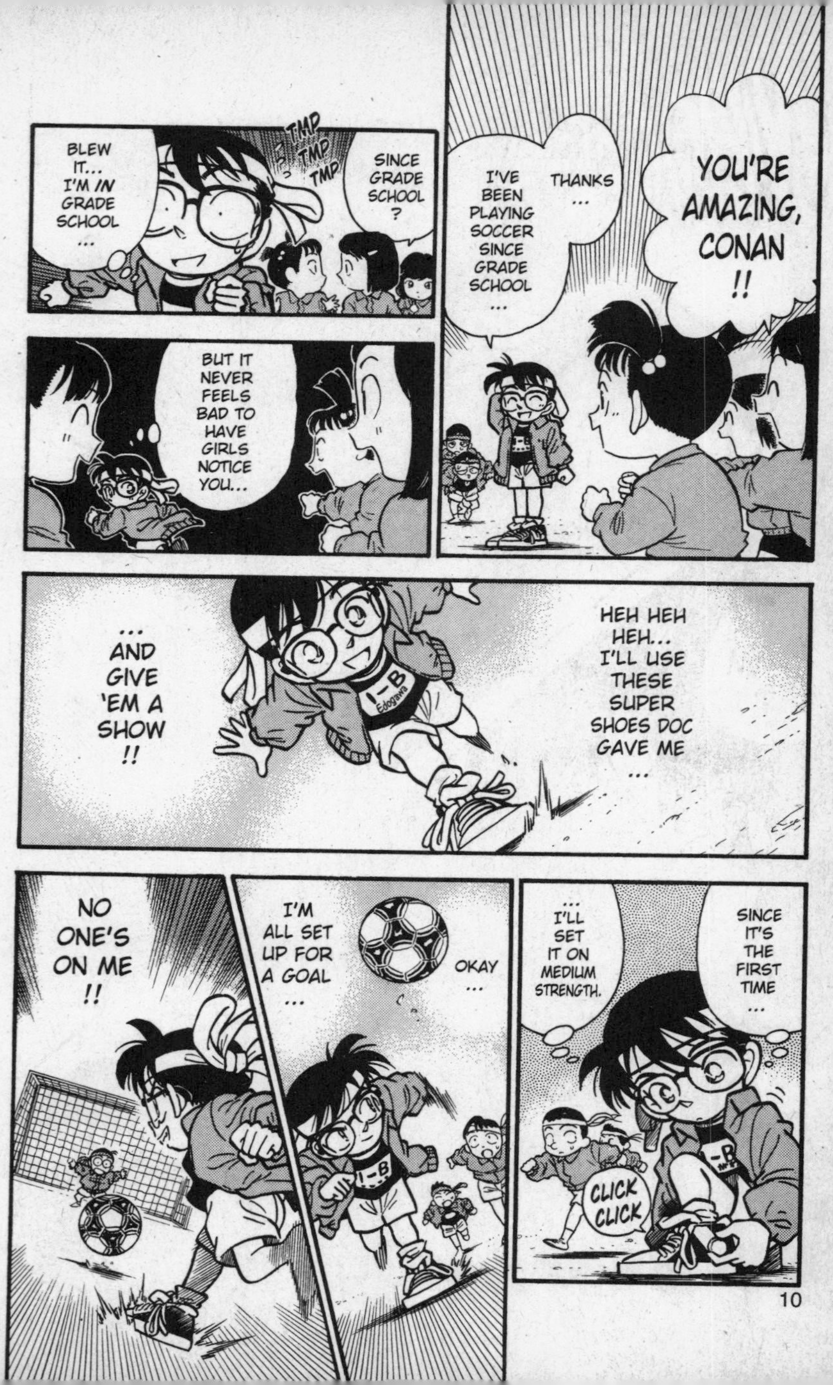

YOU'RE AMAZING, CONAN !!
THANKS ...
I'VE BEEN PLAYING SOCCER SINCE GRADE SCHOOL ...
SINCE GRADE SCHOOL ?
TMP TMP TMP
BLEW IT... I'M *IN* GRADE SCHOOL ...
BUT IT NEVER FEELS BAD TO HAVE GIRLS NOTICE YOU...
HEH HEH HEH... I'LL USE THESE SUPER SHOES DOC GAVE ME ...
... AND GIVE 'EM A SHOW !!
SINCE IT'S THE FIRST TIME ...
... I'LL SET IT ON MEDIUM STRENGTH.
CLICK CLICK
OKAY ...
I'M ALL SET UP FOR A GOAL ...
NO ONE'S ON ME !!

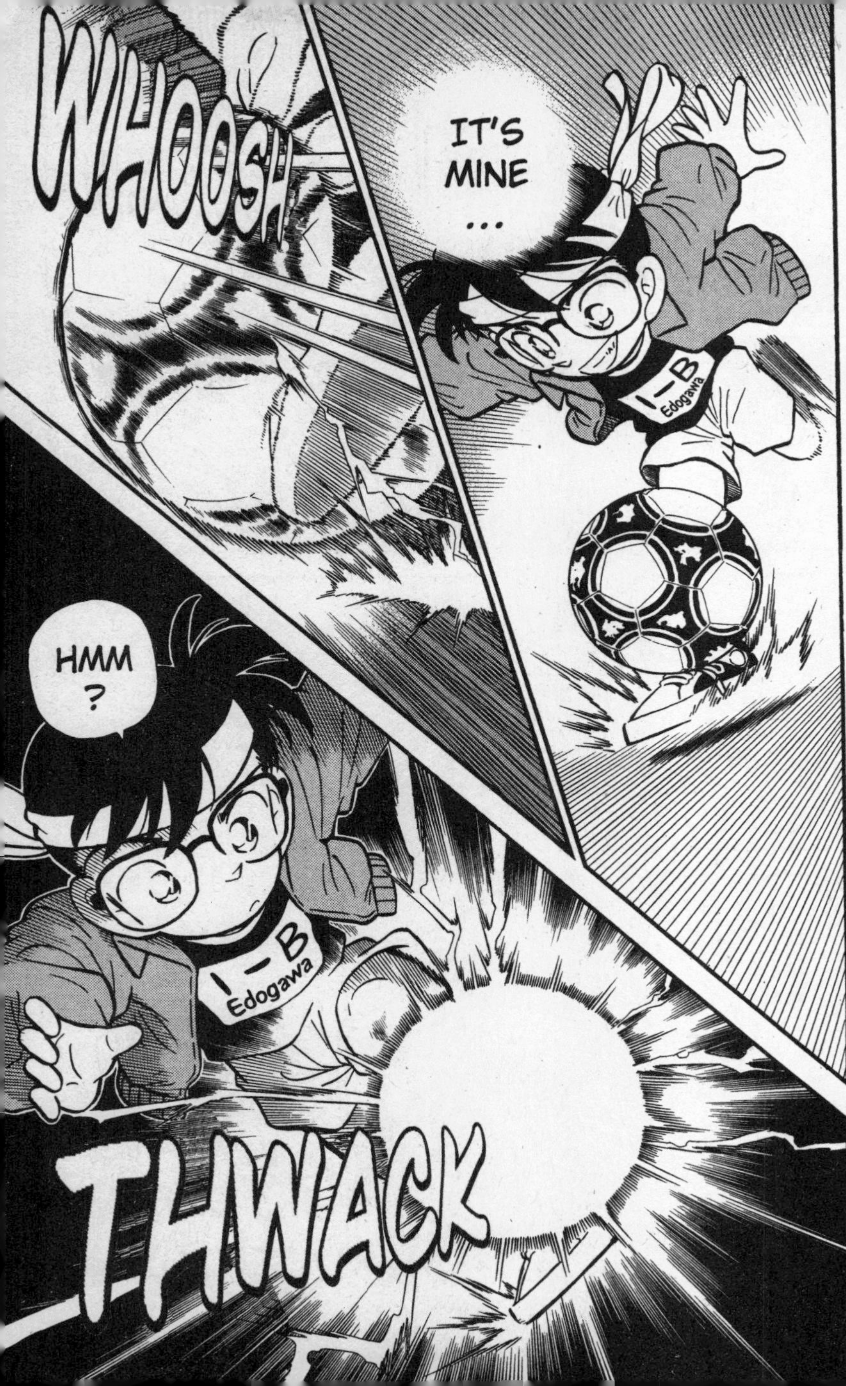
IT'S MINE ...
I—B
Edogawa
WHOOSH
HMM ?
I—B
Edogawa
THWACK

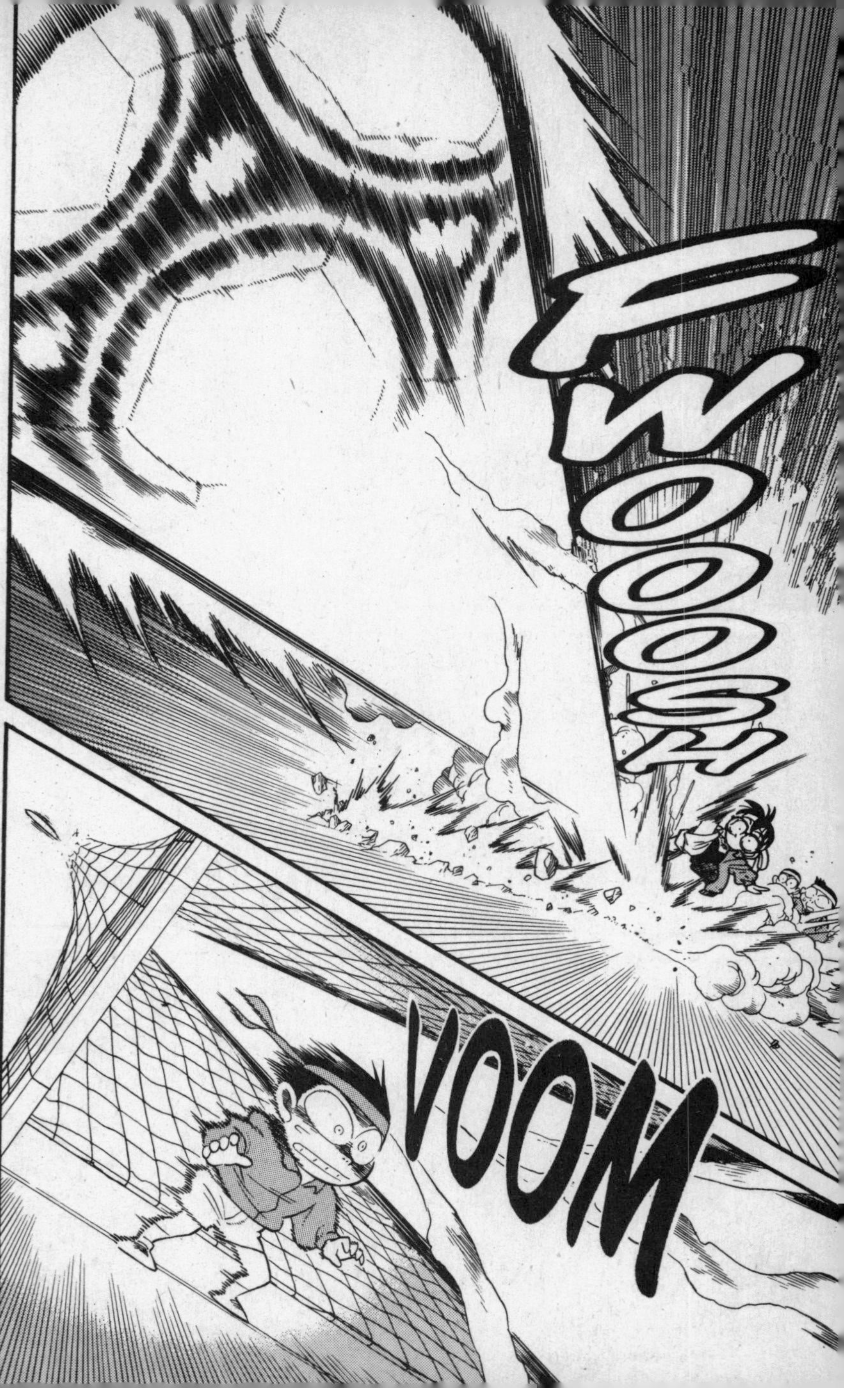
WHOOOSH
VOOM

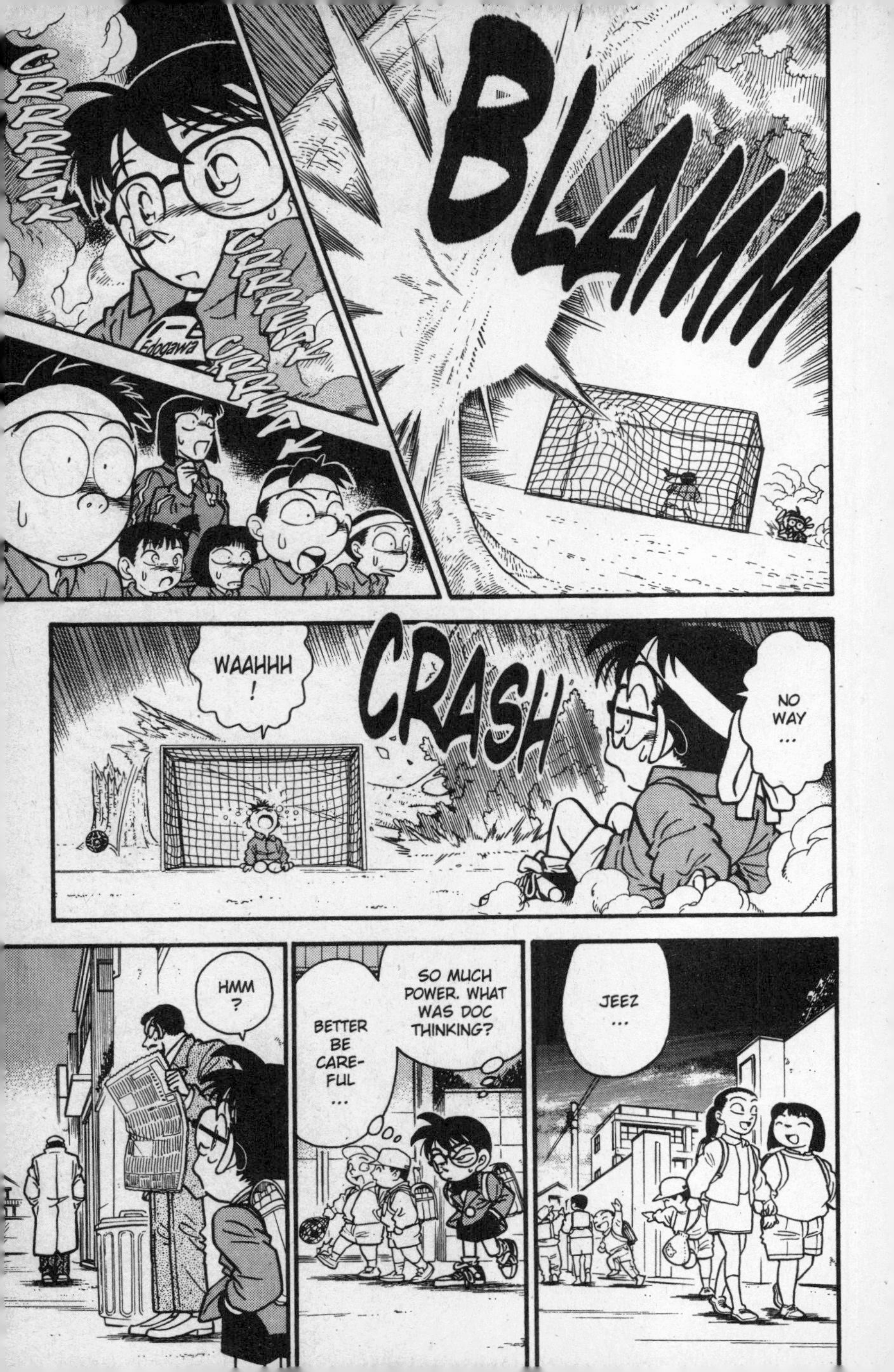
BLAMM
CRRREAK
CRRREAK
CRRREAK
Edogawa
NO WAY ...
CRASH
WAAHHH !
JEEZ ...
SO MUCH POWER. WHAT WAS DOC THINKING?
BETTER BE CARE-FUL ...
HMM ?

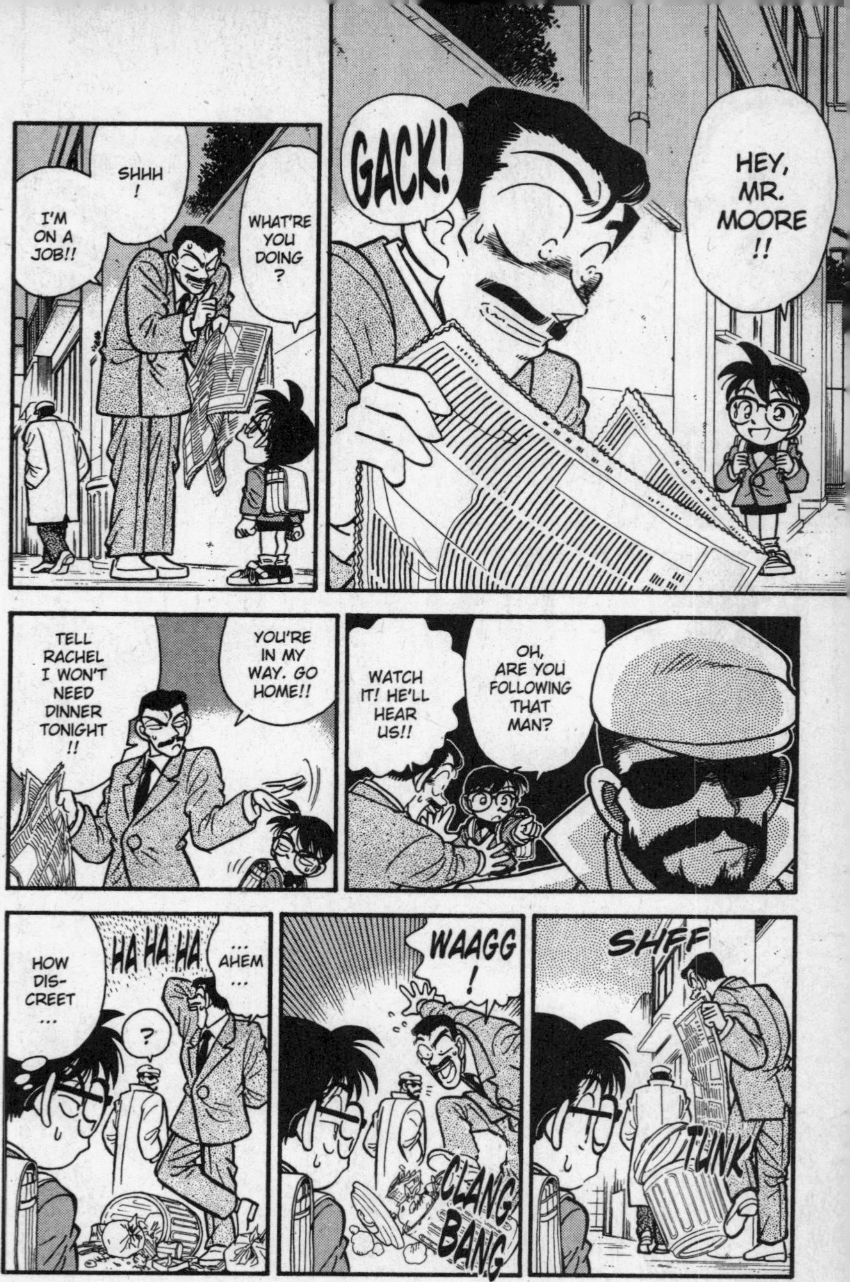
HEY, MR. MOORE !!
GACK!
WHAT'RE YOU DOING ?
SHHH !
I'M ON A JOB!!
OH, ARE YOU FOLLOWING THAT MAN?
WATCH IT! HE'LL HEAR US!!
YOU'RE IN MY WAY. GO HOME!!
TELL RACHEL I WON'T NEED DINNER TONIGHT !!
SHFF
TUNK
WAAGG !
CLANG BANG
... AHEM ...
HA HA HA
HOW DIS-CREET ...
?

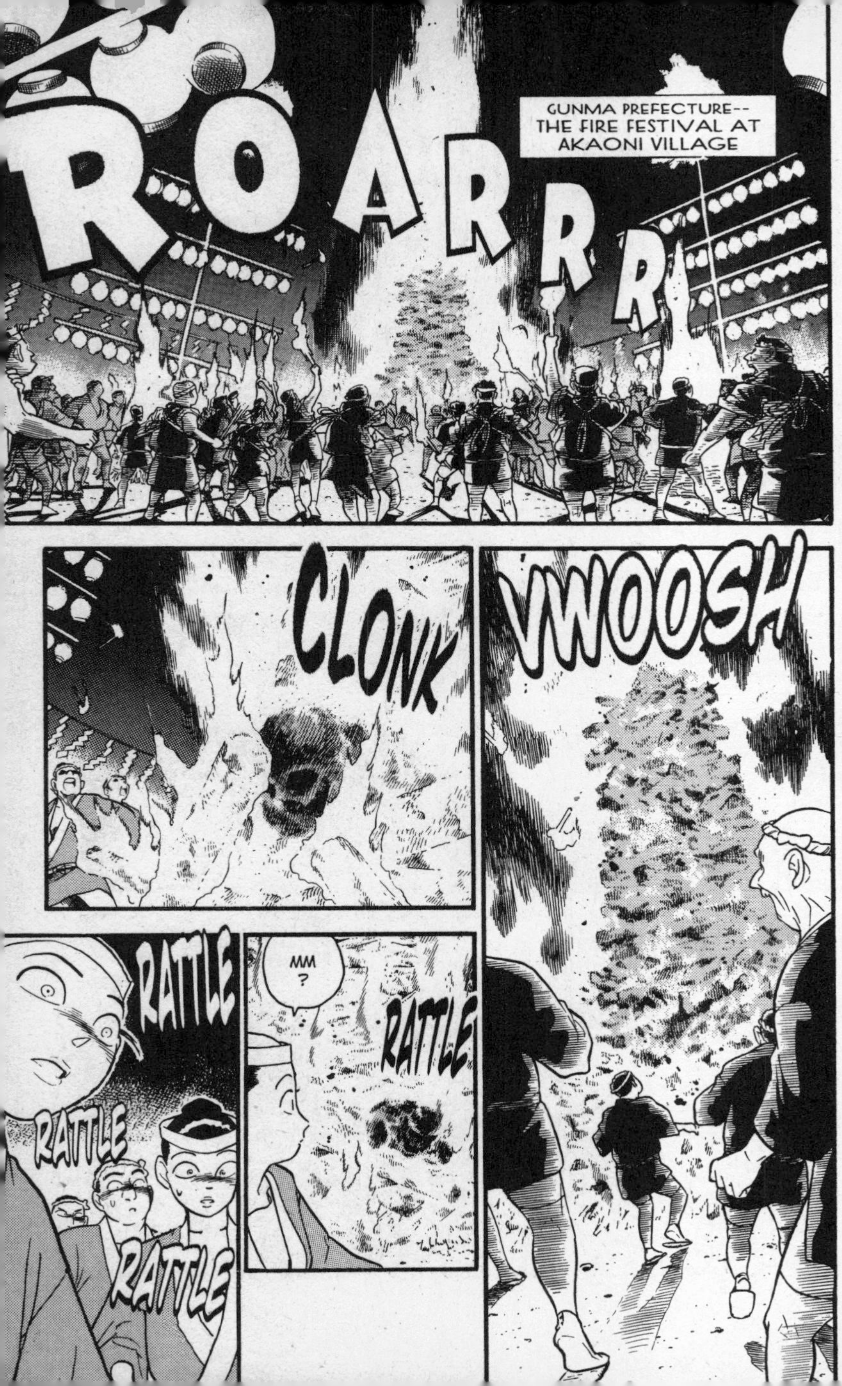
GUNMA PREFECTURE-- THE FIRE FESTIVAL AT AKAONI VILLAGE
ROARRR
VWOOSH
CLONK
MM ?
RATTLE
RATTLE
RATTLE
RATTLE

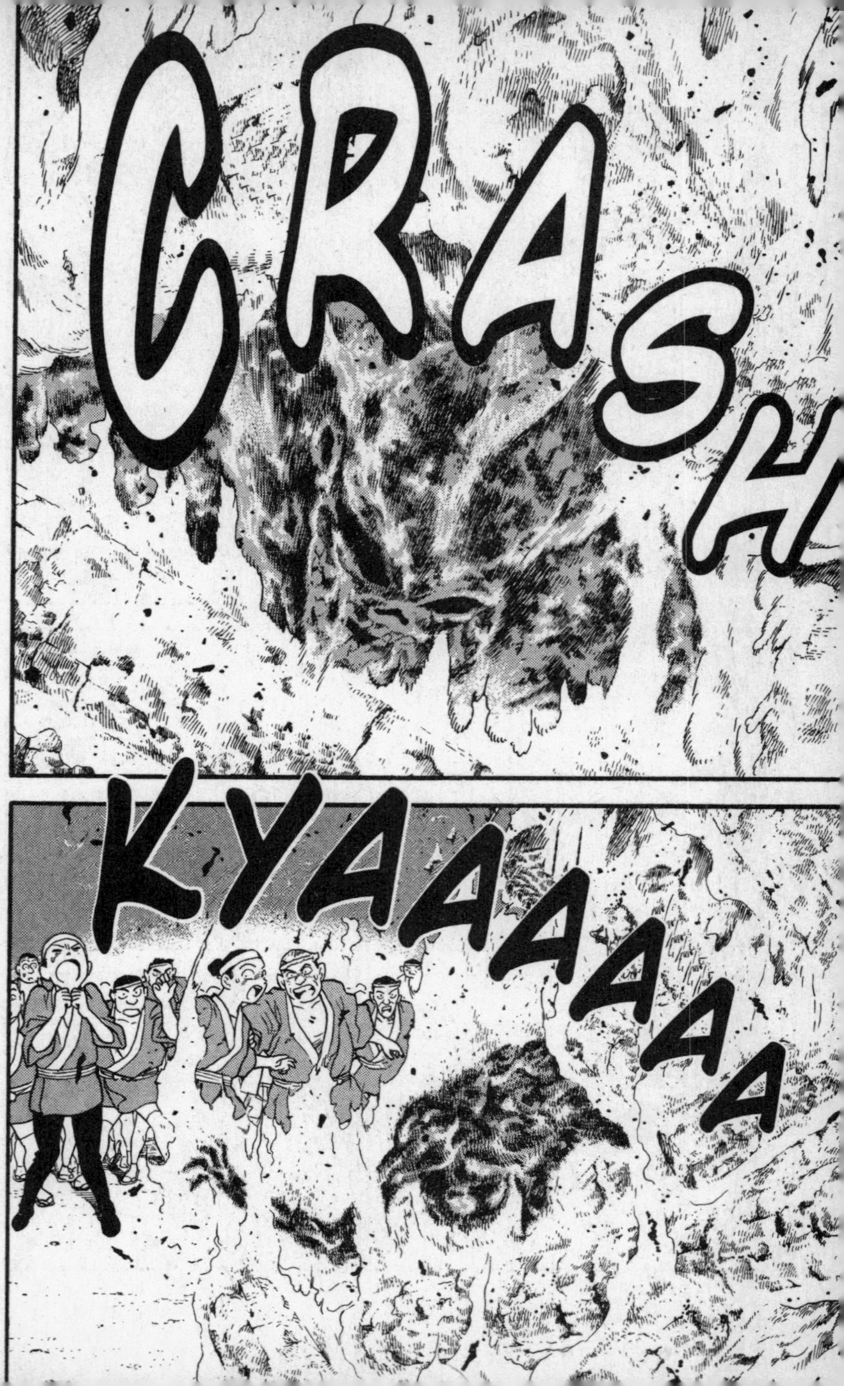
CRASH
KYAAAAAAA

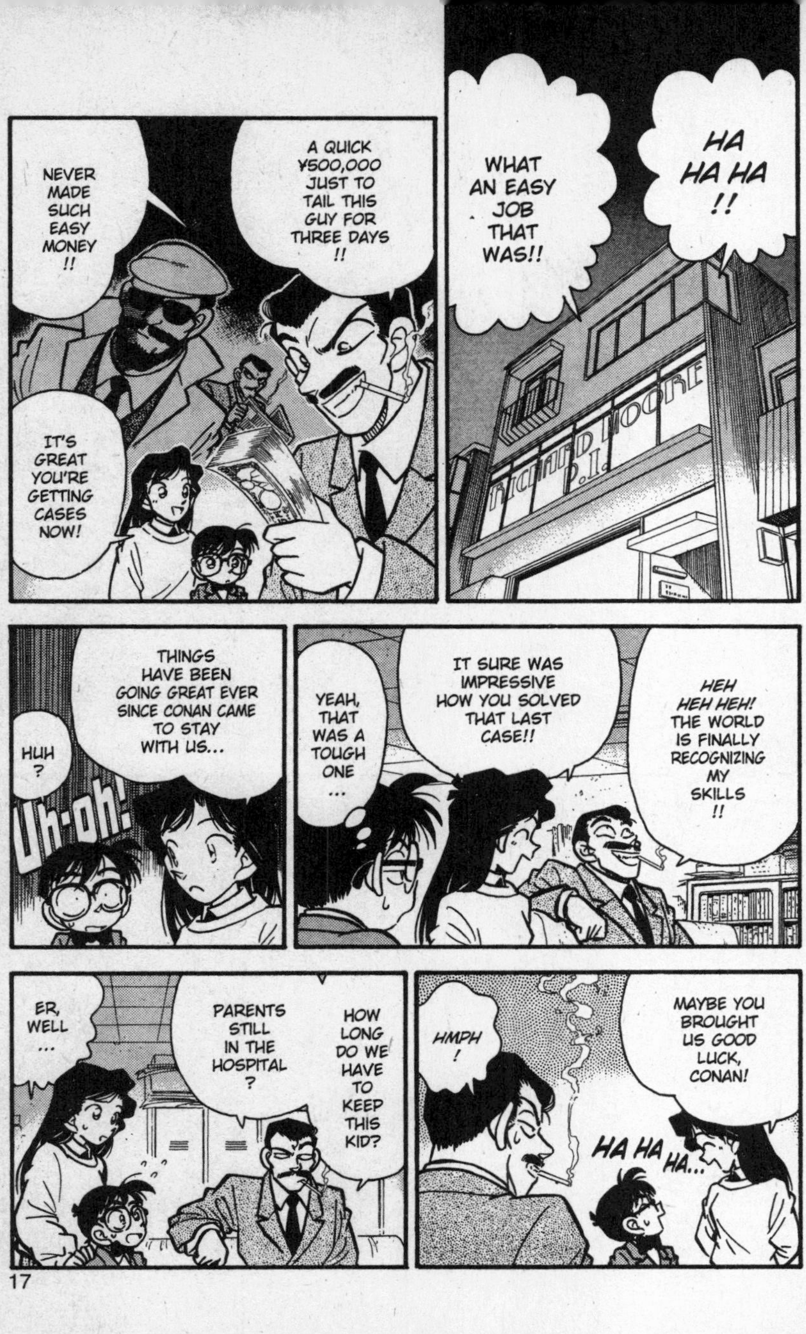

HA HA HA !!
WHAT AN EASY JOB THAT WAS!!
RICHARD MOORE P.I.
A QUICK ¥500,000 JUST TO TAIL THIS GUY FOR THREE DAYS !!
NEVER MADE SUCH EASY MONEY !!
IT'S GREAT YOU'RE GETTING CASES NOW!
HEH HEH HEH! THE WORLD IS FINALLY RECOGNIZING MY SKILLS !!
IT SURE WAS IMPRESSIVE HOW YOU SOLVED THAT LAST CASE!!
YEAH, THAT WAS A TOUGH ONE ...
THINGS HAVE BEEN GOING GREAT EVER SINCE CONAN CAME TO STAY WITH US...
HUH ?
Uh-oh!
MAYBE YOU BROUGHT US GOOD LUCK, CONAN!
HMPH !
HA HA HA...
HOW LONG DO WE HAVE TO KEEP THIS KID?
PARENTS STILL IN THE HOSPITAL ?
ER, WELL ...

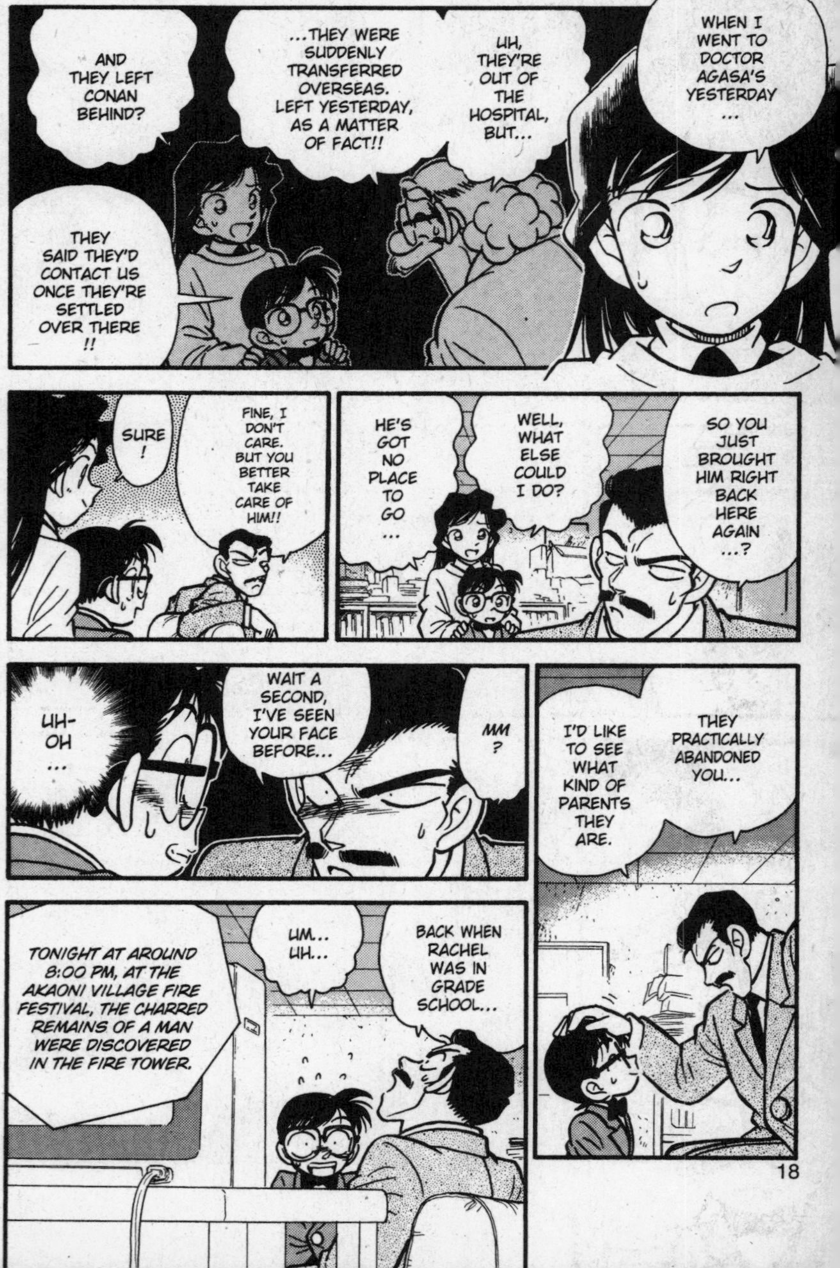

WHEN I WENT TO DOCTOR AGASA'S YESTERDAY ...
UH, THEY'RE OUT OF THE HOSPITAL, BUT...
...THEY WERE SUDDENLY TRANSFERRED OVERSEAS. LEFT YESTERDAY, AS A MATTER OF FACT!!
AND THEY LEFT CONAN BEHIND?
THEY SAID THEY'D CONTACT US ONCE THEY'RE SETTLED OVER THERE !!
SO YOU JUST BROUGHT HIM RIGHT BACK HERE AGAIN ...?
WELL, WHAT ELSE COULD I DO?
HE'S GOT NO PLACE TO GO ...
FINE, I DON'T CARE. BUT YOU BETTER TAKE CARE OF HIM!!
SURE !
THEY PRACTICALLY ABANDONED YOU...
I'D LIKE TO SEE WHAT KIND OF PARENTS THEY ARE.
MM ?
WAIT A SECOND, I'VE SEEN YOUR FACE BEFORE...
UH-OH ...
BACK WHEN RACHEL WAS IN GRADE SCHOOL...
UM... UH...
TONIGHT AT AROUND 8:00 PM, AT THE AKAONI VILLAGE FIRE FESTIVAL, THE CHARRED REMAINS OF A MAN WERE DISCOVERED IN THE FIRE TOWER.

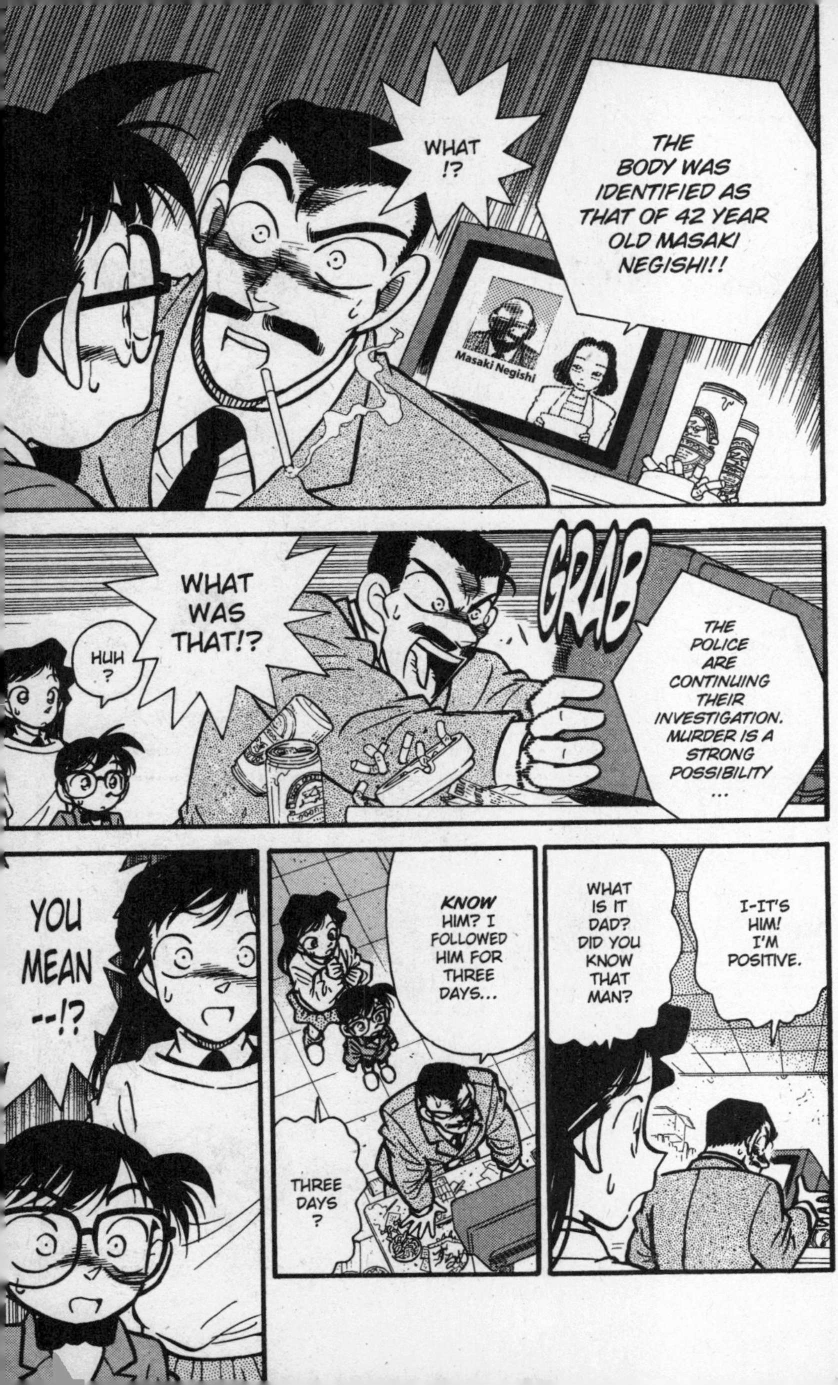
THE BODY WAS IDENTIFIED AS THAT OF 42 YEAR OLD MASAKI NEGISHI!!
WHAT !?
Masaki Negishi
THE POLICE ARE CONTINUING THEIR INVESTIGATION. MURDER IS A STRONG POSSIBILITY ...
GRAB
WHAT WAS THAT!?
HUH ?
I-IT'S HIM! I'M POSITIVE.
WHAT IS IT DAD? DID YOU KNOW THAT MAN?
KNOW HIM? I FOLLOWED HIM FOR THREE DAYS...
THREE DAYS ?
YOU MEAN --!?

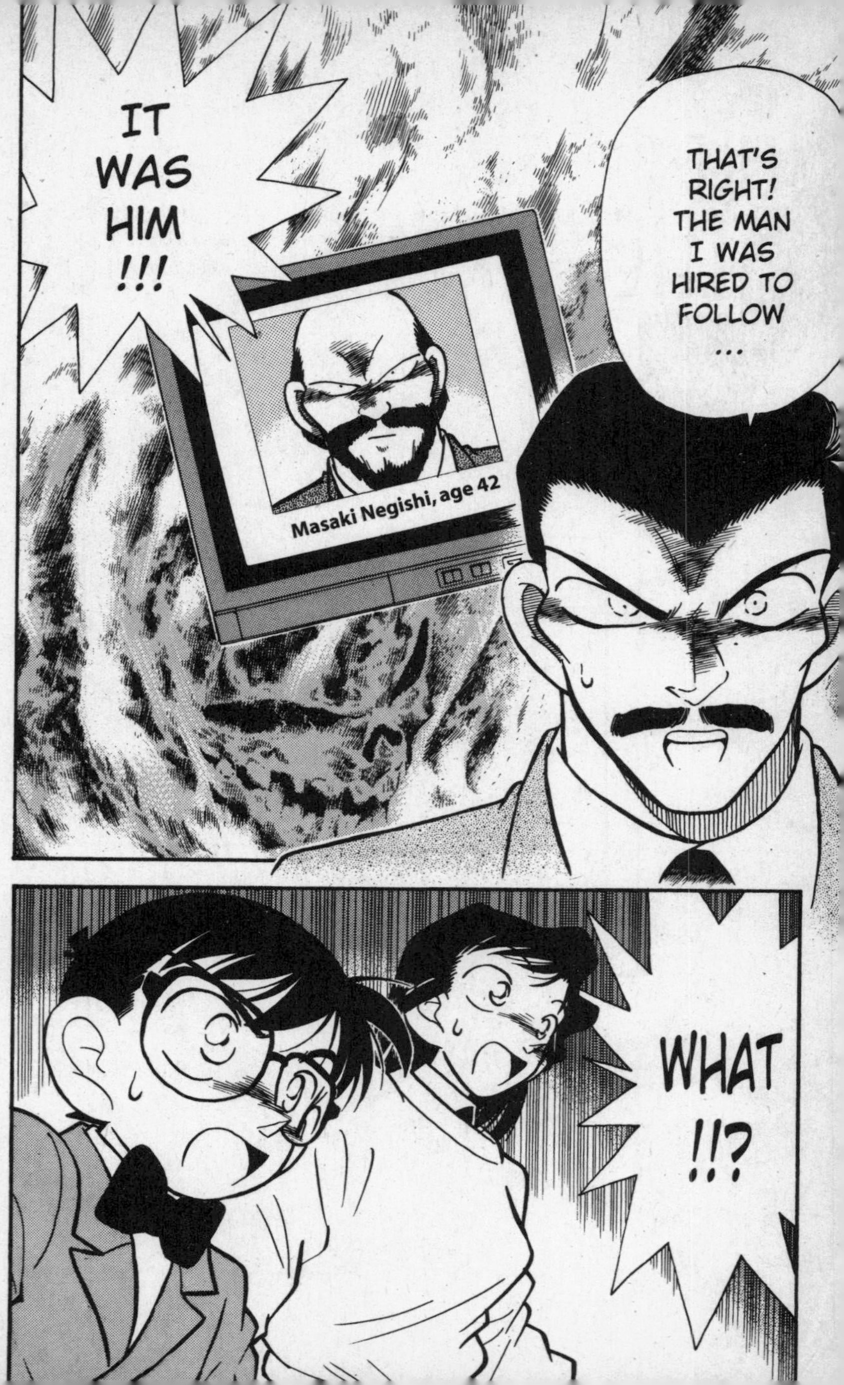
THAT'S RIGHT! THE MAN I WAS HIRED TO FOLLOW ...
IT WAS HIM !!!
Masaki Negishi, age 42
WHAT !!?

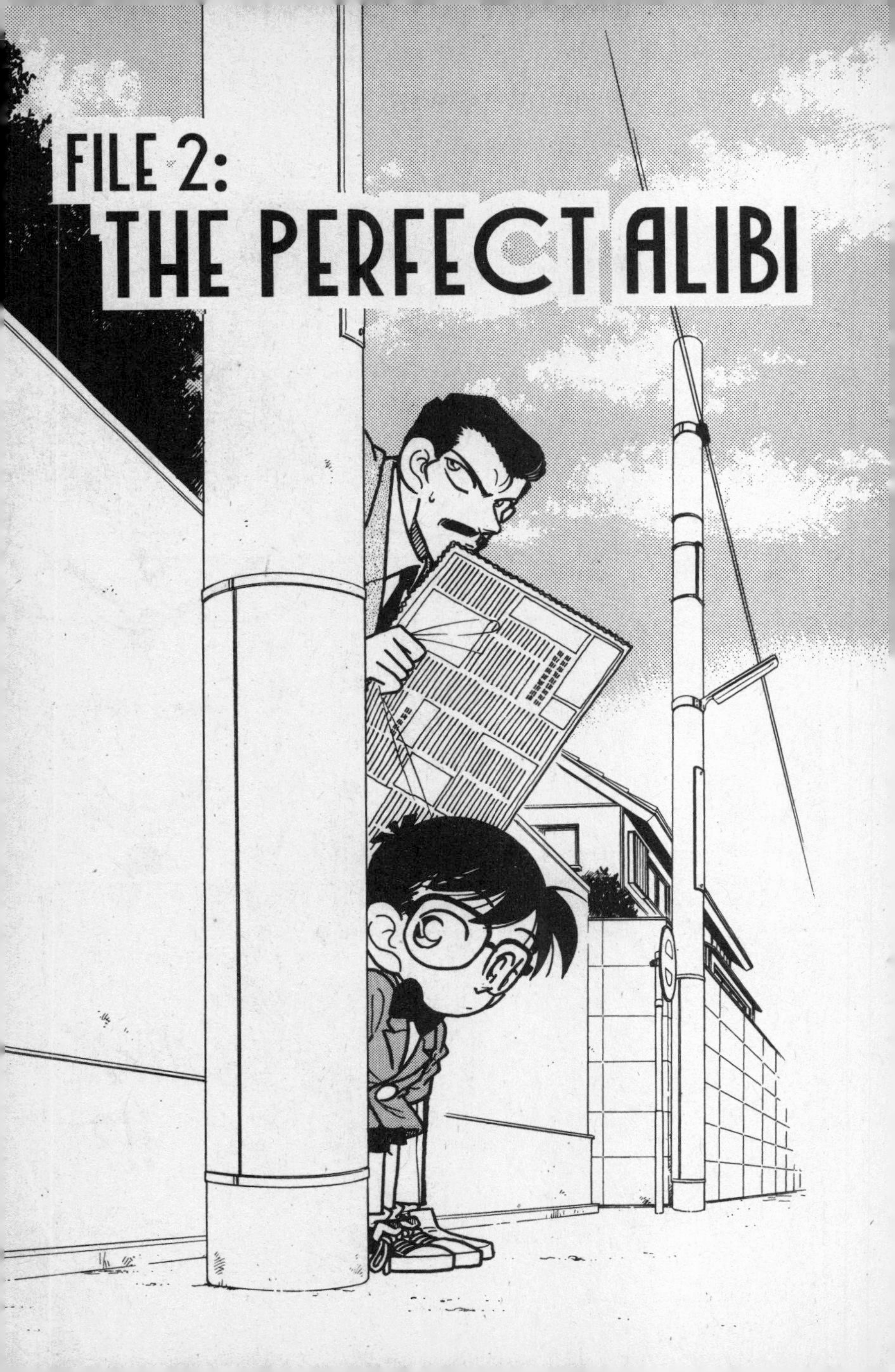
FILE 2:
THE PERFECT ALIBI

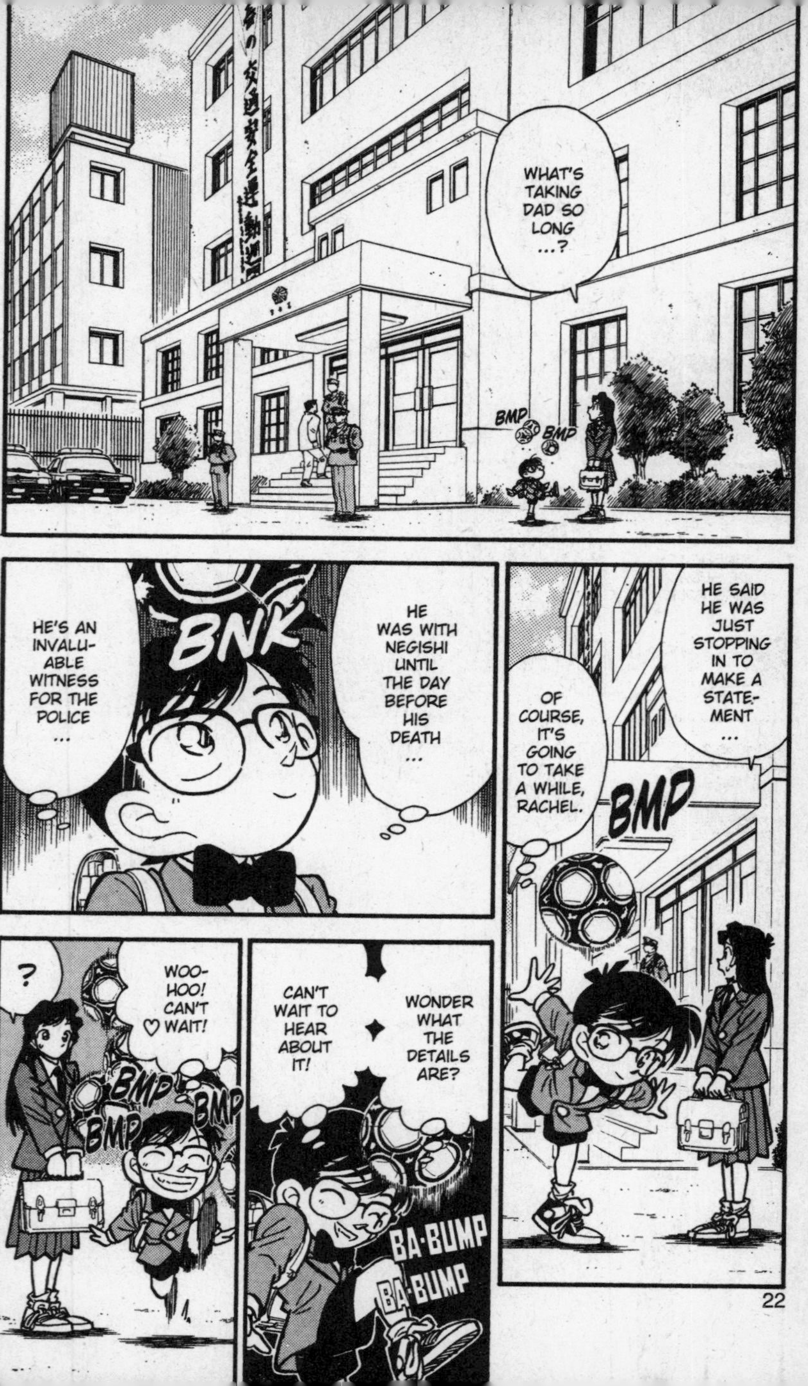
WHAT'S TAKING DAD SO LONG ...?
BMP
BMP
HE SAID HE WAS JUST STOPPING IN TO MAKE A STATEMENT ...
OF COURSE, IT'S GOING TO TAKE A WHILE, RACHEL.
BMP
BNK
HE WAS WITH NEGISHI UNTIL THE DAY BEFORE HIS DEATH ...
HE'S AN INVALUABLE WITNESS FOR THE POLICE ...
WONDER WHAT THE DETAILS ARE?
CAN'T WAIT TO HEAR ABOUT IT!
BA-BUMP
BA-BUMP
WOO-HOO! CAN'T ♡ WAIT!
?
BMP
BMP
BMP

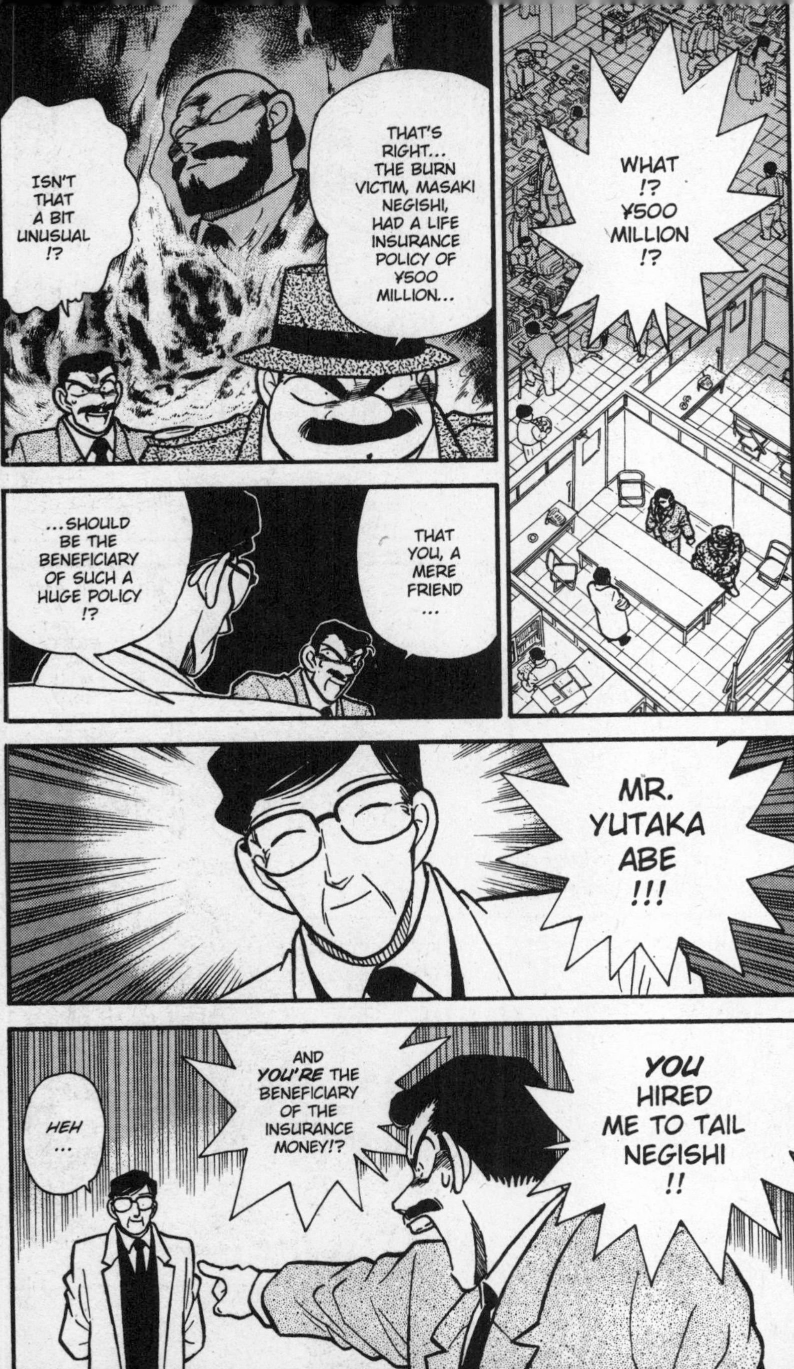

WHAT !? ¥500 MILLION !?
THAT'S RIGHT... THE BURN VICTIM, MASAKI NEGISHI, HAD A LIFE INSURANCE POLICY OF ¥500 MILLION...
ISN'T THAT A BIT UNUSUAL !?
THAT YOU, A MERE FRIEND ...
...SHOULD BE THE BENEFICIARY OF SUCH A HUGE POLICY !?
MR. YUTAKA ABE !!!
YOU HIRED ME TO TAIL NEGISHI !!
AND *YOU'RE* THE BENEFICIARY OF THE INSURANCE MONEY!?
HEH ...

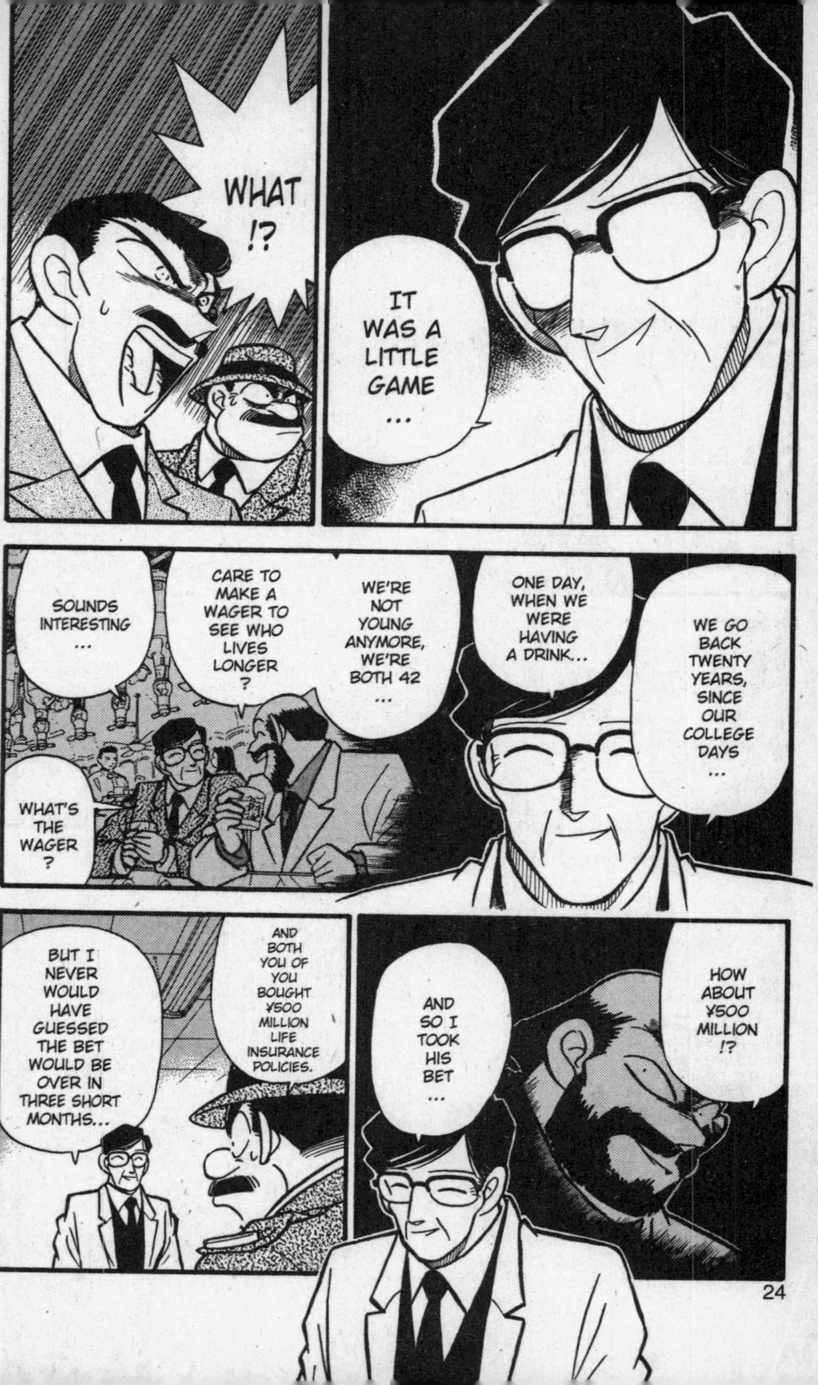
IT WAS A LITTLE GAME ...
WHAT !?
WE GO BACK TWENTY YEARS, SINCE OUR COLLEGE DAYS ...
ONE DAY, WHEN WE WERE HAVING A DRINK...
WE'RE NOT YOUNG ANYMORE, WE'RE BOTH 42 ...
CARE TO MAKE A WAGER TO SEE WHO LIVES LONGER ?
SOUNDS INTERESTING ...
WHAT'S THE WAGER ?
HOW ABOUT ¥500 MILLION !?
AND SO I TOOK HIS BET ...
AND BOTH YOU OF YOU BOUGHT ¥500 MILLION LIFE INSURANCE POLICIES.
BUT I NEVER WOULD HAVE GUESSED THE BET WOULD BE OVER IN THREE SHORT MONTHS...

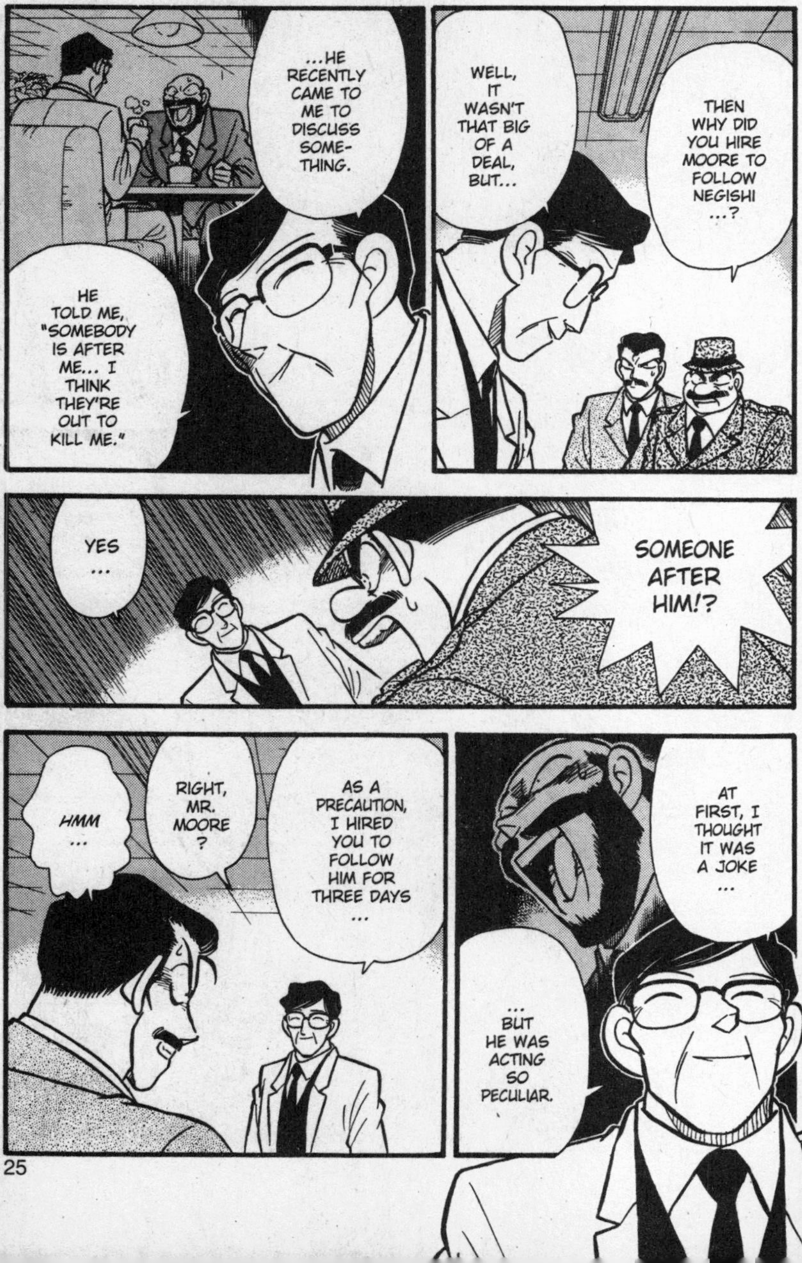
THEN WHY DID YOU HIRE MOORE TO FOLLOW NEGISHI ...?
WELL, IT WASN'T THAT BIG OF A DEAL, BUT...
...HE RECENTLY CAME TO ME TO DISCUSS SOME-THING.
HE TOLD ME, "SOMEBODY IS AFTER ME... I THINK THEY'RE OUT TO KILL ME."
SOMEONE AFTER HIM!?
YES ...
AT FIRST, I THOUGHT IT WAS A JOKE ...
... BUT HE WAS ACTING SO PECULIAR.
AS A PRECAUTION, I HIRED YOU TO FOLLOW HIM FOR THREE DAYS ...
RIGHT, MR. MOORE ?
HMM ...

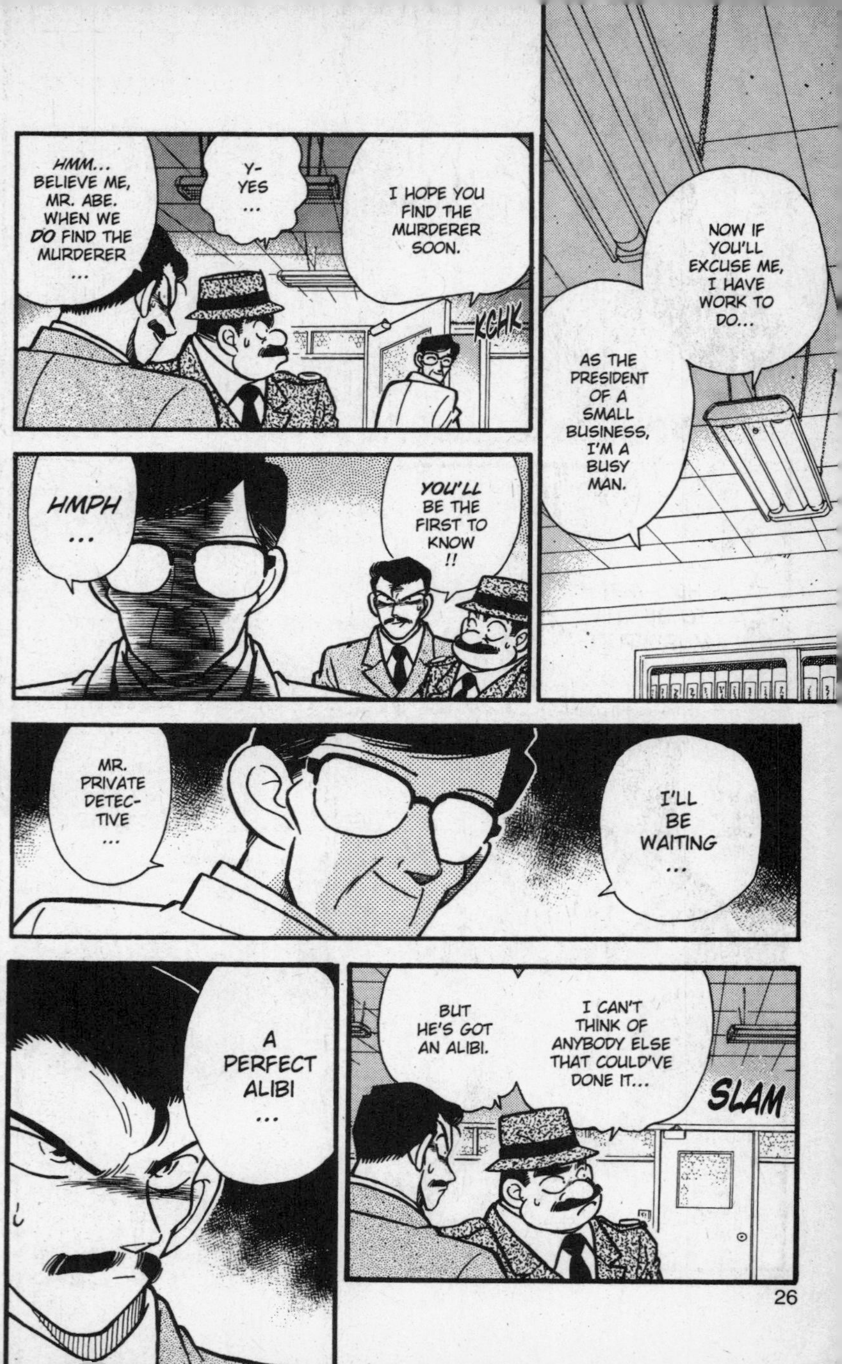
NOW IF YOU'LL EXCUSE ME, I HAVE WORK TO DO...
AS THE PRESIDENT OF A SMALL BUSINESS, I'M A BUSY MAN.
KCHK
I HOPE YOU FIND THE MURDERER SOON.
Y-YES ...
HMM... BELIEVE ME, MR. ABE. WHEN WE DO FIND THE MURDERER ...
YOU'LL BE THE FIRST TO KNOW !!
HMPH ...
I'LL BE WAITING ...
MR. PRIVATE DETECTIVE ...
SLAM
I CAN'T THINK OF ANYBODY ELSE THAT COULD'VE DONE IT...
BUT HE'S GOT AN ALIBI.
A PERFECT ALIBI ...

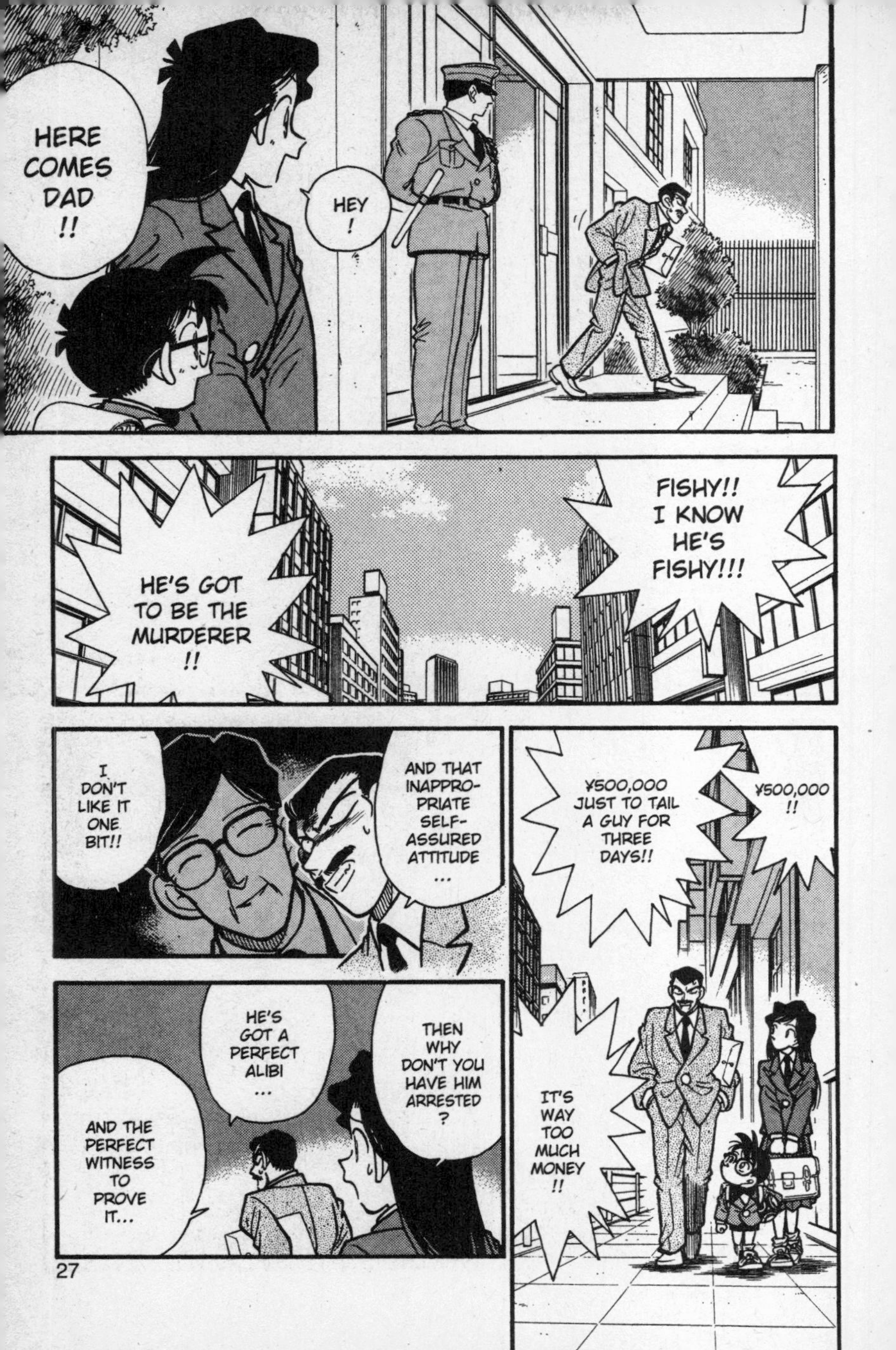
HEY !
HERE COMES DAD !!
FISHY!! I KNOW HE'S FISHY!!!
HE'S GOT TO BE THE MURDERER !!
¥500,000 !!
¥500,000 JUST TO TAIL A GUY FOR THREE DAYS!!
IT'S WAY TOO MUCH MONEY !!
AND THAT INAPPROPRIATE SELF-ASSURED ATTITUDE ...
I DON'T LIKE IT ONE BIT!!
THEN WHY DON'T YOU HAVE HIM ARRESTED ?
HE'S GOT A PERFECT ALIBI ...
AND THE PERFECT WITNESS TO PROVE IT...

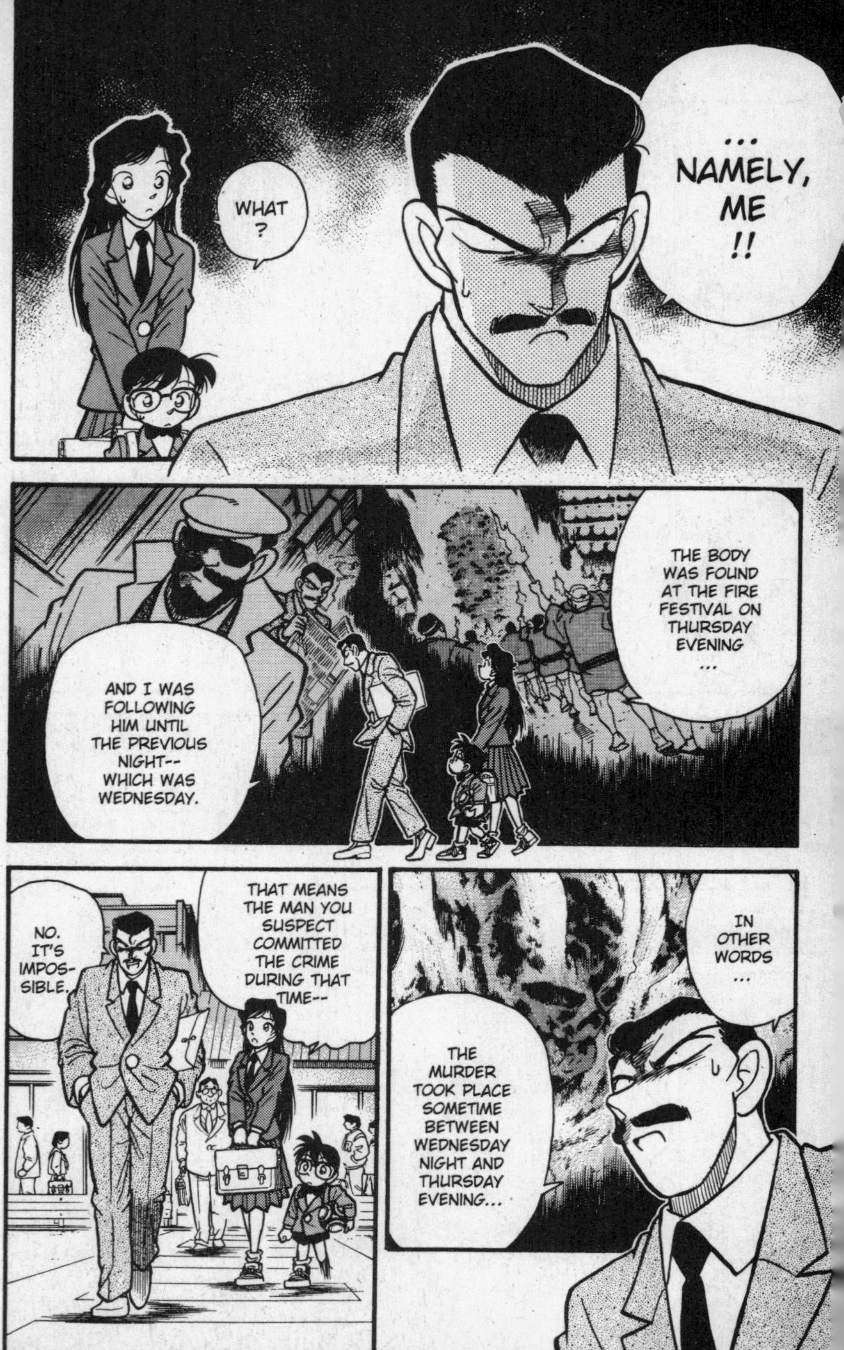
... NAMELY, ME !!
WHAT ?
THE BODY WAS FOUND AT THE FIRE FESTIVAL ON THURSDAY EVENING ...
AND I WAS FOLLOWING HIM UNTIL THE PREVIOUS NIGHT-- WHICH WAS WEDNESDAY.
IN OTHER WORDS ...
THE MURDER TOOK PLACE SOMETIME BETWEEN WEDNESDAY NIGHT AND THURSDAY EVENING...
THAT MEANS THE MAN YOU SUSPECT COMMITTED THE CRIME DURING THAT TIME--
NO. IT'S IMPOS-SIBLE.

BECAUSE ...

THEN WHY ARE YOU SO HUNG UP ON HIM?

A GROUP TRIP WITH HIS COMPANY!!

HE WAS ON A TRIP FROM WEDNESDAY MORNING TO FRIDAY NIGHT!!

I SEE ...

IS THAT SO ...

THAT'S WHAT MY DETECTIVE INSTINCTS TELL ME!!

.....

DETECTIVE MOORE TAILS THE VICTIM

POSSIBLE TIME MURDER TOOK PLACE

MONDAY	TUESDAY	WEDNESDAY	THURSDAY	FRIDAY

YUTAKA ABE'S TRIP

THE PERFECT ALIBI ...

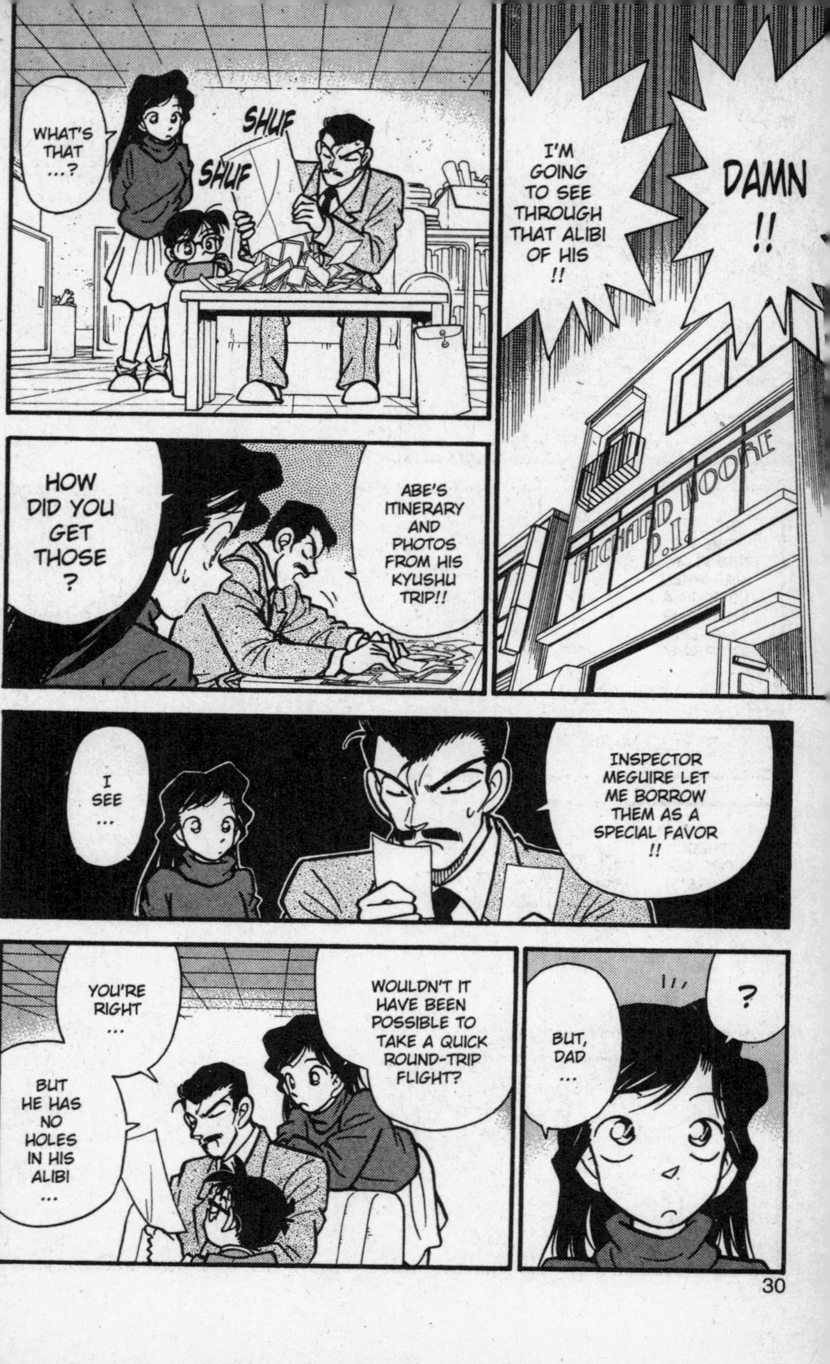
DAMN !!
I'M GOING TO SEE THROUGH THAT ALIBI OF HIS !!
RICHARD MOORE P.I.
SHUF
SHUF
WHAT'S THAT ...?
ABE'S ITINERARY AND PHOTOS FROM HIS KYUSHU TRIP!!
HOW DID YOU GET THOSE ?
INSPECTOR MEGUIRE LET ME BORROW THEM AS A SPECIAL FAVOR !!
I SEE ...
?
!!
BUT, DAD ...
WOULDN'T IT HAVE BEEN POSSIBLE TO TAKE A QUICK ROUND-TRIP FLIGHT?
YOU'RE RIGHT ...
BUT HE HAS NO HOLES IN HIS ALIBI ...

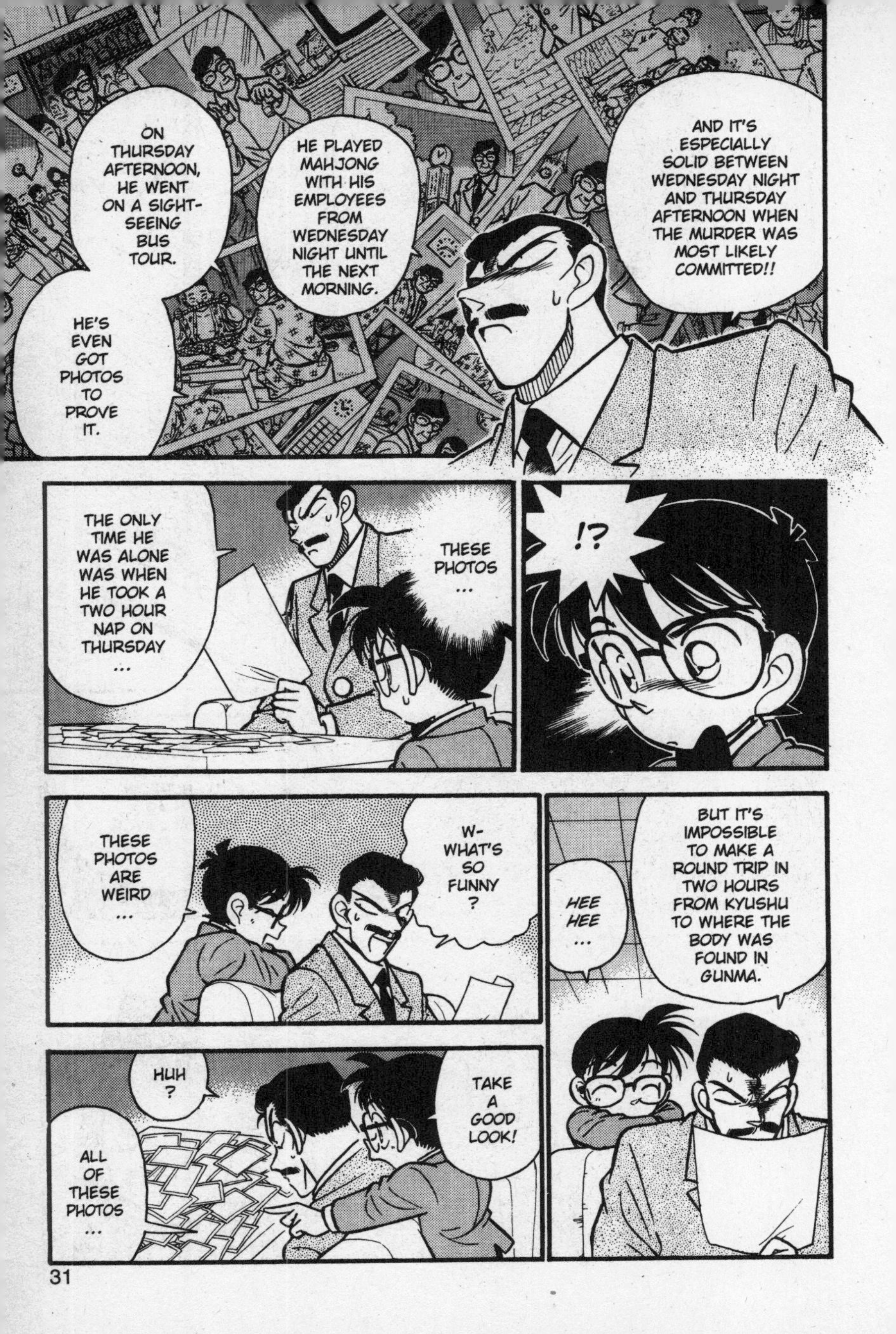
AND IT'S ESPECIALLY SOLID BETWEEN WEDNESDAY NIGHT AND THURSDAY AFTERNOON WHEN THE MURDER WAS MOST LIKELY COMMITTED!!
HE PLAYED MAHJONG WITH HIS EMPLOYEES FROM WEDNESDAY NIGHT UNTIL THE NEXT MORNING.
ON THURSDAY AFTERNOON, HE WENT ON A SIGHT-SEEING BUS TOUR.
HE'S EVEN GOT PHOTOS TO PROVE IT.
!?
THESE PHOTOS ...
THE ONLY TIME HE WAS ALONE WAS WHEN HE TOOK A TWO HOUR NAP ON THURSDAY ...
BUT IT'S IMPOSSIBLE TO MAKE A ROUND TRIP IN TWO HOURS FROM KYUSHU TO WHERE THE BODY WAS FOUND IN GUNMA.
HEE HEE ...
W-WHAT'S SO FUNNY?
THESE PHOTOS ARE WEIRD ...
TAKE A GOOD LOOK!
HUH?
ALL OF THESE PHOTOS ...

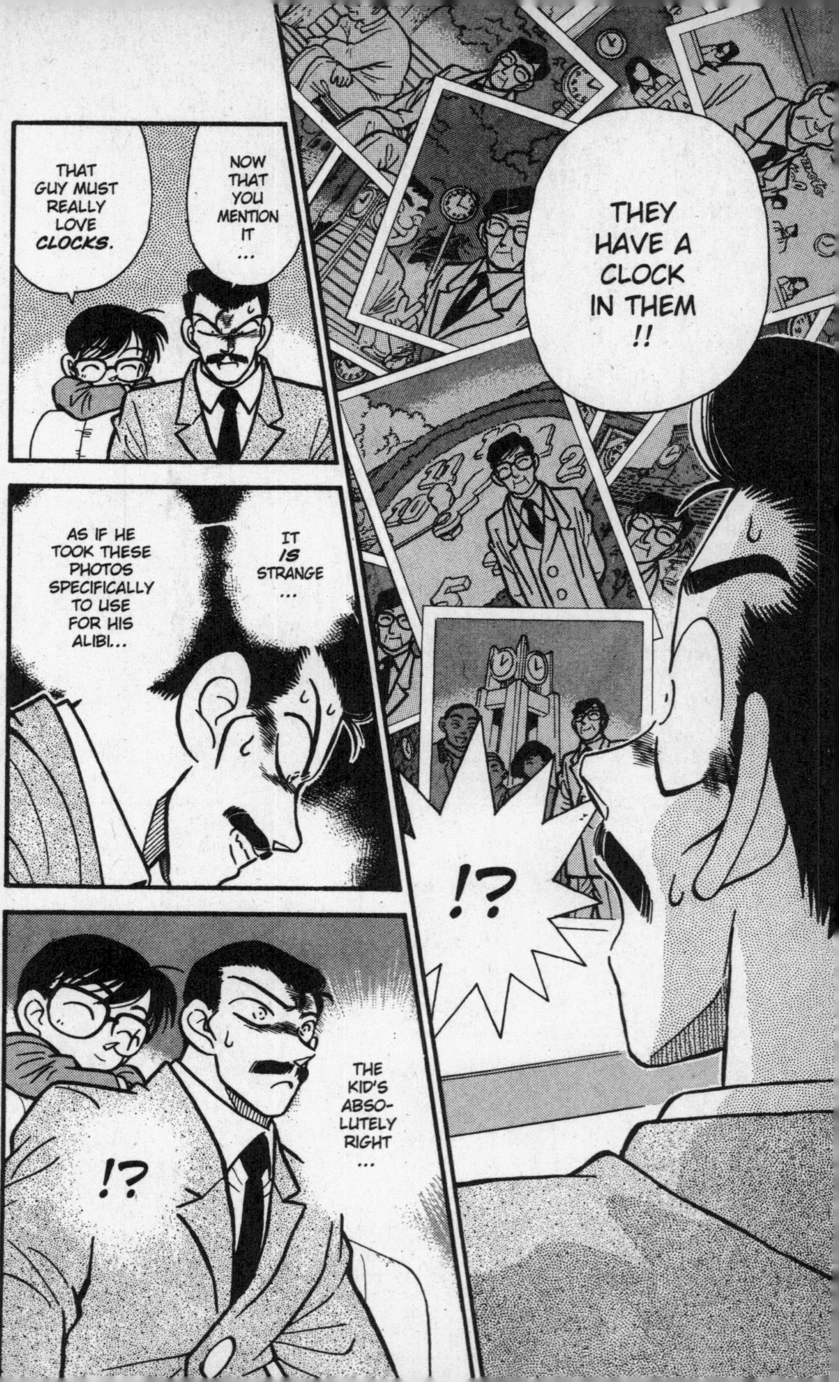
THEY HAVE A CLOCK IN THEM !!
!?
NOW THAT YOU MENTION IT ...
THAT GUY MUST REALLY LOVE CLOCKS.
IT IS STRANGE ...
AS IF HE TOOK THESE PHOTOS SPECIFICALLY TO USE FOR HIS ALIBI...
THE KID'S ABSO-LUTELY RIGHT ...
!?

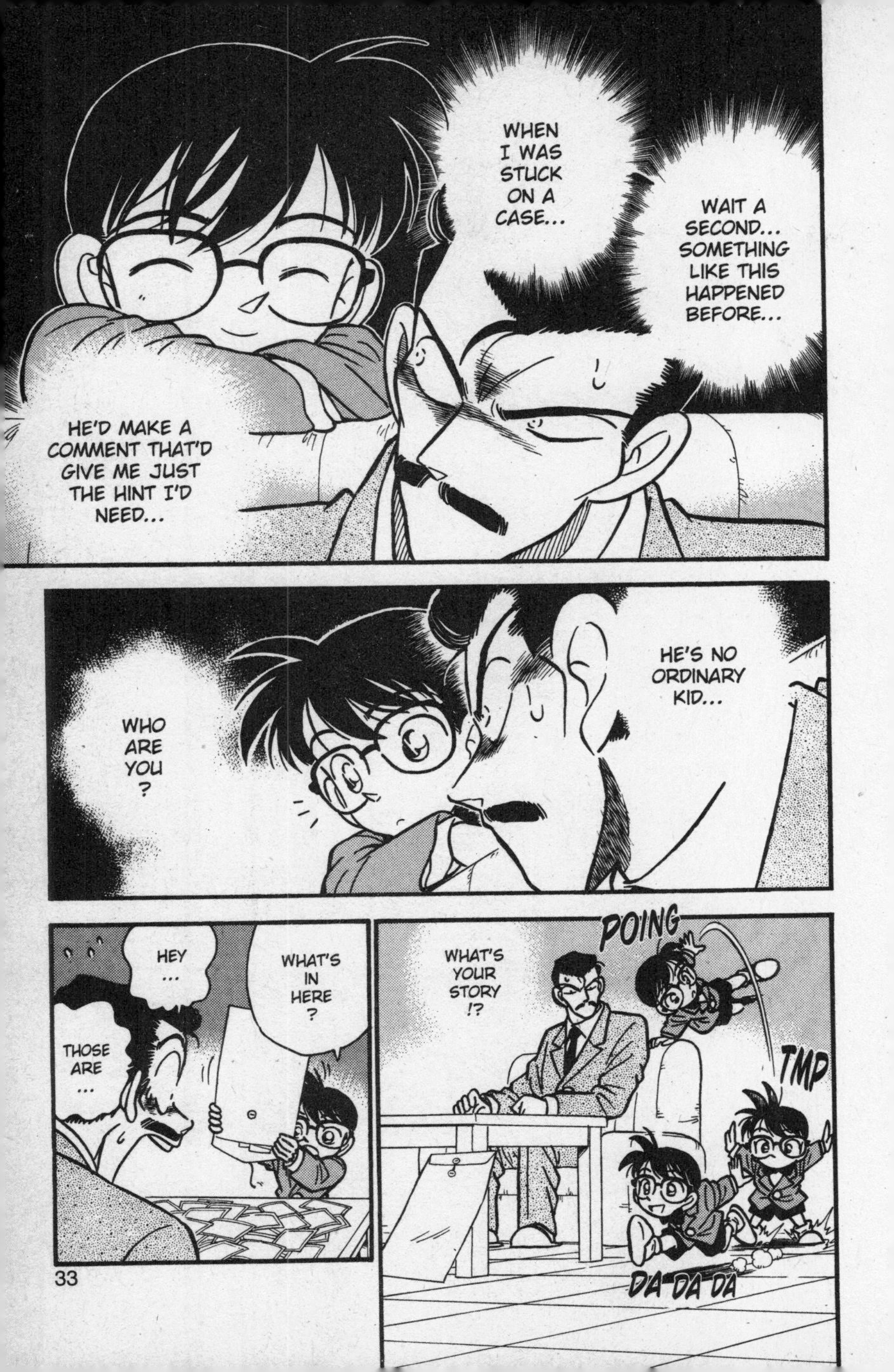
WAIT A SECOND... SOMETHING LIKE THIS HAPPENED BEFORE...
WHEN I WAS STUCK ON A CASE...
HE'D MAKE A COMMENT THAT'D GIVE ME JUST THE HINT I'D NEED...
HE'S NO ORDINARY KID...
WHO ARE YOU ?
POING
WHAT'S YOUR STORY !?
TMP
DA DA DA
WHAT'S IN HERE ?
HEY ...
THOSE ARE ...

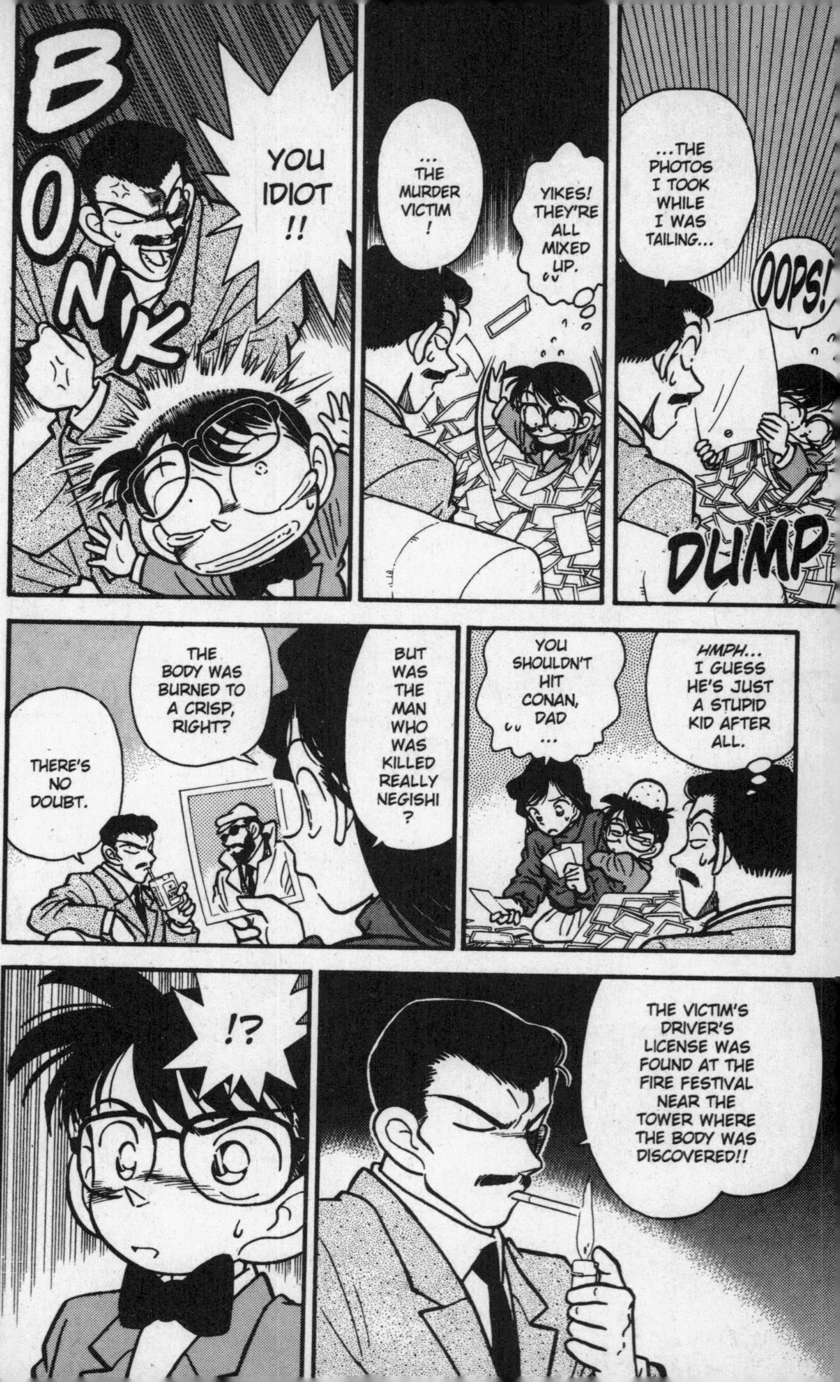
...THE PHOTOS I TOOK WHILE I WAS TAILING...
OOPS!
DUMP
...THE MURDER VICTIM!
YIKES! THEY'RE ALL MIXED UP.
BONK
YOU IDIOT!!
HMPH... I GUESS HE'S JUST A STUPID KID AFTER ALL.
YOU SHOULDN'T HIT CONAN, DAD...
BUT WAS THE MAN WHO WAS KILLED REALLY NEGISHI?
THE BODY WAS BURNED TO A CRISP, RIGHT?
THERE'S NO DOUBT.
THE VICTIM'S DRIVER'S LICENSE WAS FOUND AT THE FIRE FESTIVAL NEAR THE TOWER WHERE THE BODY WAS DISCOVERED!!
!?

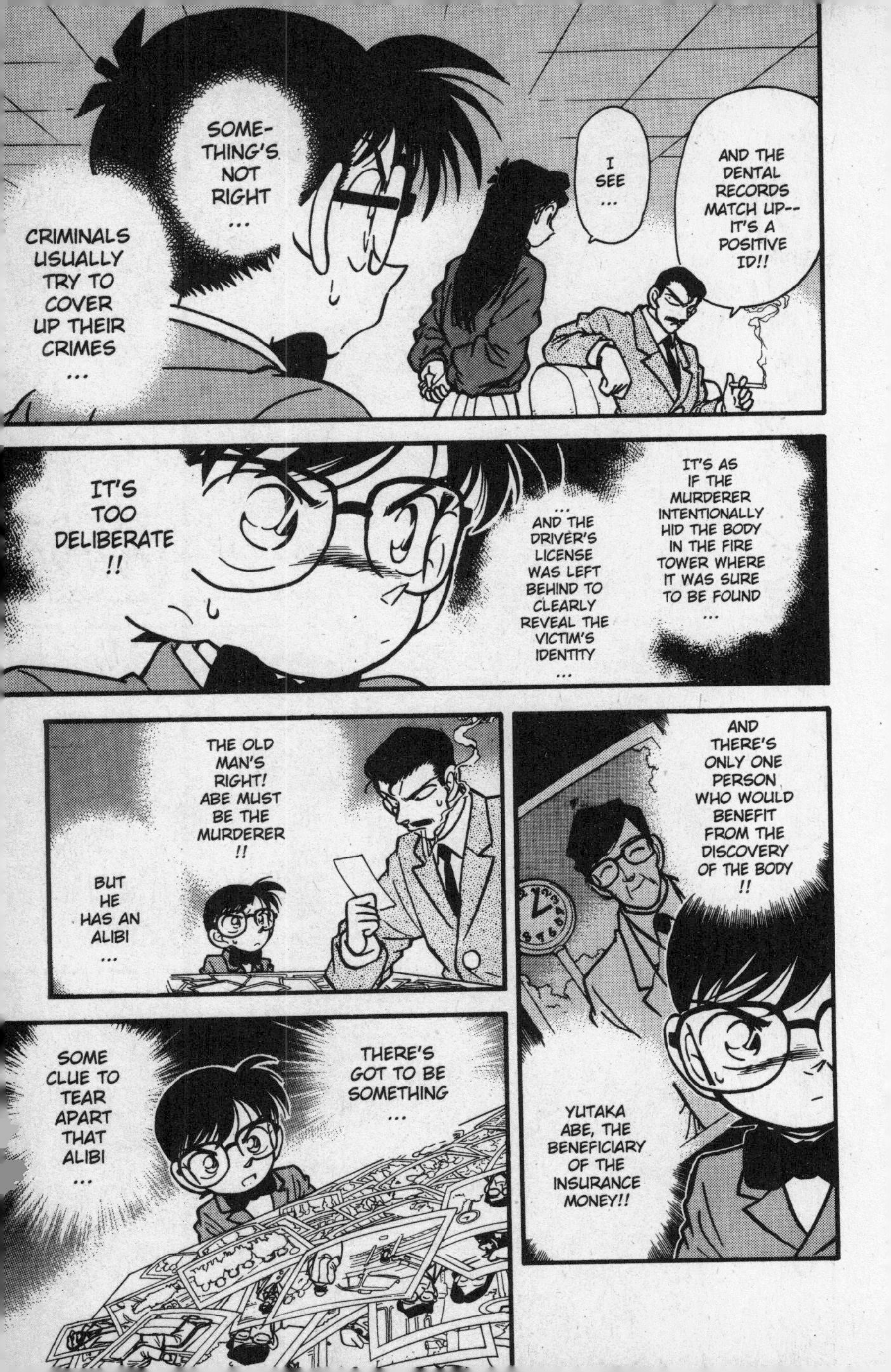
AND THE DENTAL RECORDS MATCH UP-- IT'S A POSITIVE ID!!
I SEE ...
SOME-THING'S NOT RIGHT ...
CRIMINALS USUALLY TRY TO COVER UP THEIR CRIMES ...
IT'S AS IF THE MURDERER INTENTIONALLY HID THE BODY IN THE FIRE TOWER WHERE IT WAS SURE TO BE FOUND ...
... AND THE DRIVER'S LICENSE WAS LEFT BEHIND TO CLEARLY REVEAL THE VICTIM'S IDENTITY ...
IT'S TOO DELIBERATE !!
AND THERE'S ONLY ONE PERSON WHO WOULD BENEFIT FROM THE DISCOVERY OF THE BODY !!
YUTAKA ABE, THE BENEFICIARY OF THE INSURANCE MONEY!!
THE OLD MAN'S RIGHT! ABE MUST BE THE MURDERER !!
BUT HE HAS AN ALIBI ...
THERE'S GOT TO BE SOMETHING ...
SOME CLUE TO TEAR APART THAT ALIBI ...

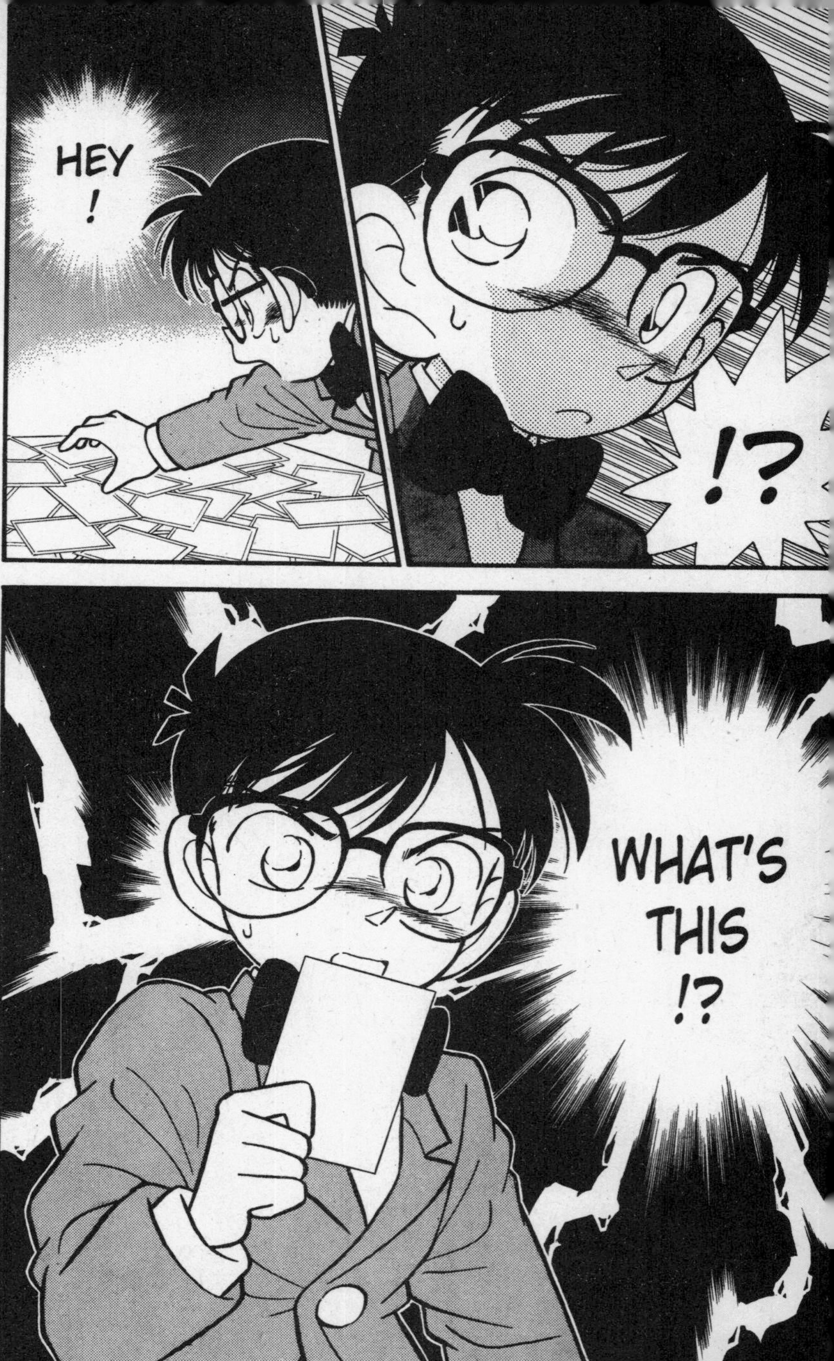
!?
HEY !
WHAT'S THIS !?

FILE 3:
THE PHOTO SPEAKS

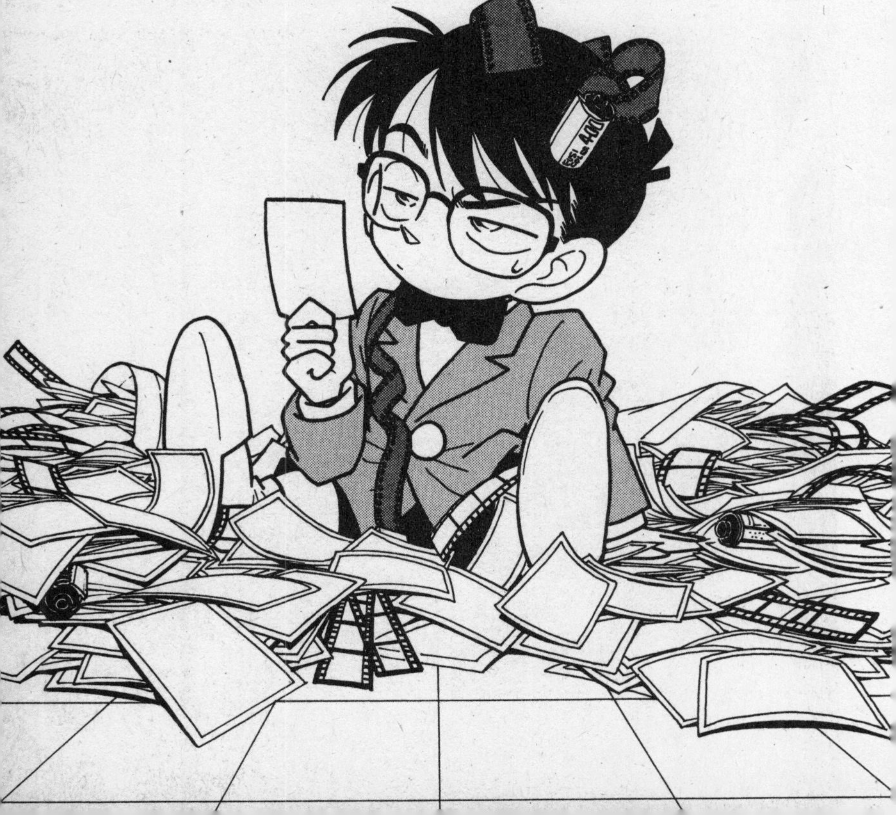

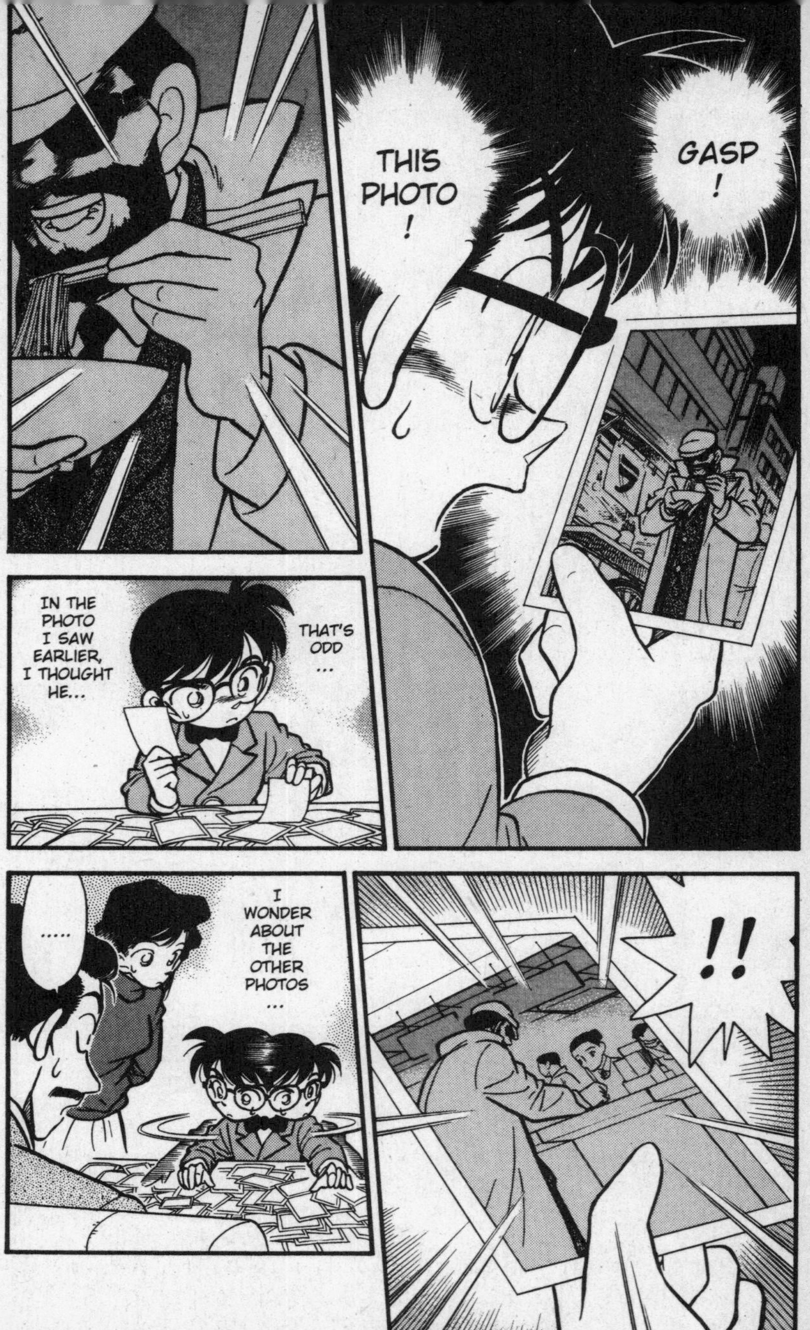
GASP!
THIS PHOTO!
THAT'S ODD...
IN THE PHOTO I SAW EARLIER, I THOUGHT HE...
!!
I WONDER ABOUT THE OTHER PHOTOS...
.....

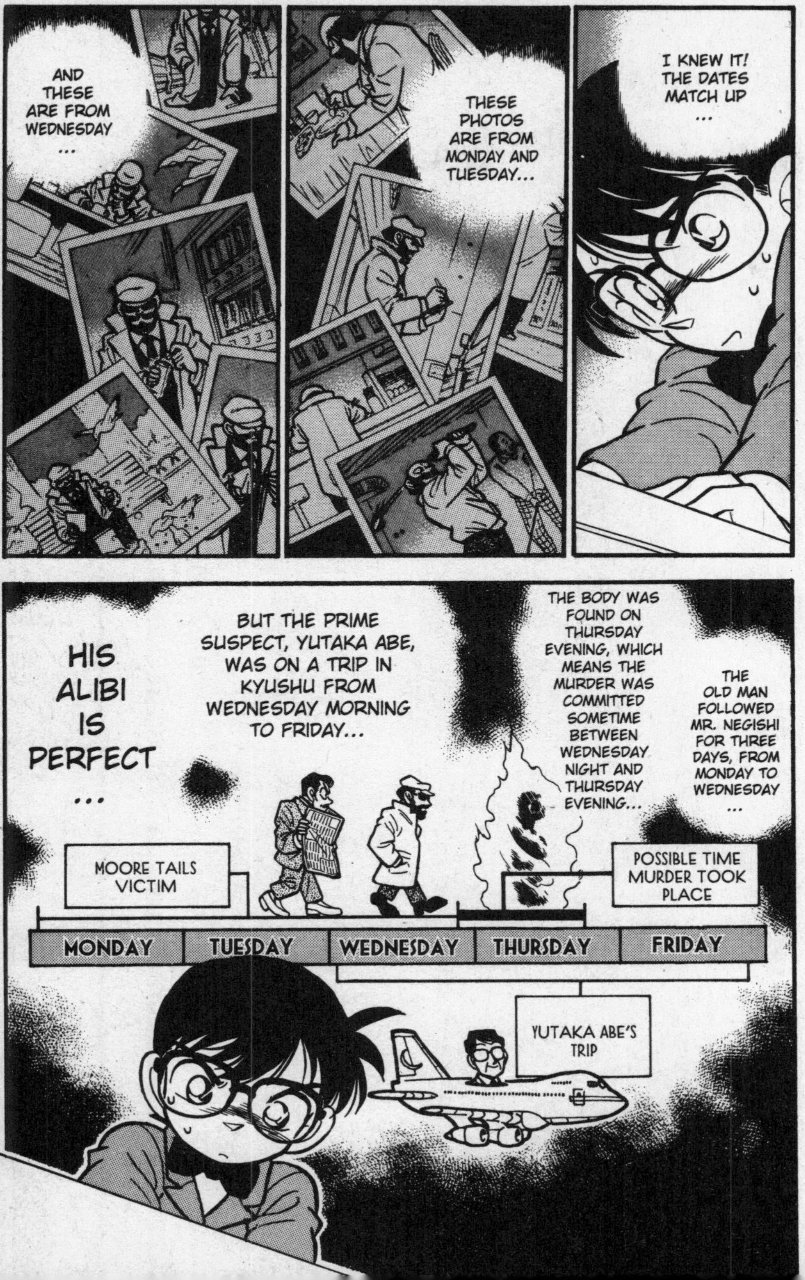

I KNEW IT! THE DATES MATCH UP ...
THESE PHOTOS ARE FROM MONDAY AND TUESDAY...
AND THESE ARE FROM WEDNESDAY ...
THE OLD MAN FOLLOWED MR. NEGISHI FOR THREE DAYS, FROM MONDAY TO WEDNESDAY ...
THE BODY WAS FOUND ON THURSDAY EVENING, WHICH MEANS THE MURDER WAS COMMITTED SOMETIME BETWEEN WEDNESDAY NIGHT AND THURSDAY EVENING...
BUT THE PRIME SUSPECT, YUTAKA ABE, WAS ON A TRIP IN KYUSHU FROM WEDNESDAY MORNING TO FRIDAY...
HIS ALIBI IS PERFECT ...
POSSIBLE TIME MURDER TOOK PLACE
MOORE TAILS VICTIM
MONDAY
TUESDAY
WEDNESDAY
THURSDAY
FRIDAY
YUTAKA ABE'S TRIP

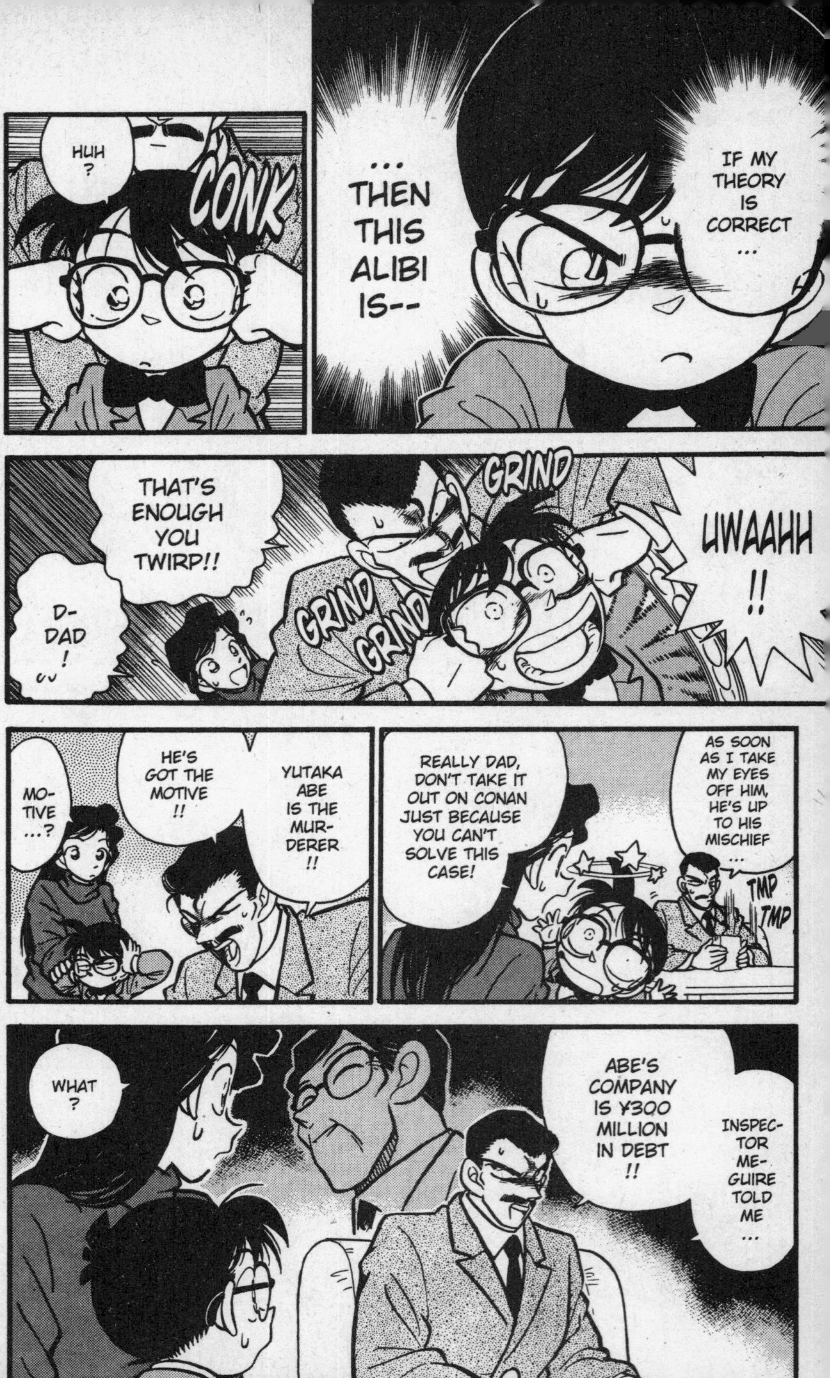
IF MY THEORY IS CORRECT ...
... THEN THIS ALIBI IS--
CONK
HUH ?
UWAAHH !!
GRIND
GRIND GRIND
THAT'S ENOUGH YOU TWIRP!!
D-DAD !
AS SOON AS I TAKE MY EYES OFF HIM, HE'S UP TO HIS MISCHIEF ...
TMP TMP
REALLY DAD, DON'T TAKE IT OUT ON CONAN JUST BECAUSE YOU CAN'T SOLVE THIS CASE!
YUTAKA ABE IS THE MUR-DERER !!
HE'S GOT THE MOTIVE !!
MO-TIVE ...?
INSPEC-TOR ME-GUIRE TOLD ME ...
ABE'S COMPANY IS ¥300 MILLION IN DEBT !!
WHAT ?

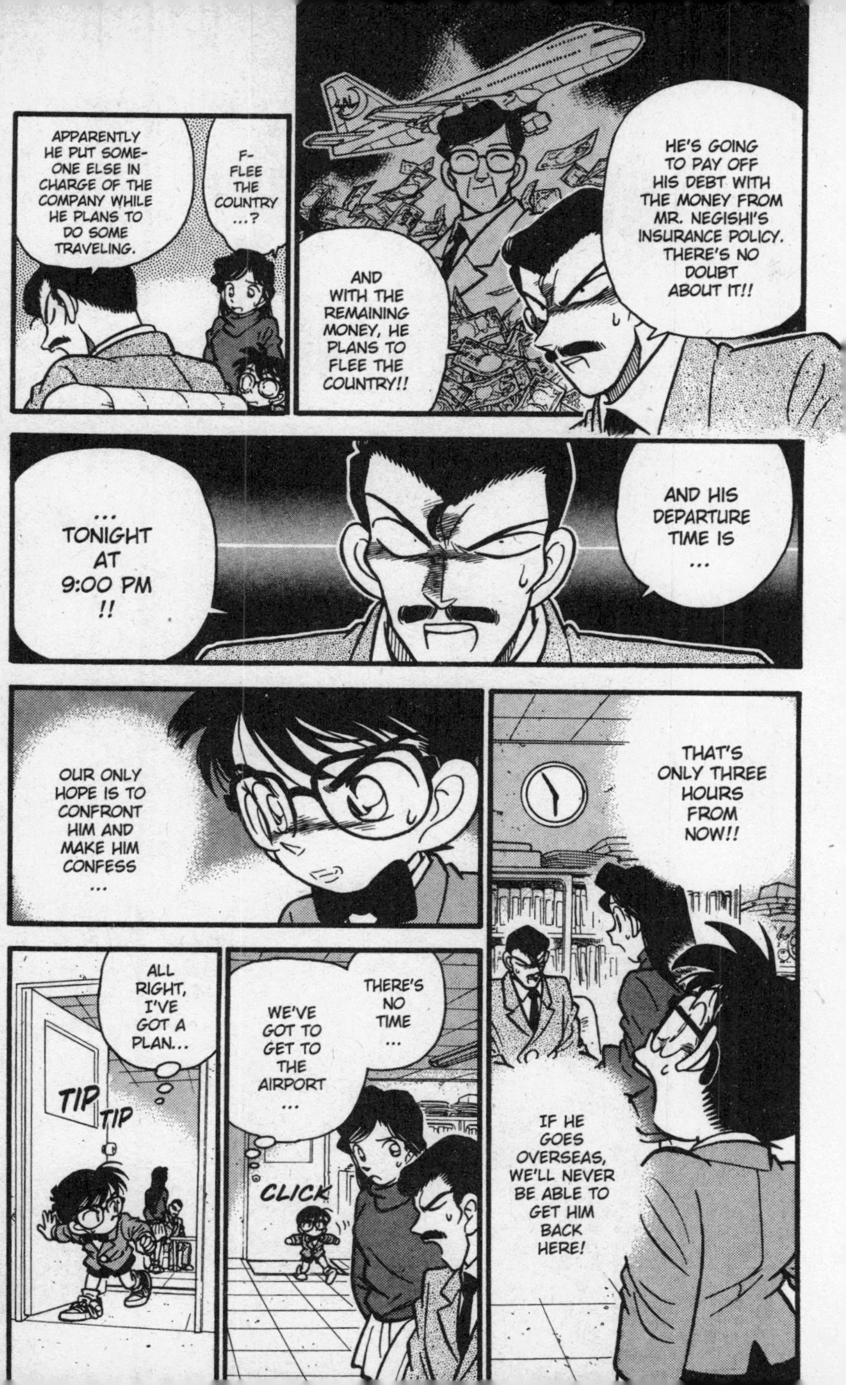
HE'S GOING TO PAY OFF HIS DEBT WITH THE MONEY FROM MR. NEGISHI'S INSURANCE POLICY. THERE'S NO DOUBT ABOUT IT!!
AND WITH THE REMAINING MONEY, HE PLANS TO FLEE THE COUNTRY!!
F- FLEE THE COUNTRY ...?
APPARENTLY HE PUT SOME-ONE ELSE IN CHARGE OF THE COMPANY WHILE HE PLANS TO DO SOME TRAVELING.
AND HIS DEPARTURE TIME IS ...
... TONIGHT AT 9:00 PM !!
THAT'S ONLY THREE HOURS FROM NOW!!
IF HE GOES OVERSEAS, WE'LL NEVER BE ABLE TO GET HIM BACK HERE!
OUR ONLY HOPE IS TO CONFRONT HIM AND MAKE HIM CONFESS ...
THERE'S NO TIME ...
WE'VE GOT TO GET TO THE AIRPORT ...
CLICK
ALL RIGHT, I'VE GOT A PLAN...
TIP TIP

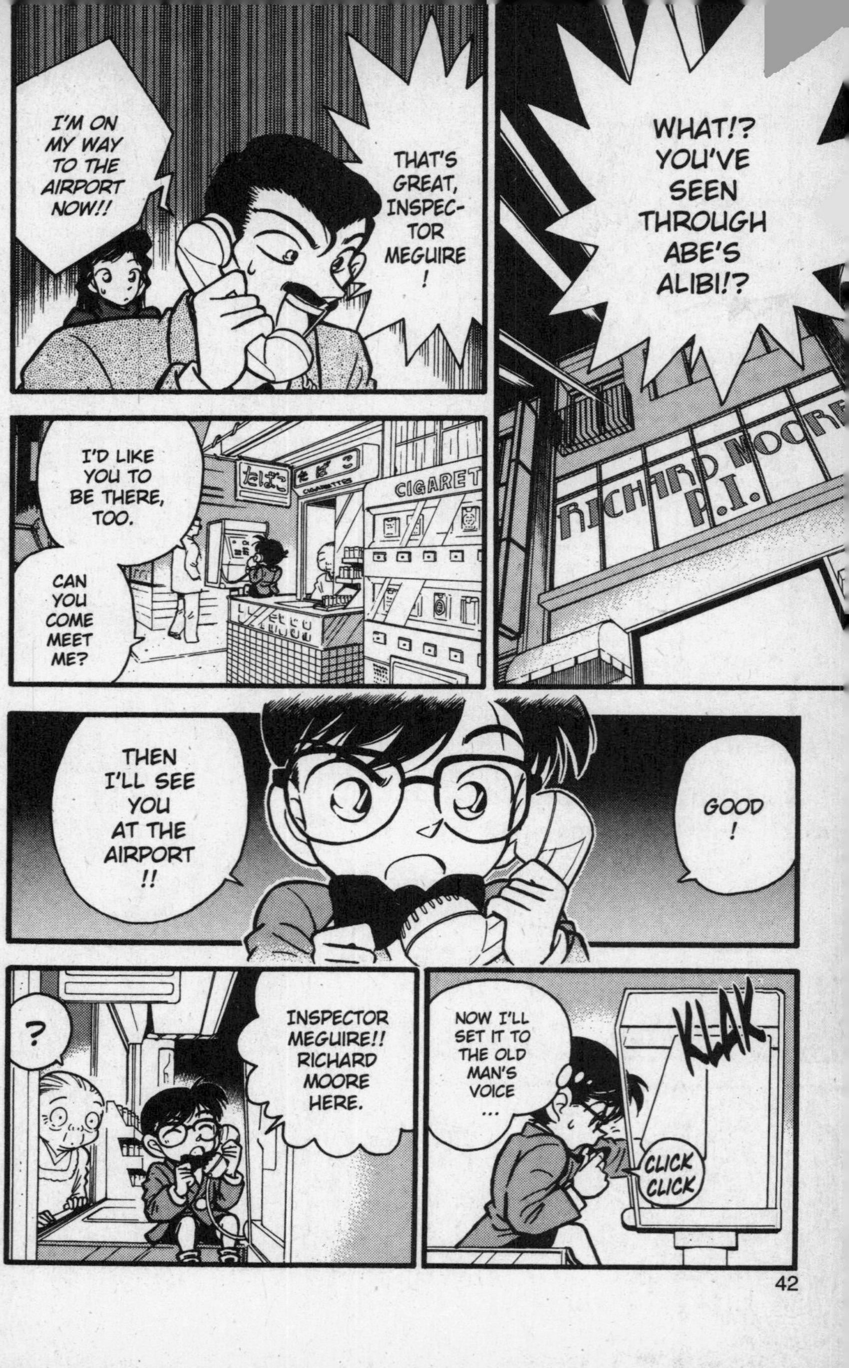
WHAT!? YOU'VE SEEN THROUGH ABE'S ALIBI!?
RICHARD MOORE P.I.
THAT'S GREAT, INSPECTOR MEGUIRE!
I'M ON MY WAY TO THE AIRPORT NOW!!
CIGARET
I'D LIKE YOU TO BE THERE, TOO.
CAN YOU COME MEET ME?
GOOD!
THEN I'LL SEE YOU AT THE AIRPORT!!
KLAK
NOW I'LL SET IT TO THE OLD MAN'S VOICE...
CLICK CLICK
INSPECTOR MEGUIRE!! RICHARD MOORE HERE.
?

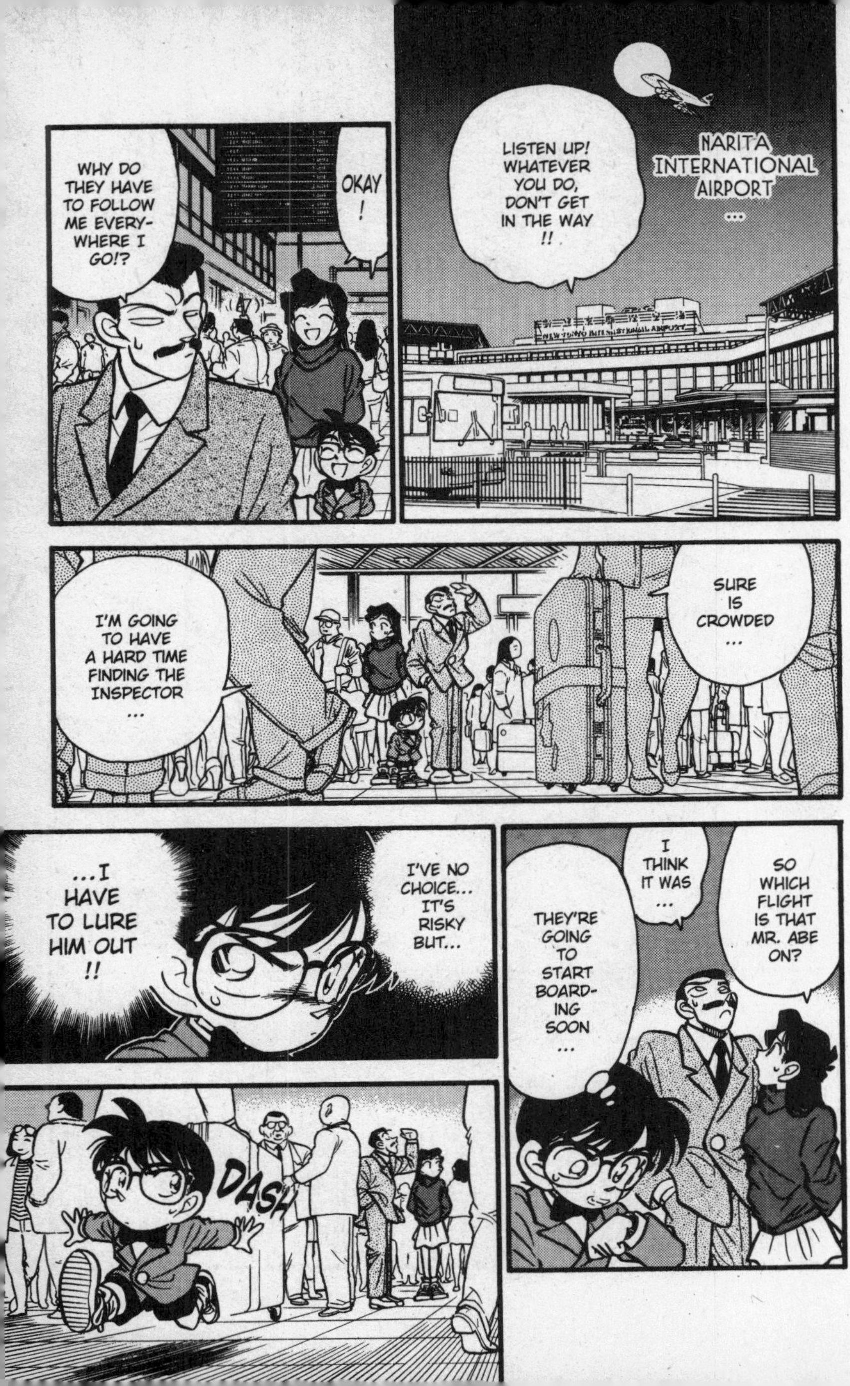
NARITA INTERNATIONAL AIRPORT ...
LISTEN UP! WHATEVER YOU DO, DON'T GET IN THE WAY !!
OKAY !
WHY DO THEY HAVE TO FOLLOW ME EVERY-WHERE I GO!?
SURE IS CROWDED ...
I'M GOING TO HAVE A HARD TIME FINDING THE INSPECTOR ...
SO WHICH FLIGHT IS THAT MR. ABE ON?
I THINK IT WAS ...
THEY'RE GOING TO START BOARD-ING SOON ...
I'VE NO CHOICE... IT'S RISKY BUT...
...I HAVE TO LURE HIM OUT !!
DASH

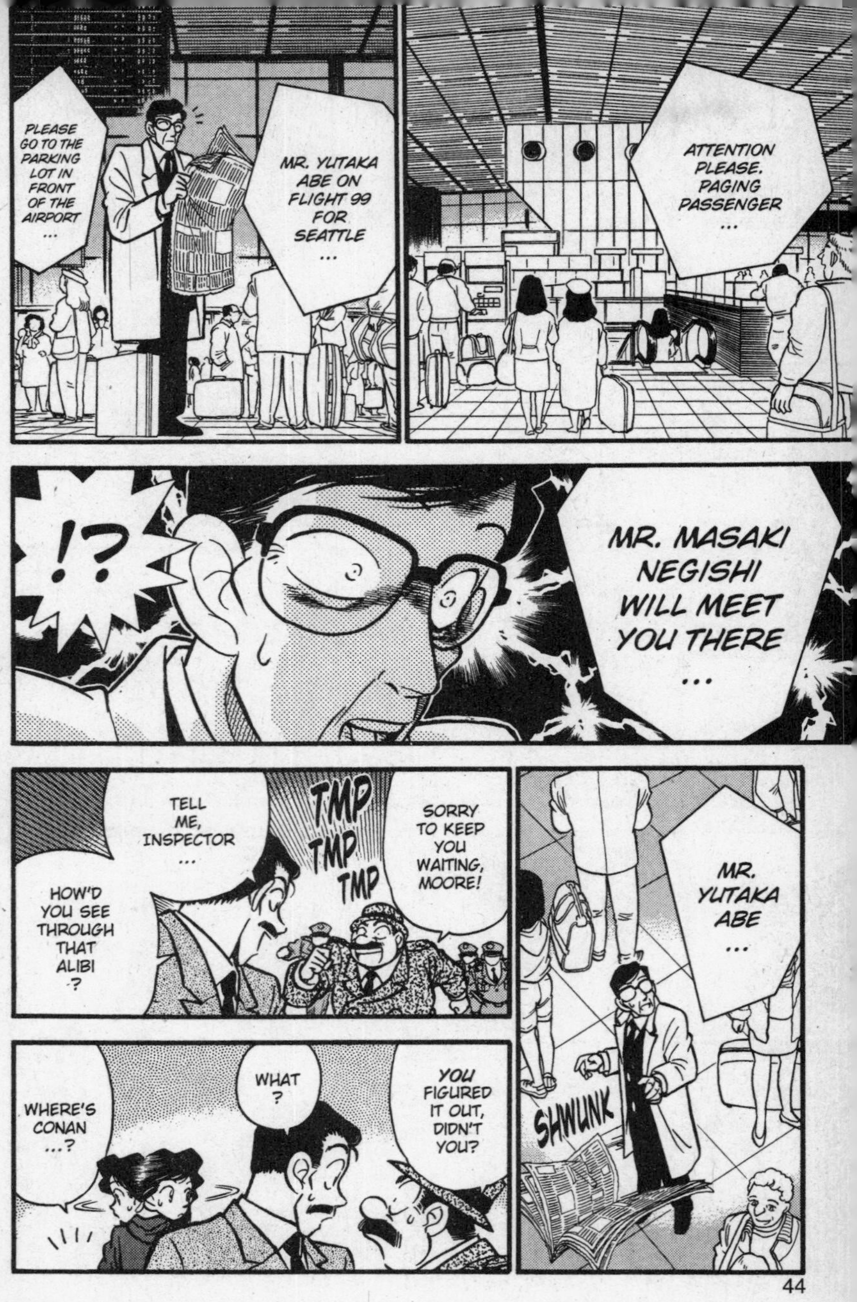
ATTENTION PLEASE. PAGING PASSENGER ...
MR. YUTAKA ABE ON FLIGHT 99 FOR SEATTLE ...
PLEASE GO TO THE PARKING LOT IN FRONT OF THE AIRPORT ...
MR. MASAKI NEGISHI WILL MEET YOU THERE ...
!?
MR. YUTAKA ABE ...
SHWUNK
SORRY TO KEEP YOU WAITING, MOORE!
TMP TMP TMP
TELL ME, INSPECTOR ...
HOW'D YOU SEE THROUGH THAT ALIBI ?
YOU FIGURED IT OUT, DIDN'T YOU?
WHAT ?
WHERE'S CONAN ...?

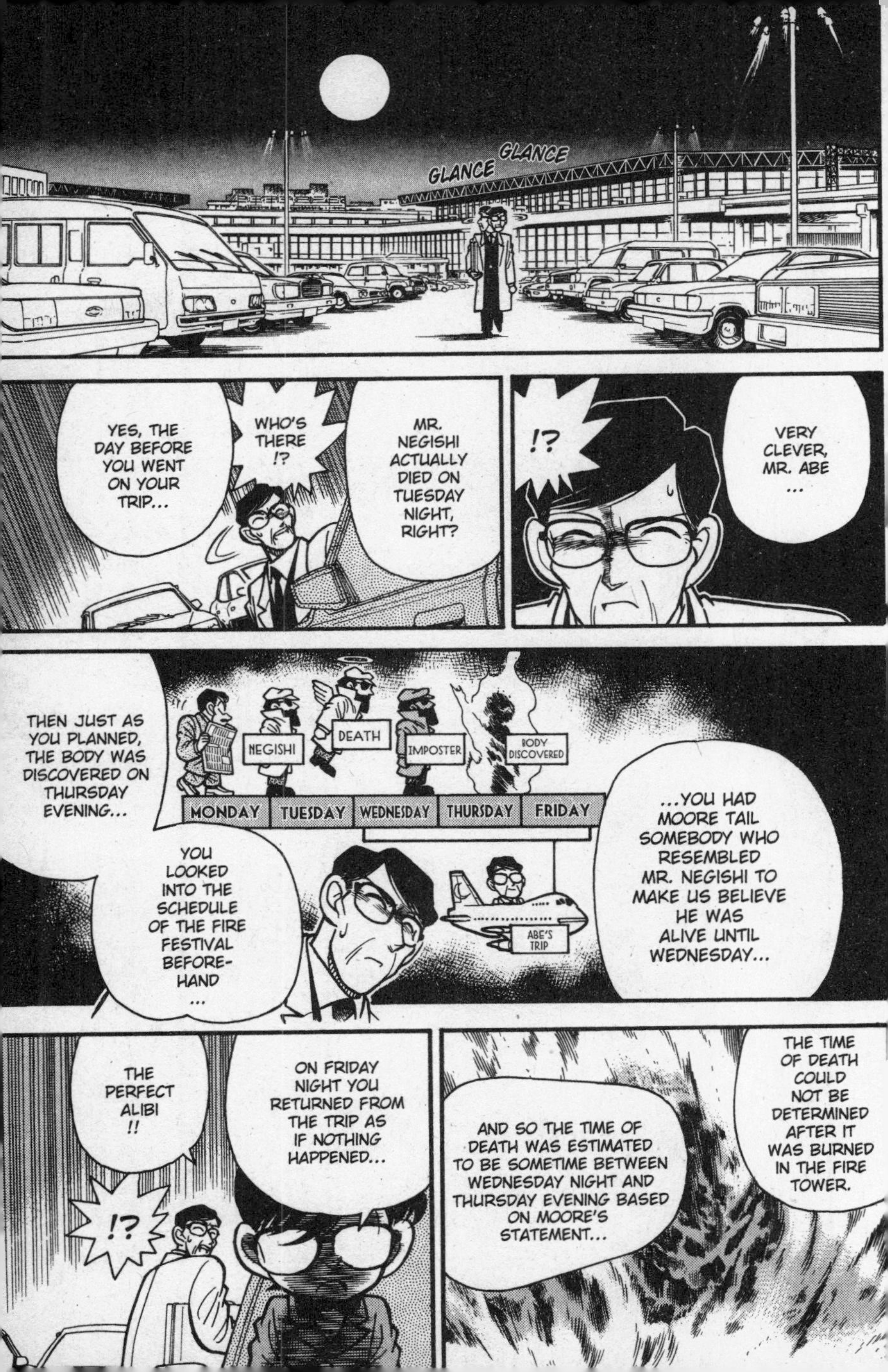
GLANCE GLANCE
VERY CLEVER, MR. ABE ...
!?
MR. NEGISHI ACTUALLY DIED ON TUESDAY NIGHT, RIGHT?
WHO'S THERE !?
YES, THE DAY BEFORE YOU WENT ON YOUR TRIP...
...YOU HAD MOORE TAIL SOMEBODY WHO RESEMBLED MR. NEGISHI TO MAKE US BELIEVE HE WAS ALIVE UNTIL WEDNESDAY...
BODY DISCOVERED
IMPOSTER
DEATH
NEGISHI
MONDAY
TUESDAY
WEDNESDAY
THURSDAY
FRIDAY
ABE'S TRIP
THEN JUST AS YOU PLANNED, THE BODY WAS DISCOVERED ON THURSDAY EVENING...
YOU LOOKED INTO THE SCHEDULE OF THE FIRE FESTIVAL BEFORE-HAND ...
THE TIME OF DEATH COULD NOT BE DETERMINED AFTER IT WAS BURNED IN THE FIRE TOWER.
AND SO THE TIME OF DEATH WAS ESTIMATED TO BE SOMETIME BETWEEN WEDNESDAY NIGHT AND THURSDAY EVENING BASED ON MOORE'S STATEMENT...
ON FRIDAY NIGHT YOU RETURNED FROM THE TRIP AS IF NOTHING HAPPENED...
!?
THE PERFECT ALIBI !!

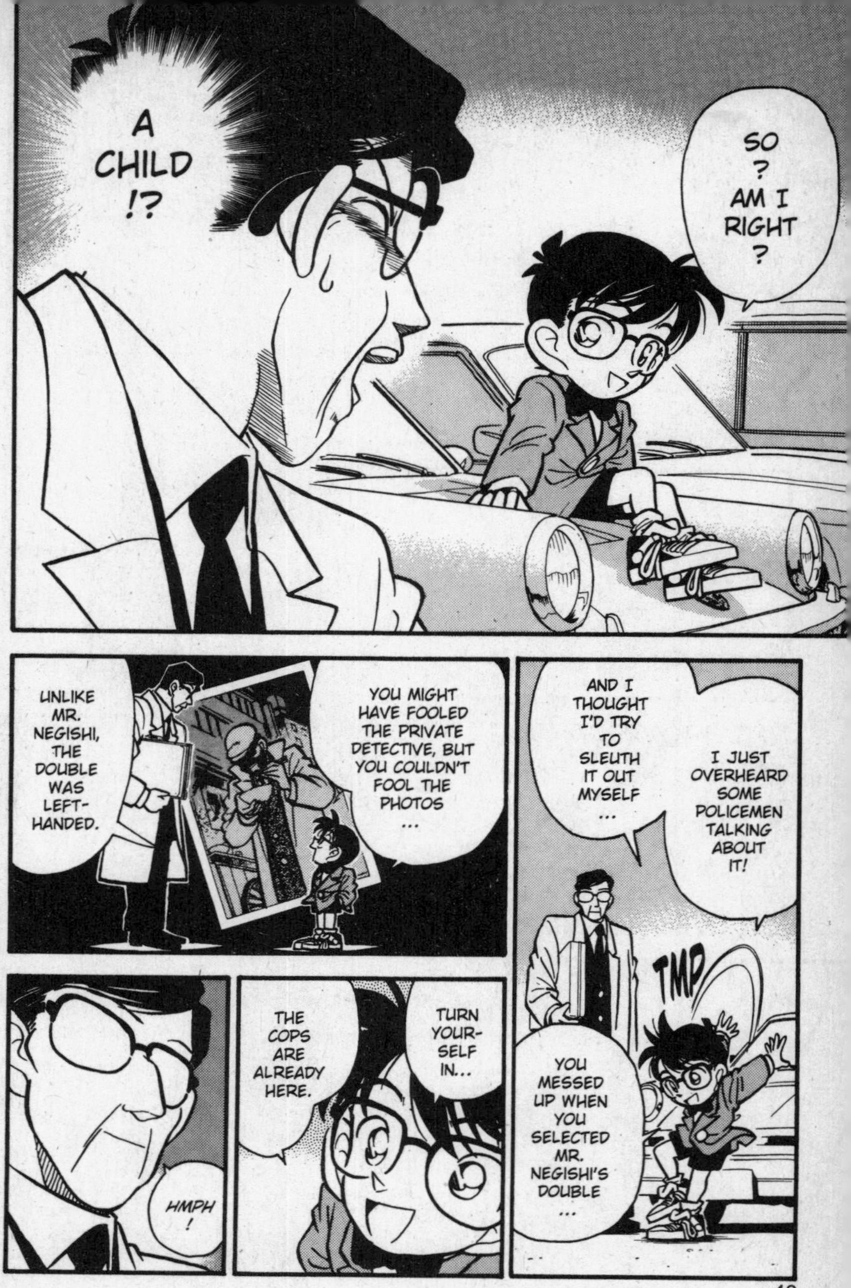
SO? AM I RIGHT?
A CHILD!?
I JUST OVERHEARD SOME POLICEMEN TALKING ABOUT IT!
AND I THOUGHT I'D TRY TO SLEUTH IT OUT MYSELF...
TMP
YOU MESSED UP WHEN YOU SELECTED MR. NEGISHI'S DOUBLE...
YOU MIGHT HAVE FOOLED THE PRIVATE DETECTIVE, BUT YOU COULDN'T FOOL THE PHOTOS...
UNLIKE MR. NEGISHI, THE DOUBLE WAS LEFT-HANDED.
TURN YOURSELF IN...
THE COPS ARE ALREADY HERE.
HMPH!

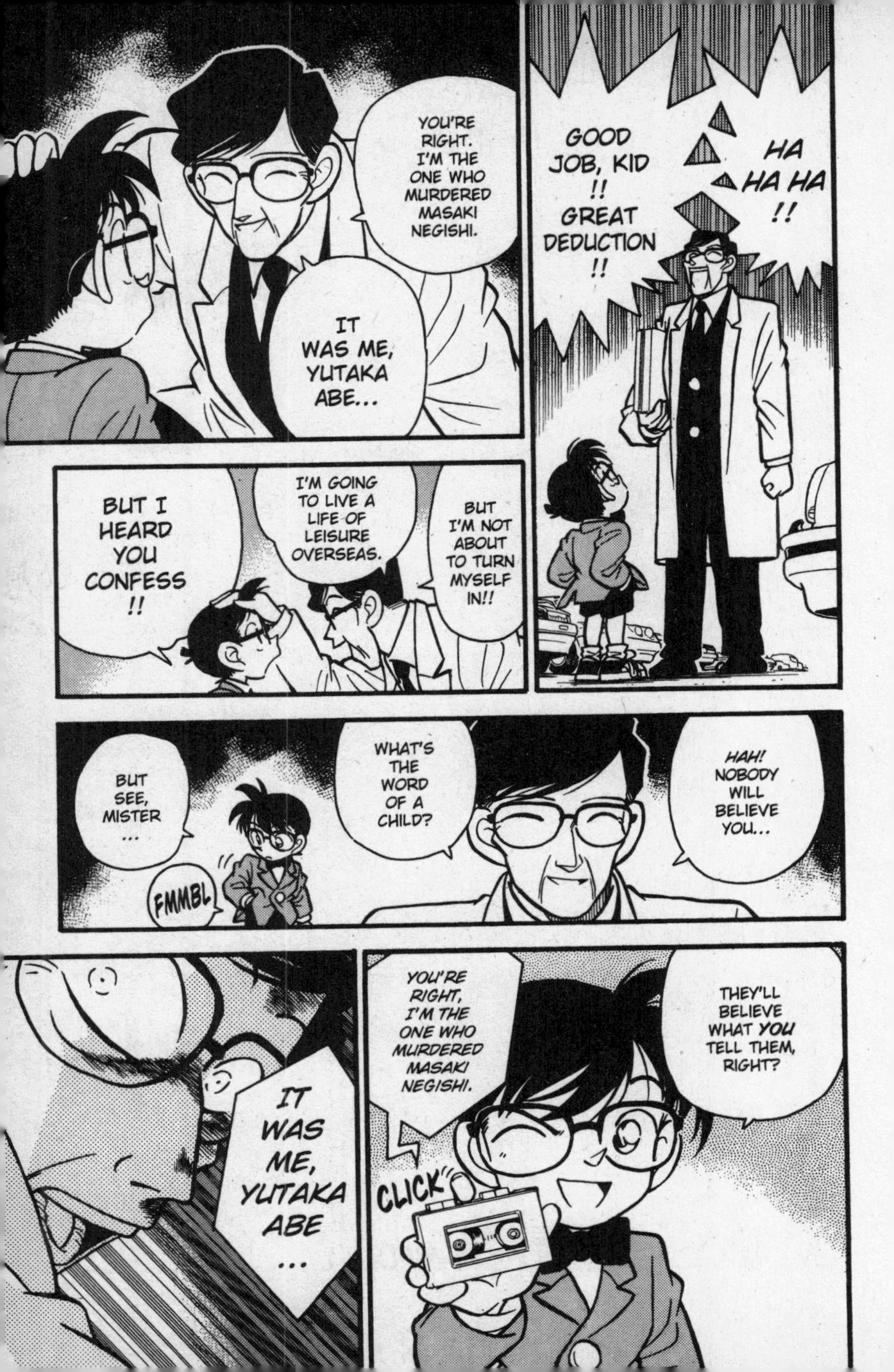
HA HA HA !!
GOOD JOB, KID !! GREAT DEDUCTION !!
YOU'RE RIGHT. I'M THE ONE WHO MURDERED MASAKI NEGISHI.
IT WAS ME, YUTAKA ABE...
BUT I'M NOT ABOUT TO TURN MYSELF IN!!
I'M GOING TO LIVE A LIFE OF LEISURE OVERSEAS.
BUT I HEARD YOU CONFESS !!
HAH! NOBODY WILL BELIEVE YOU...
WHAT'S THE WORD OF A CHILD?
BUT SEE, MISTER ...
FMMBL
THEY'LL BELIEVE WHAT YOU TELL THEM, RIGHT?
YOU'RE RIGHT, I'M THE ONE WHO MURDERED MASAKI NEGISHI.
CLICK
IT WAS ME, YUTAKA ABE ...

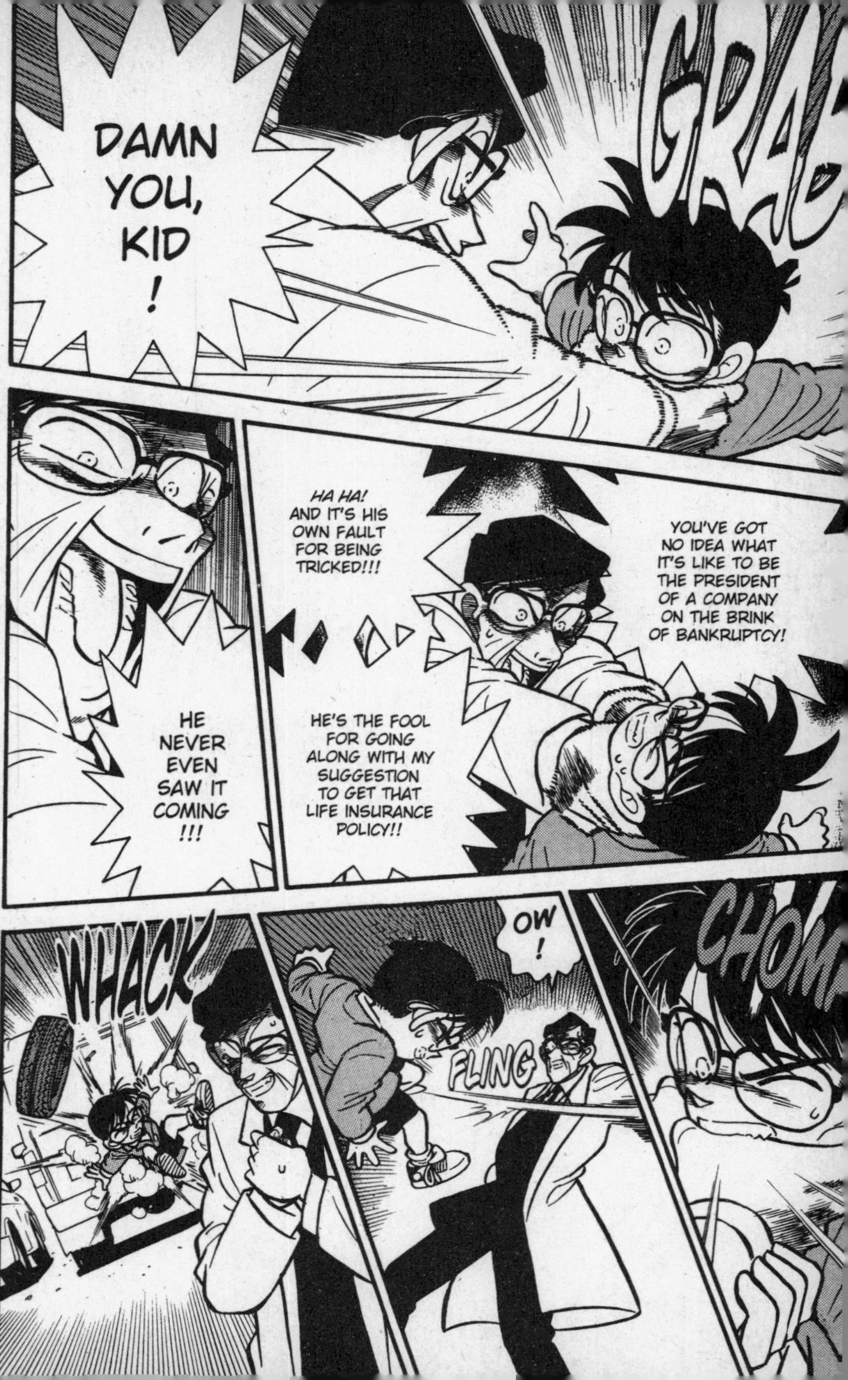
GRAB
DAMN YOU, KID!
YOU'VE GOT NO IDEA WHAT IT'S LIKE TO BE THE PRESIDENT OF A COMPANY ON THE BRINK OF BANKRUPTCY!
HA HA! AND IT'S HIS OWN FAULT FOR BEING TRICKED!!!
HE'S THE FOOL FOR GOING ALONG WITH MY SUGGESTION TO GET THAT LIFE INSURANCE POLICY!!
HE NEVER EVEN SAW IT COMING!!!
CHOM
OW!
FLING
WHACK

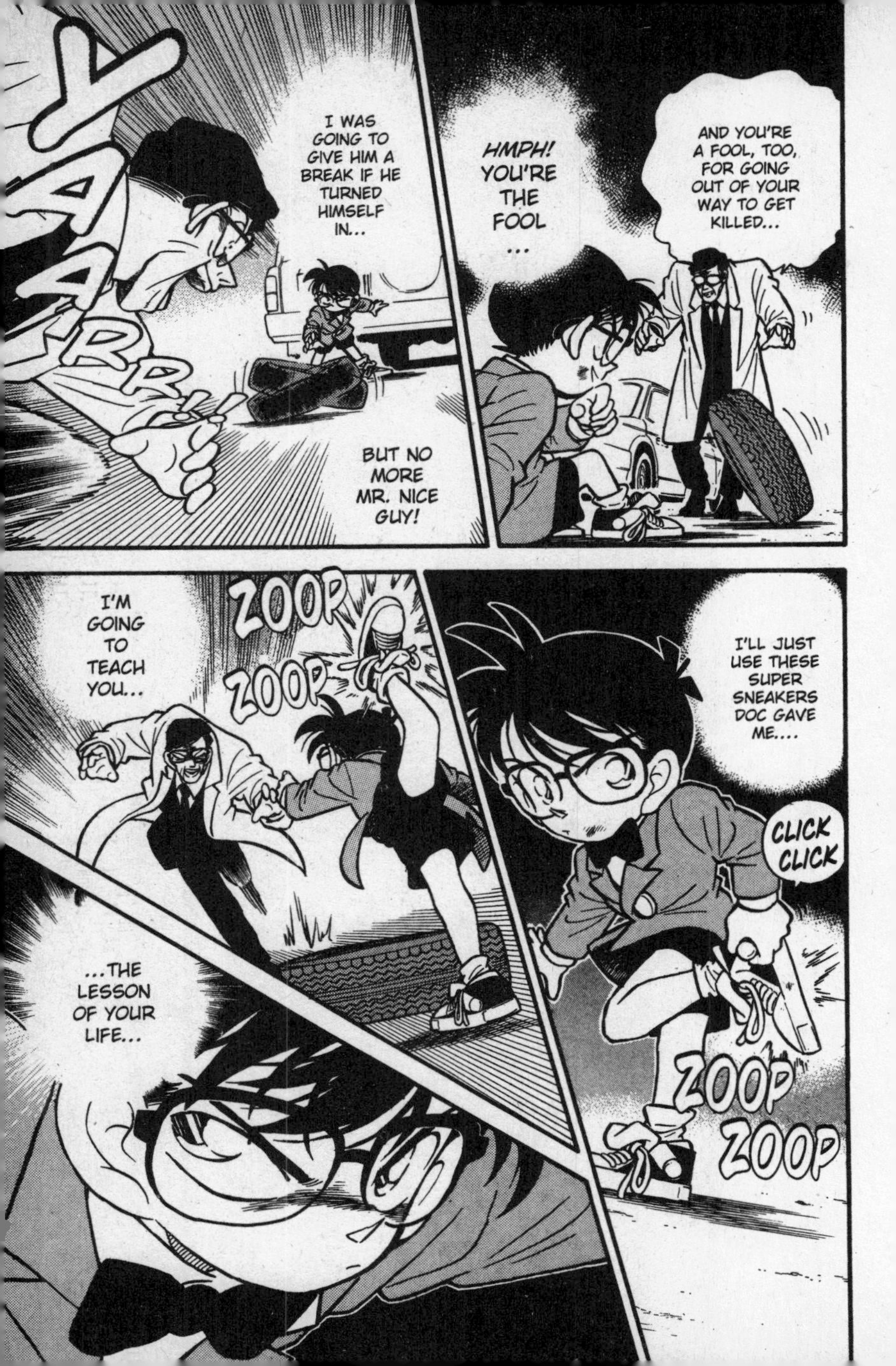
AND YOU'RE A FOOL, TOO, FOR GOING OUT OF YOUR WAY TO GET KILLED...
HMPH! YOU'RE THE FOOL ...
YAARR!!
I WAS GOING TO GIVE HIM A BREAK IF HE TURNED HIMSELF IN...
BUT NO MORE MR. NICE GUY!
I'LL JUST USE THESE SUPER SNEAKERS DOC GAVE ME....
CLICK CLICK
ZOOP
ZOOP
I'M GOING TO TEACH YOU...
ZOOP
ZOOP
...THE LESSON OF YOUR LIFE...

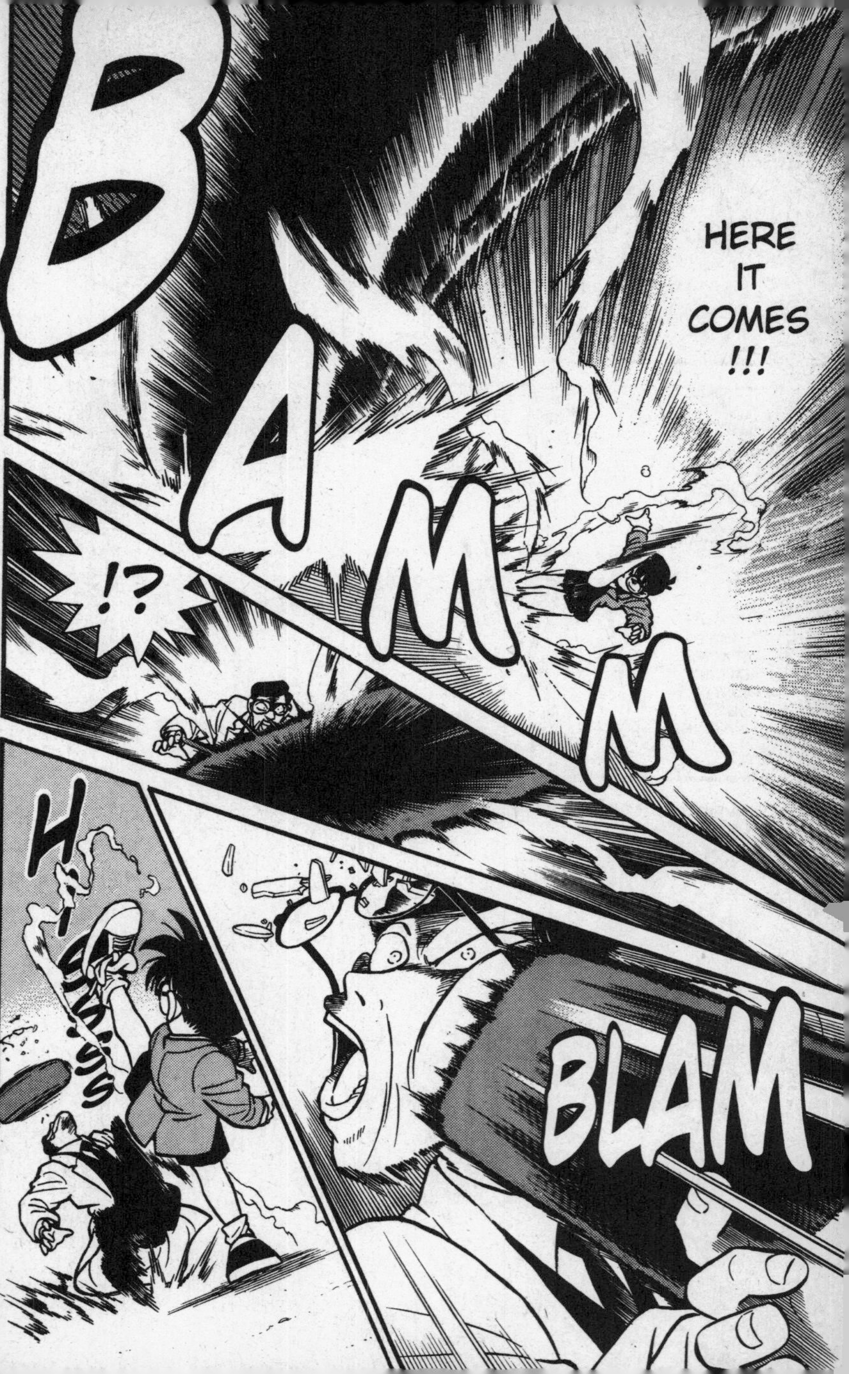
BAMMM
HERE IT COMES!!!
!?
BLAM
HISSSS

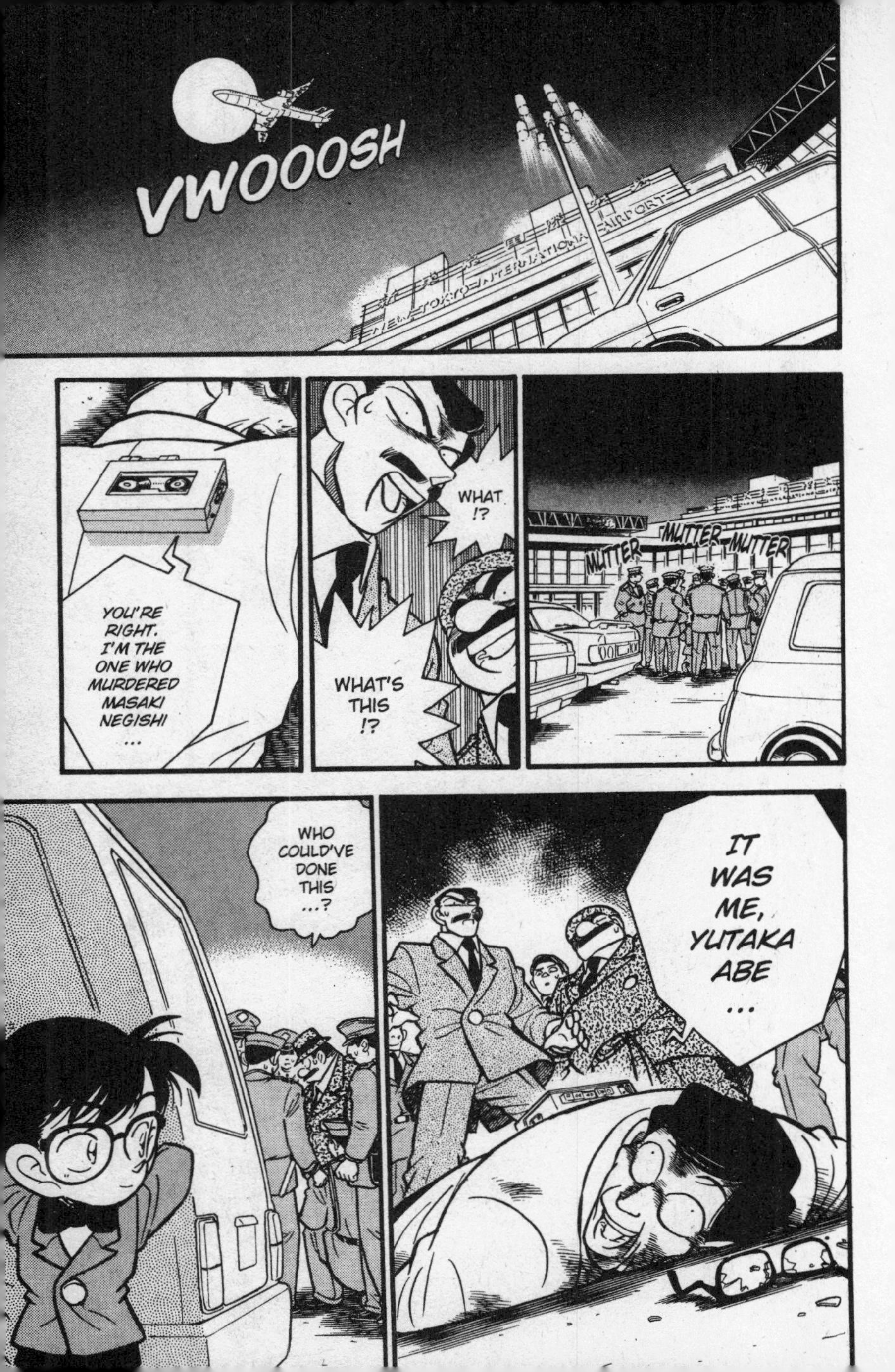
VWOOOSH
MUTTER MUTTER MUTTER
WHAT !?
WHAT'S THIS !?
YOU'RE RIGHT. I'M THE ONE WHO MURDERED MASAKI NEGISHI ...
IT WAS ME, YUTAKA ABE ...
WHO COULD'VE DONE THIS ...?

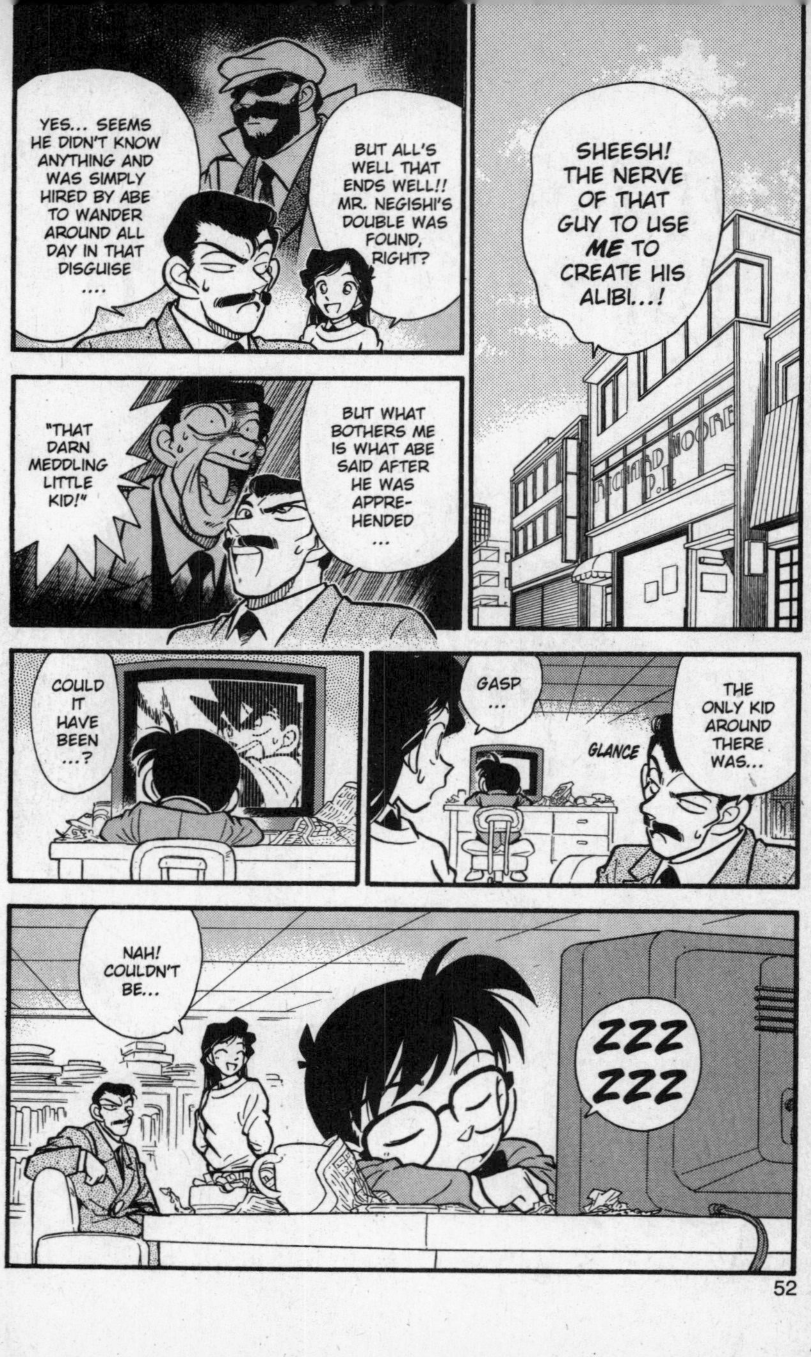
SHEESH! THE NERVE OF THAT GUY TO USE *ME* TO CREATE HIS ALIBI...!
RICHARD MOORE P.I.
BUT ALL'S WELL THAT ENDS WELL!! MR. NEGISHI'S DOUBLE WAS FOUND, RIGHT?
YES... SEEMS HE DIDN'T KNOW ANYTHING AND WAS SIMPLY HIRED BY ABE TO WANDER AROUND ALL DAY IN THAT DISGUISE ....
BUT WHAT BOTHERS ME IS WHAT ABE SAID AFTER HE WAS APPRE-HENDED ...
"THAT DARN MEDDLING LITTLE KID!"
THE ONLY KID AROUND THERE WAS...
GLANCE
GASP ...
COULD IT HAVE BEEN ...?
NAH! COULDN'T BE...
ZZZ ZZZ

FILE 4:
THE MISSING MAN

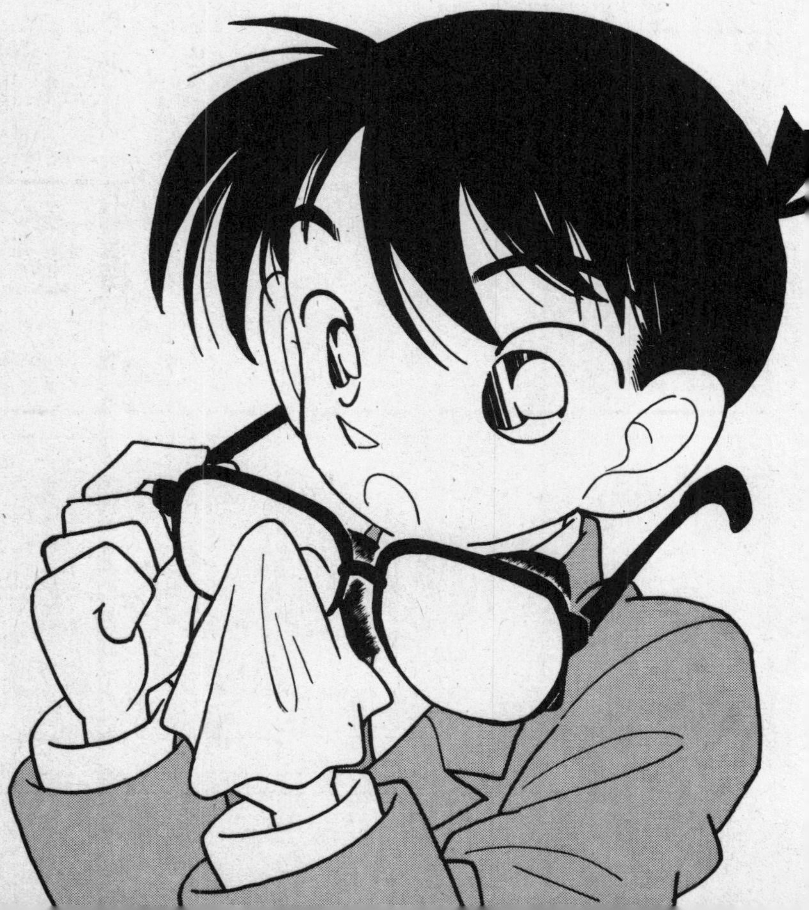

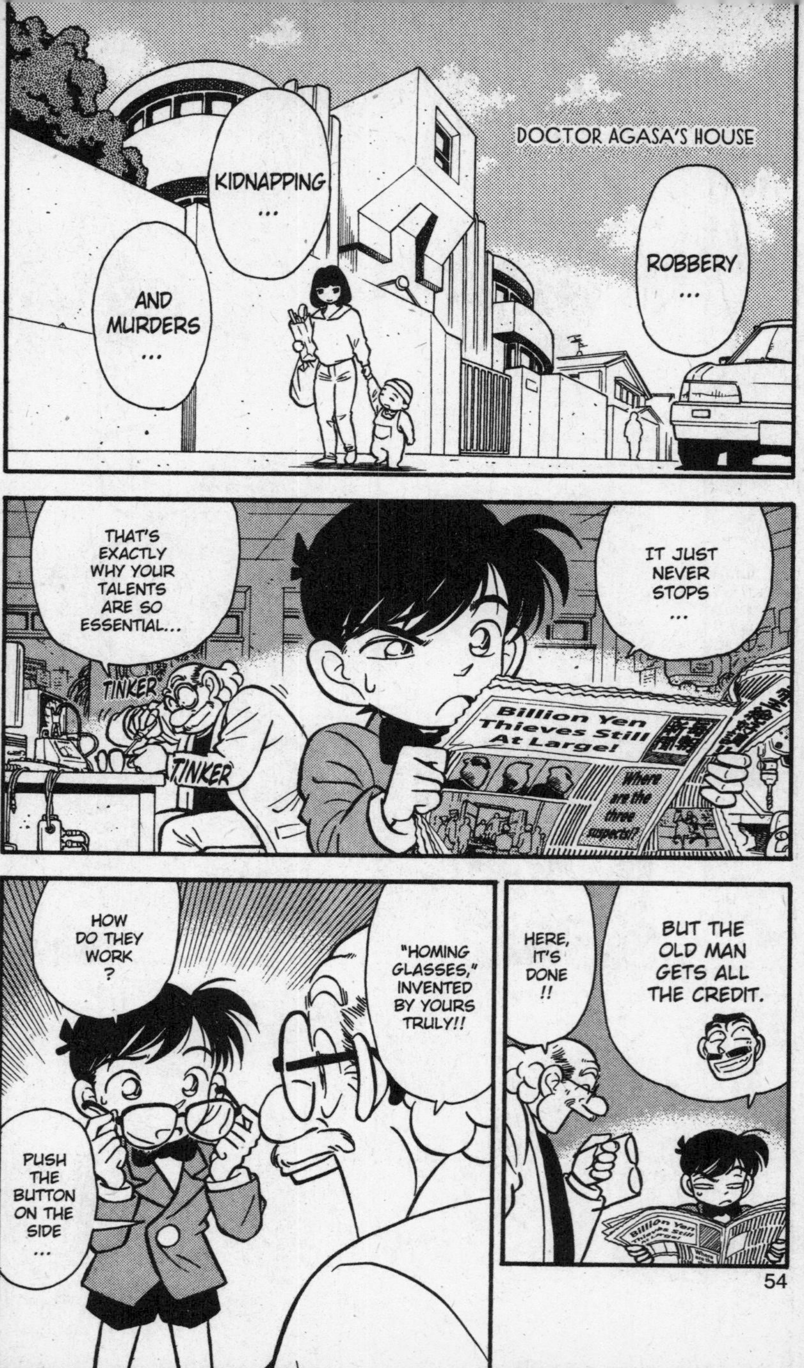
DOCTOR AGASA'S HOUSE
ROBBERY ...
KIDNAPPING ...
AND MURDERS ...
IT JUST NEVER STOPS ...
Billion Yen Thieves Still At Large!
Where are the three suspects!?
THAT'S EXACTLY WHY YOUR TALENTS ARE SO ESSENTIAL...
TINKER
TINKER
BUT THE OLD MAN GETS ALL THE CREDIT.
HERE, IT'S DONE !!
"HOMING GLASSES," INVENTED BY YOURS TRULY!!
HOW DO THEY WORK ?
PUSH THE BUTTON ON THE SIDE ...

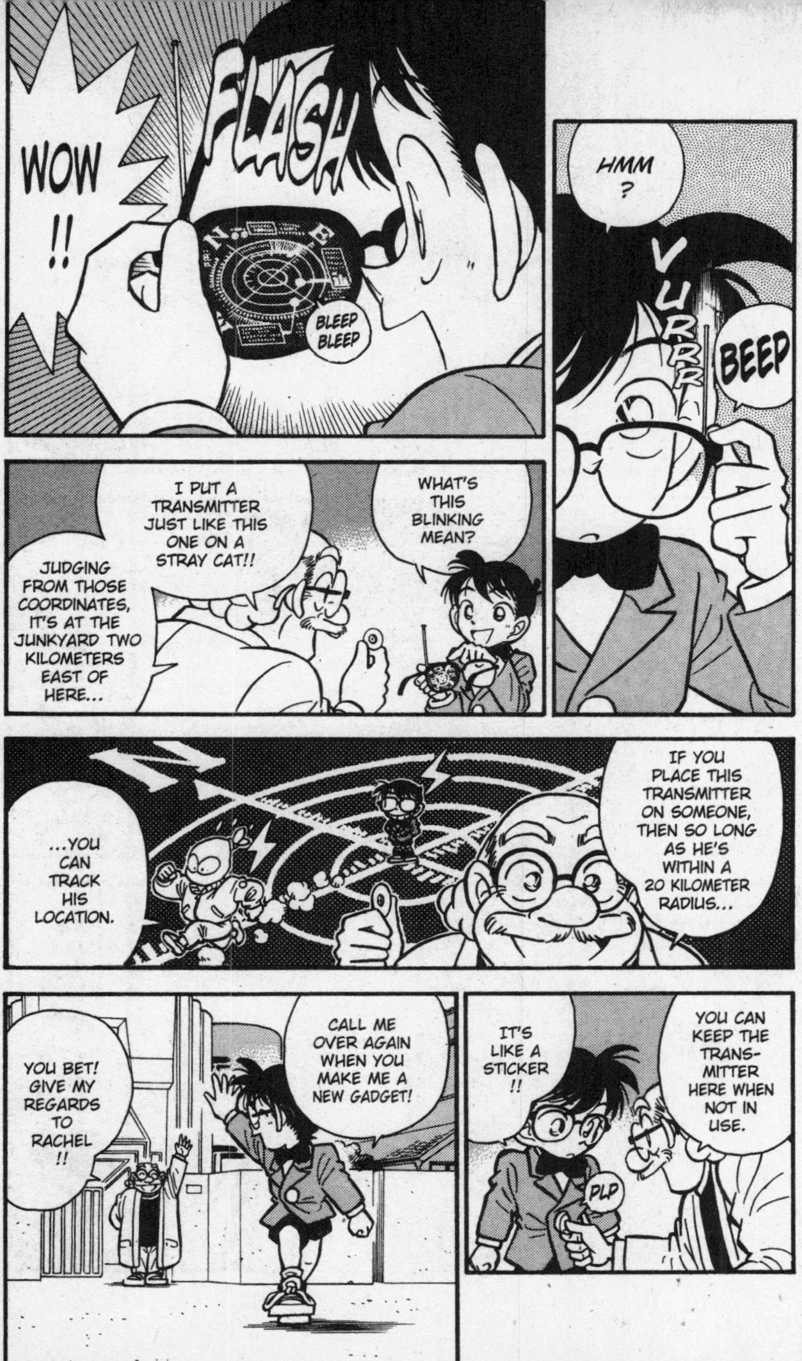
HMM ?
VURRR
BEEP
FLASH
BLEEP BLEEP
WOW !!
WHAT'S THIS BLINKING MEAN?
I PUT A TRANSMITTER JUST LIKE THIS ONE ON A STRAY CAT!!
JUDGING FROM THOSE COORDINATES, IT'S AT THE JUNKYARD TWO KILOMETERS EAST OF HERE...
IF YOU PLACE THIS TRANSMITTER ON SOMEONE, THEN SO LONG AS HE'S WITHIN A 20 KILOMETER RADIUS...
...YOU CAN TRACK HIS LOCATION.
YOU CAN KEEP THE TRANS-MITTER HERE WHEN NOT IN USE.
PLP
IT'S LIKE A STICKER !!
CALL ME OVER AGAIN WHEN YOU MAKE ME A NEW GADGET!
YOU BET! GIVE MY REGARDS TO RACHEL !!

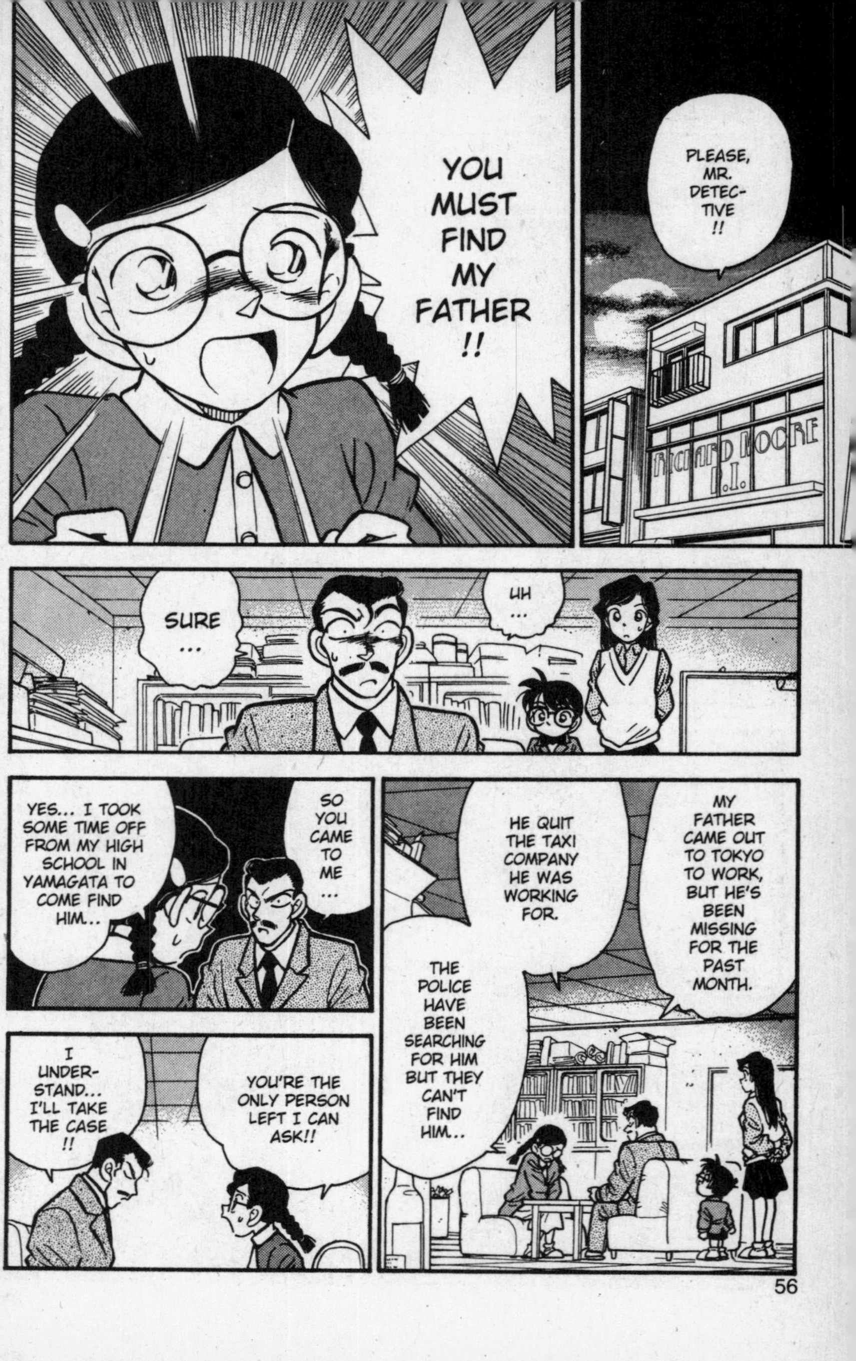
PLEASE, MR. DETECTIVE!!
RICHARD MOORE P.I.
YOU MUST FIND MY FATHER!!
UH ...
SURE ...
MY FATHER CAME OUT TO TOKYO TO WORK, BUT HE'S BEEN MISSING FOR THE PAST MONTH.
HE QUIT THE TAXI COMPANY HE WAS WORKING FOR.
THE POLICE HAVE BEEN SEARCHING FOR HIM BUT THEY CAN'T FIND HIM...
SO YOU CAME TO ME ...
YES... I TOOK SOME TIME OFF FROM MY HIGH SCHOOL IN YAMAGATA TO COME FIND HIM...
YOU'RE THE ONLY PERSON LEFT I CAN ASK!!
I UNDERSTAND... I'LL TAKE THE CASE!!

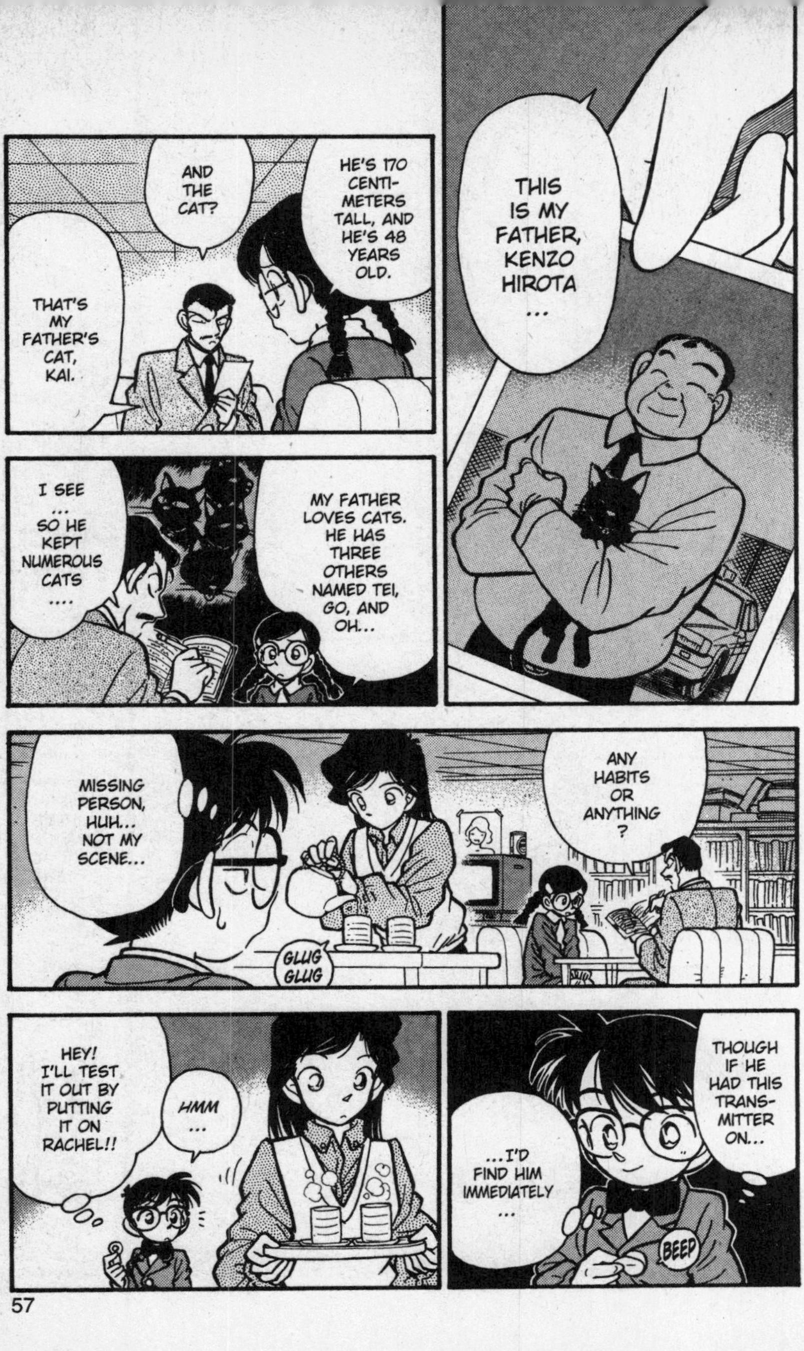
THIS IS MY FATHER, KENZO HIROTA ...
HE'S 170 CENTIMETERS TALL, AND HE'S 48 YEARS OLD.
AND THE CAT?
THAT'S MY FATHER'S CAT, KAI.
MY FATHER LOVES CATS. HE HAS THREE OTHERS NAMED TEI, GO, AND OH...
I SEE ... SO HE KEPT NUMEROUS CATS ....
ANY HABITS OR ANYTHING?
MISSING PERSON, HUH... NOT MY SCENE...
GLUG GLUG
THOUGH IF HE HAD THIS TRANSMITTER ON...
...I'D FIND HIM IMMEDIATELY ...
BEEP
HMM ...
HEY! I'LL TEST IT OUT BY PUTTING IT ON RACHEL!!

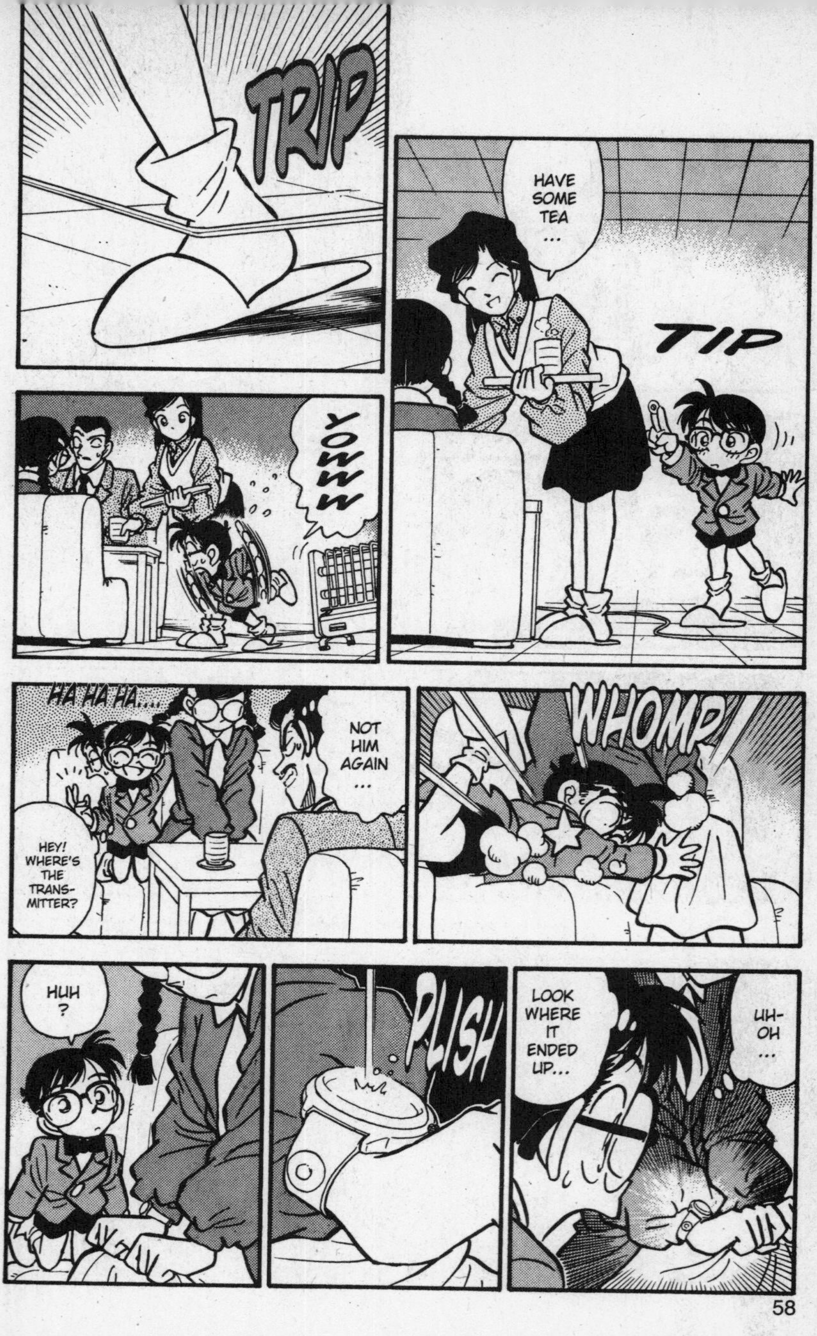
HAVE SOME TEA ...
TIP
TRIP
YOWWW
WHOMP
NOT HIM AGAIN ...
HA HA HA...
HEY! WHERE'S THE TRANS-MITTER?
LOOK WHERE IT ENDED UP...
UH-OH ...
PLISH
HUH ?

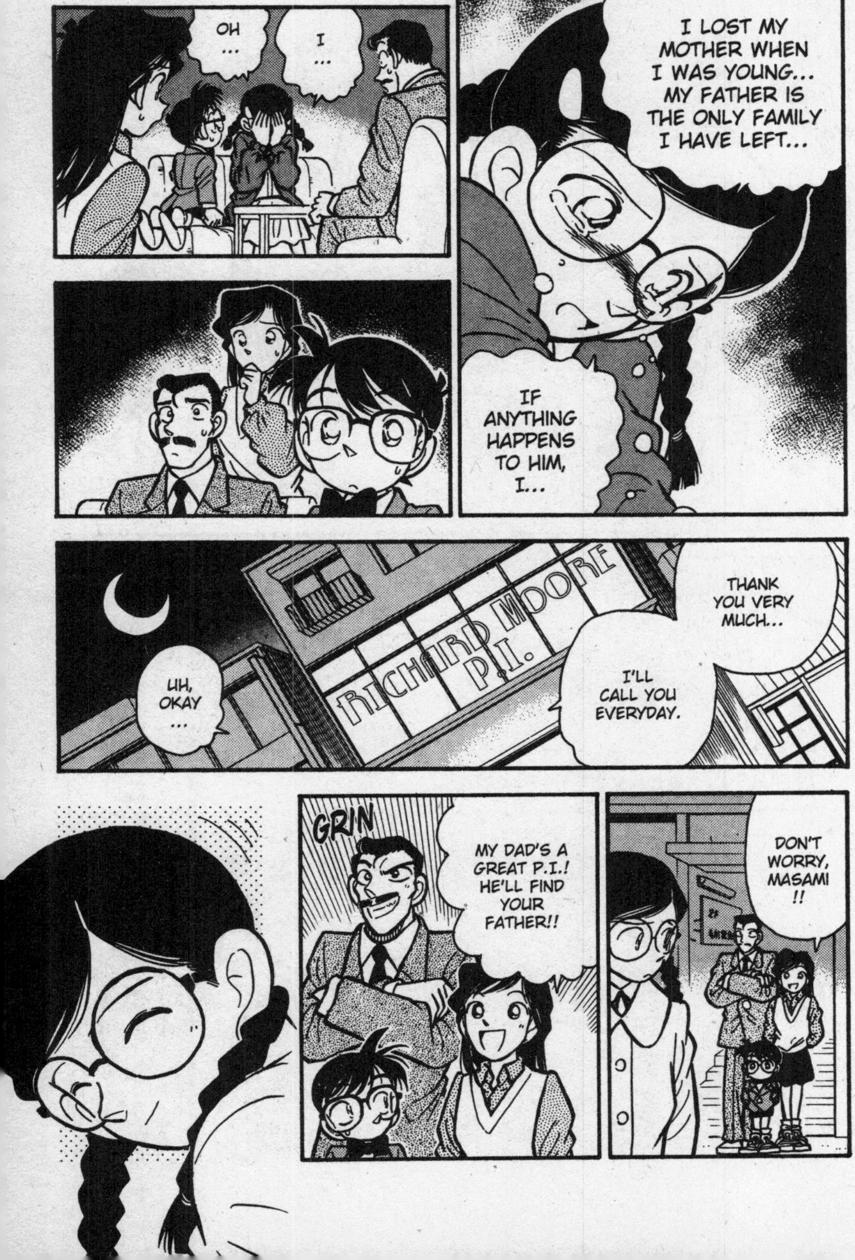
I LOST MY MOTHER WHEN I WAS YOUNG... MY FATHER IS THE ONLY FAMILY I HAVE LEFT...
IF ANYTHING HAPPENS TO HIM, I...
I ...
OH ...
THANK YOU VERY MUCH...
I'LL CALL YOU EVERYDAY.
RICHARD MOORE P.I.
UH, OKAY ...
DON'T WORRY, MASAMI !!
GRIN
MY DAD'S A GREAT P.I.! HE'LL FIND YOUR FATHER!!

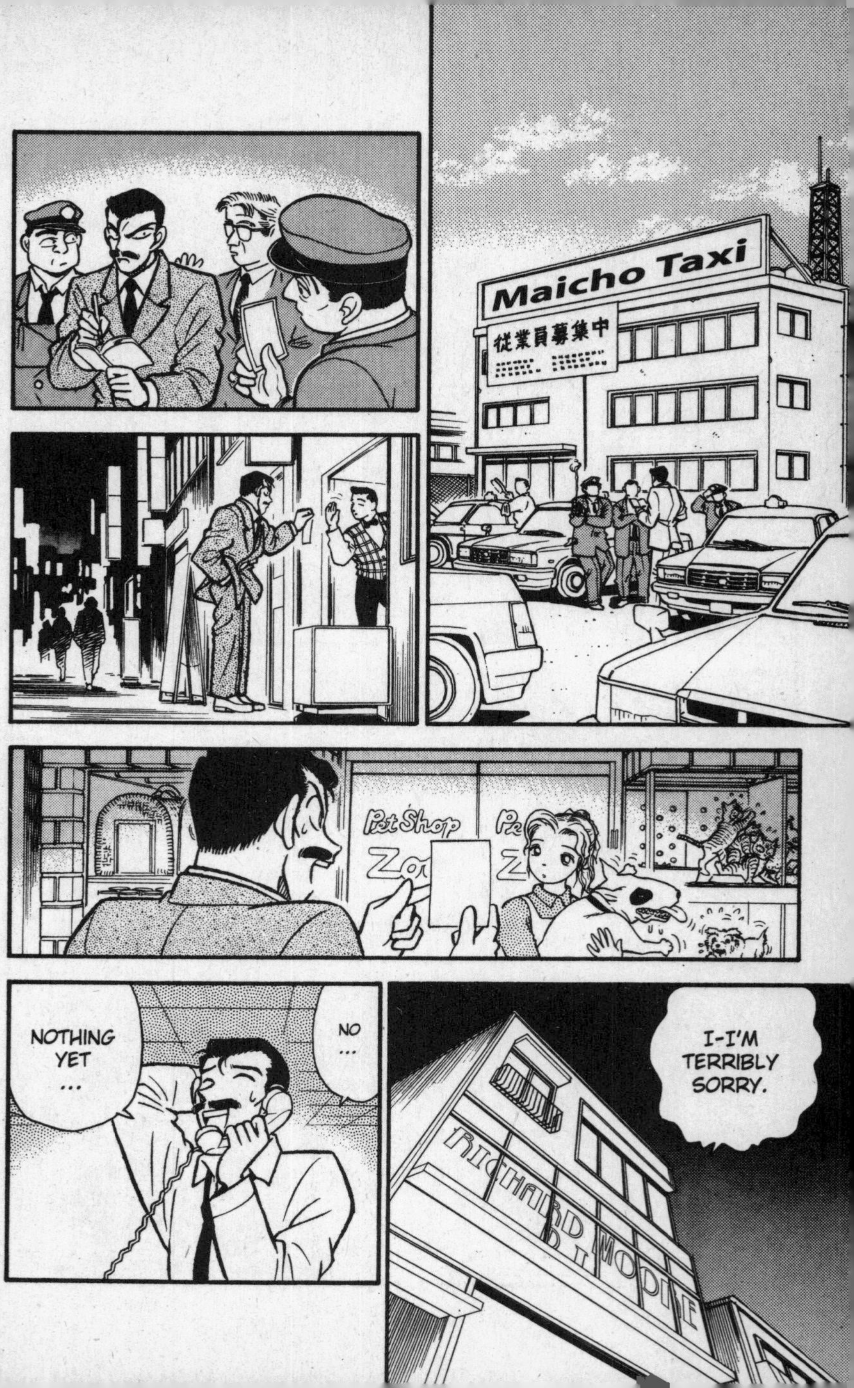

Maicho Taxi
従業員募集中
Pet Shop
RICHARD
I-I'M TERRIBLY SORRY.
NO ...
NOTHING YET ...

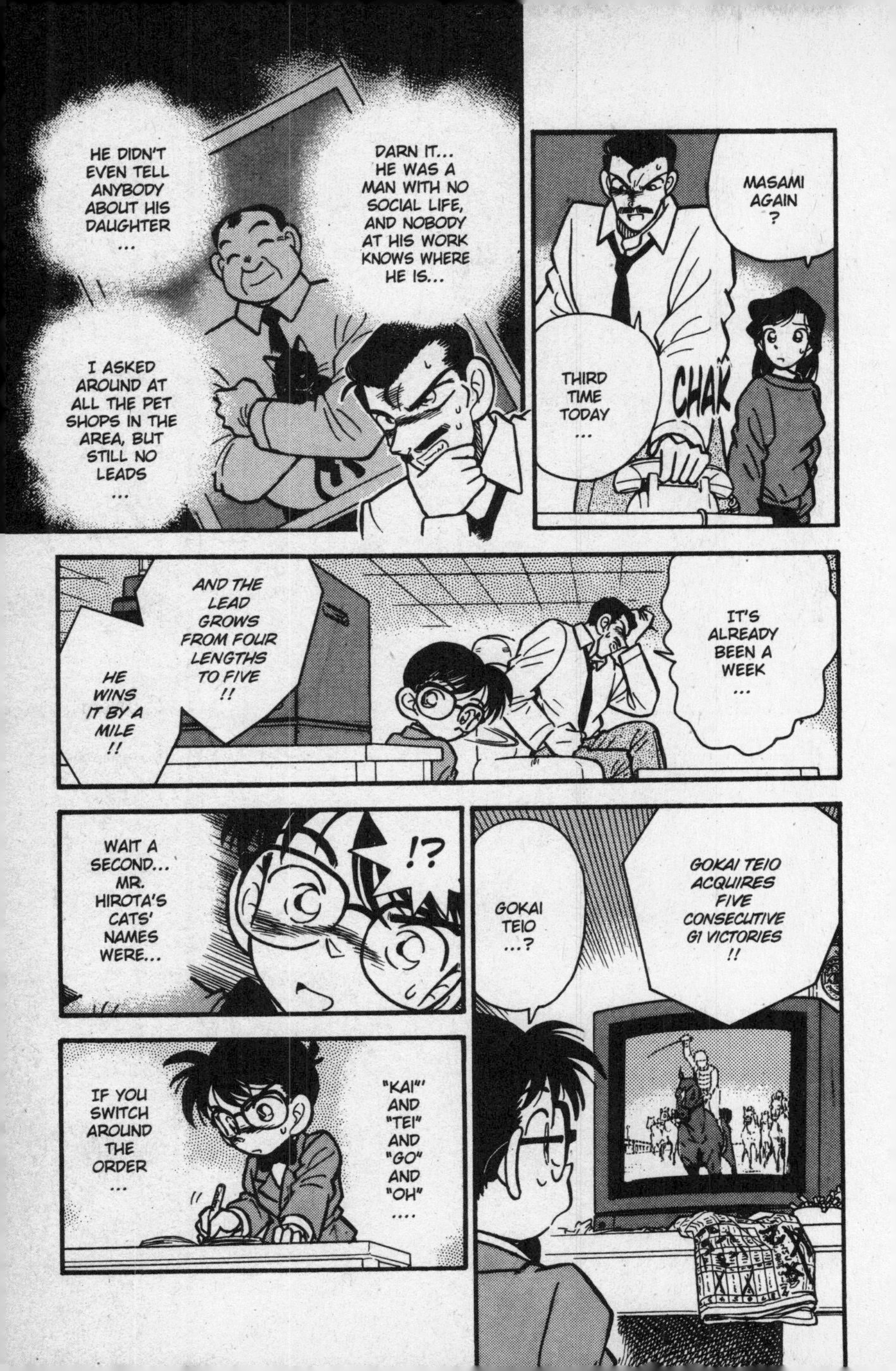
MASAMI AGAIN ?
CHAK
THIRD TIME TODAY ...
DARN IT... HE WAS A MAN WITH NO SOCIAL LIFE, AND NOBODY AT HIS WORK KNOWS WHERE HE IS...
HE DIDN'T EVEN TELL ANYBODY ABOUT HIS DAUGHTER ...
I ASKED AROUND AT ALL THE PET SHOPS IN THE AREA, BUT STILL NO LEADS ...
IT'S ALREADY BEEN A WEEK ...
AND THE LEAD GROWS FROM FOUR LENGTHS TO FIVE !!
HE WINS IT BY A MILE !!
GOKAI TEIO ACQUIRES FIVE CONSECUTIVE G1 VICTORIES !!
GOKAI TEIO ...?
!?
WAIT A SECOND... MR. HIROTA'S CATS' NAMES WERE...
"KAI" AND "TEI" AND "GO" AND "OH" ....
IF YOU SWITCH AROUND THE ORDER ...

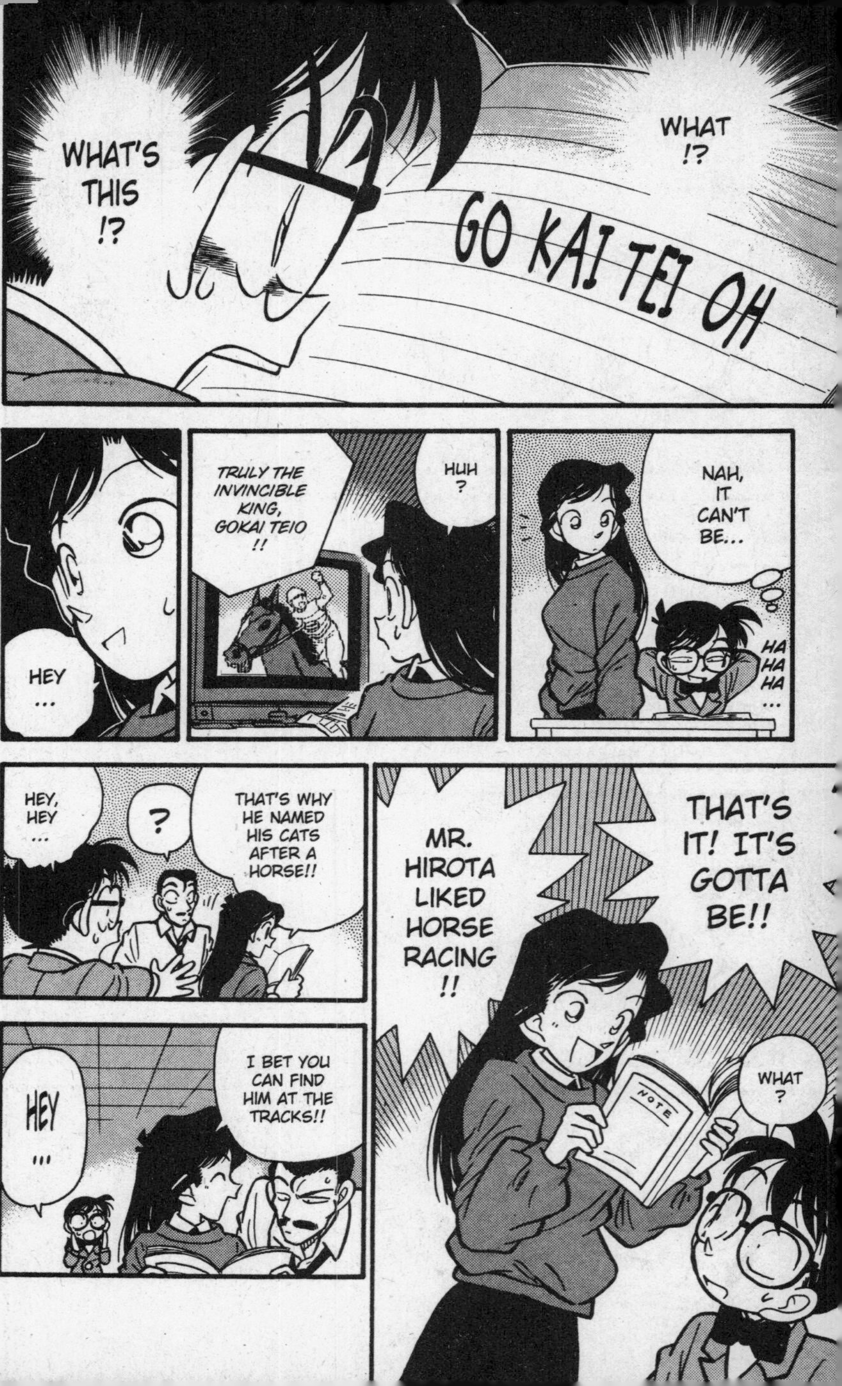
WHAT !?
GO KAI TEI OH
WHAT'S THIS !?
NAH, IT CAN'T BE...
HA HA HA ...
HUH ?
TRULY THE INVINCIBLE KING, GOKAI TEIO !!
HEY ...
THAT'S IT! IT'S GOTTA BE!!
MR. HIROTA LIKED HORSE RACING !!
NOTE
WHAT ?
THAT'S WHY HE NAMED HIS CATS AFTER A HORSE!!
?
HEY, HEY ...
I BET YOU CAN FIND HIM AT THE TRACKS!!
HEY ...

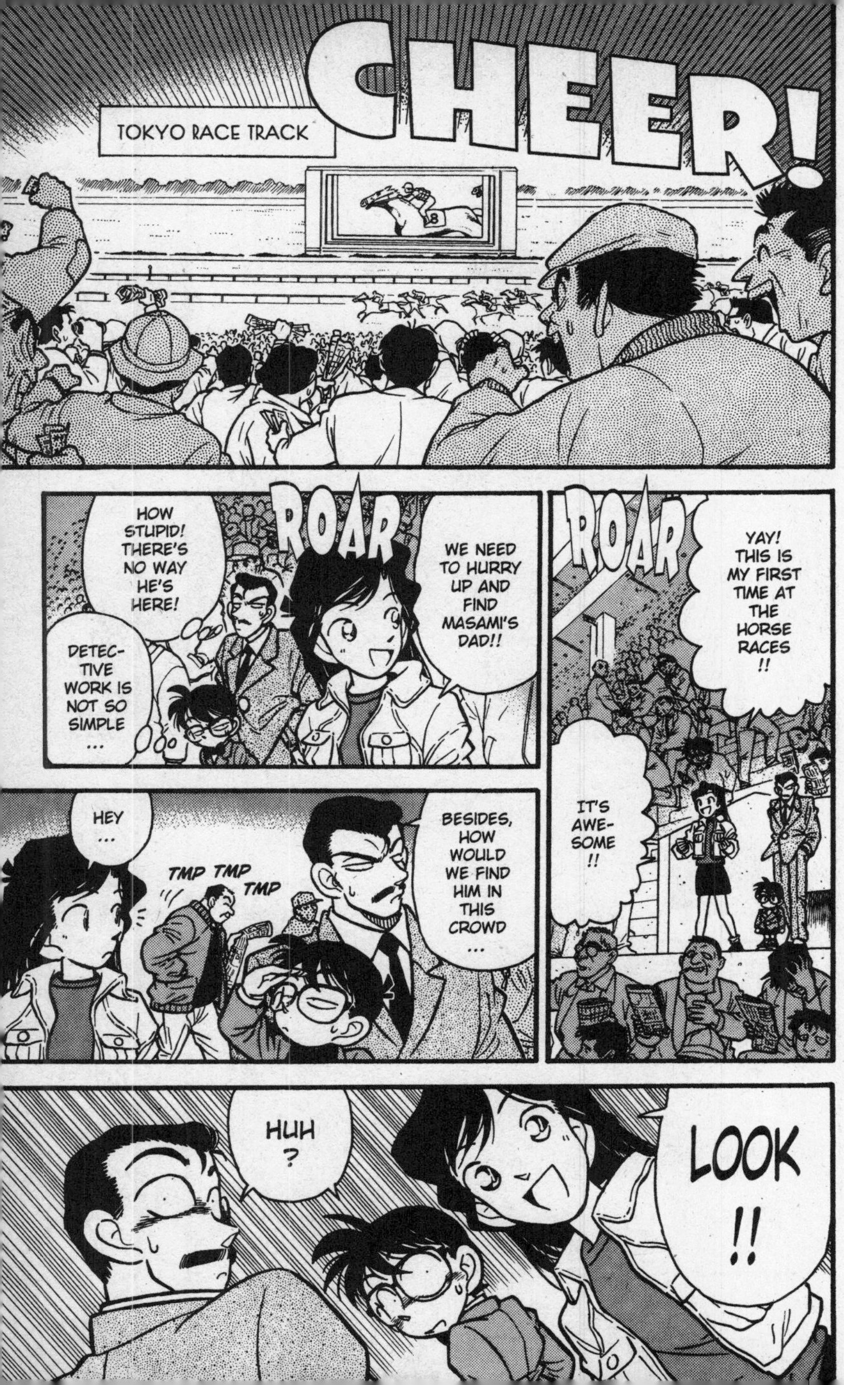
CHEER!
TOKYO RACE TRACK
ROAR
YAY! THIS IS MY FIRST TIME AT THE HORSE RACES!!
IT'S AWE-SOME!!
WE NEED TO HURRY UP AND FIND MASAMI'S DAD!!
ROAR
HOW STUPID! THERE'S NO WAY HE'S HERE!
DETEC-TIVE WORK IS NOT SO SIMPLE...
BESIDES, HOW WOULD WE FIND HIM IN THIS CROWD...
TMP TMP TMP
HEY...
LOOK!!
HUH?

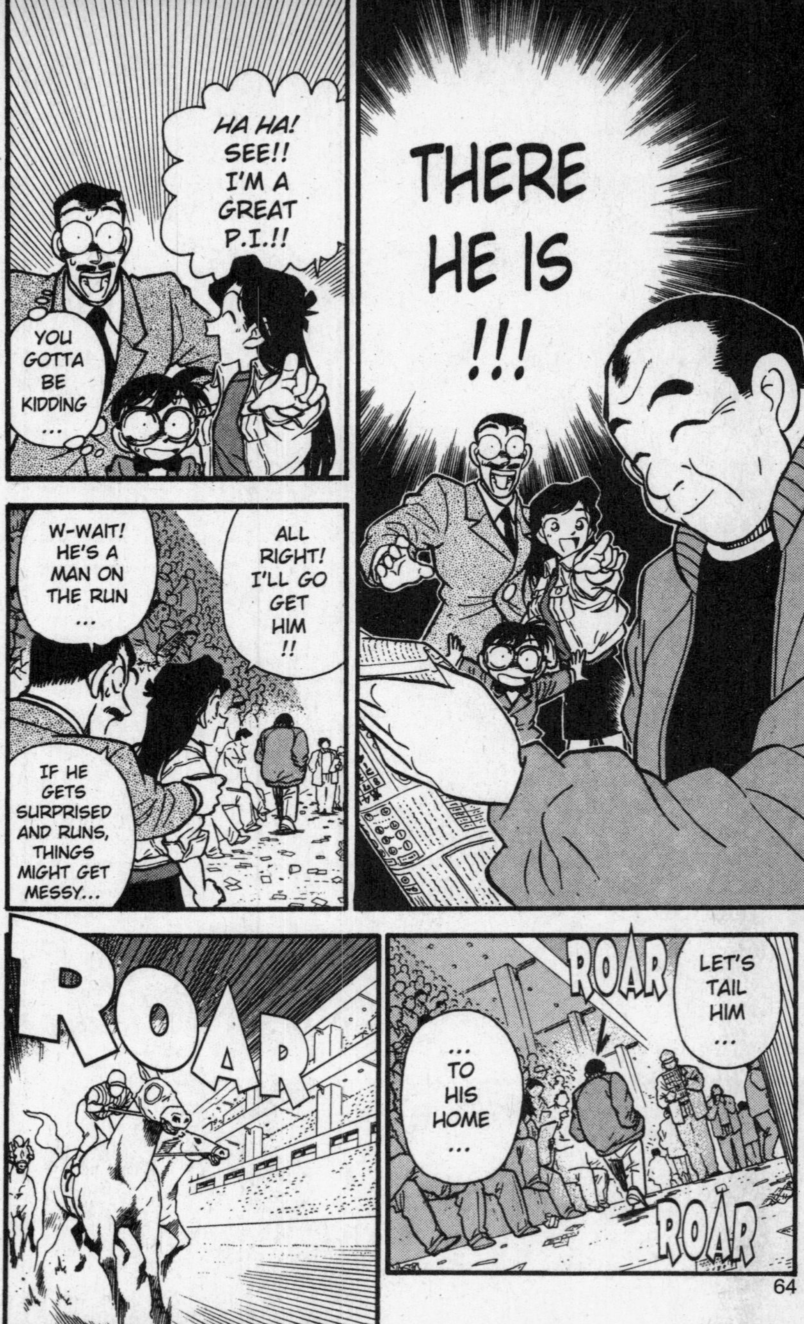
THERE HE IS !!!
HA HA! SEE!! I'M A GREAT P.I.!!
YOU GOTTA BE KIDDING ...
ALL RIGHT! I'LL GO GET HIM !!
W-WAIT! HE'S A MAN ON THE RUN ...
IF HE GETS SURPRISED AND RUNS, THINGS MIGHT GET MESSY...
ROAR
LET'S TAIL HIM ...
... TO HIS HOME ...
ROAR
ROAR

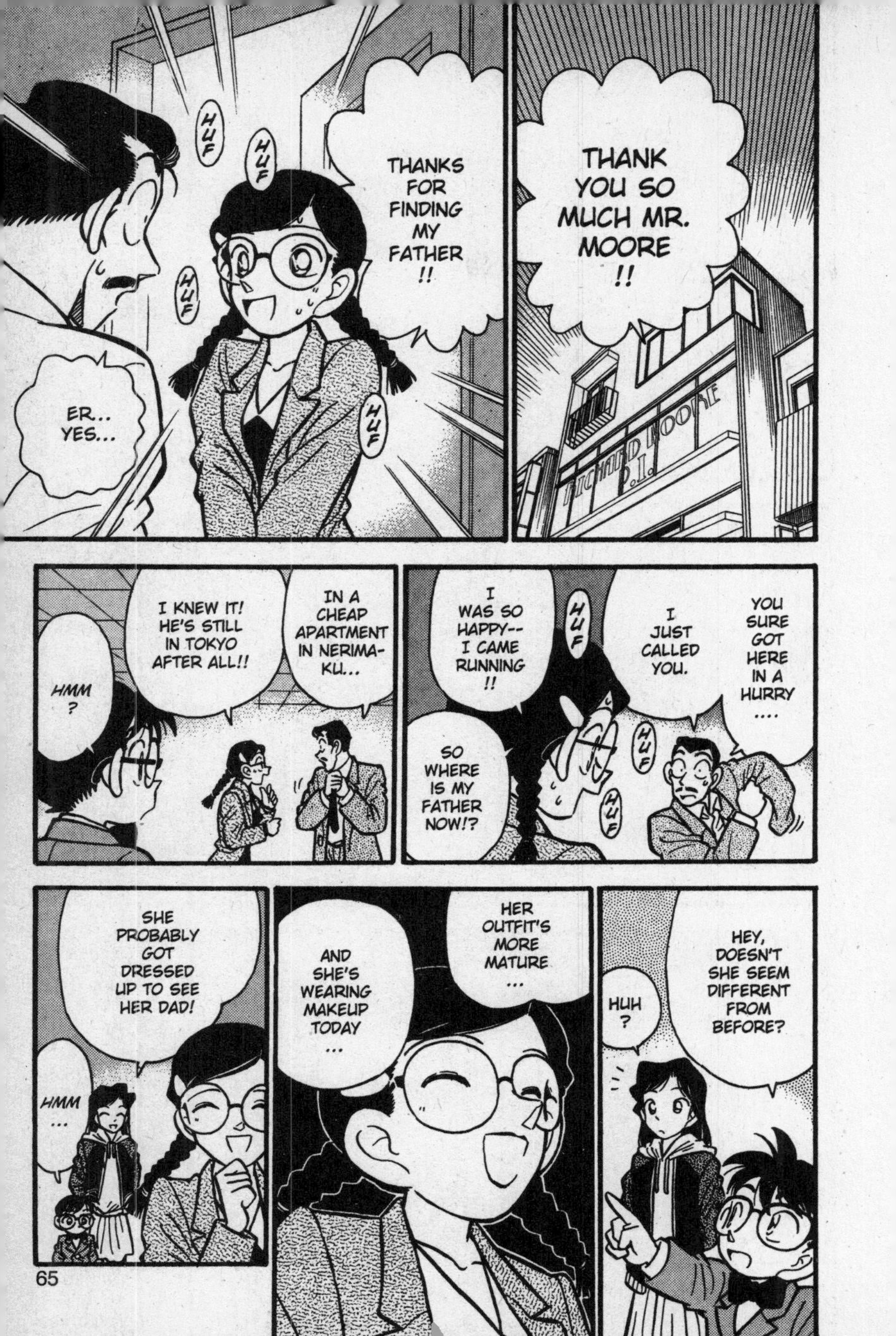
THANK YOU SO MUCH MR. MOORE !!
HUF
HUF
THANKS FOR FINDING MY FATHER !!
HUF
HUF
ER... YES...
YOU SURE GOT HERE IN A HURRY ....
I JUST CALLED YOU.
I WAS SO HAPPY-- I CAME RUNNING !!
HUF
HUF
HUF
SO WHERE IS MY FATHER NOW!?
IN A CHEAP APARTMENT IN NERIMA-KU...
I KNEW IT! HE'S STILL IN TOKYO AFTER ALL!!
HMM ?
HEY, DOESN'T SHE SEEM DIFFERENT FROM BEFORE?
HUH ?
HER OUTFIT'S MORE MATURE ...
AND SHE'S WEARING MAKEUP TODAY ...
SHE PROBABLY GOT DRESSED UP TO SEE HER DAD!
HMM ...

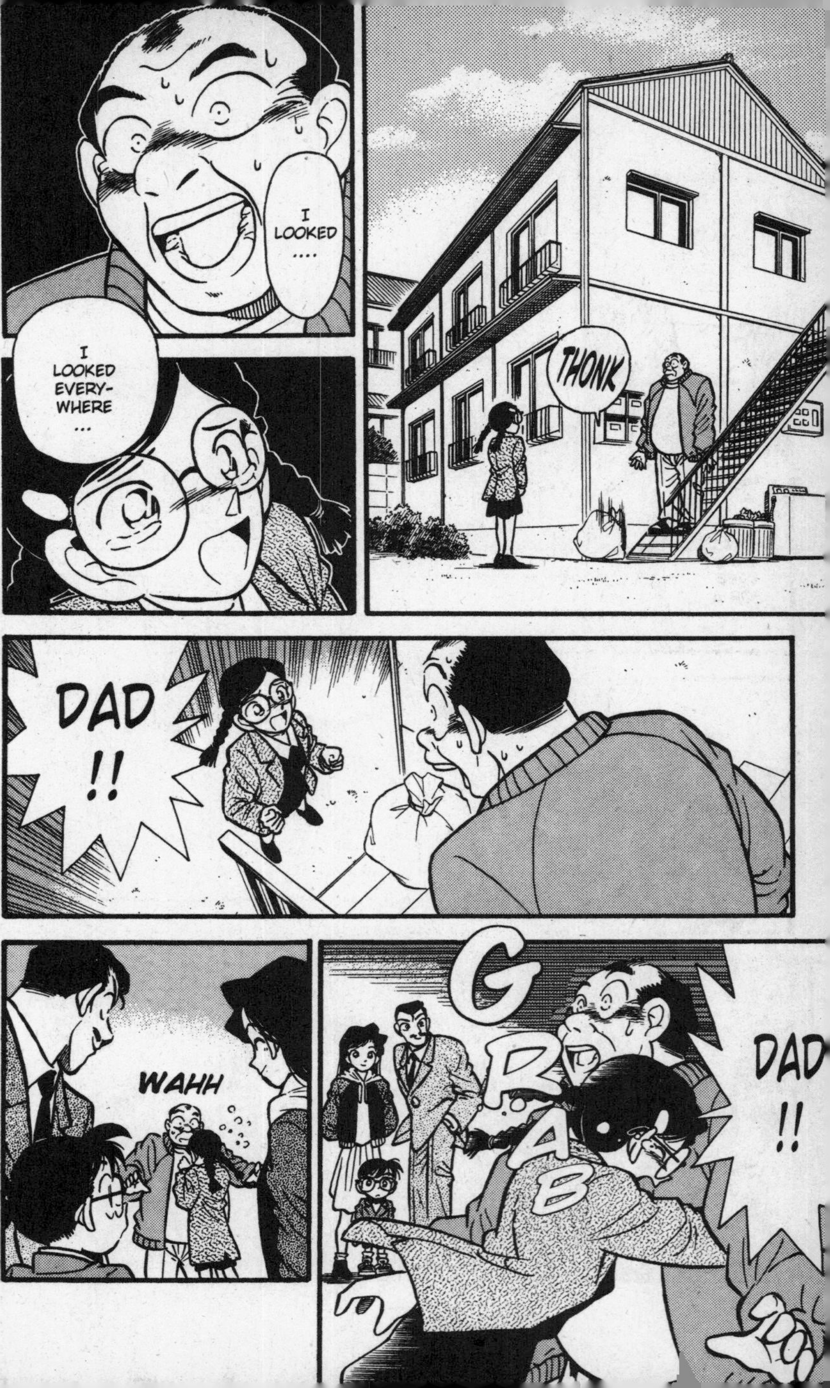
THONK
I LOOKED ....
I LOOKED EVERY-WHERE ...
DAD !!
DAD !!
GRAB
WAHH

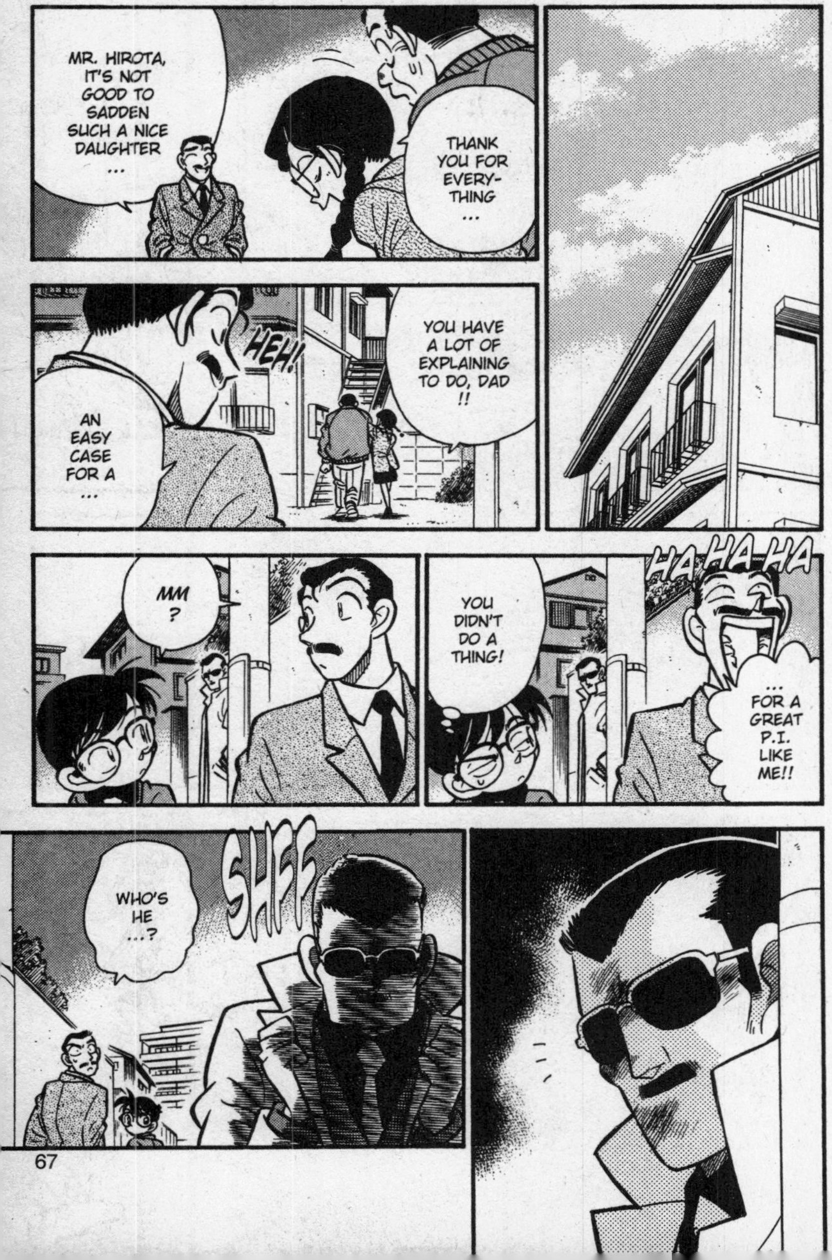
THANK YOU FOR EVERYTHING ...
MR. HIROTA, IT'S NOT GOOD TO SADDEN SUCH A NICE DAUGHTER ...
YOU HAVE A LOT OF EXPLAINING TO DO, DAD !!
HEH!
AN EASY CASE FOR A ...
HA HA HA HA
... FOR A GREAT P.I. LIKE ME!!
YOU DIDN'T DO A THING!
MM ?
SHFF
WHO'S HE ...?

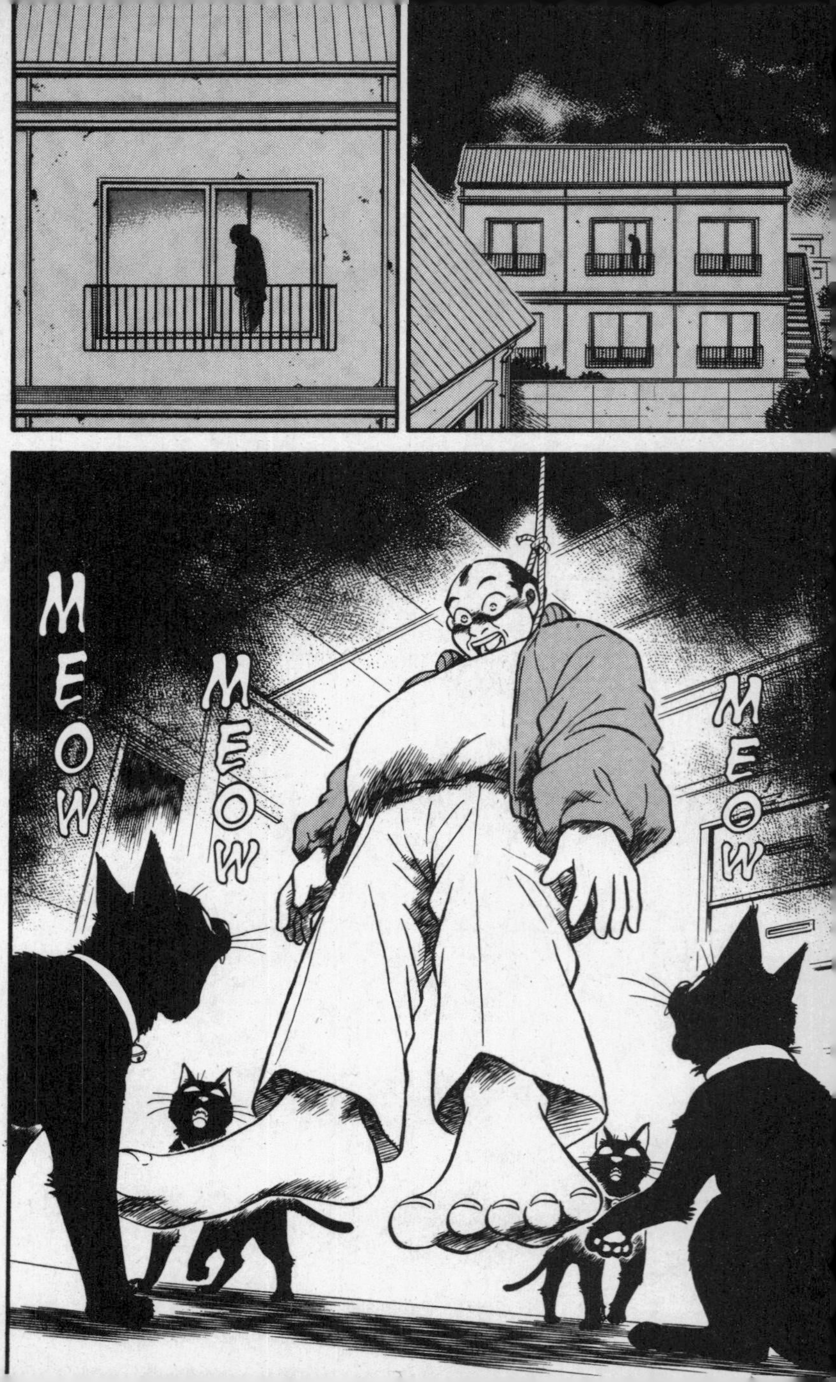
MEOW
MEOW
MEOW

FILE 5: THE POOR GIRL

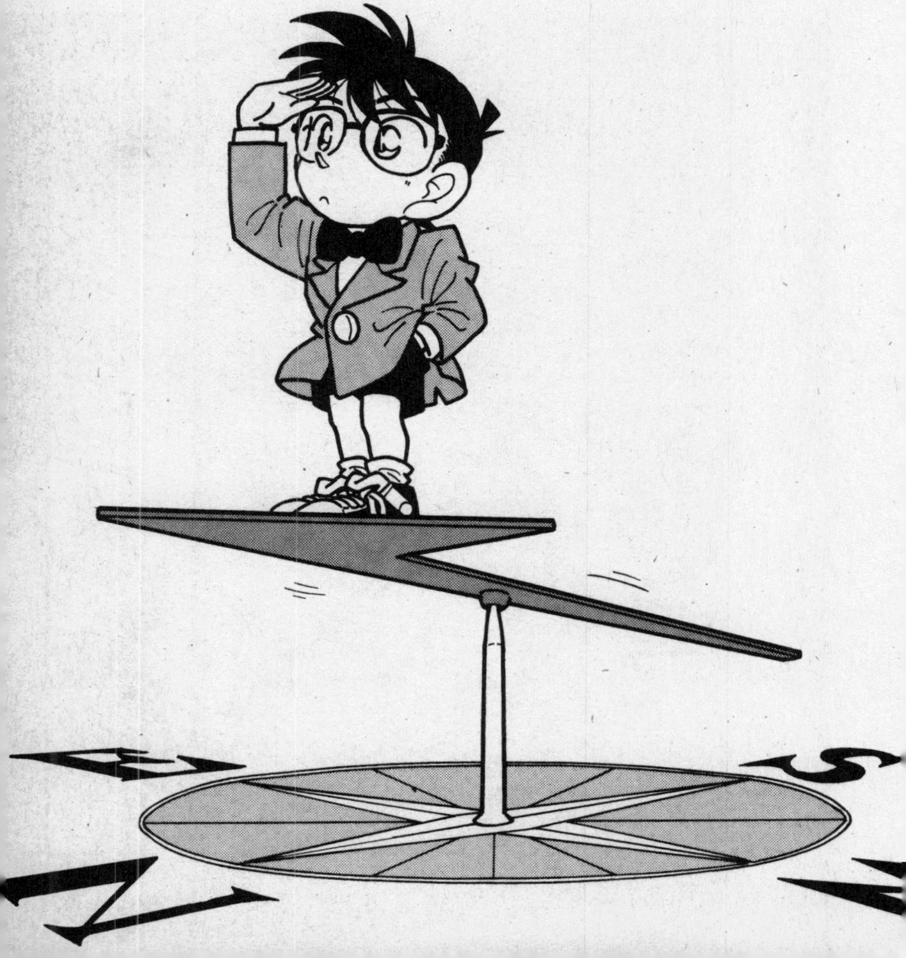

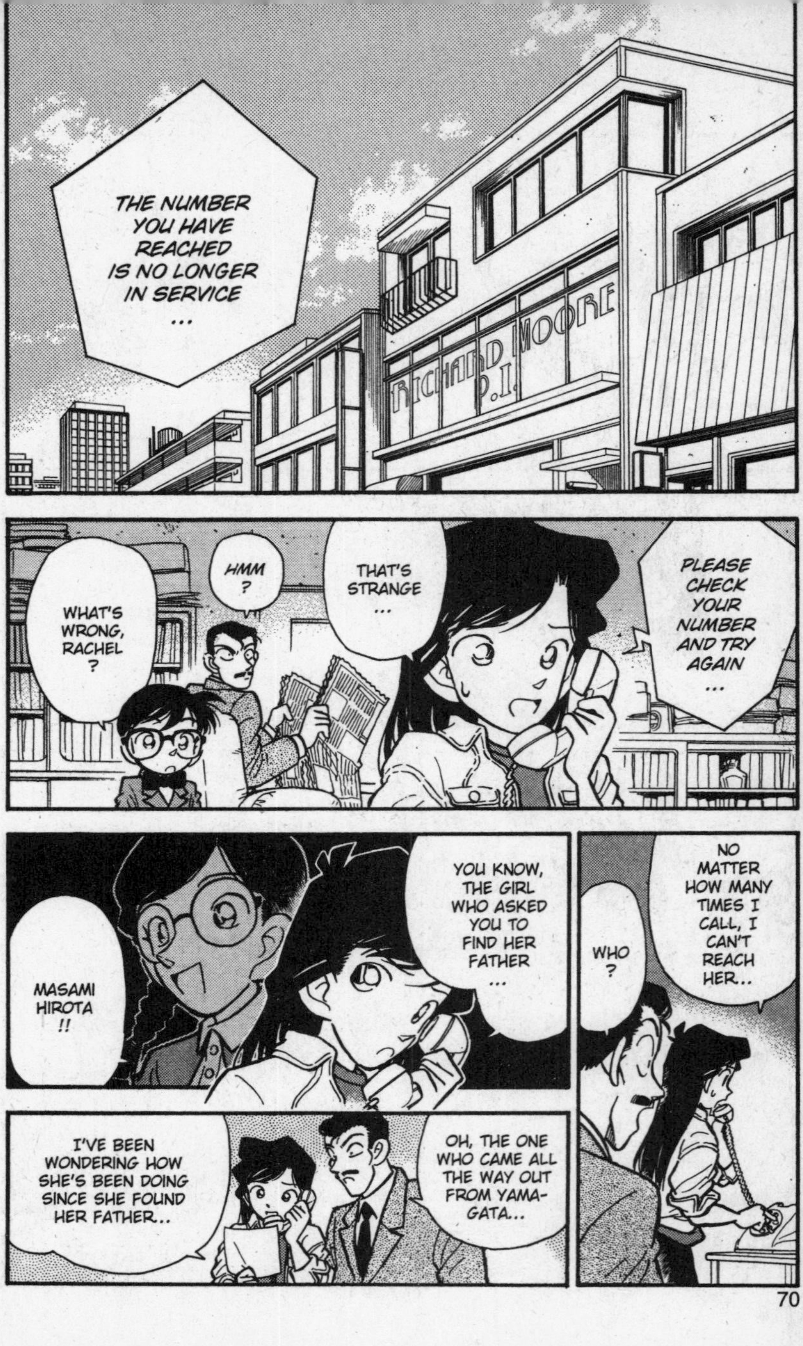
THE NUMBER YOU HAVE REACHED IS NO LONGER IN SERVICE ...
RICHARD MOORE P.I.
PLEASE CHECK YOUR NUMBER AND TRY AGAIN ...
THAT'S STRANGE ...
HMM ?
WHAT'S WRONG, RACHEL ?
NO MATTER HOW MANY TIMES I CALL, I CAN'T REACH HER...
WHO ?
YOU KNOW, THE GIRL WHO ASKED YOU TO FIND HER FATHER ...
MASAMI HIROTA !!
OH, THE ONE WHO CAME ALL THE WAY OUT FROM YAMA-GATA...
I'VE BEEN WONDERING HOW SHE'S BEEN DOING SINCE SHE FOUND HER FATHER...

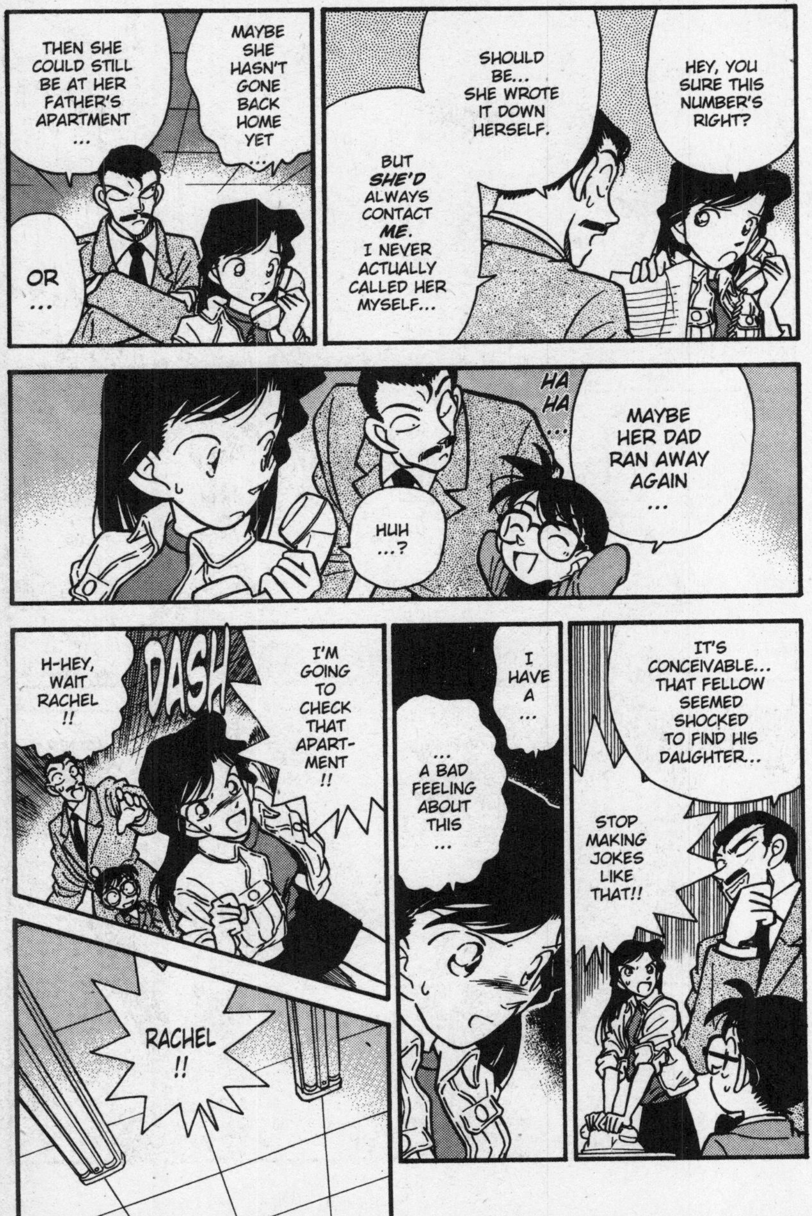
HEY, YOU SURE THIS NUMBER'S RIGHT?
SHOULD BE... SHE WROTE IT DOWN HERSELF.
BUT *SHE'D* ALWAYS CONTACT *ME*. I NEVER ACTUALLY CALLED HER MYSELF...
MAYBE SHE HASN'T GONE BACK HOME YET...
THEN SHE COULD STILL BE AT HER FATHER'S APARTMENT...
OR...
HA HA...
MAYBE HER DAD RAN AWAY AGAIN...
HUH...?
IT'S CONCEIVABLE... THAT FELLOW SEEMED SHOCKED TO FIND HIS DAUGHTER...
STOP MAKING JOKES LIKE THAT!!
I HAVE A...
...A BAD FEELING ABOUT THIS...
I'M GOING TO CHECK THAT APART-MENT!!
DASH
H-HEY, WAIT RACHEL!!
RACHEL!!

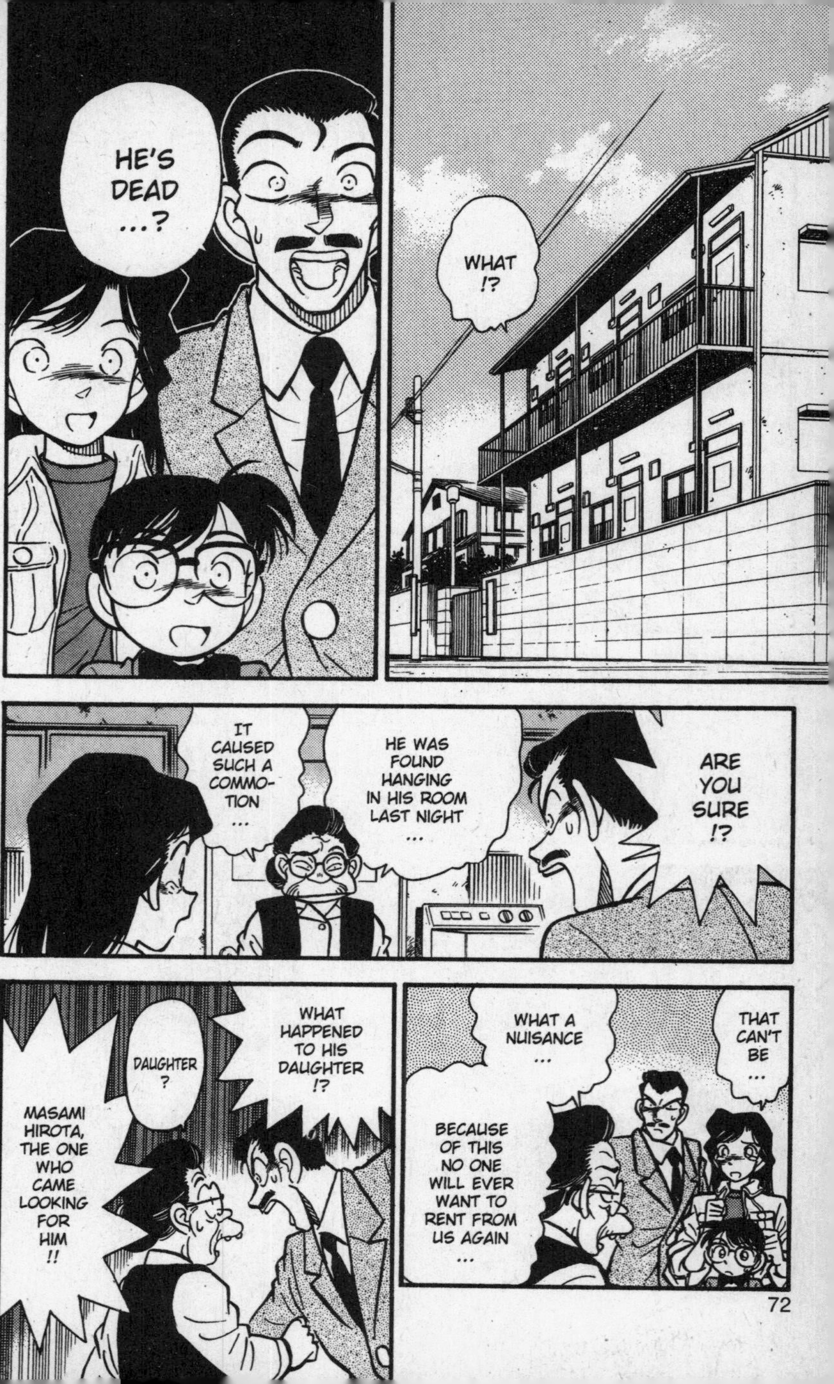
WHAT !?
HE'S DEAD ...?
ARE YOU SURE !?
HE WAS FOUND HANGING IN HIS ROOM LAST NIGHT ...
IT CAUSED SUCH A COMMOTION ...
THAT CAN'T BE ...
WHAT A NUISANCE ...
BECAUSE OF THIS NO ONE WILL EVER WANT TO RENT FROM US AGAIN ...
WHAT HAPPENED TO HIS DAUGHTER !?
DAUGHTER ?
MASAMI HIROTA, THE ONE WHO CAME LOOKING FOR HIM !!

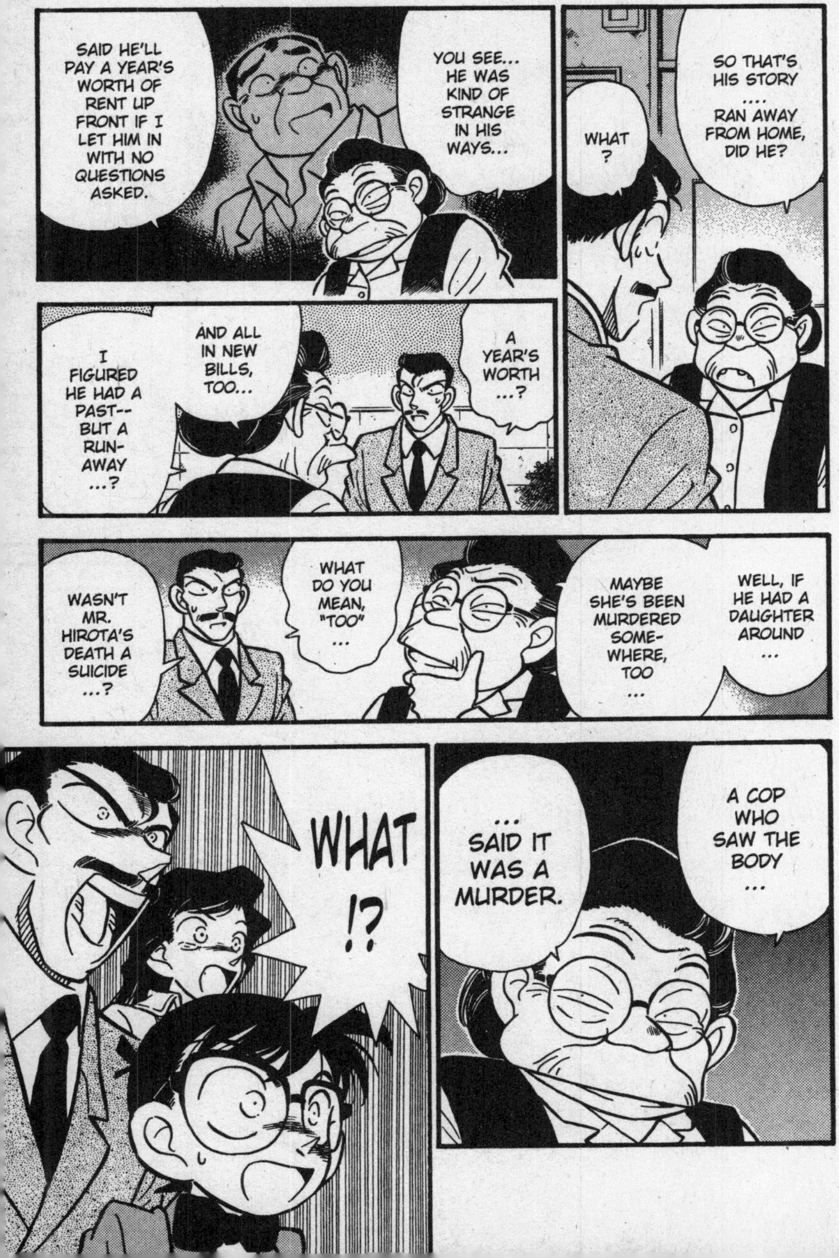
SO THAT'S HIS STORY .... RAN AWAY FROM HOME, DID HE?
WHAT ?
YOU SEE... HE WAS KIND OF STRANGE IN HIS WAYS...
SAID HE'LL PAY A YEAR'S WORTH OF RENT UP FRONT IF I LET HIM IN WITH NO QUESTIONS ASKED.
A YEAR'S WORTH ...?
AND ALL IN NEW BILLS, TOO...
I FIGURED HE HAD A PAST-- BUT A RUN-AWAY ...?
WELL, IF HE HAD A DAUGHTER AROUND ...
MAYBE SHE'S BEEN MURDERED SOME-WHERE, TOO ...
WHAT DO YOU MEAN, "TOO" ...
WASN'T MR. HIROTA'S DEATH A SUICIDE ...?
A COP WHO SAW THE BODY ...
... SAID IT WAS A MURDER.
WHAT !?

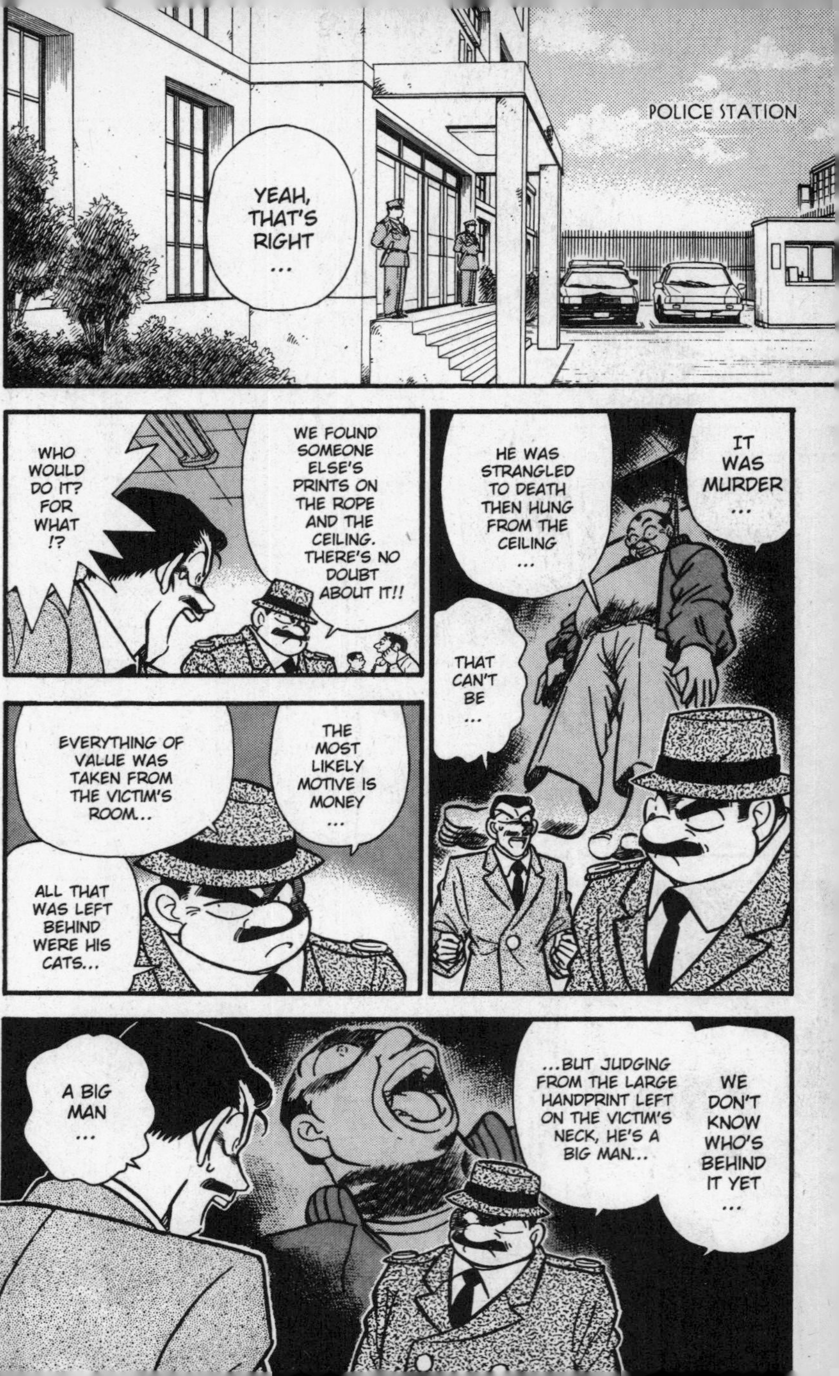
POLICE STATION
YEAH, THAT'S RIGHT ...
IT WAS MURDER ...
HE WAS STRANGLED TO DEATH THEN HUNG FROM THE CEILING ...
THAT CAN'T BE ...
WE FOUND SOMEONE ELSE'S PRINTS ON THE ROPE AND THE CEILING. THERE'S NO DOUBT ABOUT IT!!
WHO WOULD DO IT? FOR WHAT !?
THE MOST LIKELY MOTIVE IS MONEY ...
EVERYTHING OF VALUE WAS TAKEN FROM THE VICTIM'S ROOM...
ALL THAT WAS LEFT BEHIND WERE HIS CATS...
WE DON'T KNOW WHO'S BEHIND IT YET ...
...BUT JUDGING FROM THE LARGE HANDPRINT LEFT ON THE VICTIM'S NECK, HE'S A BIG MAN...
A BIG MAN ...

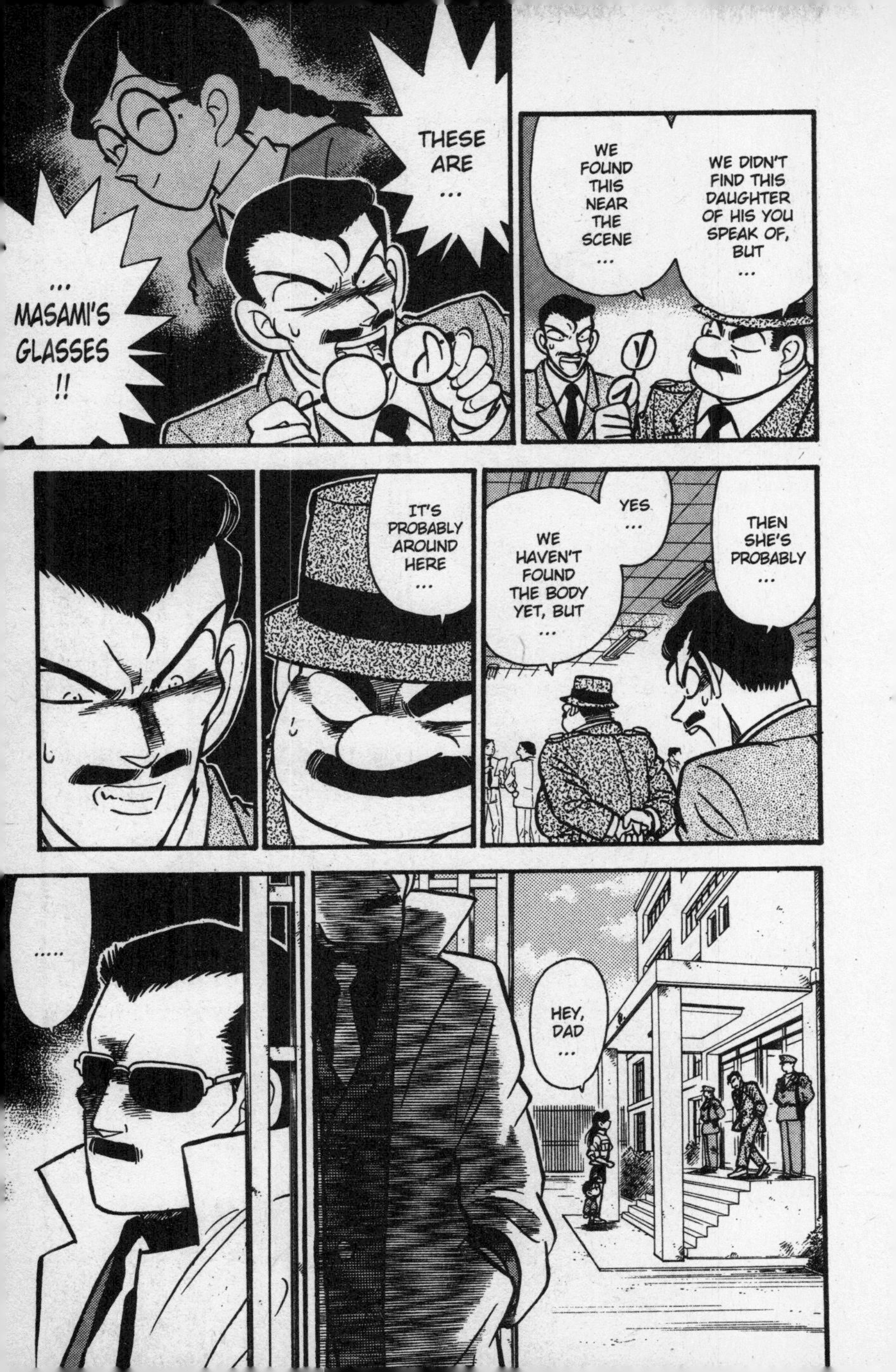
WE DIDN'T FIND THIS DAUGHTER OF HIS YOU SPEAK OF, BUT ...
WE FOUND THIS NEAR THE SCENE ...
THESE ARE ...
... MASAMI'S GLASSES !!
THEN SHE'S PROBABLY ...
YES ...
WE HAVEN'T FOUND THE BODY YET, BUT ...
IT'S PROBABLY AROUND HERE ...
HEY, DAD ...
.....

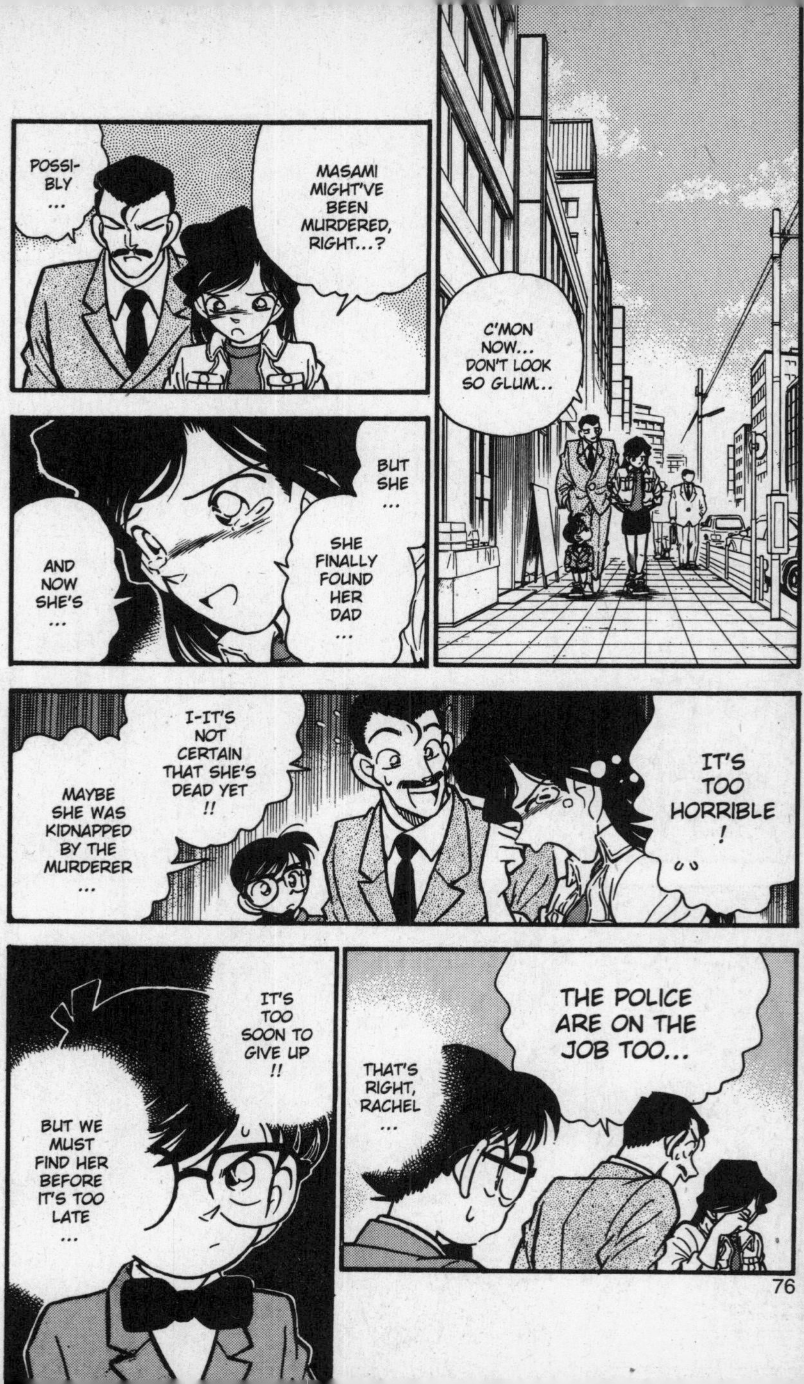
C'MON NOW... DON'T LOOK SO GLUM...
MASAMI MIGHT'VE BEEN MURDERED, RIGHT...?
POSSI-BLY ...
BUT SHE ...
SHE FINALLY FOUND HER DAD ...
AND NOW SHE'S ...
IT'S TOO HORRIBLE !
I-IT'S NOT CERTAIN THAT SHE'S DEAD YET !!
MAYBE SHE WAS KIDNAPPED BY THE MURDERER ...
THE POLICE ARE ON THE JOB TOO...
THAT'S RIGHT, RACHEL ...
IT'S TOO SOON TO GIVE UP !!
BUT WE MUST FIND HER BEFORE IT'S TOO LATE ...

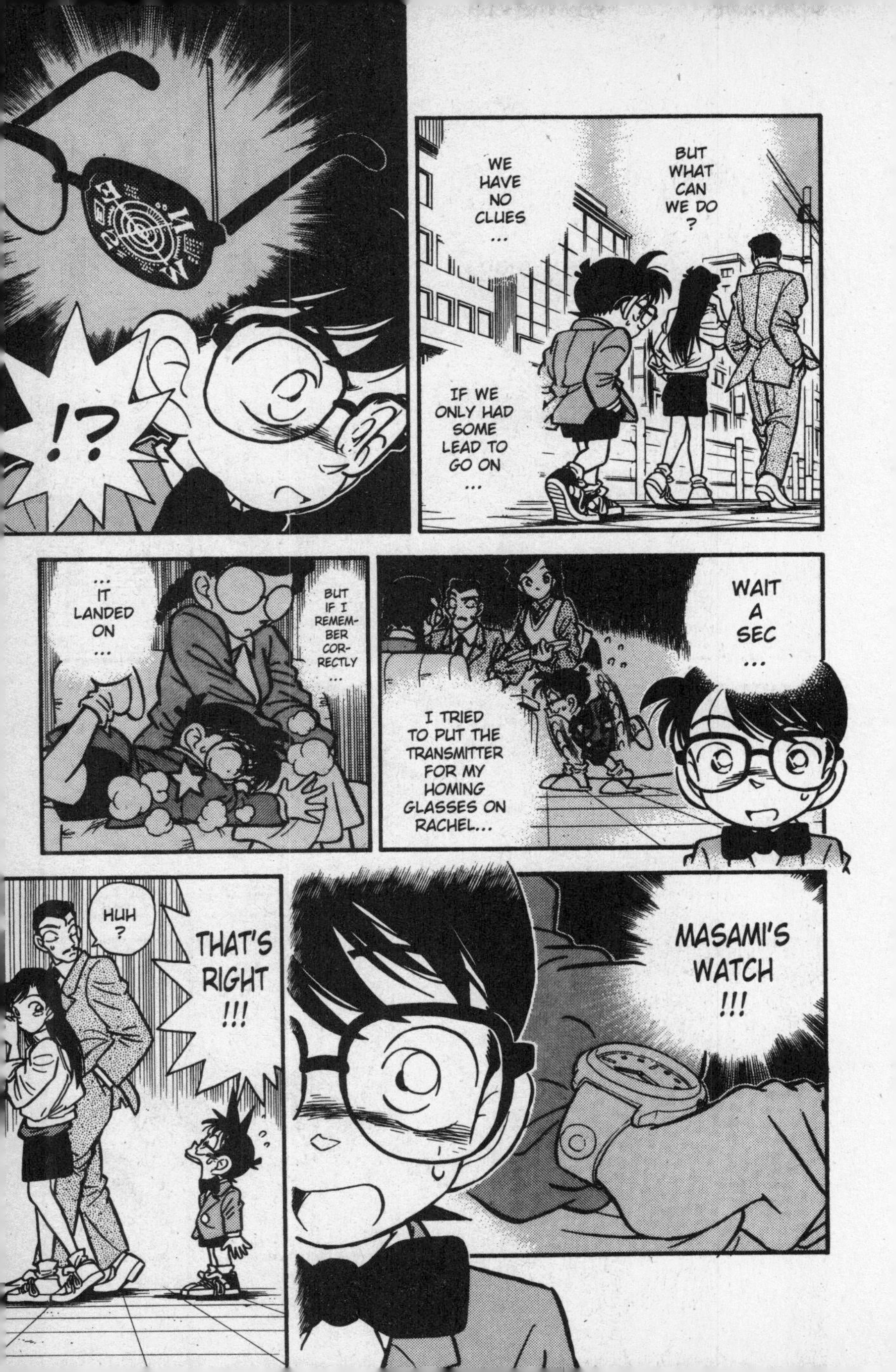
BUT WHAT CAN WE DO?
WE HAVE NO CLUES...
IF WE ONLY HAD SOME LEAD TO GO ON...
!?
WAIT A SEC...
I TRIED TO PUT THE TRANSMITTER FOR MY HOMING GLASSES ON RACHEL...
BUT IF I REMEMBER CORRECTLY...
...IT LANDED ON...
MASAMI'S WATCH!!!
THAT'S RIGHT!!!
HUH?

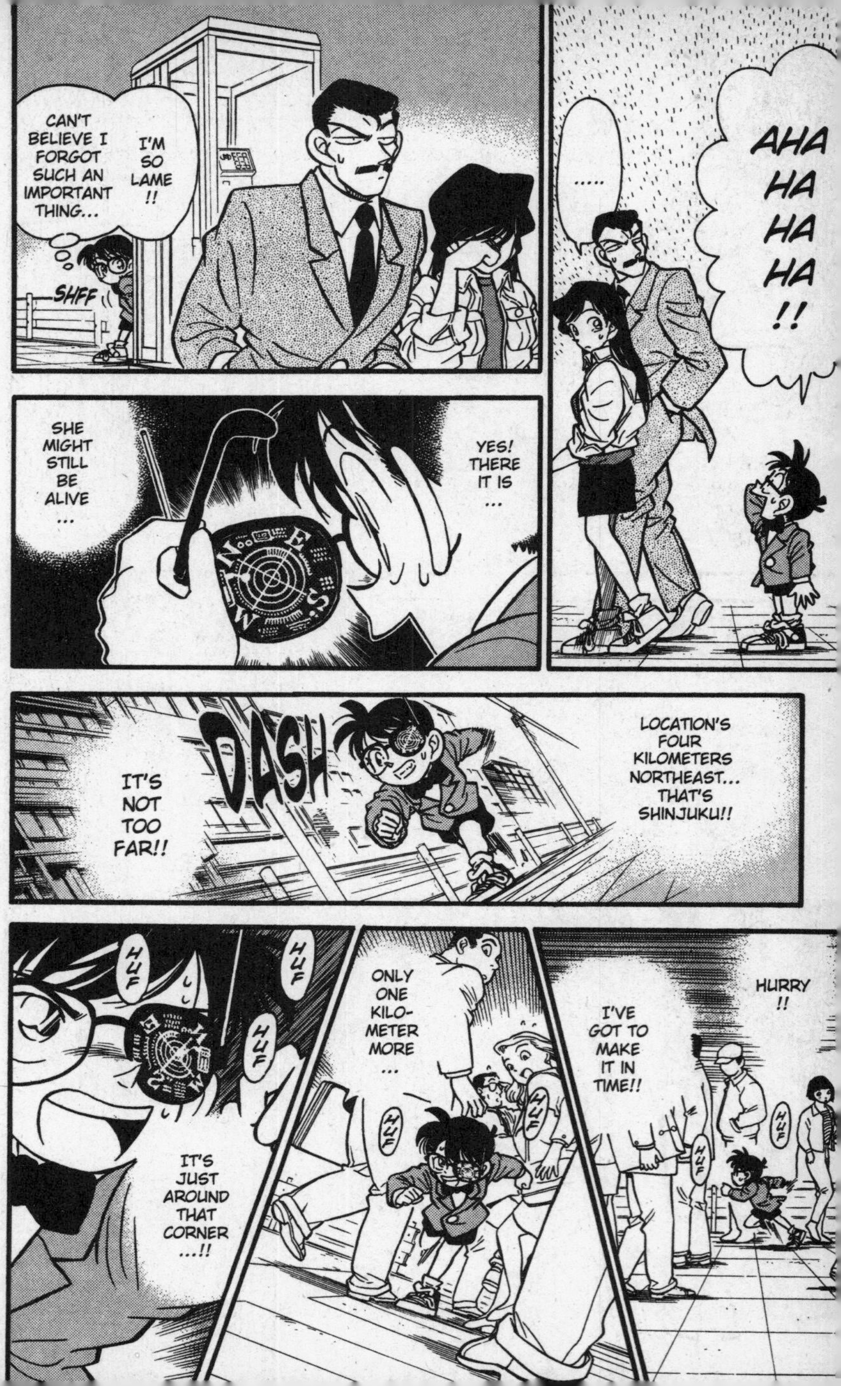

AHA HA HA HA!!
.....
I'M SO LAME!!
CAN'T BELIEVE I FORGOT SUCH AN IMPORTANT THING...
SHFF
YES! THERE IT IS...
SHE MIGHT STILL BE ALIVE...
LOCATION'S FOUR KILOMETERS NORTHEAST... THAT'S SHINJUKU!!
DASH
IT'S NOT TOO FAR!!
HURRY!!
I'VE GOT TO MAKE IT IN TIME!!
HUF
HUF
ONLY ONE KILO-METER MORE...
HUF
HUF
HUF
HUF
IT'S JUST AROUND THAT CORNER...!!

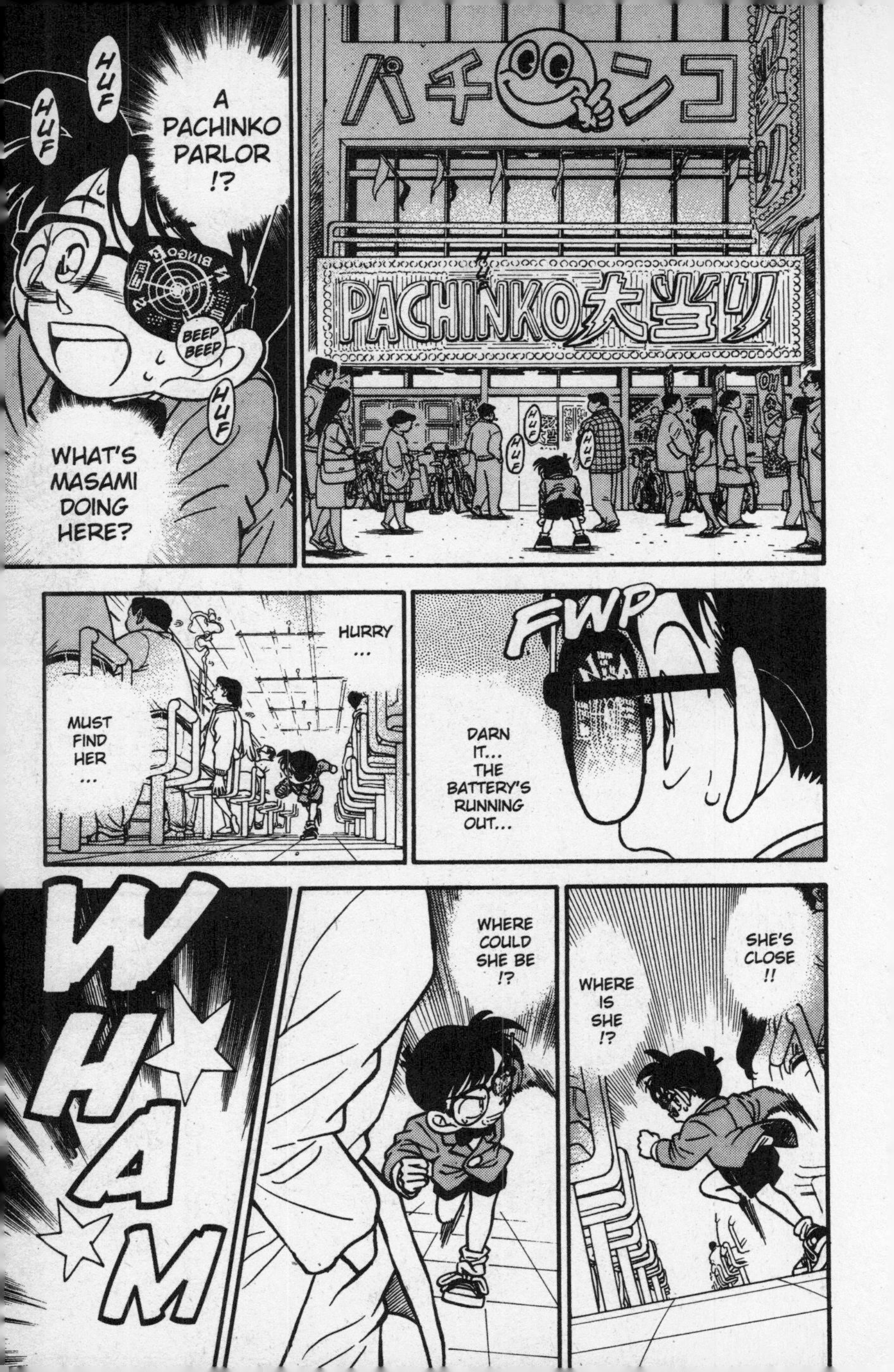

パチンコ
PACHINKO 大当り
HUF
HUF
HUF
HUF
A PACHINKO PARLOR !?
HUF
BINGO
BEEP BEEP
HUF
WHAT'S MASAMI DOING HERE?
FWP
DARN IT... THE BATTERY'S RUNNING OUT...
HURRY ...
MUST FIND HER ...
SHE'S CLOSE !!
WHERE IS SHE !?
WHERE COULD SHE BE !?
WHAM

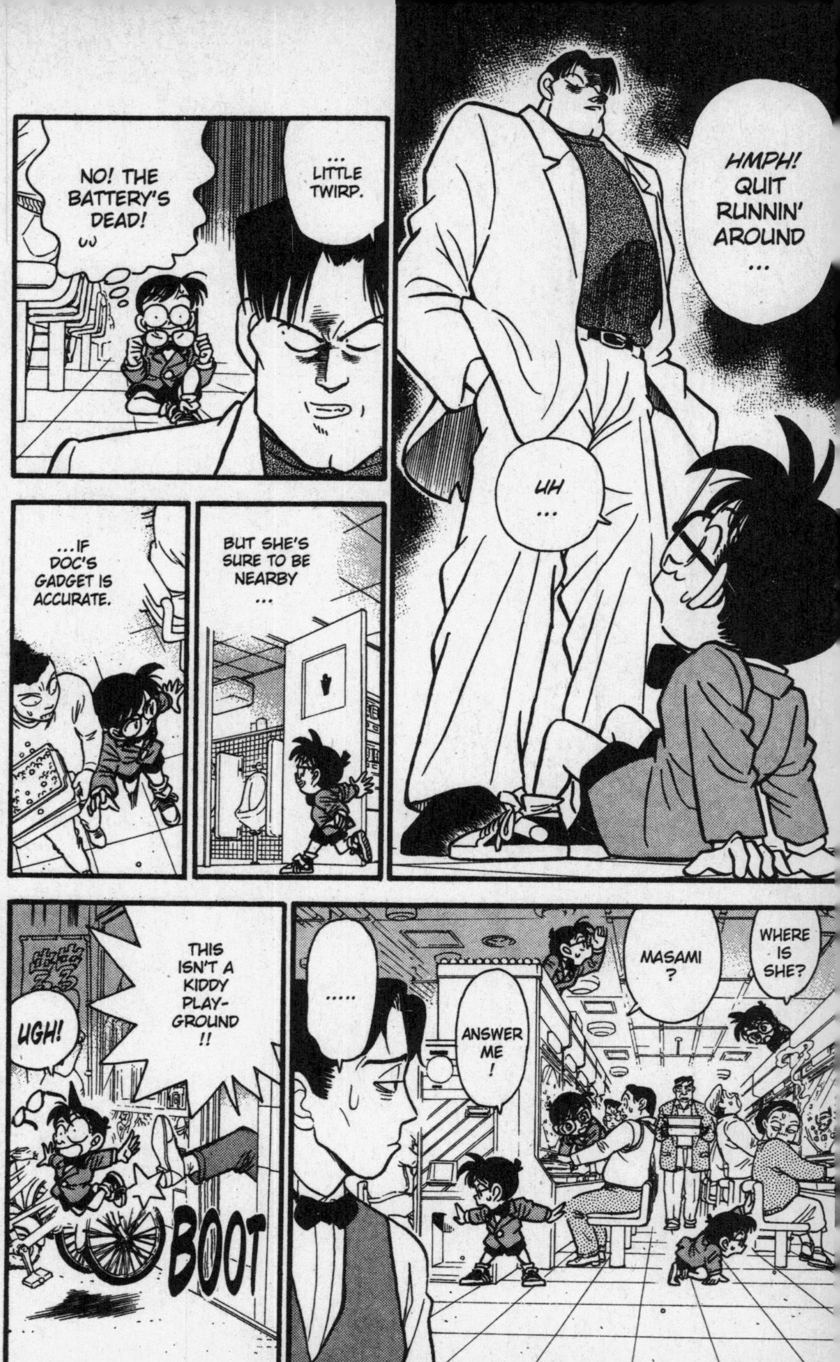
HMPH! QUIT RUNNIN' AROUND ...
UH ...
... LITTLE TWIRP.
NO! THE BATTERY'S DEAD!
BUT SHE'S SURE TO BE NEARBY ...
...IF DOC'S GADGET IS ACCURATE.
WHERE IS SHE?
MASAMI ?
ANSWER ME !
.....
THIS ISN'T A KIDDY PLAY-GROUND !!
UGH!
BOOT

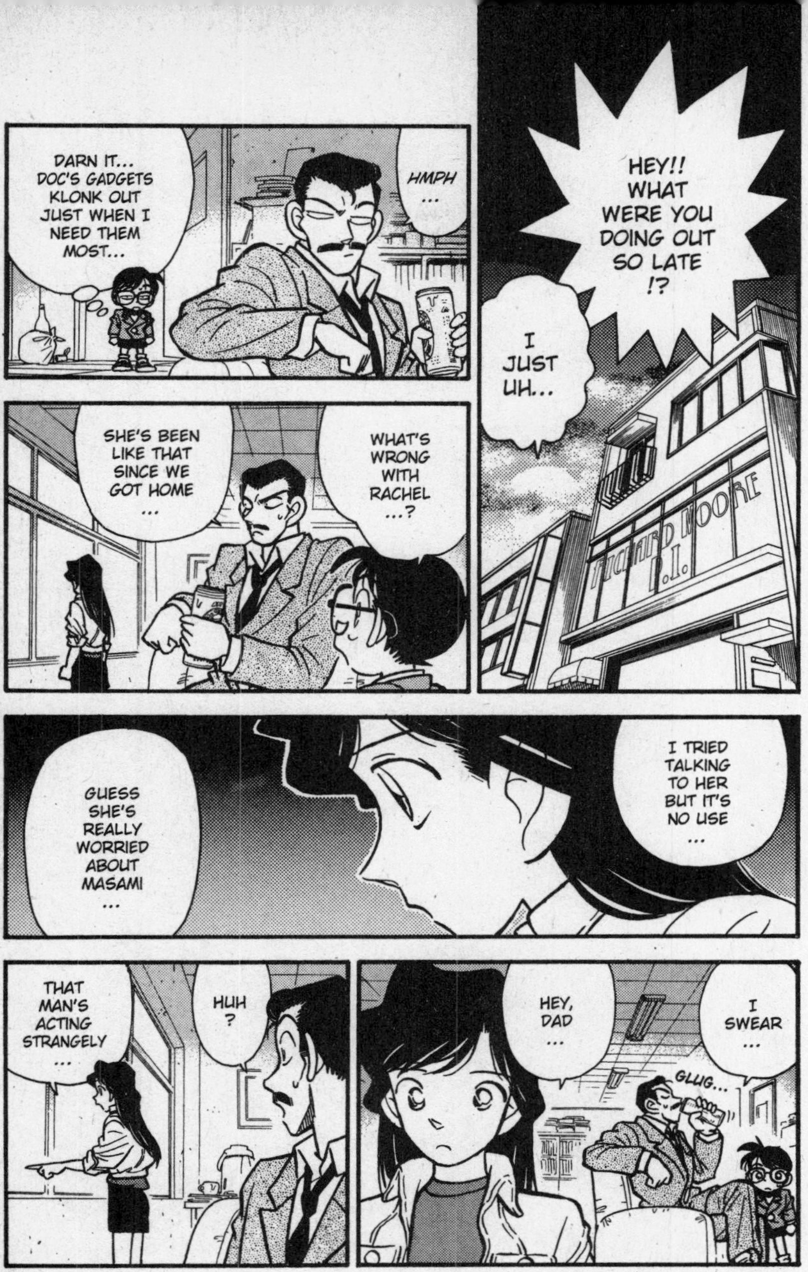
HEY!! WHAT WERE YOU DOING OUT SO LATE !?
I JUST UH...
RICHARD MOORE P.I.
HMPH ...
DARN IT... DOC'S GADGETS KLONK OUT JUST WHEN I NEED THEM MOST...
WHAT'S WRONG WITH RACHEL ...?
SHE'S BEEN LIKE THAT SINCE WE GOT HOME ...
I TRIED TALKING TO HER BUT IT'S NO USE ...
GUESS SHE'S REALLY WORRIED ABOUT MASAMI ...
I SWEAR ...
GLUG...
HEY, DAD ...
HUH ?
THAT MAN'S ACTING STRANGELY ...

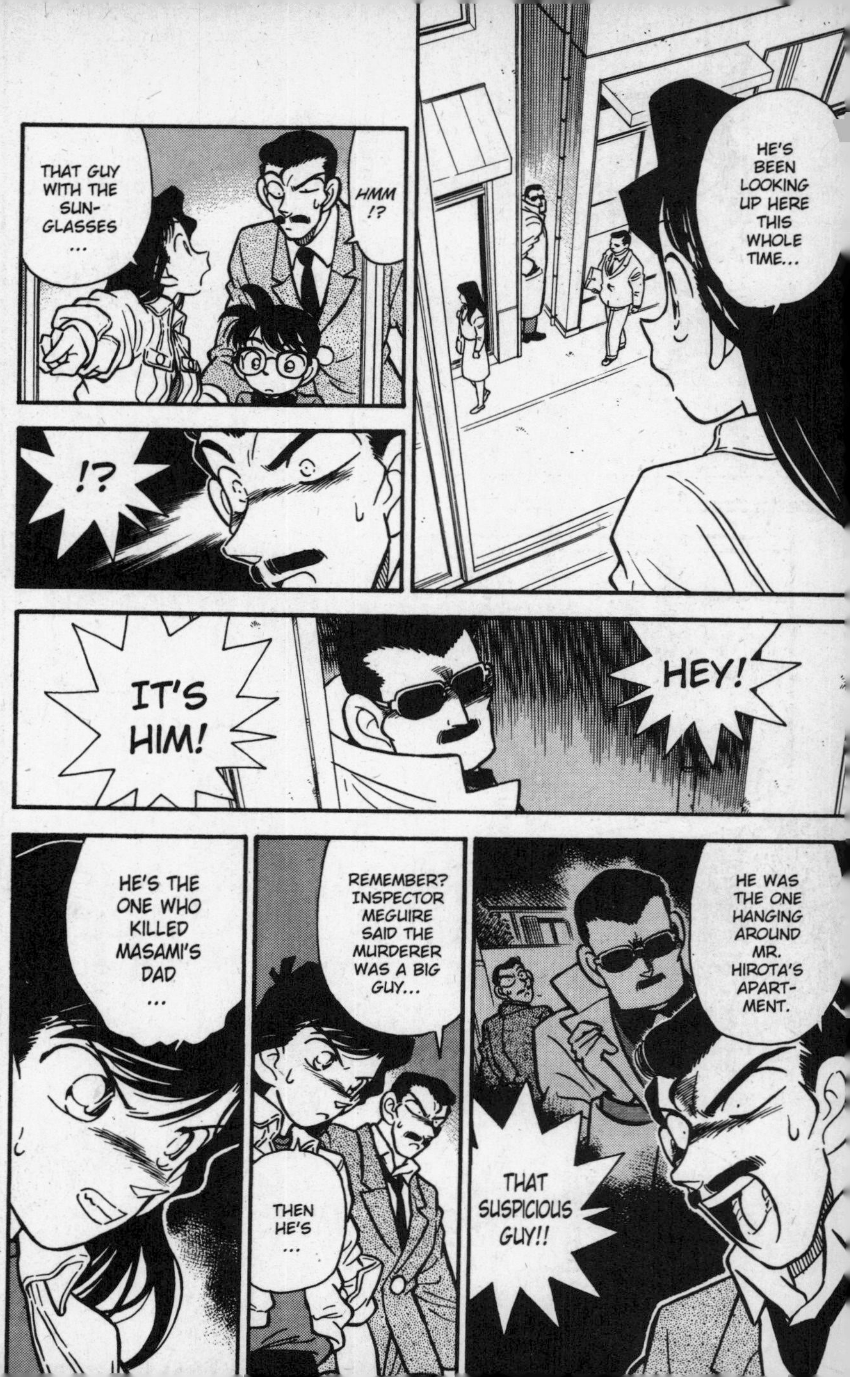
HE'S BEEN LOOKING UP HERE THIS WHOLE TIME...
HMM!?
THAT GUY WITH THE SUN-GLASSES ...
!?
HEY!
IT'S HIM!
HE WAS THE ONE HANGING AROUND MR. HIROTA'S APART-MENT.
THAT SUSPICIOUS GUY!!
REMEMBER? INSPECTOR MEGUIRE SAID THE MURDERER WAS A BIG GUY...
THEN HE'S ...
HE'S THE ONE WHO KILLED MASAMI'S DAD ...

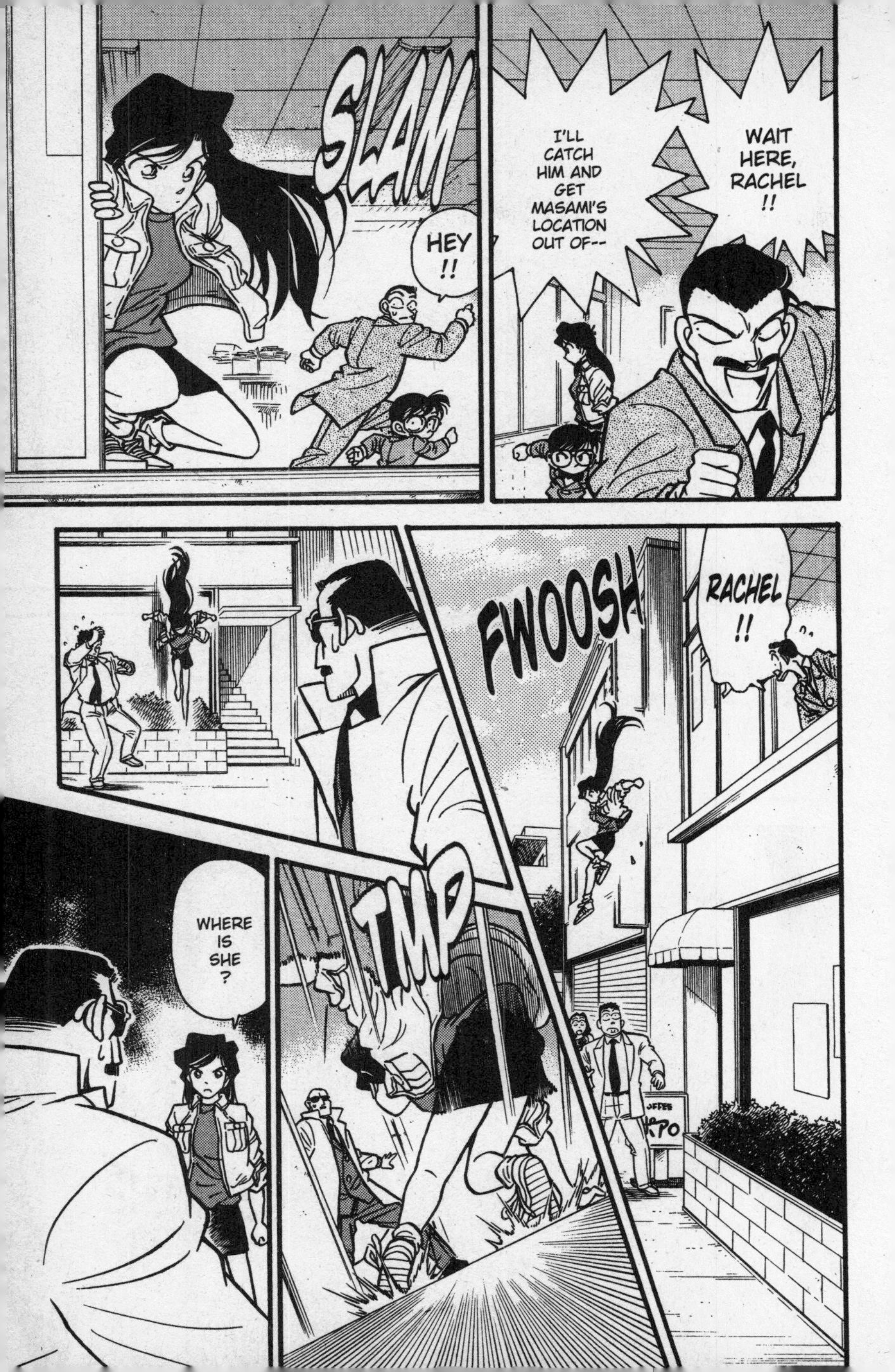
WAIT HERE, RACHEL !!
I'LL CATCH HIM AND GET MASAMI'S LOCATION OUT OF--
SLAM
HEY !!
RACHEL !!
FWOOSH
TMP
WHERE IS SHE ?

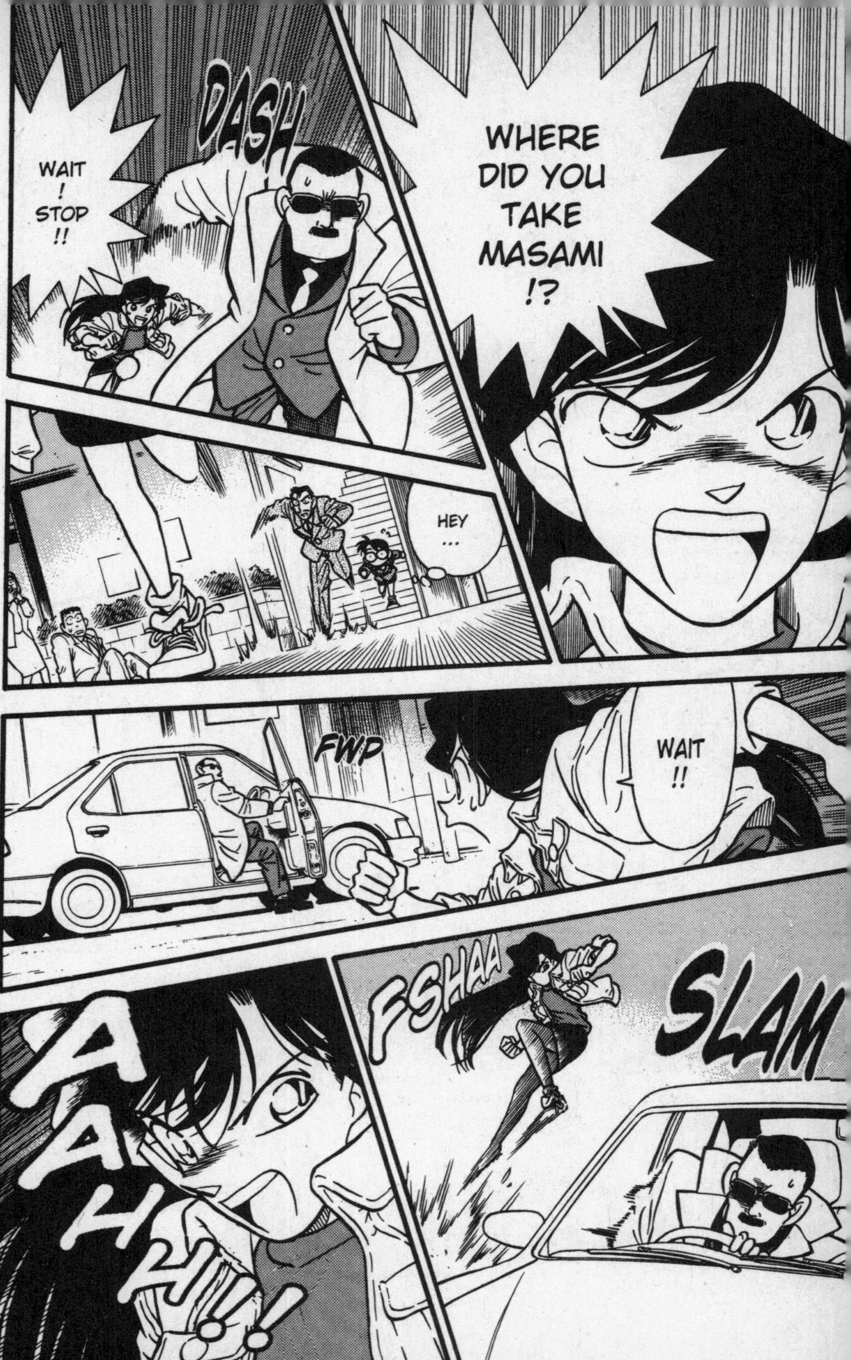
WHERE DID YOU TAKE MASAMI !?
DASH
WAIT ! STOP !!
HEY ...
WAIT !!
FWP
SLAM
FSHAA
AAHH!!

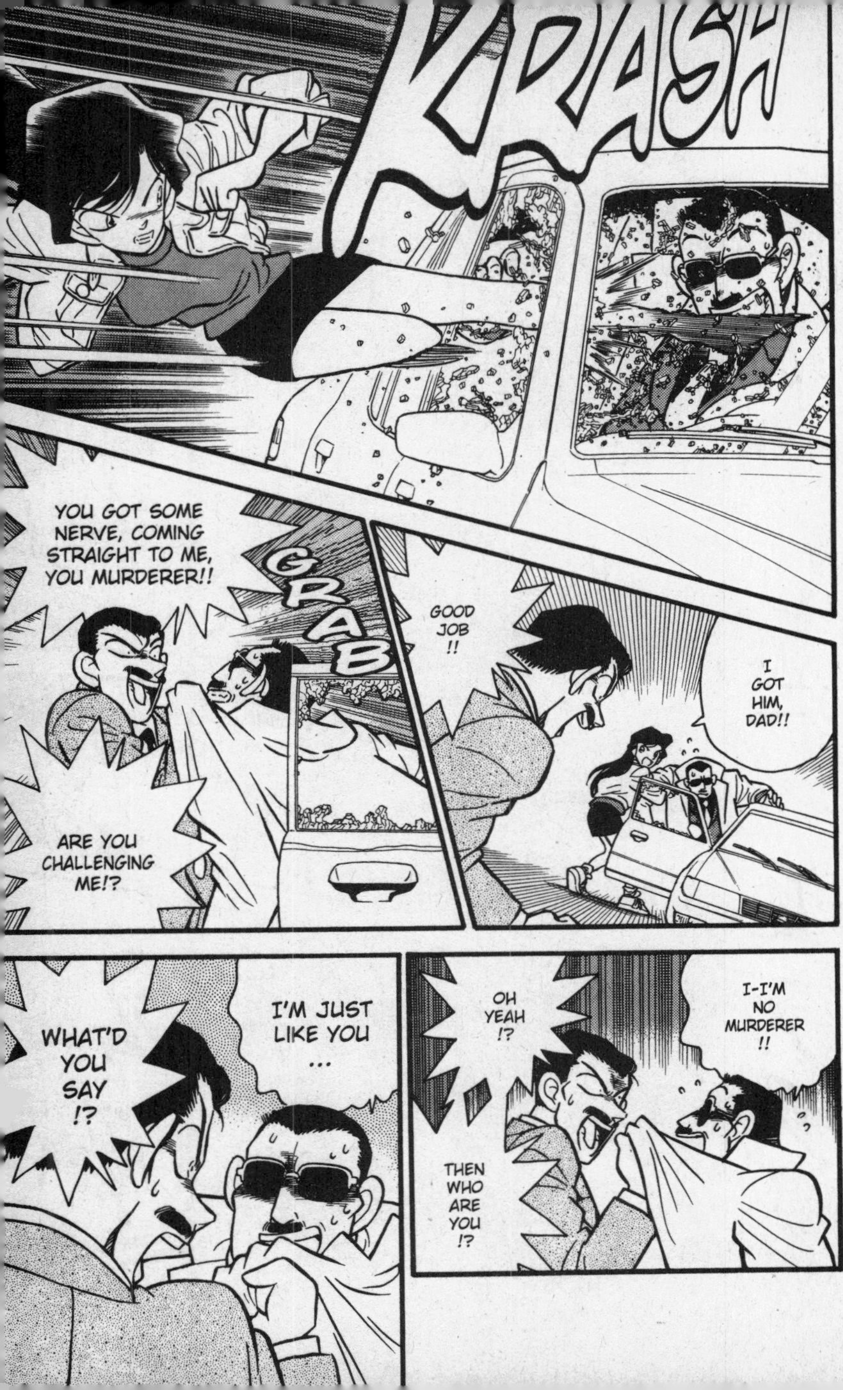
KRASH
I GOT HIM, DAD!!
GOOD JOB!!
GRAB
YOU GOT SOME NERVE, COMING STRAIGHT TO ME, YOU MURDERER!!
ARE YOU CHALLENGING ME!?
I-I'M NO MURDERER!!
OH YEAH!?
THEN WHO ARE YOU!?
I'M JUST LIKE YOU ...
WHAT'D YOU SAY!?

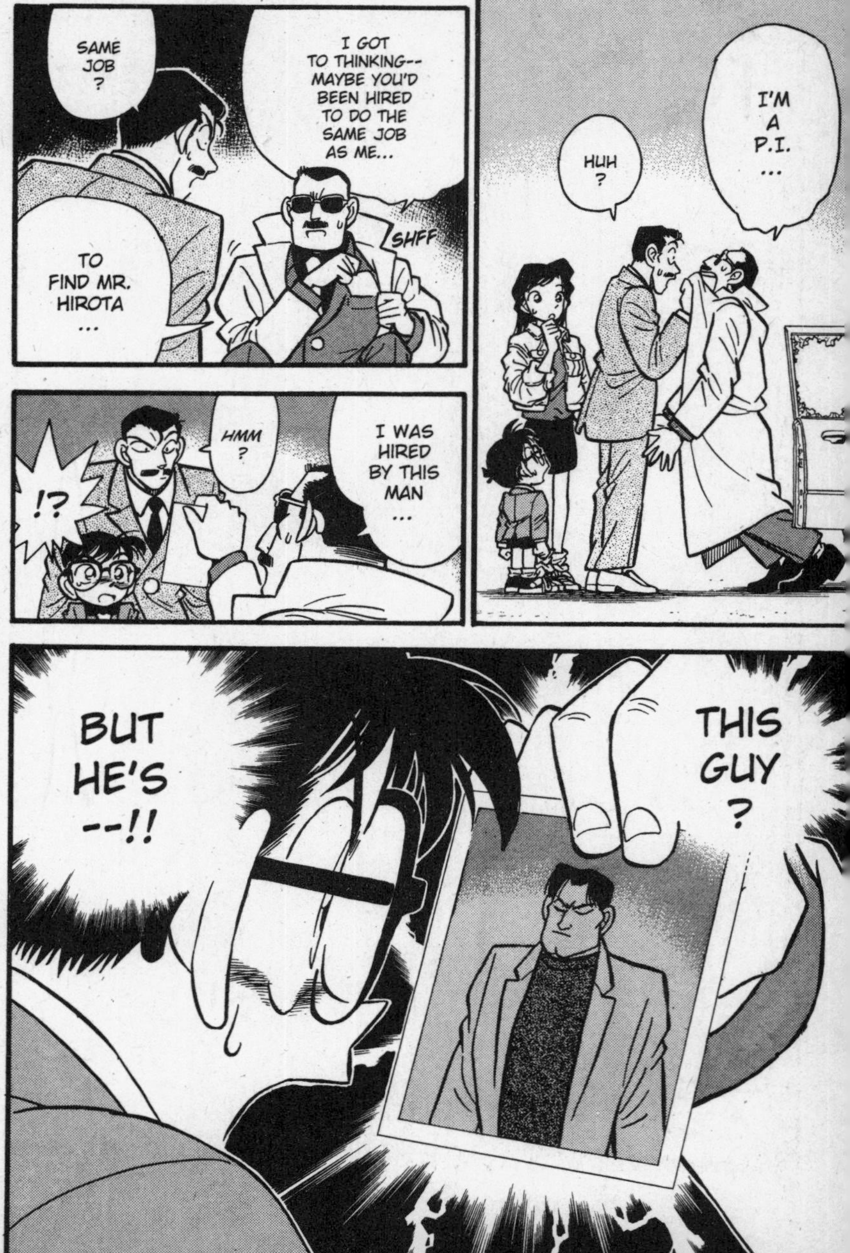

I'M A P.I. ...
HUH ?
I GOT TO THINKING-- MAYBE YOU'D BEEN HIRED TO DO THE SAME JOB AS ME...
SAME JOB ?
SHFF
TO FIND MR. HIROTA ...
I WAS HIRED BY THIS MAN ...
HMM ?
!?
THIS GUY ?
BUT HE'S --!!

FILE 6: FOLLOW THE BIG MAN!

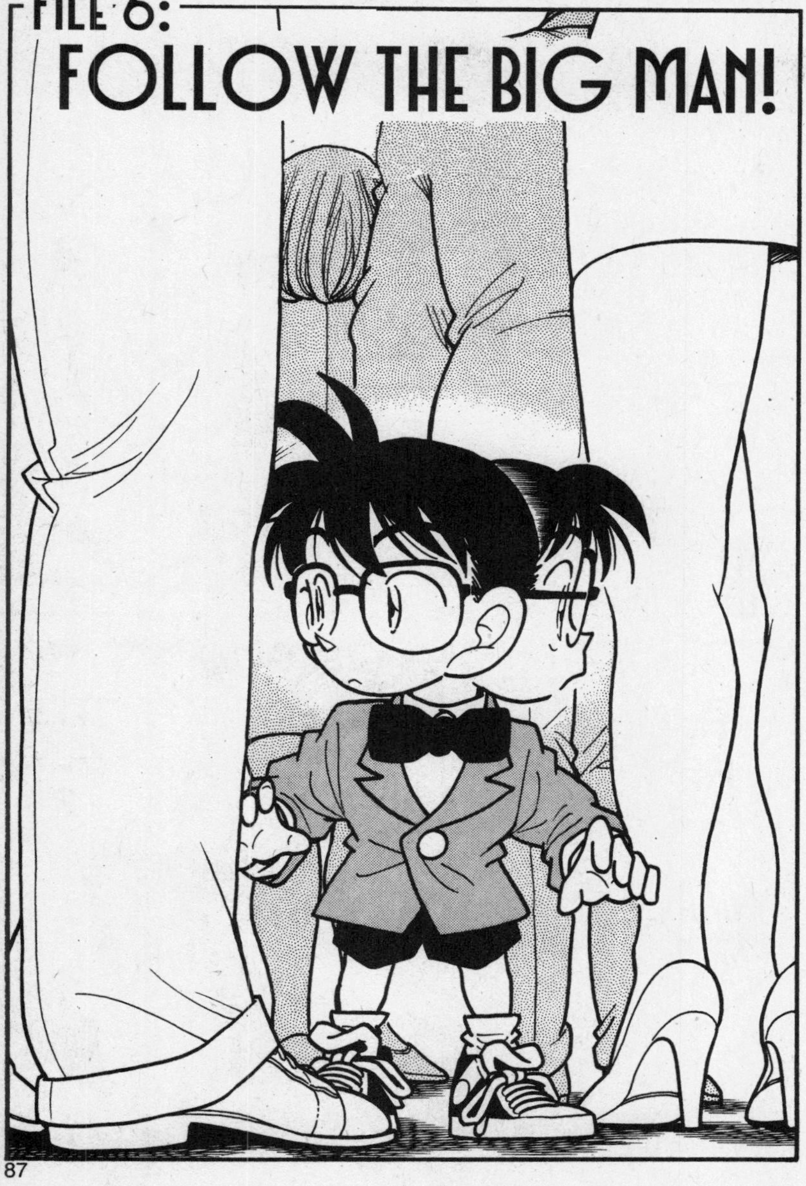

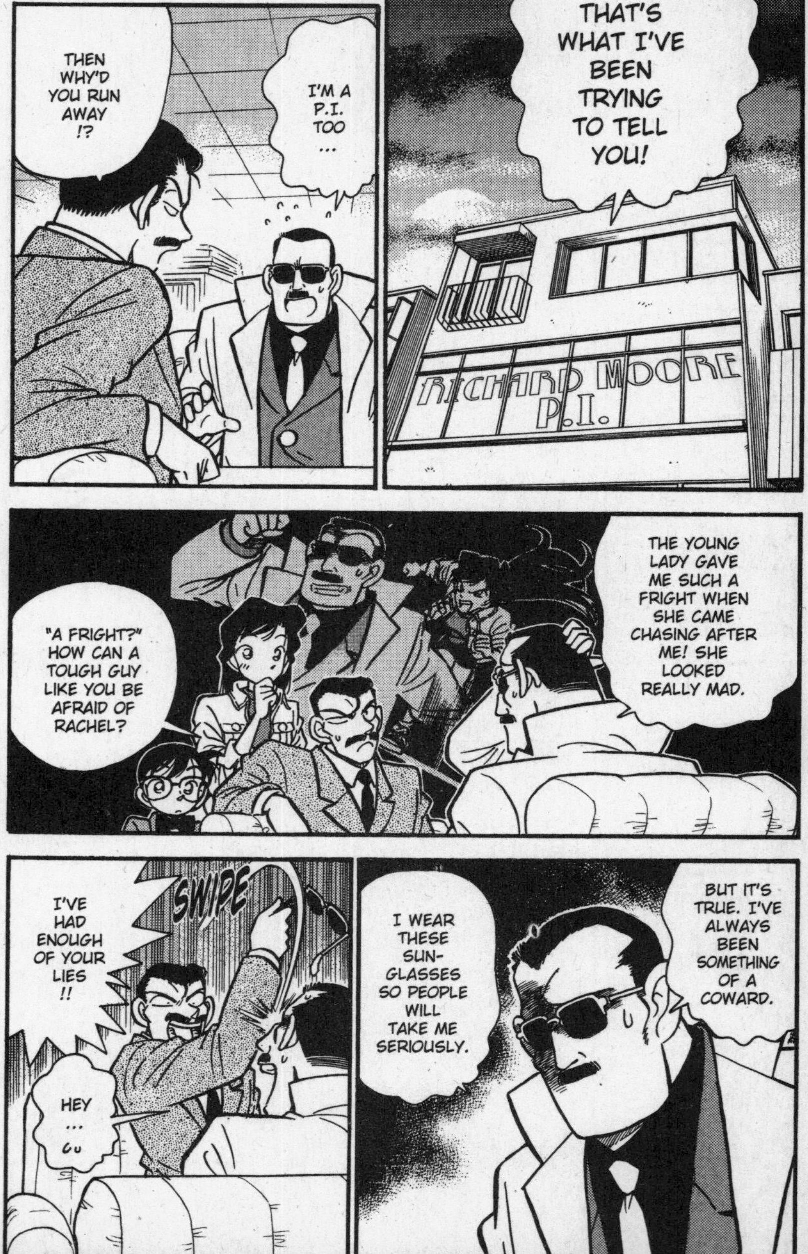
THAT'S WHAT I'VE BEEN TRYING TO TELL YOU!
RICHARD MOORE P.I.
I'M A P.I. TOO ...
THEN WHY'D YOU RUN AWAY !?
THE YOUNG LADY GAVE ME SUCH A FRIGHT WHEN SHE CAME CHASING AFTER ME! SHE LOOKED REALLY MAD.
"A FRIGHT?" HOW CAN A TOUGH GUY LIKE YOU BE AFRAID OF RACHEL?
BUT IT'S TRUE. I'VE ALWAYS BEEN SOMETHING OF A COWARD.
I WEAR THESE SUN-GLASSES SO PEOPLE WILL TAKE ME SERIOUSLY.
SWIPE
I'VE HAD ENOUGH OF YOUR LIES !!
HEY ...

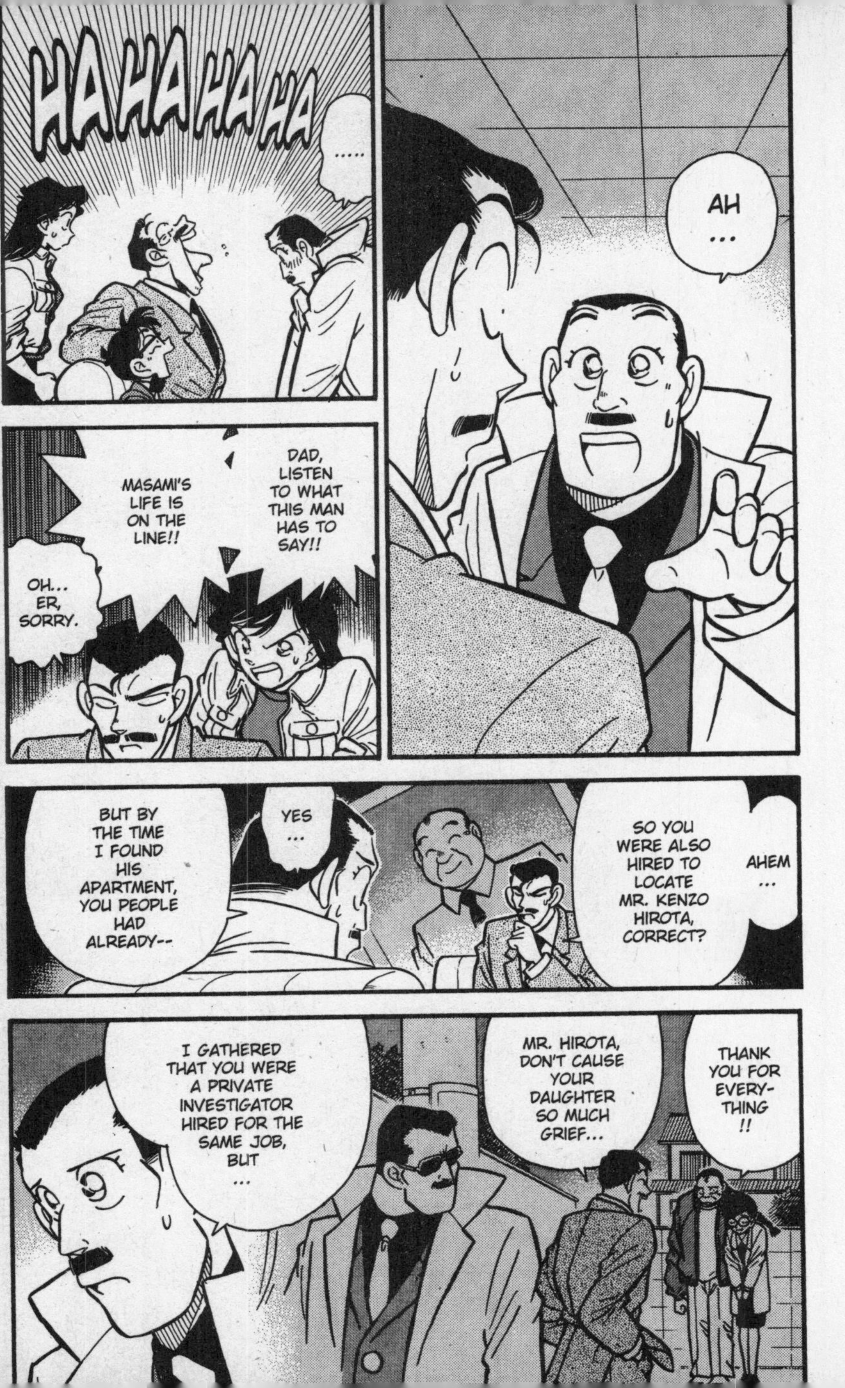
AH ...
HAHA HA HA HA
.....
DAD, LISTEN TO WHAT THIS MAN HAS TO SAY!!
MASAMI'S LIFE IS ON THE LINE!!
OH... ER, SORRY.
AHEM ...
SO YOU WERE ALSO HIRED TO LOCATE MR. KENZO HIROTA, CORRECT?
YES ...
BUT BY THE TIME I FOUND HIS APARTMENT, YOU PEOPLE HAD ALREADY--
THANK YOU FOR EVERY-THING !!
MR. HIROTA, DON'T CAUSE YOUR DAUGHTER SO MUCH GRIEF...
I GATHERED THAT YOU WERE A PRIVATE INVESTIGATOR HIRED FOR THE SAME JOB, BUT ...

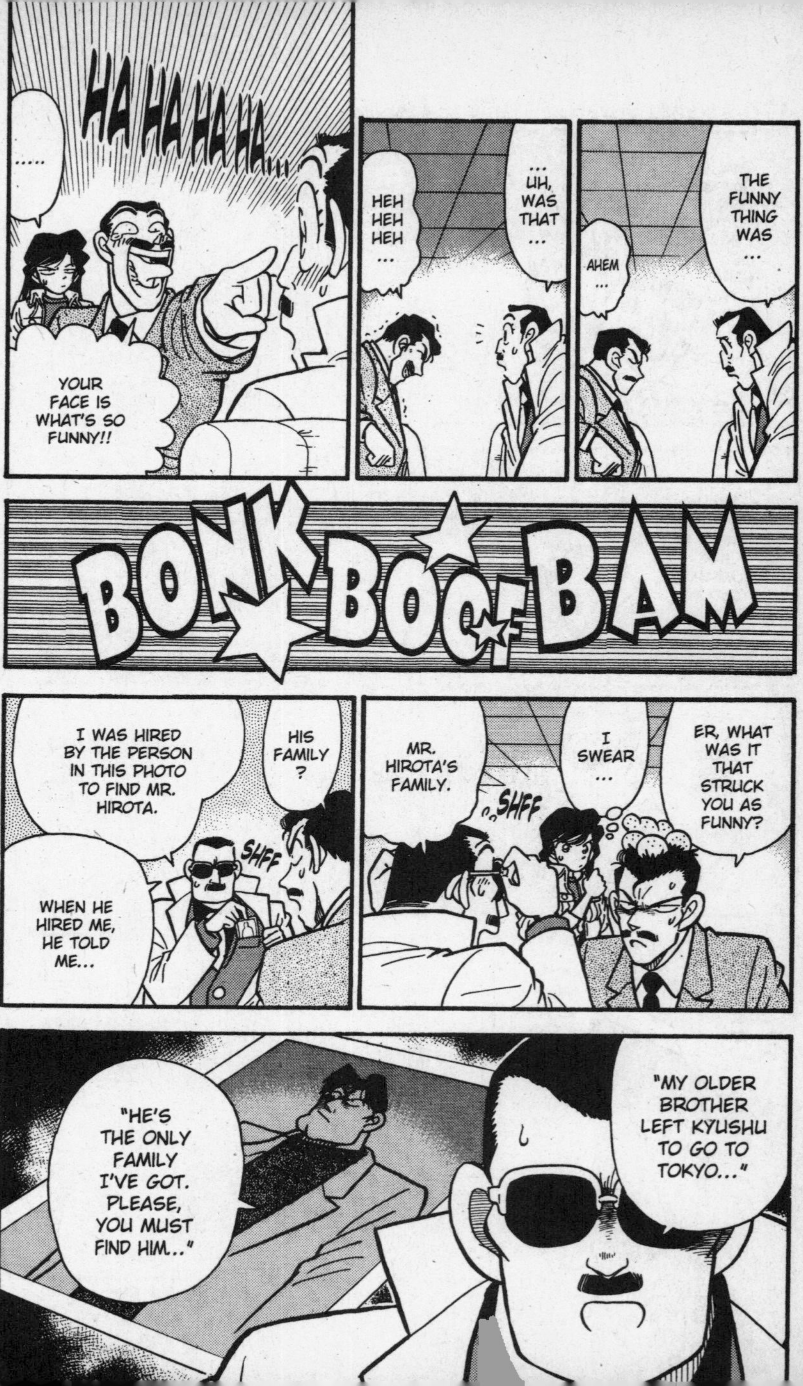
THE FUNNY THING WAS ...
AHEM ...
... UH, WAS THAT ...
HEH HEH HEH ...
HA HA HA HA...
.....
YOUR FACE IS WHAT'S SO FUNNY!!
BONK BOOF BAM
ER, WHAT WAS IT THAT STRUCK YOU AS FUNNY?
I SWEAR ...
MR. HIROTA'S FAMILY.
SHFF
HIS FAMILY ?
I WAS HIRED BY THE PERSON IN THIS PHOTO TO FIND MR. HIROTA.
SHFF
WHEN HE HIRED ME, HE TOLD ME...
"MY OLDER BROTHER LEFT KYUSHU TO GO TO TOKYO..."
"HE'S THE ONLY FAMILY I'VE GOT. PLEASE, YOU MUST FIND HIM..."

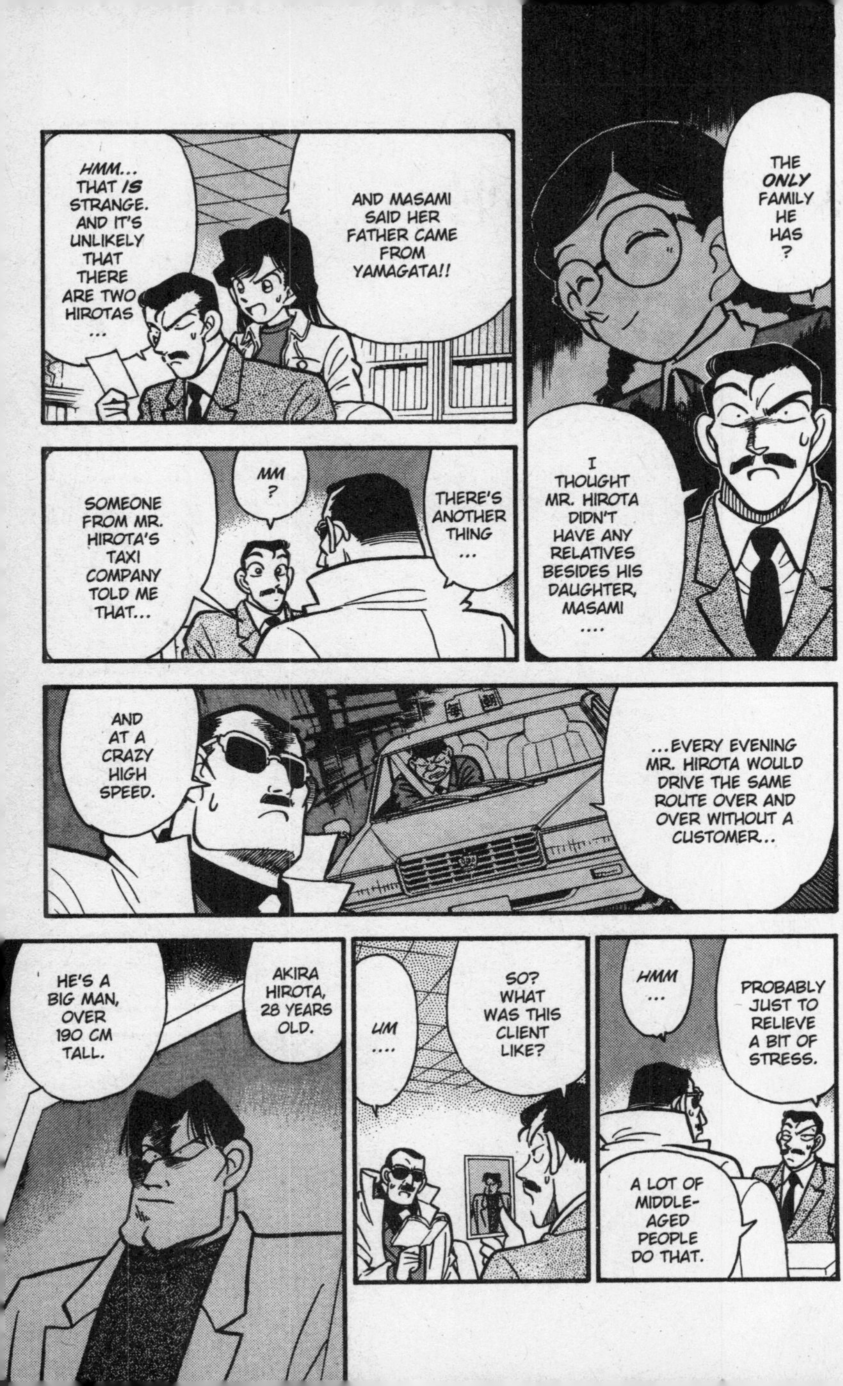
THE ONLY FAMILY HE HAS?
I THOUGHT MR. HIROTA DIDN'T HAVE ANY RELATIVES BESIDES HIS DAUGHTER, MASAMI ....
AND MASAMI SAID HER FATHER CAME FROM YAMAGATA!!
HMM... THAT IS STRANGE. AND IT'S UNLIKELY THAT THERE ARE TWO HIROTAS ...
THERE'S ANOTHER THING ...
MM ?
SOMEONE FROM MR. HIROTA'S TAXI COMPANY TOLD ME THAT...
...EVERY EVENING MR. HIROTA WOULD DRIVE THE SAME ROUTE OVER AND OVER WITHOUT A CUSTOMER...
AND AT A CRAZY HIGH SPEED.
PROBABLY JUST TO RELIEVE A BIT OF STRESS.
HMM ...
A LOT OF MIDDLE-AGED PEOPLE DO THAT.
SO? WHAT WAS THIS CLIENT LIKE?
UM ....
AKIRA HIROTA, 28 YEARS OLD.
HE'S A BIG MAN, OVER 190 CM TALL.

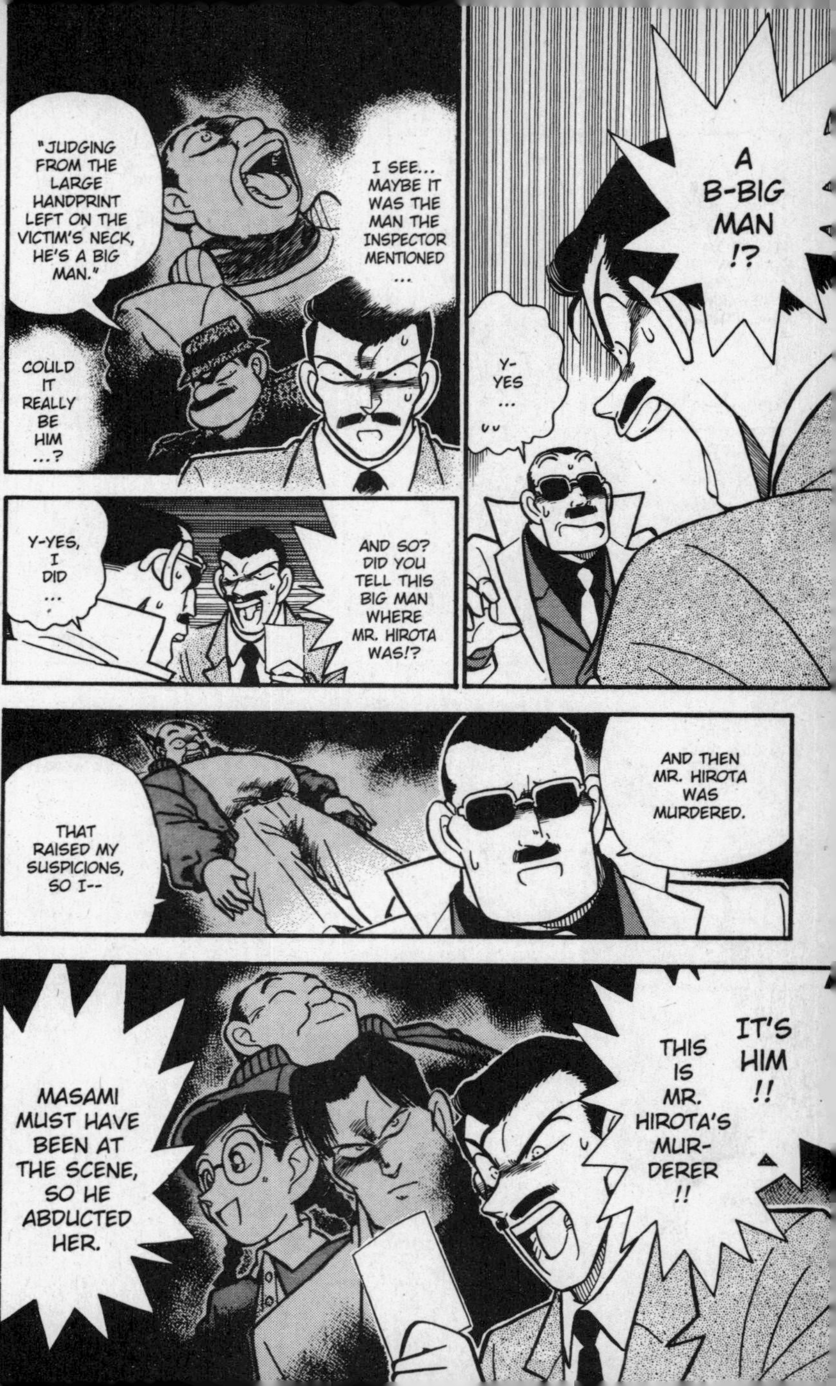
A B-BIG MAN !?
Y-YES ...
I SEE... MAYBE IT WAS THE MAN THE INSPECTOR MENTIONED ...
"JUDGING FROM THE LARGE HANDPRINT LEFT ON THE VICTIM'S NECK, HE'S A BIG MAN."
COULD IT REALLY BE HIM ...?
AND SO? DID YOU TELL THIS BIG MAN WHERE MR. HIROTA WAS!?
Y-YES, I DID ...
AND THEN MR. HIROTA WAS MURDERED.
THAT RAISED MY SUSPICIONS, SO I--
IT'S HIM !!
THIS IS MR. HIROTA'S MUR-DERER !!
MASAMI MUST HAVE BEEN AT THE SCENE, SO HE ABDUCTED HER.

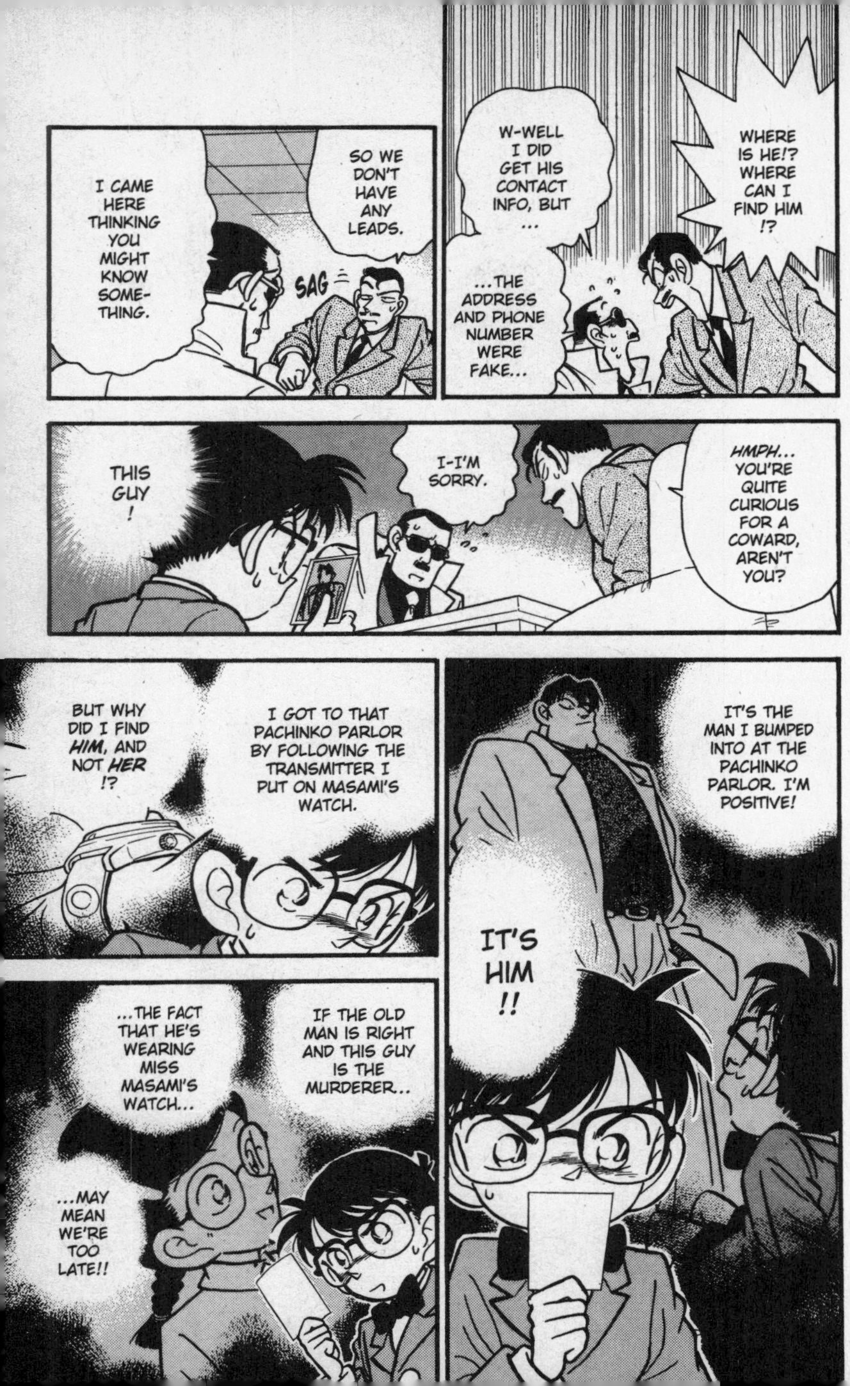
WHERE IS HE!? WHERE CAN I FIND HIM!?
W-WELL I DID GET HIS CONTACT INFO, BUT...
...THE ADDRESS AND PHONE NUMBER WERE FAKE...
SO WE DON'T HAVE ANY LEADS.
SAG
I CAME HERE THINKING YOU MIGHT KNOW SOME-THING.
HMPH... YOU'RE QUITE CURIOUS FOR A COWARD, AREN'T YOU?
I-I'M SORRY.
THIS GUY!
IT'S THE MAN I BUMPED INTO AT THE PACHINKO PARLOR. I'M POSITIVE!
IT'S HIM!!
I GOT TO THAT PACHINKO PARLOR BY FOLLOWING THE TRANSMITTER I PUT ON MASAMI'S WATCH.
BUT WHY DID I FIND *HIM*, AND NOT *HER*!?
IF THE OLD MAN IS RIGHT AND THIS GUY IS THE MURDERER...
...THE FACT THAT HE'S WEARING MISS MASAMI'S WATCH...
...MAY MEAN WE'RE TOO LATE!!

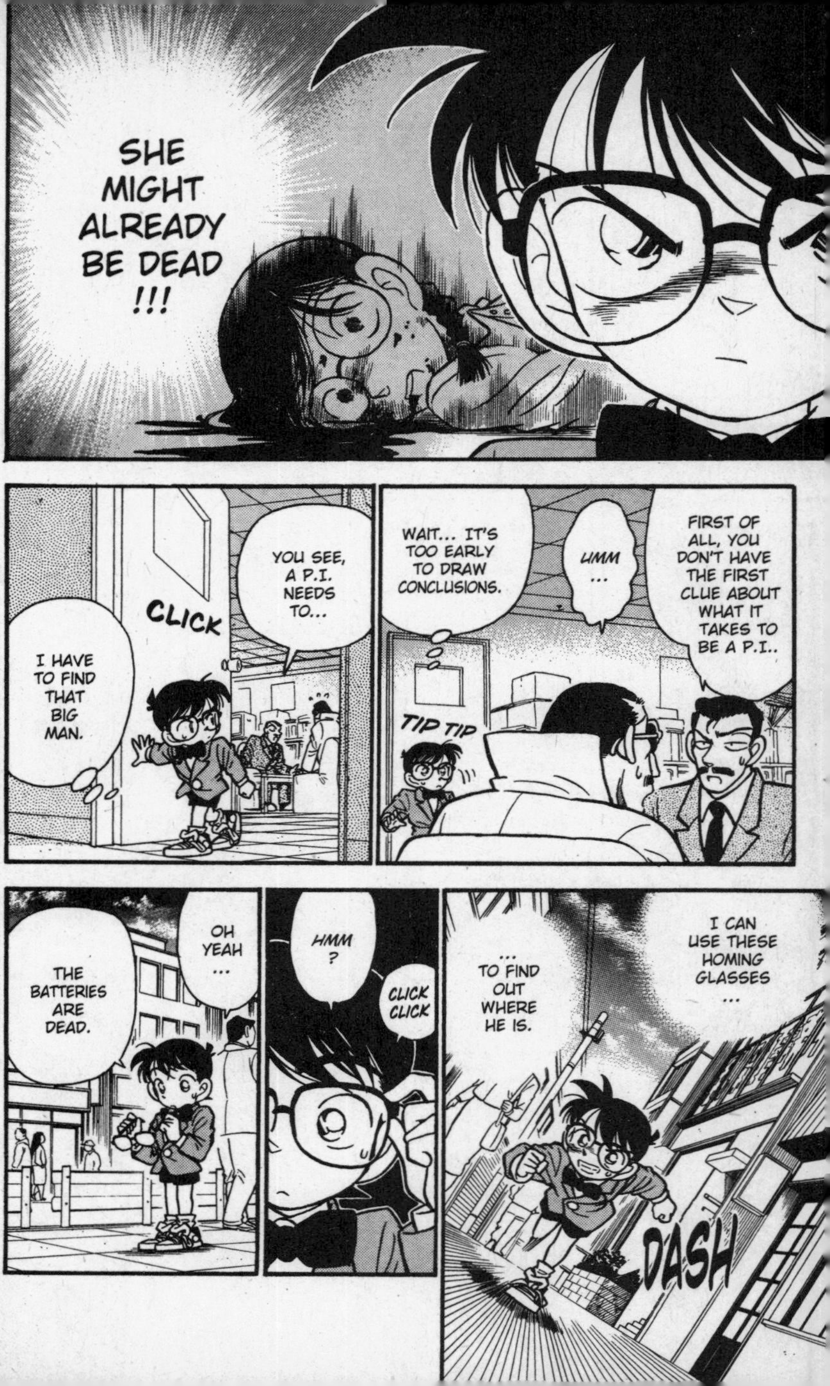
SHE MIGHT ALREADY BE DEAD !!!
FIRST OF ALL, YOU DON'T HAVE THE FIRST CLUE ABOUT WHAT IT TAKES TO BE A P.I..
UMM ...
WAIT... IT'S TOO EARLY TO DRAW CONCLUSIONS.
TIP TIP
YOU SEE, A P.I. NEEDS TO...
CLICK
I HAVE TO FIND THAT BIG MAN.
I CAN USE THESE HOMING GLASSES ...
... TO FIND OUT WHERE HE IS.
DASH
HMM ?
CLICK CLICK
OH YEAH ...
THE BATTERIES ARE DEAD.

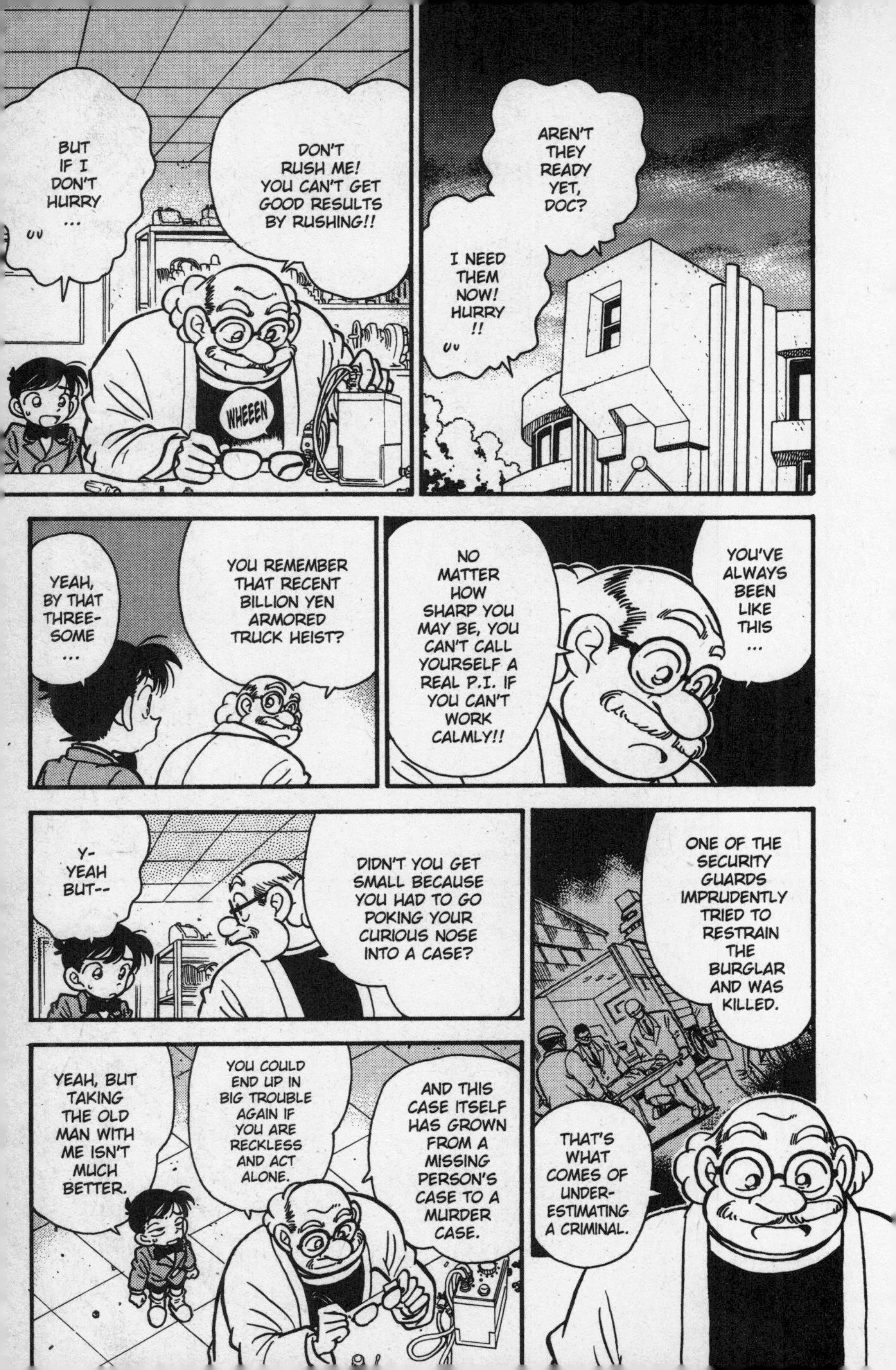
AREN'T THEY READY YET, DOC?
I NEED THEM NOW! HURRY!!
DON'T RUSH ME! YOU CAN'T GET GOOD RESULTS BY RUSHING!!
WHEEEN
BUT IF I DON'T HURRY ...
YOU'VE ALWAYS BEEN LIKE THIS ...
NO MATTER HOW SHARP YOU MAY BE, YOU CAN'T CALL YOURSELF A REAL P.I. IF YOU CAN'T WORK CALMLY!!
YOU REMEMBER THAT RECENT BILLION YEN ARMORED TRUCK HEIST?
YEAH, BY THAT THREE-SOME ...
ONE OF THE SECURITY GUARDS IMPRUDENTLY TRIED TO RESTRAIN THE BURGLAR AND WAS KILLED.
THAT'S WHAT COMES OF UNDER-ESTIMATING A CRIMINAL.
DIDN'T YOU GET SMALL BECAUSE YOU HAD TO GO POKING YOUR CURIOUS NOSE INTO A CASE?
Y-YEAH BUT--
AND THIS CASE ITSELF HAS GROWN FROM A MISSING PERSON'S CASE TO A MURDER CASE.
YOU COULD END UP IN BIG TROUBLE AGAIN IF YOU ARE RECKLESS AND ACT ALONE.
YEAH, BUT TAKING THE OLD MAN WITH ME ISN'T MUCH BETTER.

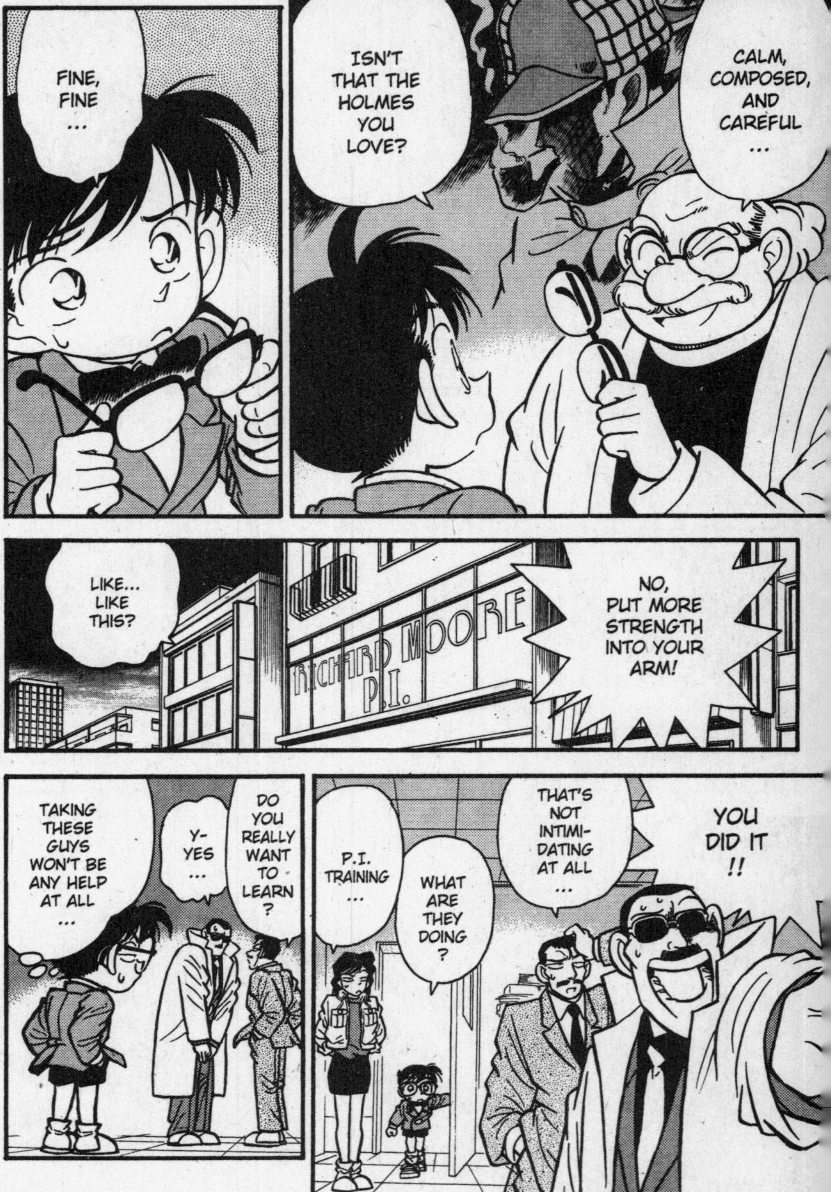
CALM, COMPOSED, AND CAREFUL ...
ISN'T THAT THE HOLMES YOU LOVE?
FINE, FINE ...
NO, PUT MORE STRENGTH INTO YOUR ARM!
RICHARD MOORE P.I.
LIKE... LIKE THIS?
YOU DID IT !!
THAT'S NOT INTIMI-DATING AT ALL ...
WHAT ARE THEY DOING ?
P.I. TRAINING ...
DO YOU REALLY WANT TO LEARN ?
Y-YES ...
TAKING THESE GUYS WON'T BE ANY HELP AT ALL ...

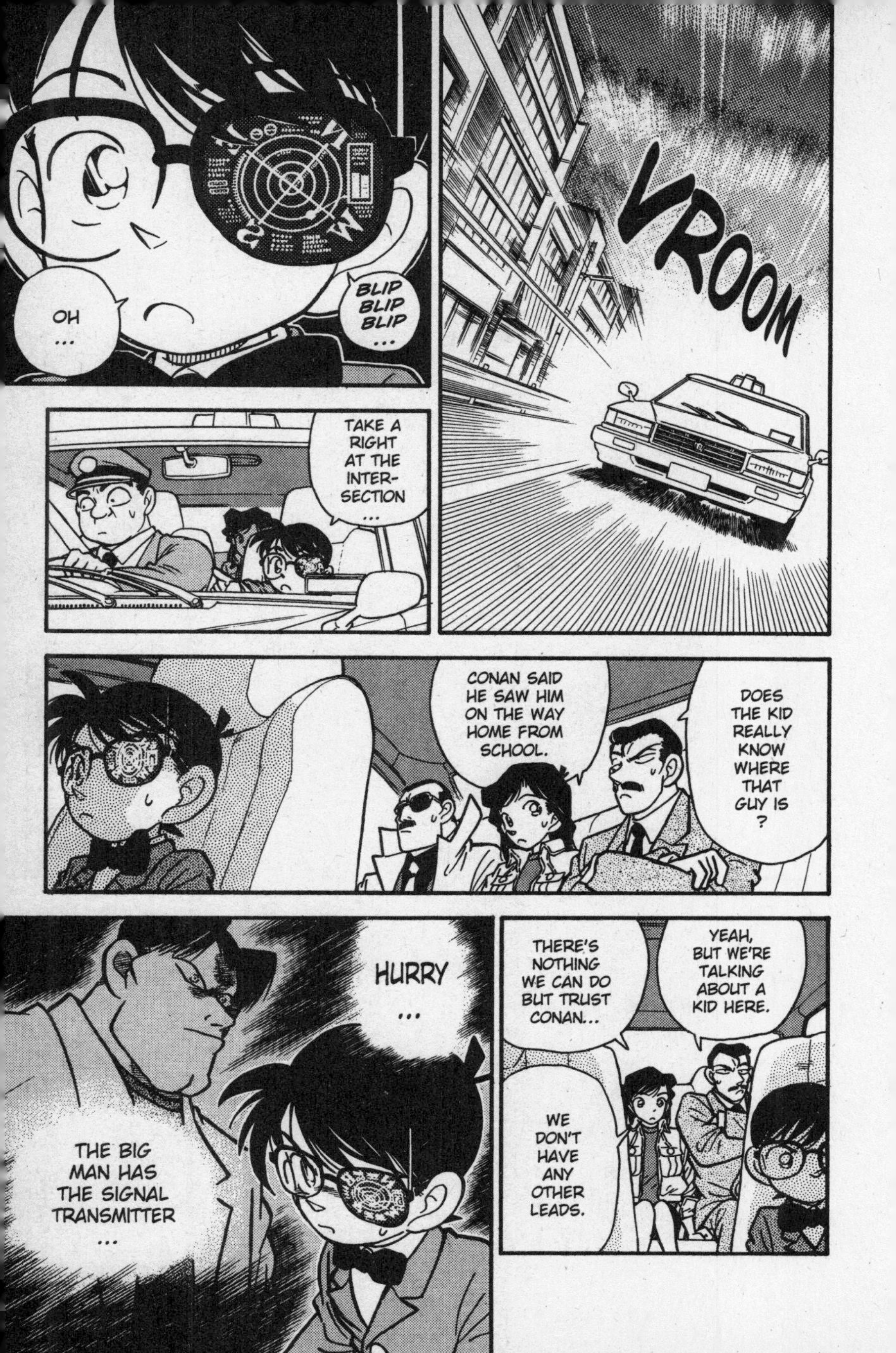
VROOM
BLIP BLIP BLIP ...
OH ...
TAKE A RIGHT AT THE INTER-SECTION ...
DOES THE KID REALLY KNOW WHERE THAT GUY IS ?
CONAN SAID HE SAW HIM ON THE WAY HOME FROM SCHOOL.
YEAH, BUT WE'RE TALKING ABOUT A KID HERE.
THERE'S NOTHING WE CAN DO BUT TRUST CONAN...
WE DON'T HAVE ANY OTHER LEADS.
HURRY ...
THE BIG MAN HAS THE SIGNAL TRANSMITTER ...

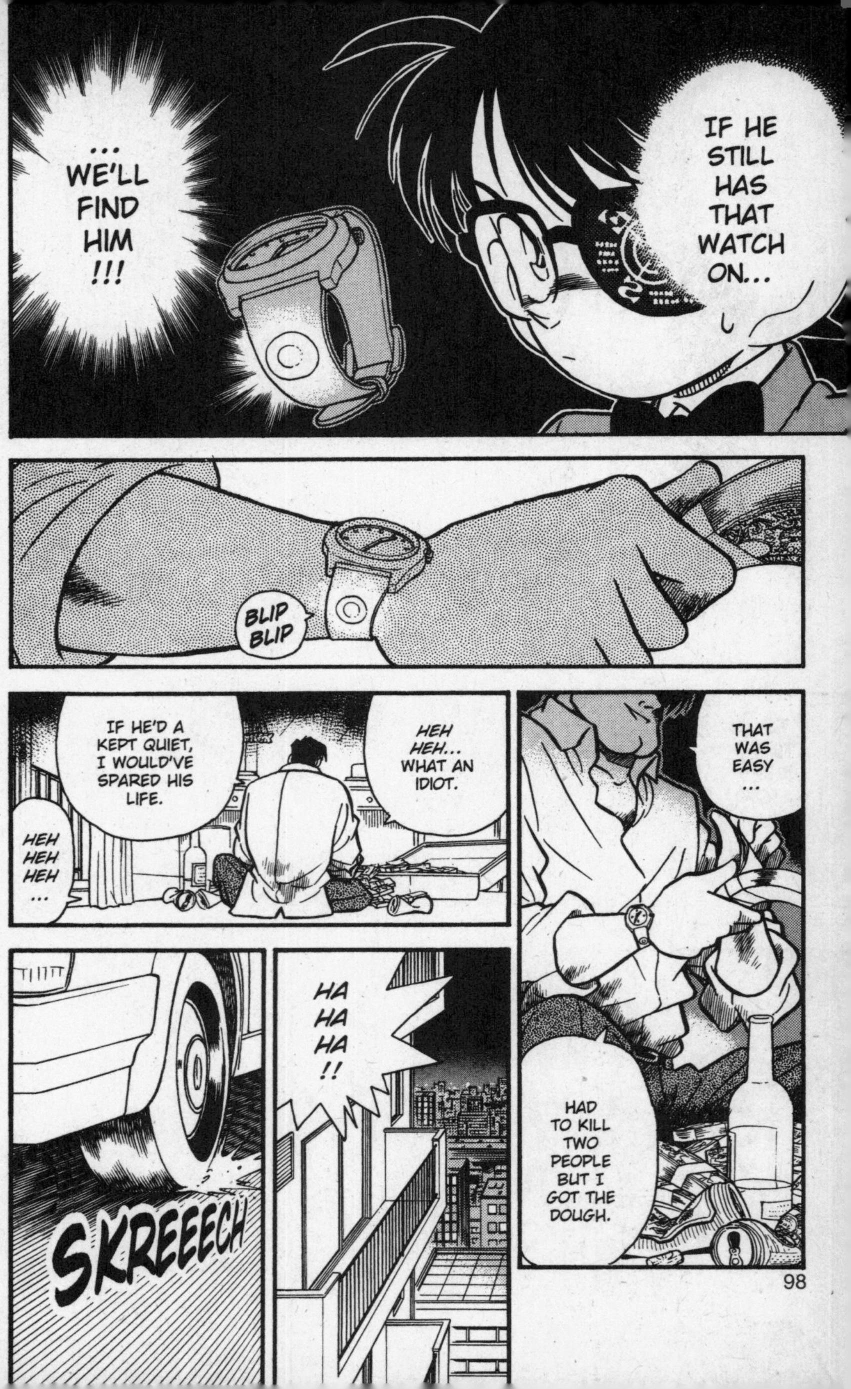
IF HE STILL HAS THAT WATCH ON...
... WE'LL FIND HIM !!!
BLIP BLIP
THAT WAS EASY ...
HAD TO KILL TWO PEOPLE BUT I GOT THE DOUGH.
HEH HEH... WHAT AN IDIOT.
IF HE'D A KEPT QUIET, I WOULD'VE SPARED HIS LIFE.
HEH HEH HEH ...
HA HA HA !!
SKREEECH

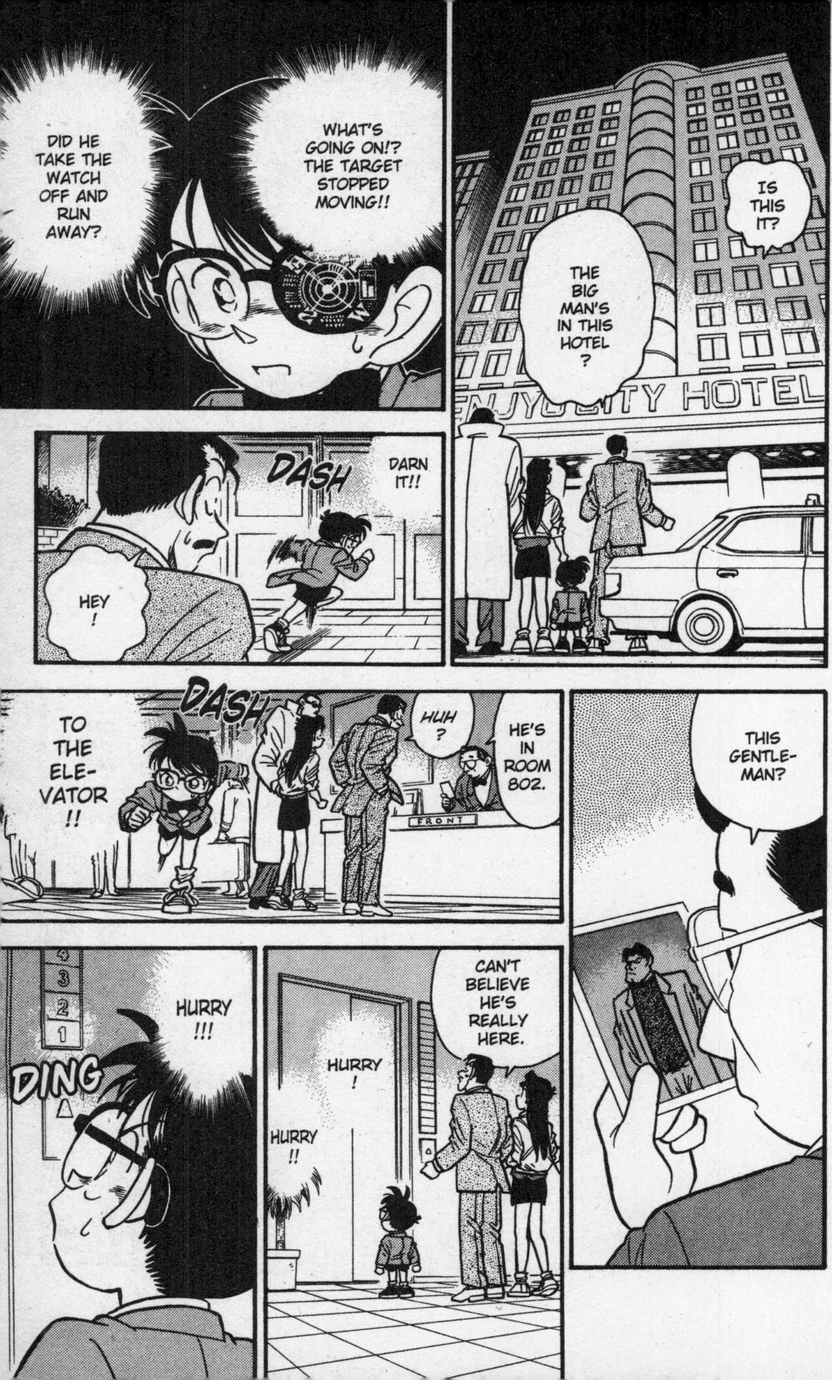
IS THIS IT?
THE BIG MAN'S IN THIS HOTEL?
ENJYU CITY HOTEL
WHAT'S GOING ON!? THE TARGET STOPPED MOVING!!
DID HE TAKE THE WATCH OFF AND RUN AWAY?
DARN IT!!
DASH
HEY!
THIS GENTLEMAN?
HE'S IN ROOM 802.
HUH?
FRONT
DASH
TO THE ELEVATOR!!
CAN'T BELIEVE HE'S REALLY HERE.
HURRY!
HURRY!!
HURRY!!!
DING

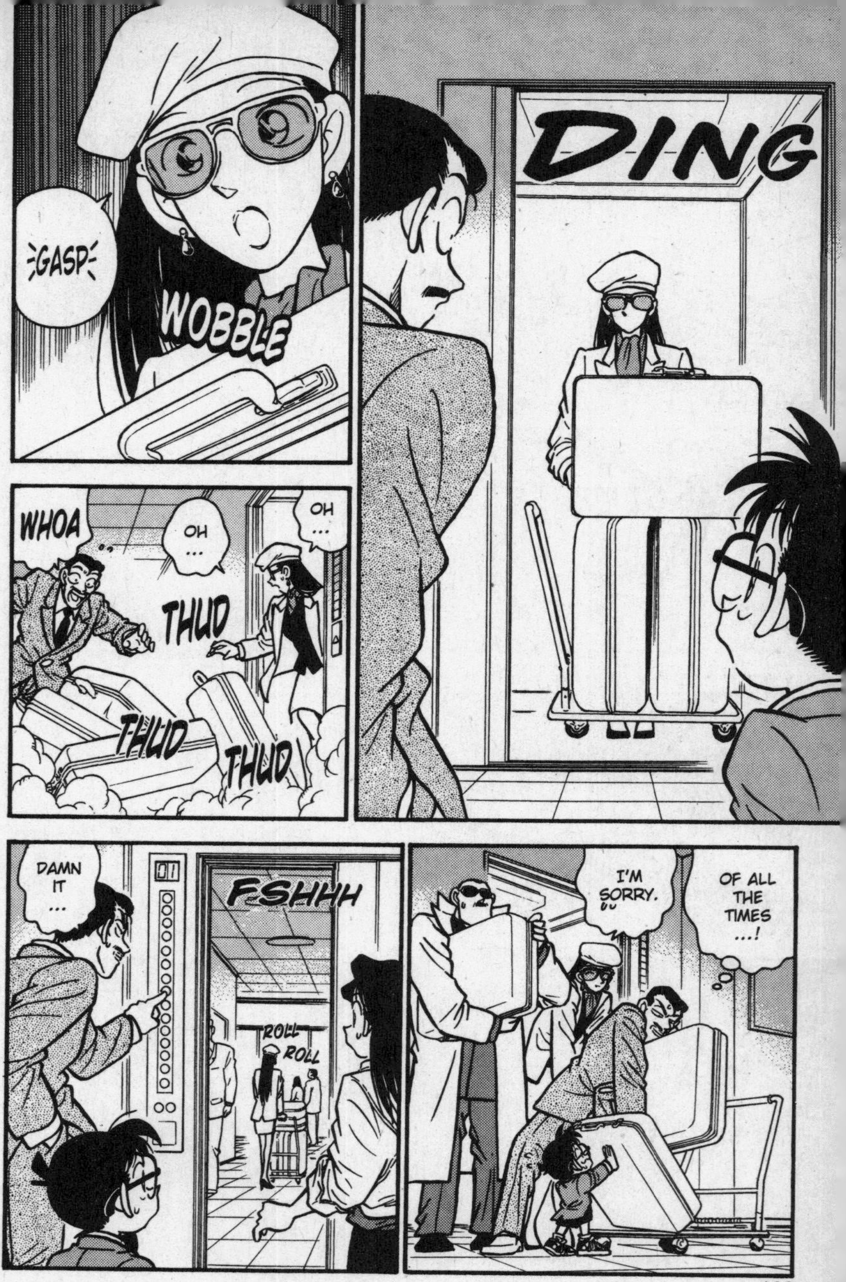
DING
GASP
WOBBLE
OH ...
OH ...
WHOA
THUD
THUD
THUD
OF ALL THE TIMES ...!
I'M SORRY.
FSHHH
DAMN IT ...
ROLL ROLL

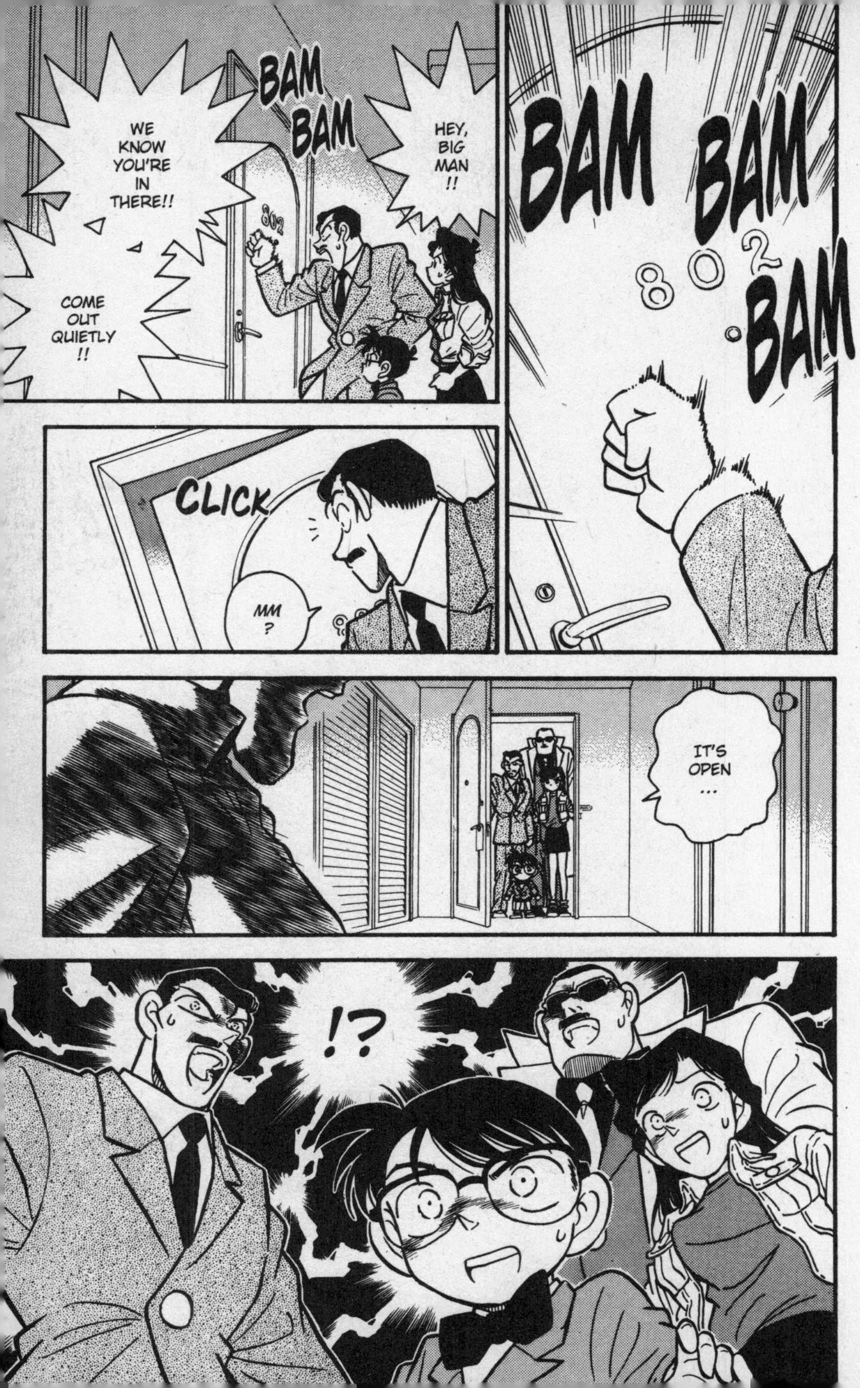
BAM BAM BAM BAM
802
HEY, BIG MAN !!
BAM BAM
WE KNOW YOU'RE IN THERE!!
COME OUT QUIETLY !!
CLICK
MM ?
IT'S OPEN ...
!?

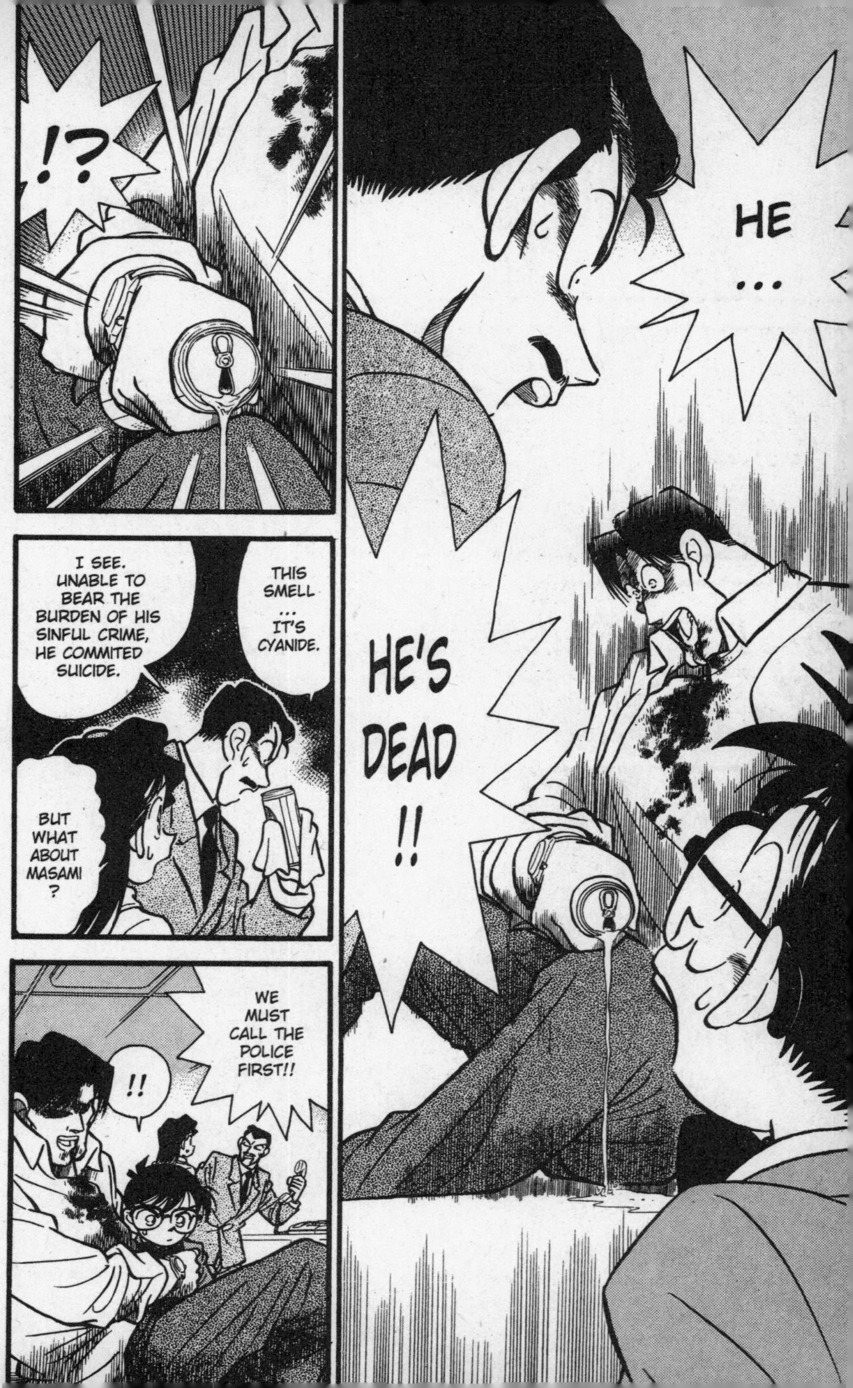
HE ...
HE'S DEAD !!
!?
THIS SMELL ... IT'S CYANIDE.
I SEE. UNABLE TO BEAR THE BURDEN OF HIS SINFUL CRIME, HE COMMITED SUICIDE.
BUT WHAT ABOUT MASAMI ?
WE MUST CALL THE POLICE FIRST!!
!!

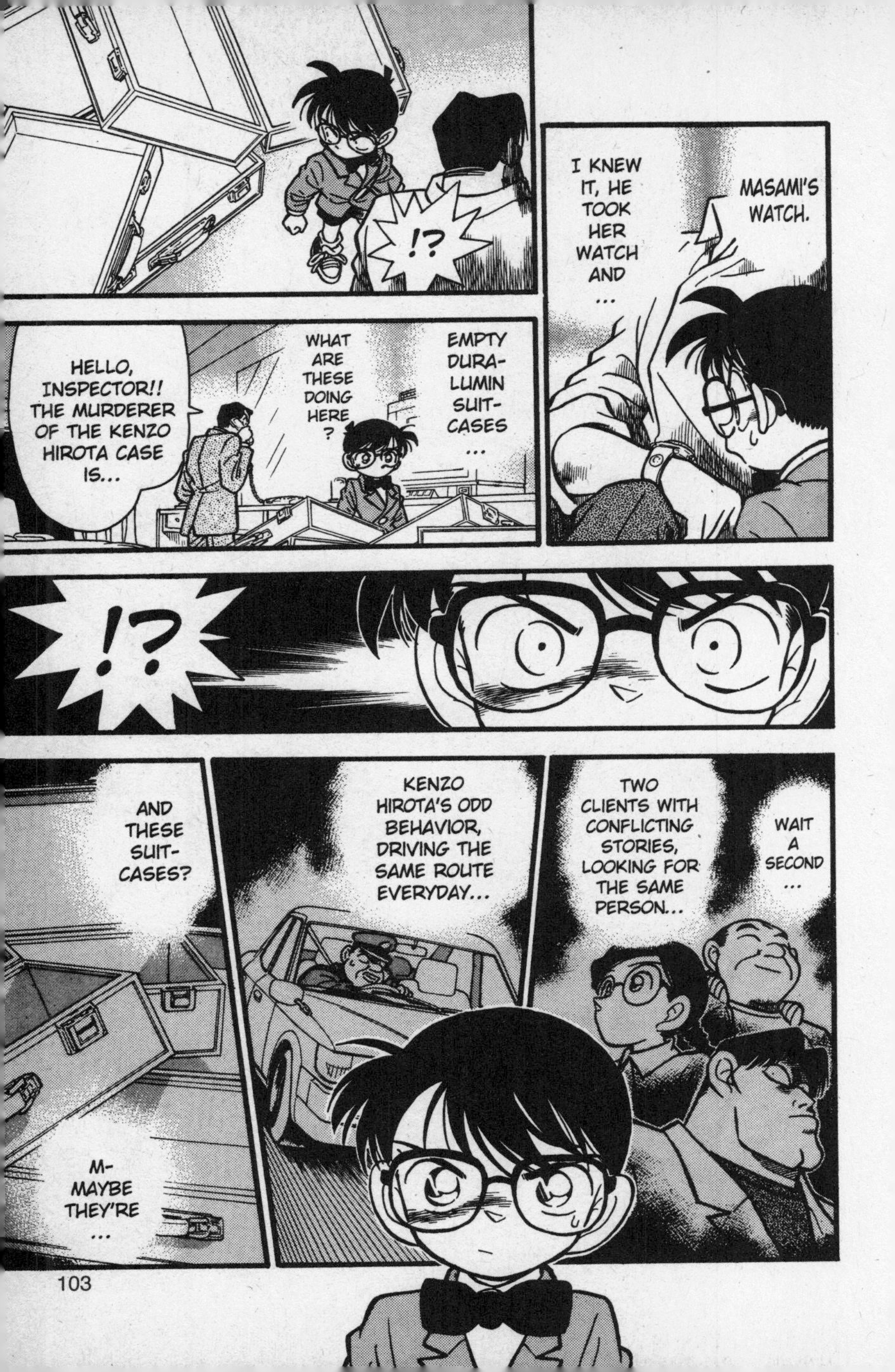
MASAMI'S WATCH.
I KNEW IT, HE TOOK HER WATCH AND ...
!?
EMPTY DURA-LUMIN SUIT-CASES ...
WHAT ARE THESE DOING HERE ?
HELLO, INSPECTOR!! THE MURDERER OF THE KENZO HIROTA CASE IS...
!?
WAIT A SECOND ...
TWO CLIENTS WITH CONFLICTING STORIES, LOOKING FOR THE SAME PERSON...
KENZO HIROTA'S ODD BEHAVIOR, DRIVING THE SAME ROUTE EVERYDAY...
AND THESE SUIT-CASES?
M-MAYBE THEY'RE ...

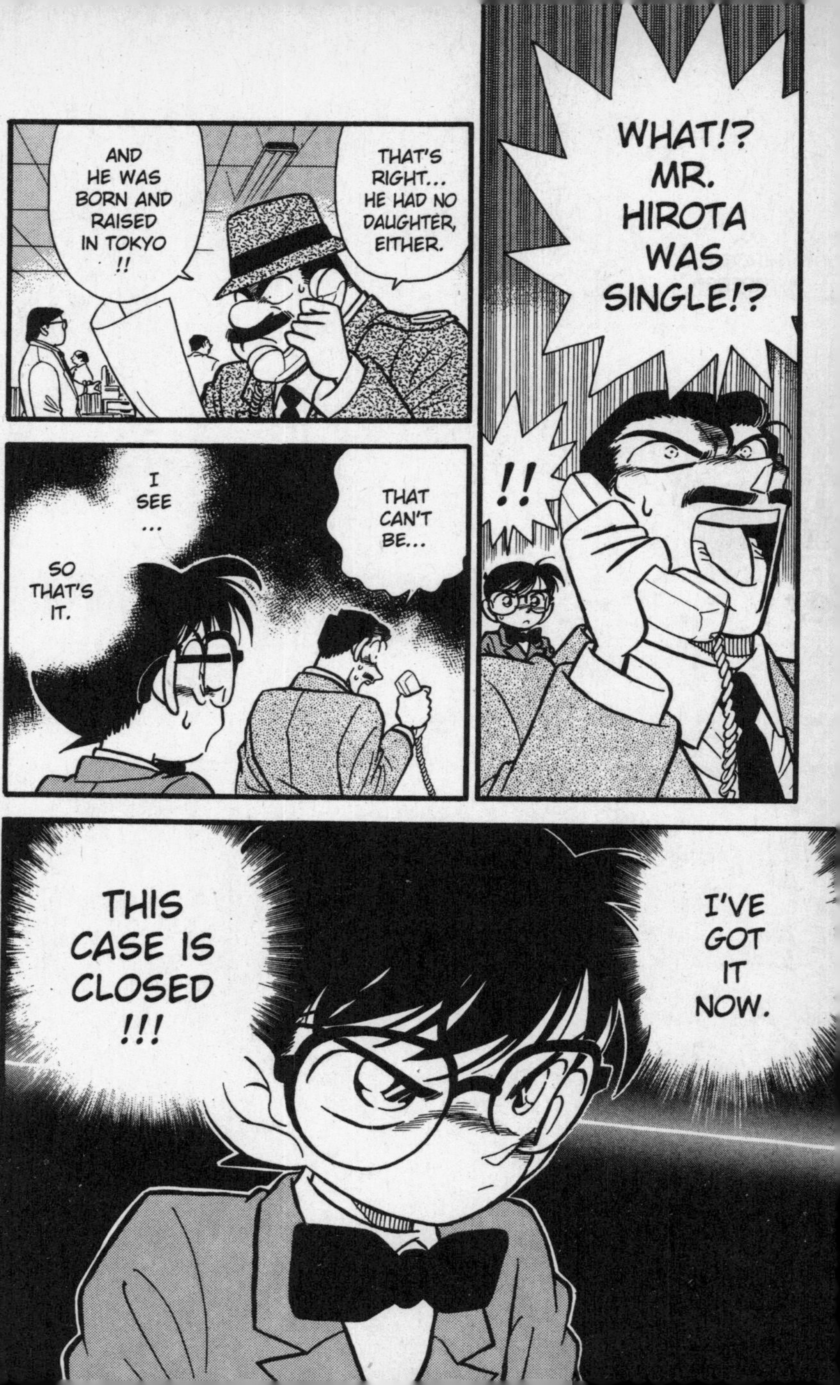
WHAT!? MR. HIROTA WAS SINGLE!?
!!
THAT'S RIGHT... HE HAD NO DAUGHTER, EITHER.
AND HE WAS BORN AND RAISED IN TOKYO !!
THAT CAN'T BE...
I SEE ...
SO THAT'S IT.
I'VE GOT IT NOW.
THIS CASE IS CLOSED !!!

FILE 7: A DEVILISH WOMAN

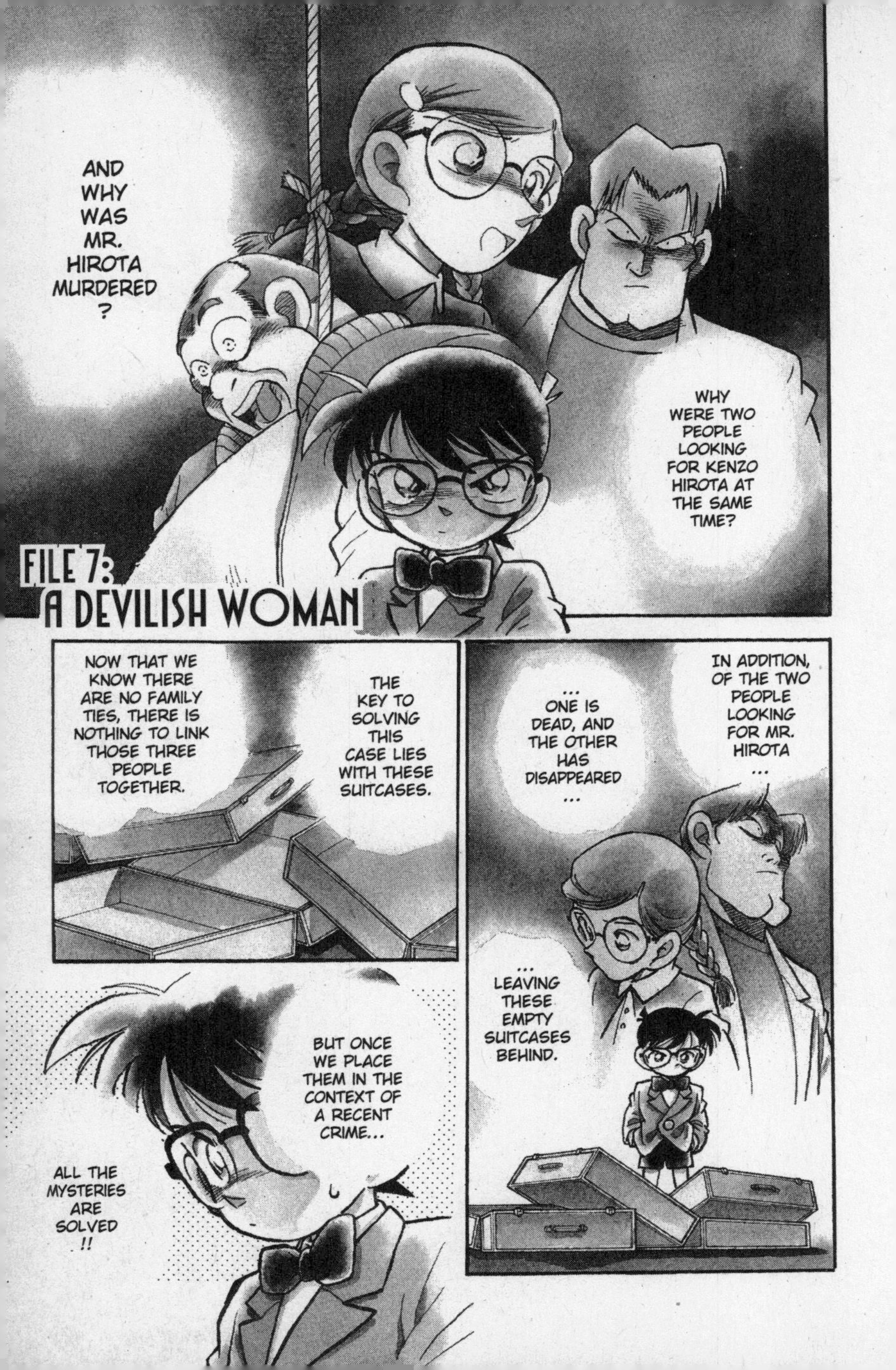

WHY WERE TWO PEOPLE LOOKING FOR KENZO HIROTA AT THE SAME TIME?
AND WHY WAS MR. HIROTA MURDERED?
IN ADDITION, OF THE TWO PEOPLE LOOKING FOR MR. HIROTA...
...ONE IS DEAD, AND THE OTHER HAS DISAPPEARED...
...LEAVING THESE EMPTY SUITCASES BEHIND.
THE KEY TO SOLVING THIS CASE LIES WITH THESE SUITCASES.
NOW THAT WE KNOW THERE ARE NO FAMILY TIES, THERE IS NOTHING TO LINK THOSE THREE PEOPLE TOGETHER.
BUT ONCE WE PLACE THEM IN THE CONTEXT OF A RECENT CRIME...
ALL THE MYSTERIES ARE SOLVED!!

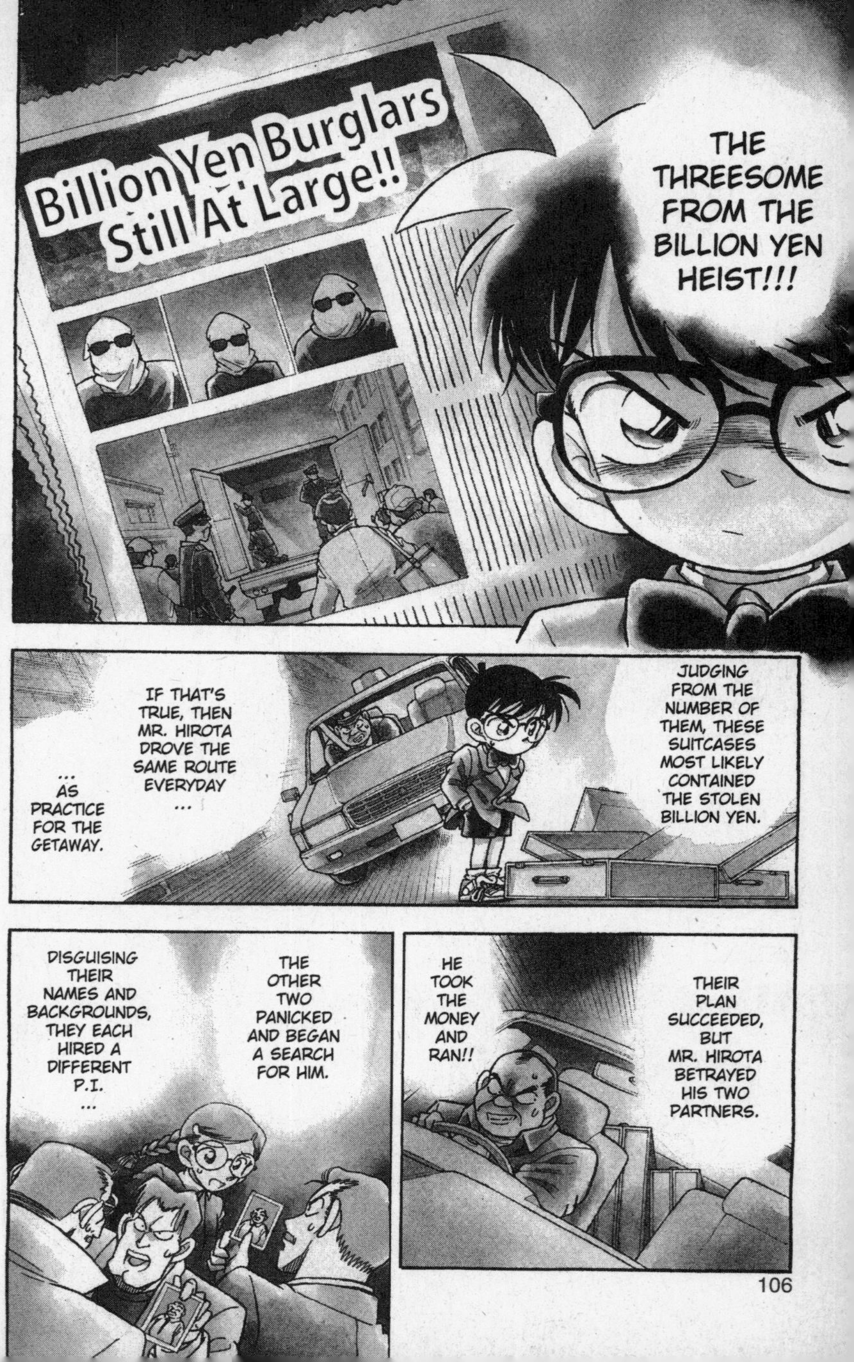
THE THREESOME FROM THE BILLION YEN HEIST!!!
Billion Yen Burglars Still At Large!!
JUDGING FROM THE NUMBER OF THEM, THESE SUITCASES MOST LIKELY CONTAINED THE STOLEN BILLION YEN.
IF THAT'S TRUE, THEN MR. HIROTA DROVE THE SAME ROUTE EVERYDAY ...
... AS PRACTICE FOR THE GETAWAY.
THEIR PLAN SUCCEEDED, BUT MR. HIROTA BETRAYED HIS TWO PARTNERS.
HE TOOK THE MONEY AND RAN!!
THE OTHER TWO PANICKED AND BEGAN A SEARCH FOR HIM.
DISGUISING THEIR NAMES AND BACKGROUNDS, THEY EACH HIRED A DIFFERENT P.I. ...

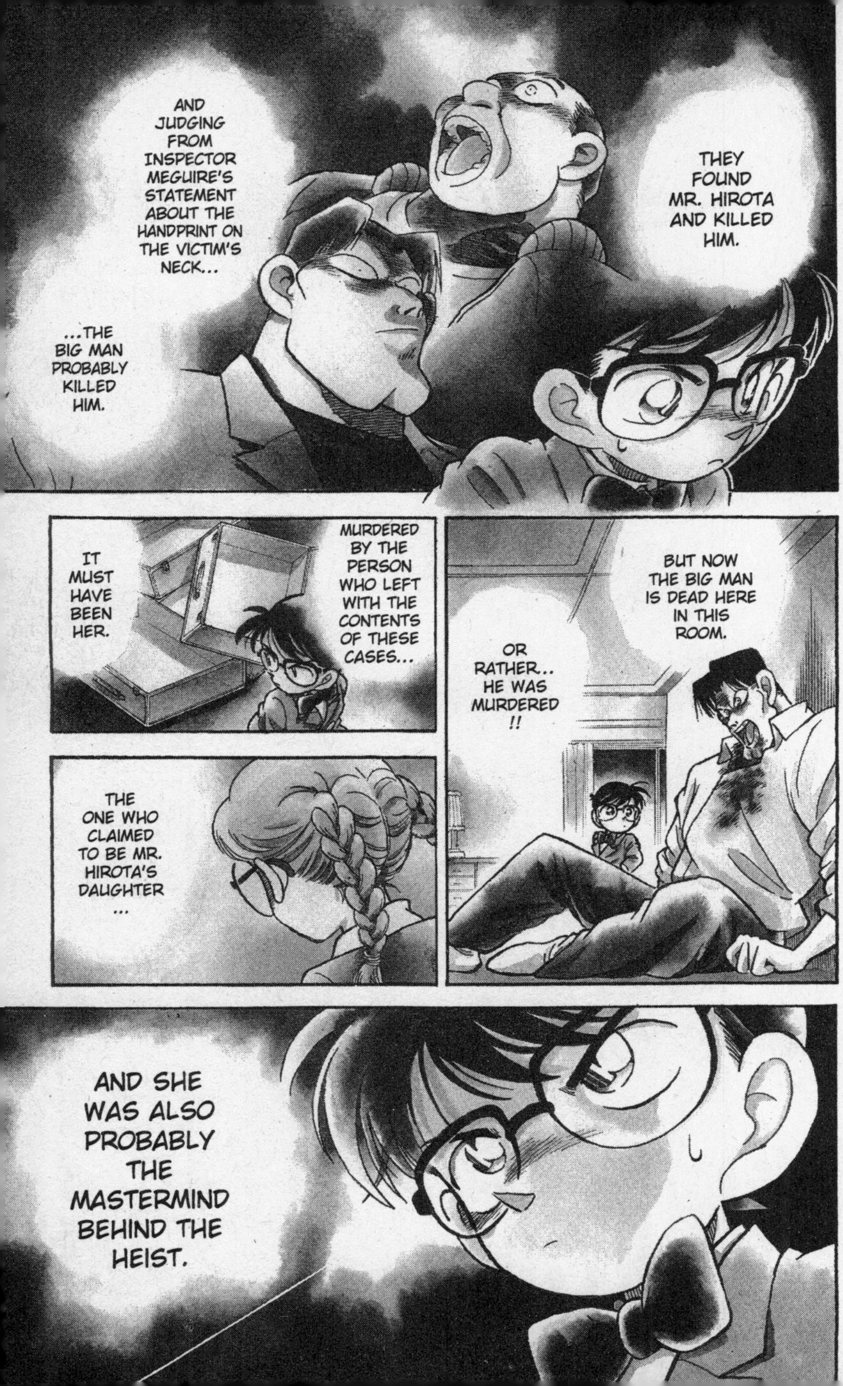
THEY FOUND MR. HIROTA AND KILLED HIM.
AND JUDGING FROM INSPECTOR MEGUIRE'S STATEMENT ABOUT THE HANDPRINT ON THE VICTIM'S NECK...
...THE BIG MAN PROBABLY KILLED HIM.
BUT NOW THE BIG MAN IS DEAD HERE IN THIS ROOM.
OR RATHER.. HE WAS MURDERED !!
MURDERED BY THE PERSON WHO LEFT WITH THE CONTENTS OF THESE CASES...
IT MUST HAVE BEEN HER.
THE ONE WHO CLAIMED TO BE MR. HIROTA'S DAUGHTER ...
AND SHE WAS ALSO PROBABLY THE MASTERMIND BEHIND THE HEIST.

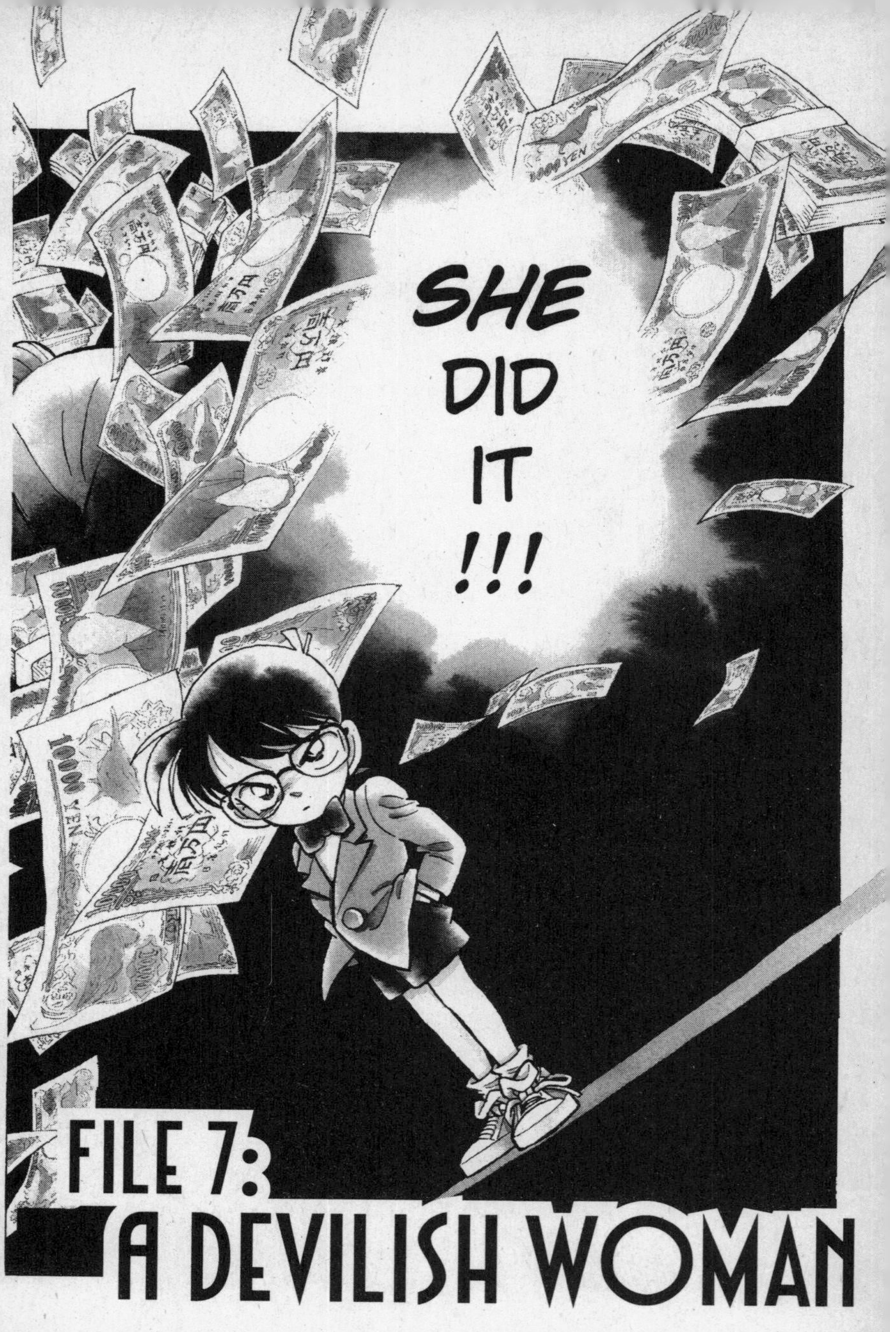
SHE DID IT !!!
FILE 7: A DEVILISH WOMAN

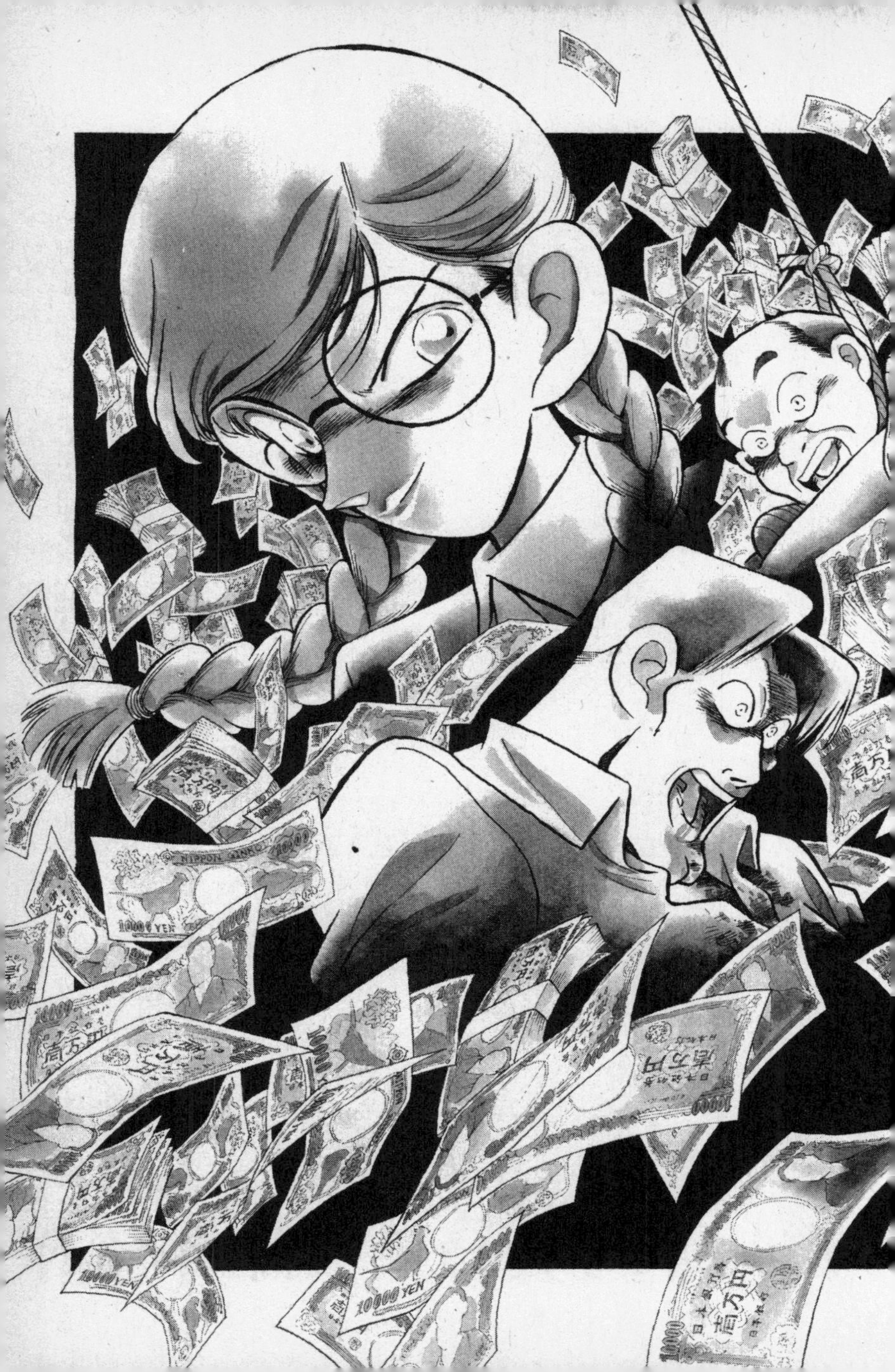
10000 YEN
壱万円

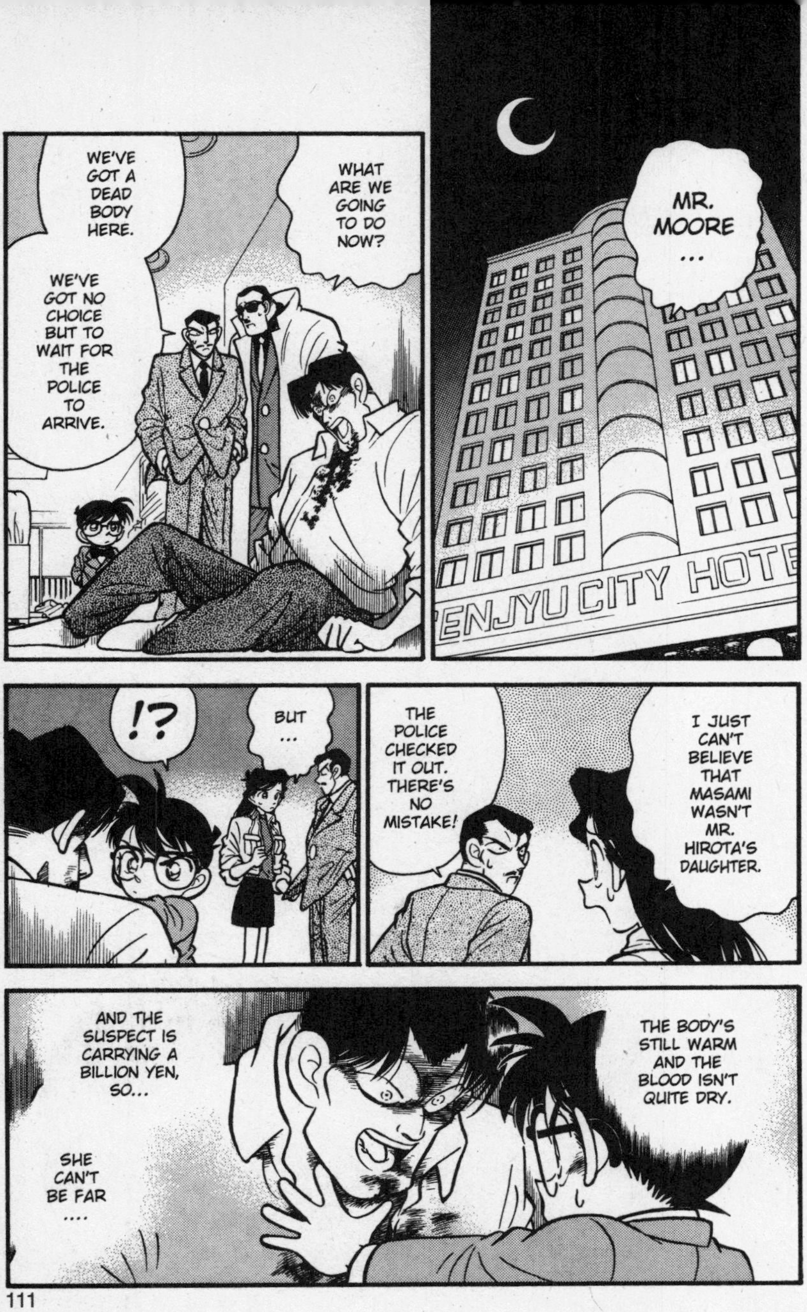
MR. MOORE ...
ENJYU CITY HOTE
WHAT ARE WE GOING TO DO NOW?
WE'VE GOT A DEAD BODY HERE.
WE'VE GOT NO CHOICE BUT TO WAIT FOR THE POLICE TO ARRIVE.
I JUST CAN'T BELIEVE THAT MASAMI WASN'T MR. HIROTA'S DAUGHTER.
THE POLICE CHECKED IT OUT. THERE'S NO MISTAKE!
BUT ...
!?
THE BODY'S STILL WARM AND THE BLOOD ISN'T QUITE DRY.
AND THE SUSPECT IS CARRYING A BILLION YEN, SO...
SHE CAN'T BE FAR ....

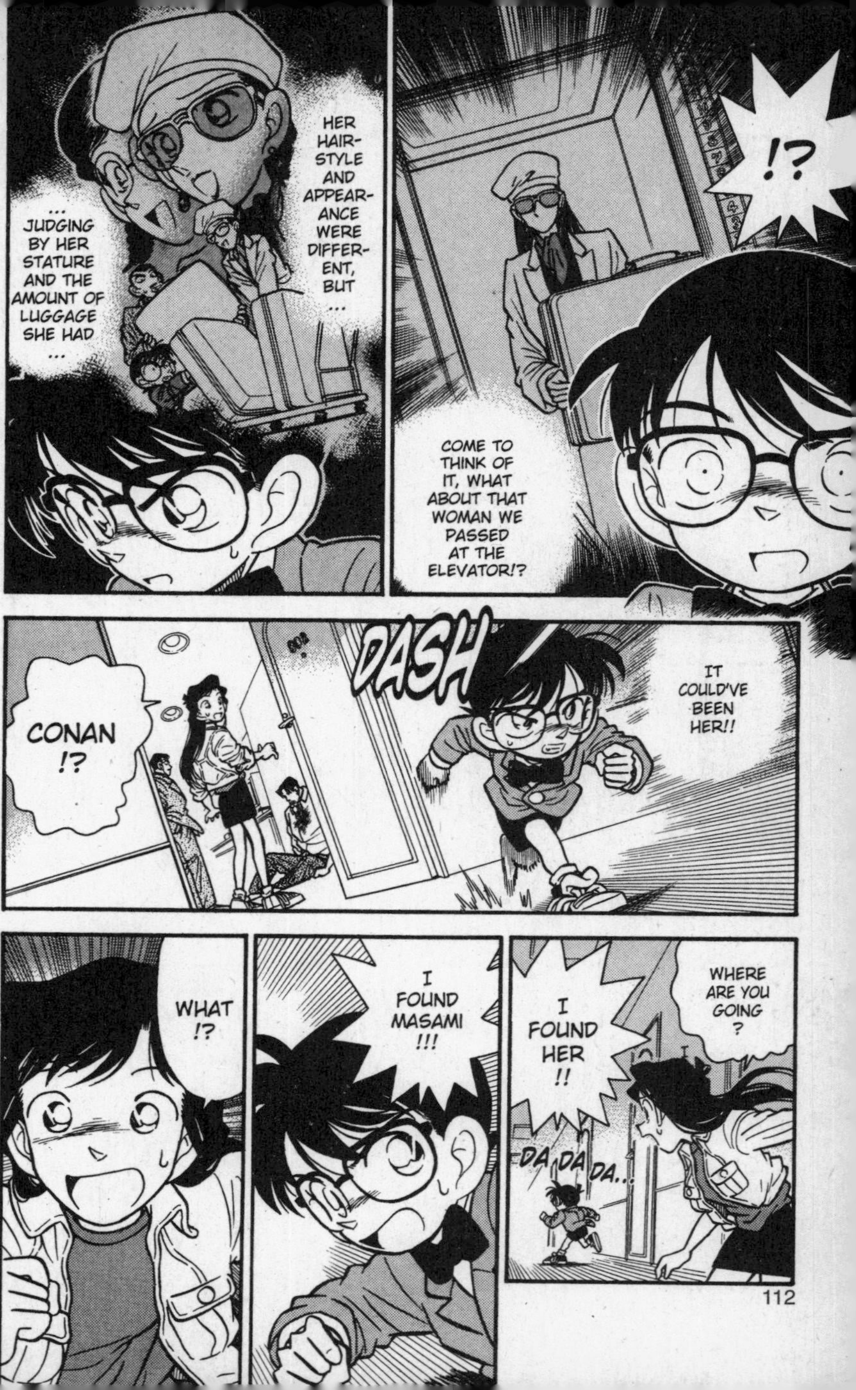
!?
COME TO THINK OF IT, WHAT ABOUT THAT WOMAN WE PASSED AT THE ELEVATOR!?
HER HAIR-STYLE AND APPEAR-ANCE WERE DIFFER-ENT, BUT ...
... JUDGING BY HER STATURE AND THE AMOUNT OF LUGGAGE SHE HAD ...
IT COULD'VE BEEN HER!!
DASH
CONAN !?
WHERE ARE YOU GOING ?
I FOUND HER !!
DA DA DA...
I FOUND MASAMI !!!
WHAT !?

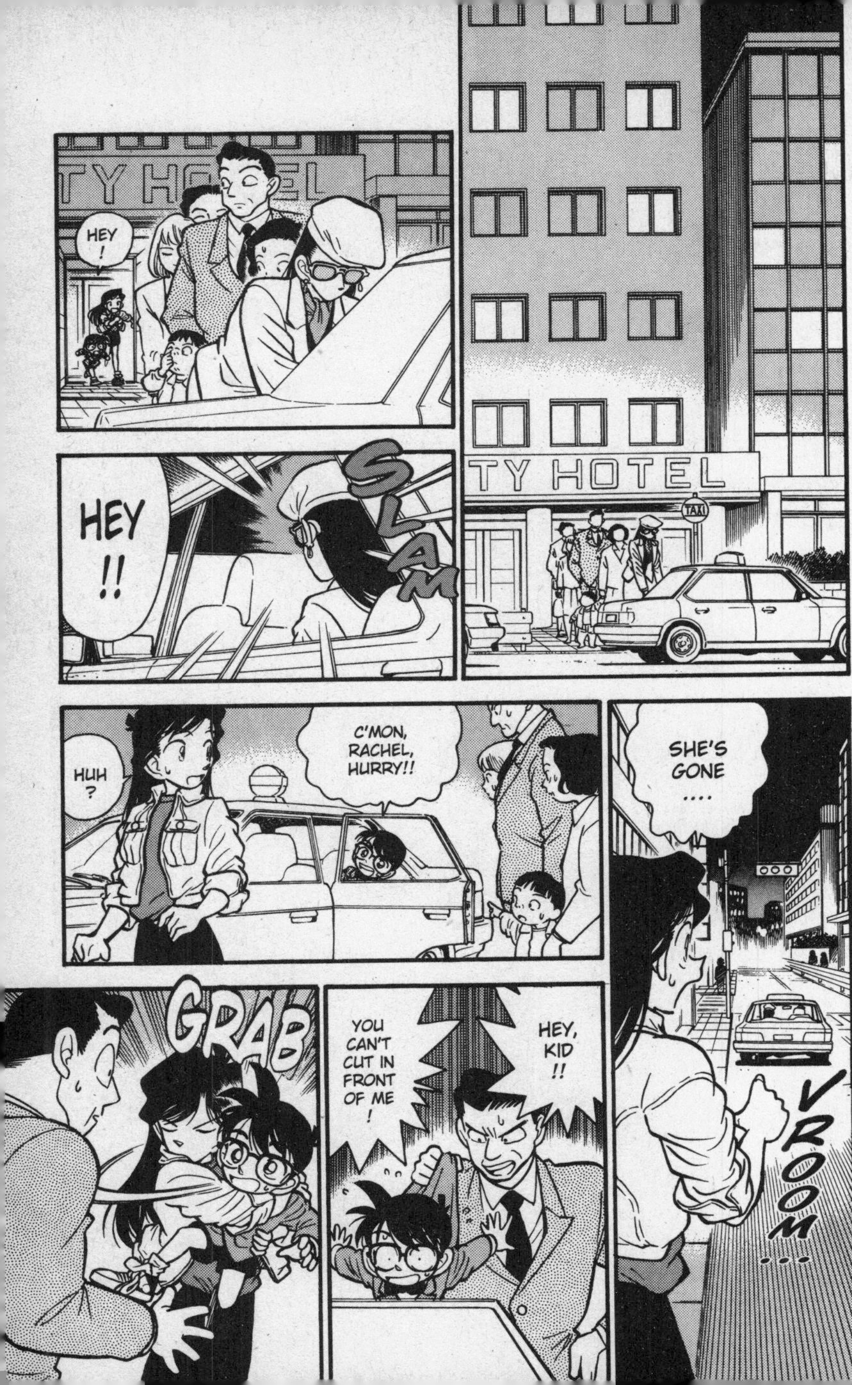
TY HOTEL
TAXI
TY HOTEL
HEY !
HEY !!
SLAM
SHE'S GONE ....
VROOM...
C'MON, RACHEL, HURRY!!
HUH ?
HEY, KID !!
YOU CAN'T CUT IN FRONT OF ME !
GRAB

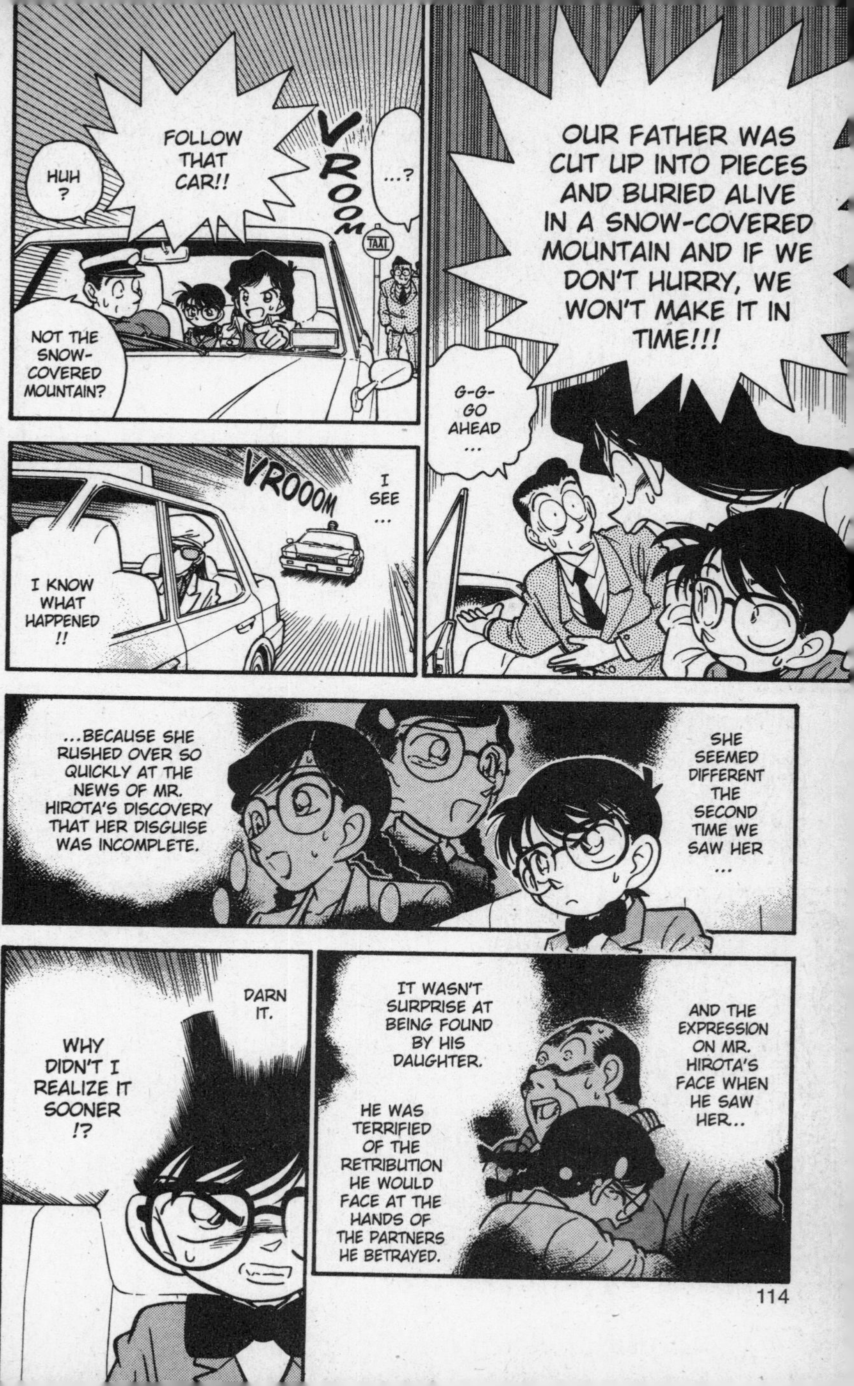
OUR FATHER WAS CUT UP INTO PIECES AND BURIED ALIVE IN A SNOW-COVERED MOUNTAIN AND IF WE DON'T HURRY, WE WON'T MAKE IT IN TIME!!!
G-G-GO AHEAD...
...?
VROOM
FOLLOW THAT CAR!!
HUH?
TAXI
NOT THE SNOW-COVERED MOUNTAIN?
I SEE...
VROOOM
I KNOW WHAT HAPPENED!!
SHE SEEMED DIFFERENT THE SECOND TIME WE SAW HER...
...BECAUSE SHE RUSHED OVER SO QUICKLY AT THE NEWS OF MR. HIROTA'S DISCOVERY THAT HER DISGUISE WAS INCOMPLETE.
AND THE EXPRESSION ON MR. HIROTA'S FACE WHEN HE SAW HER..
IT WASN'T SURPRISE AT BEING FOUND BY HIS DAUGHTER.
HE WAS TERRIFIED OF THE RETRIBUTION HE WOULD FACE AT THE HANDS OF THE PARTNERS HE BETRAYED.
DARN IT.
WHY DIDN'T I REALIZE IT SOONER!?

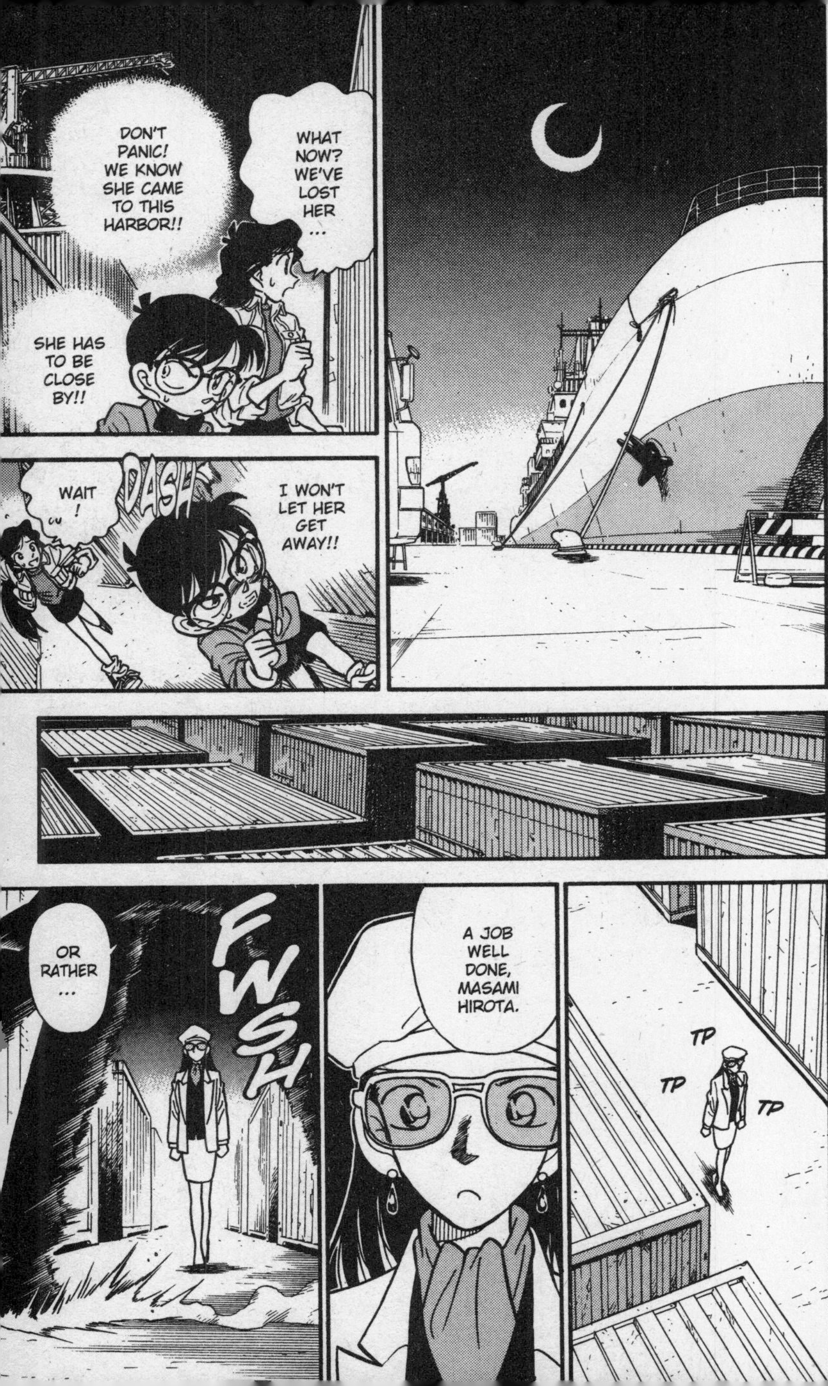
WHAT NOW? WE'VE LOST HER ...
DON'T PANIC! WE KNOW SHE CAME TO THIS HARBOR!!
SHE HAS TO BE CLOSE BY!!
I WON'T LET HER GET AWAY!!
DASH
WAIT !
TP
TP
TP
A JOB WELL DONE, MASAMI HIROTA.
FWSH
OR RATHER ...

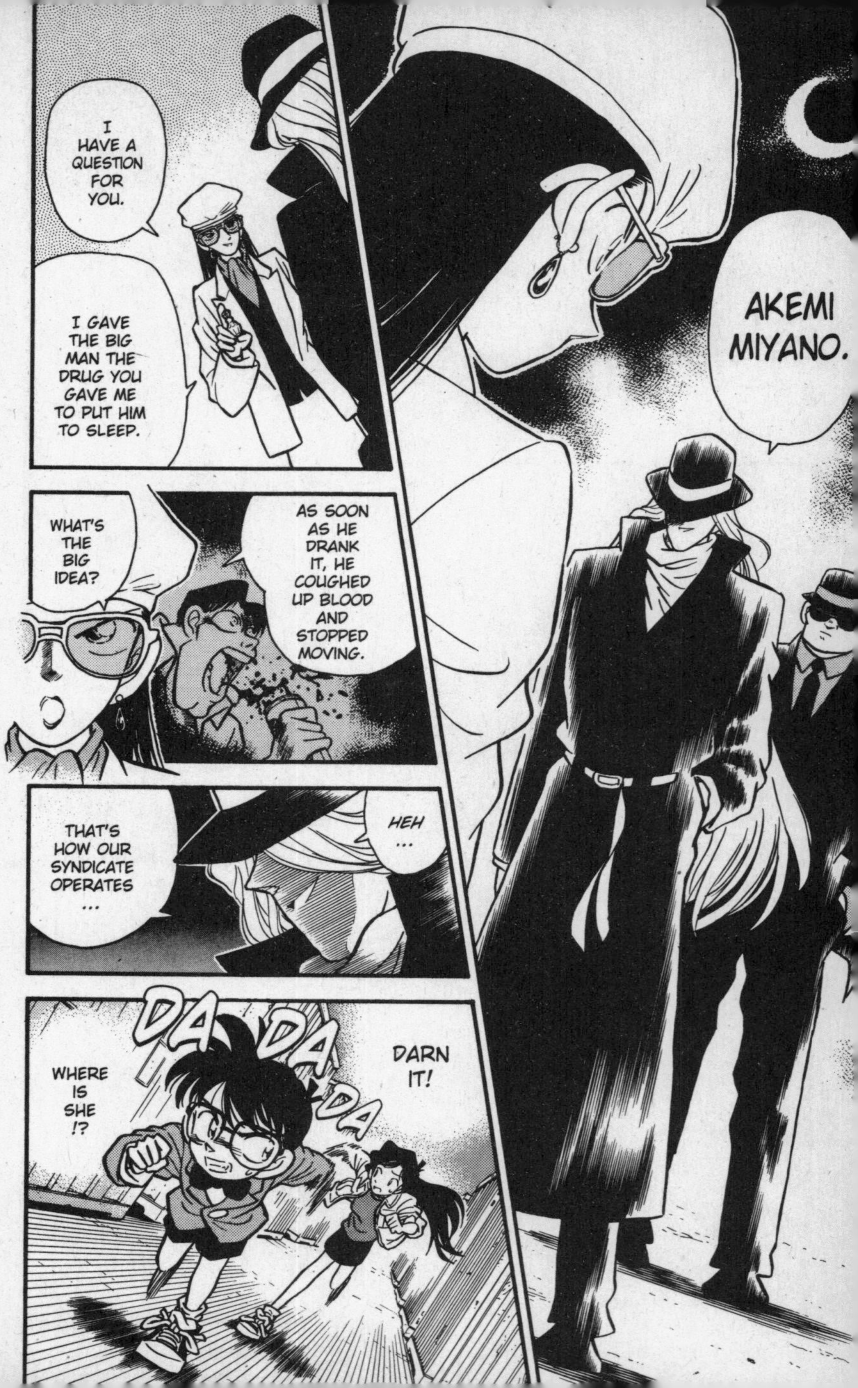
AKEMI MIYANO.
I HAVE A QUESTION FOR YOU.
I GAVE THE BIG MAN THE DRUG YOU GAVE ME TO PUT HIM TO SLEEP.
AS SOON AS HE DRANK IT, HE COUGHED UP BLOOD AND STOPPED MOVING.
WHAT'S THE BIG IDEA?
HEH ...
THAT'S HOW OUR SYNDICATE OPERATES ...
DA DA DA DA
DARN IT!
WHERE IS SHE !?

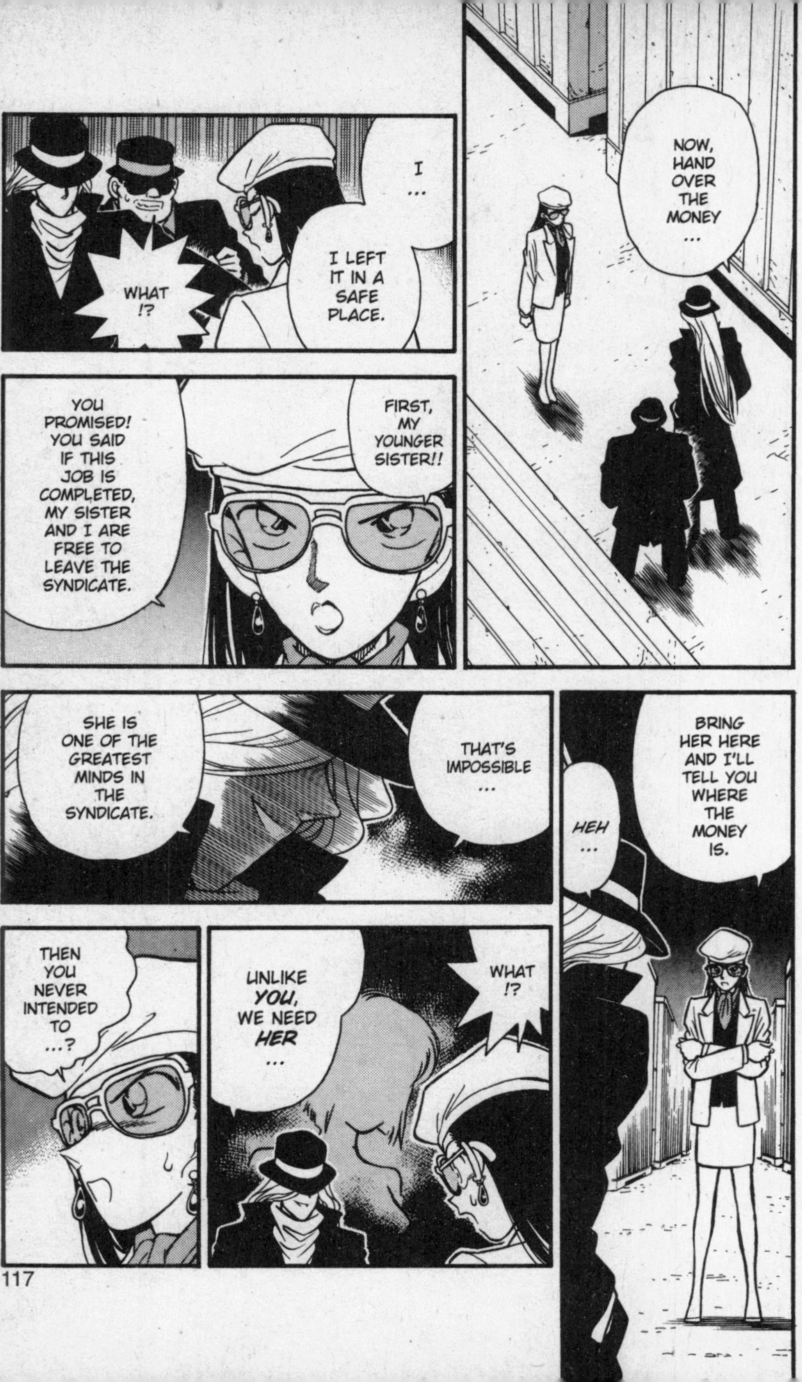
NOW, HAND OVER THE MONEY ...
I ...
I LEFT IT IN A SAFE PLACE.
WHAT !?
FIRST, MY YOUNGER SISTER!!
YOU PROMISED! YOU SAID IF THIS JOB IS COMPLETED, MY SISTER AND I ARE FREE TO LEAVE THE SYNDICATE.
BRING HER HERE AND I'LL TELL YOU WHERE THE MONEY IS.
HEH ...
THAT'S IMPOSSIBLE ...
SHE IS ONE OF THE GREATEST MINDS IN THE SYNDICATE.
WHAT !?
UNLIKE *YOU*, WE NEED *HER* ...
THEN YOU NEVER INTENDED TO ...?

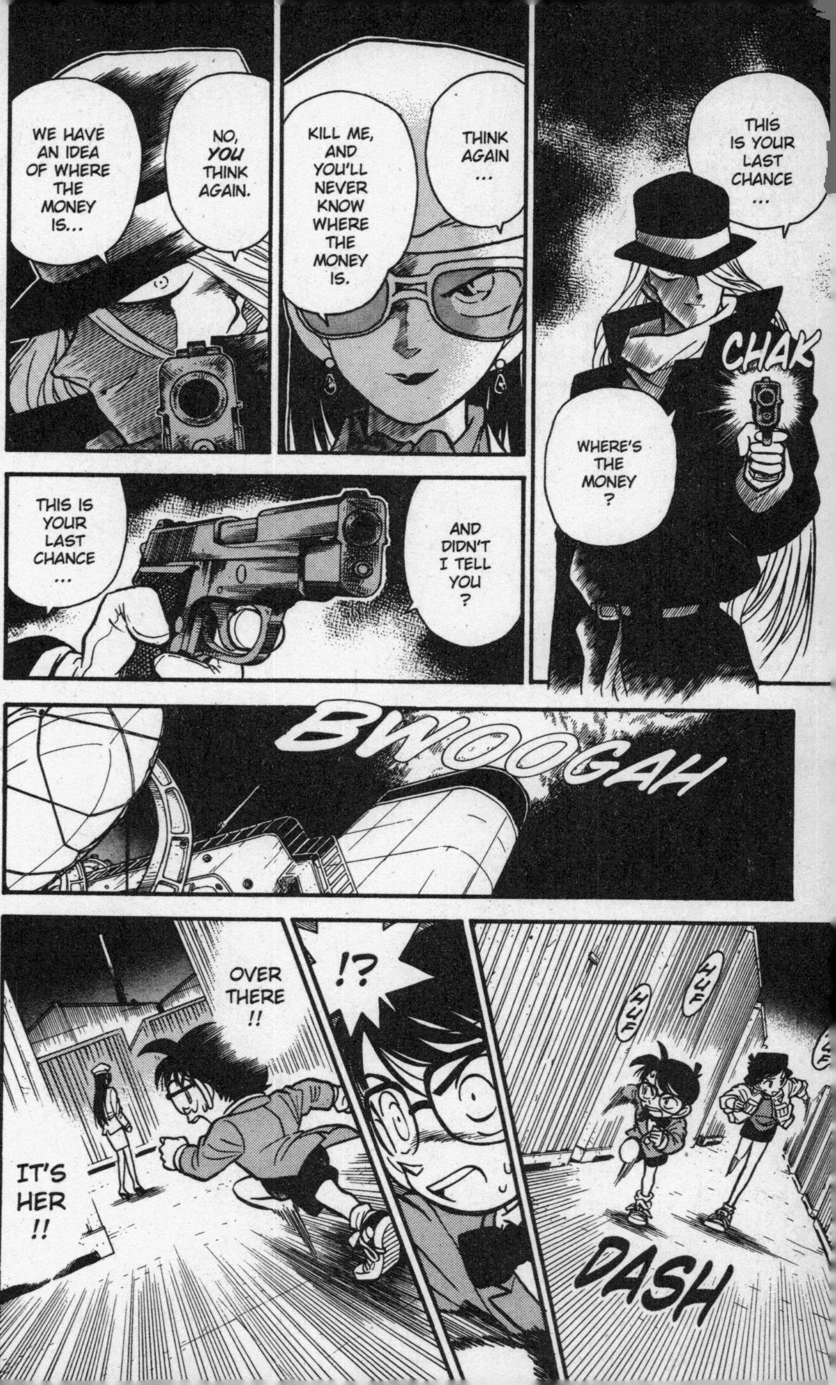
THIS IS YOUR LAST CHANCE ...
CHAK
WHERE'S THE MONEY ?
THINK AGAIN ...
KILL ME, AND YOU'LL NEVER KNOW WHERE THE MONEY IS.
NO, YOU THINK AGAIN.
WE HAVE AN IDEA OF WHERE THE MONEY IS...
AND DIDN'T I TELL YOU ?
THIS IS YOUR LAST CHANCE ...
BWOOGAH
HUF
HUF
DASH
!?
OVER THERE !!
IT'S HER !!

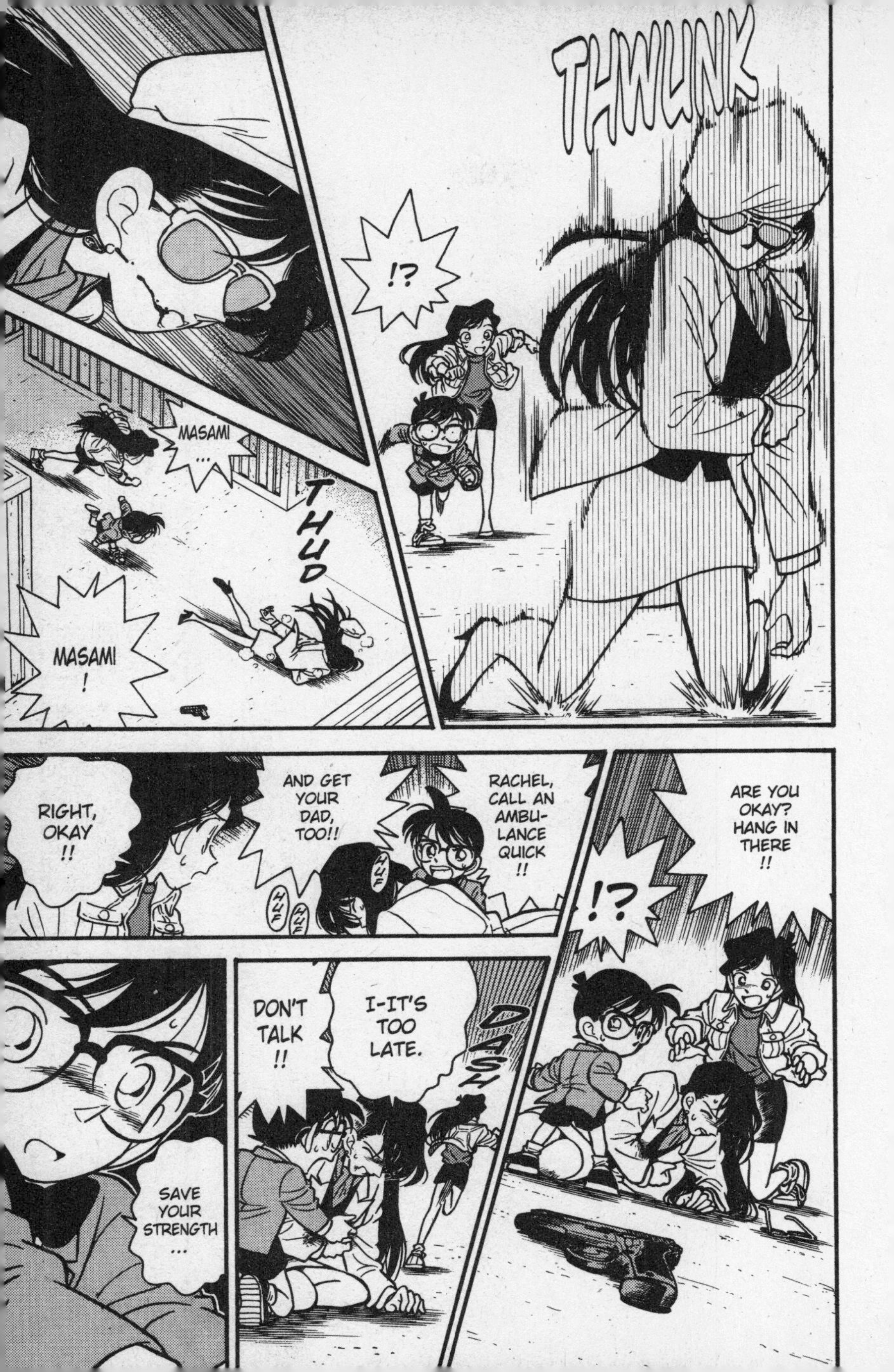
THWUNK
!?
MASAMI ...
THUD
MASAMI !
ARE YOU OKAY? HANG IN THERE !!
!?
RACHEL, CALL AN AMBU-LANCE QUICK !!
AND GET YOUR DAD, TOO!!
HUF
HUF
HUF
RIGHT, OKAY !!
I-IT'S TOO LATE.
DON'T TALK !!
DASH
SAVE YOUR STRENGTH ...

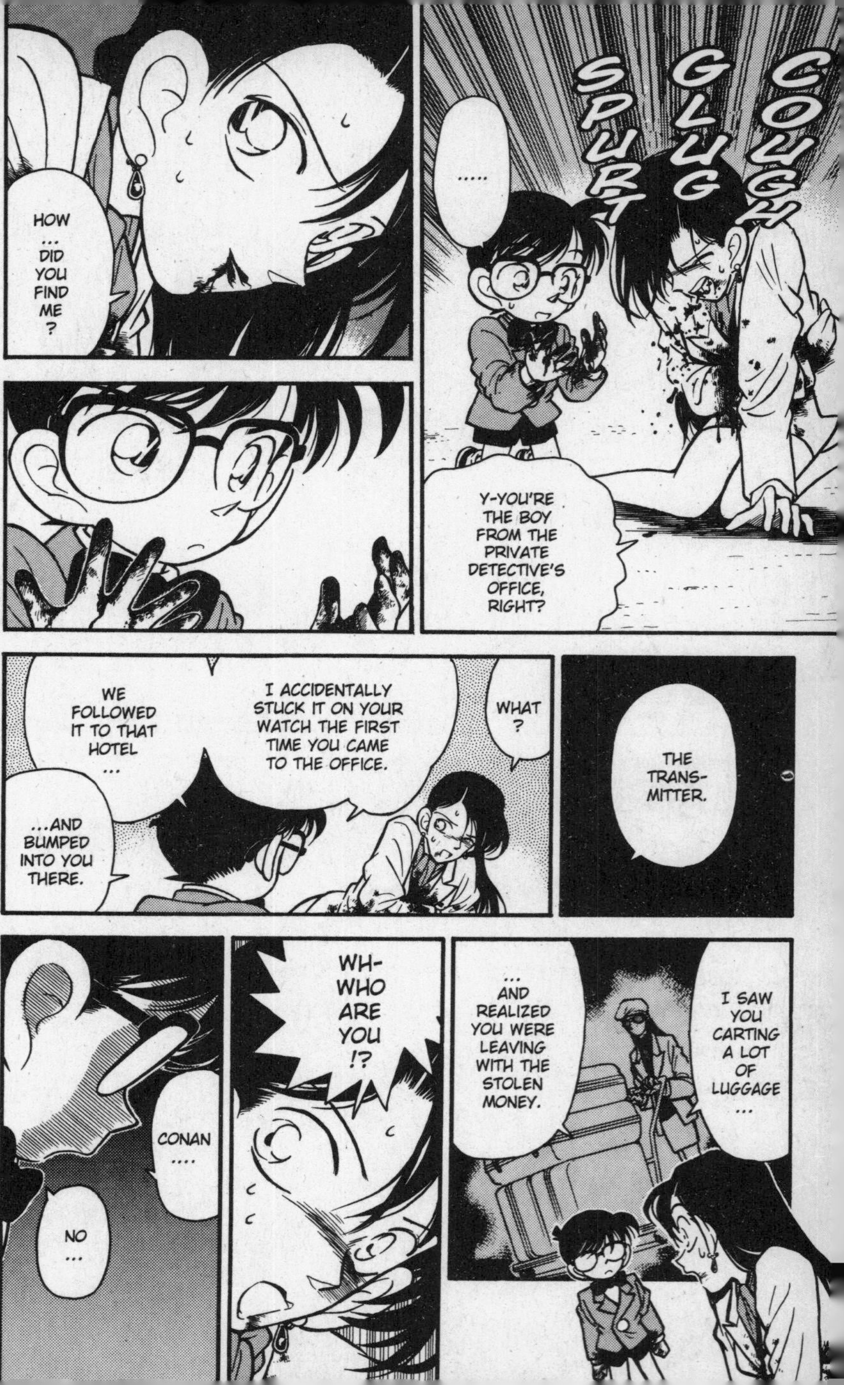
COUGH
GLUG
SPURT
.....
Y-YOU'RE THE BOY FROM THE PRIVATE DETECTIVE'S OFFICE, RIGHT?
HOW ... DID YOU FIND ME ?
THE TRANS-MITTER.
WHAT ?
I ACCIDENTALLY STUCK IT ON YOUR WATCH THE FIRST TIME YOU CAME TO THE OFFICE.
WE FOLLOWED IT TO THAT HOTEL ...
...AND BUMPED INTO YOU THERE.
I SAW YOU CARTING A LOT OF LUGGAGE ...
... AND REALIZED YOU WERE LEAVING WITH THE STOLEN MONEY.
WH-WHO ARE YOU !?
CONAN ....
NO ...

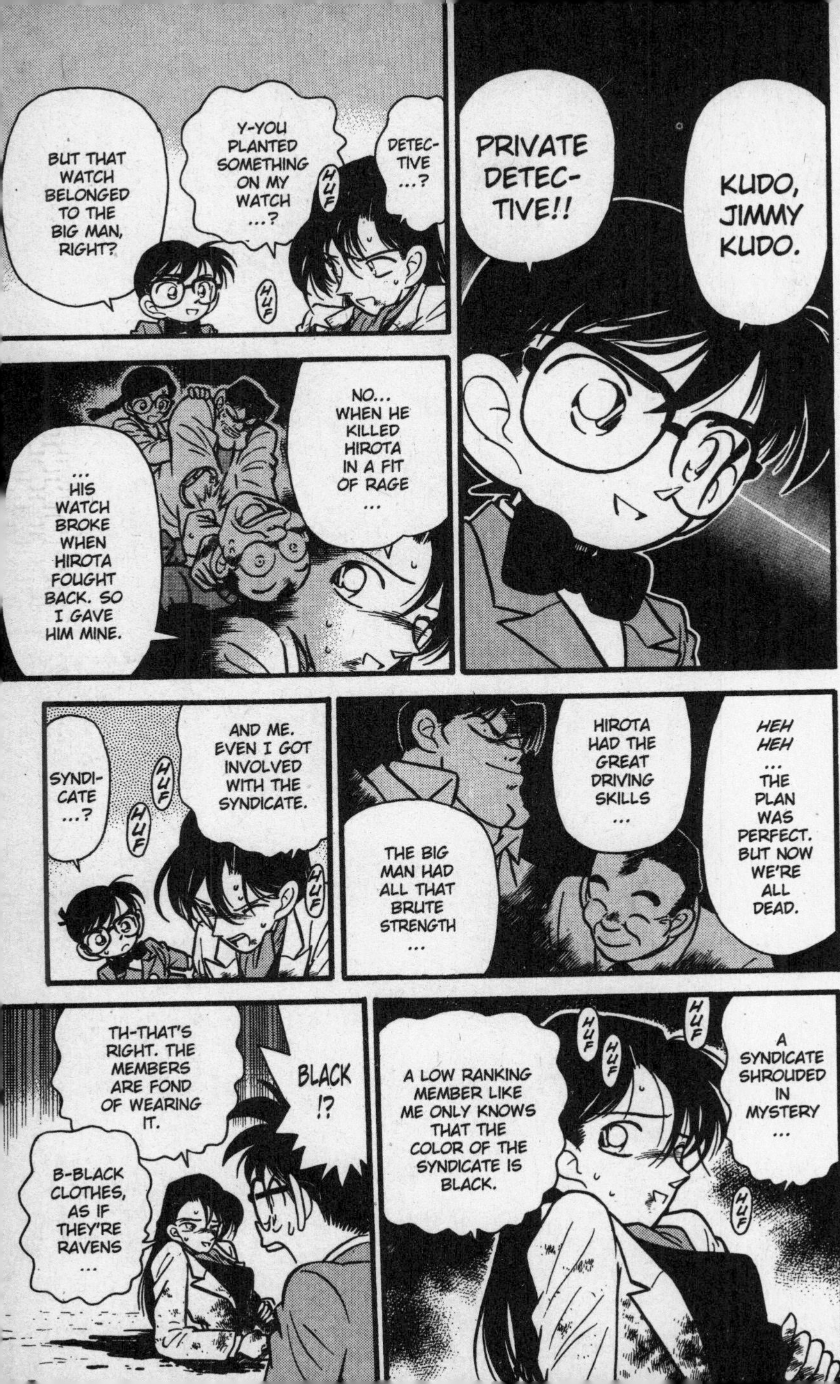
KUDO, JIMMY KUDO.
PRIVATE DETECTIVE!!
DETECTIVE ...?
HUF
Y-YOU PLANTED SOMETHING ON MY WATCH ...?
HUF
BUT THAT WATCH BELONGED TO THE BIG MAN, RIGHT?
NO... WHEN HE KILLED HIROTA IN A FIT OF RAGE ...
... HIS WATCH BROKE WHEN HIROTA FOUGHT BACK. SO I GAVE HIM MINE.
HEH HEH ... THE PLAN WAS PERFECT. BUT NOW WE'RE ALL DEAD.
HIROTA HAD THE GREAT DRIVING SKILLS ...
THE BIG MAN HAD ALL THAT BRUTE STRENGTH ...
HUF
AND ME. EVEN I GOT INVOLVED WITH THE SYNDICATE.
HUF
HUF
SYNDICATE ...?
HUF
A SYNDICATE SHROUDED IN MYSTERY ...
HUF
HUF
HUF
A LOW RANKING MEMBER LIKE ME ONLY KNOWS THAT THE COLOR OF THE SYNDICATE IS BLACK.
BLACK !?
TH-THAT'S RIGHT. THE MEMBERS ARE FOND OF WEARING IT.
B-BLACK CLOTHES, AS IF THEY'RE RAVENS ...

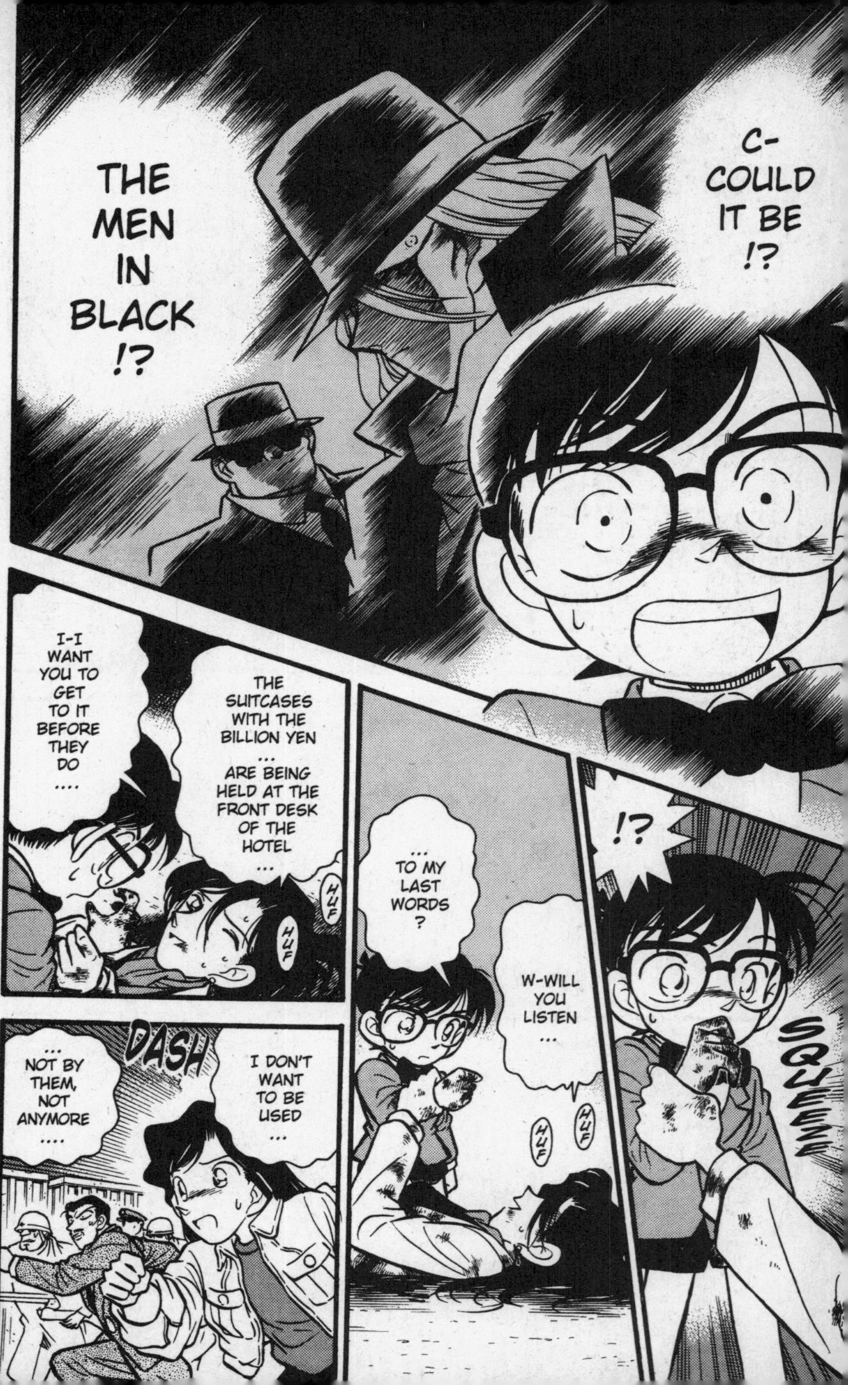
C- COULD IT BE !?
THE MEN IN BLACK !?
!?
SQUEEZE
W-WILL YOU LISTEN ...
... TO MY LAST WORDS ?
HUF
HUF
THE SUITCASES WITH THE BILLION YEN ... ARE BEING HELD AT THE FRONT DESK OF THE HOTEL ...
I-I WANT YOU TO GET TO IT BEFORE THEY DO ....
HUF
HUF
DASH
I DON'T WANT TO BE USED ...
... NOT BY THEM, NOT ANYMORE ....

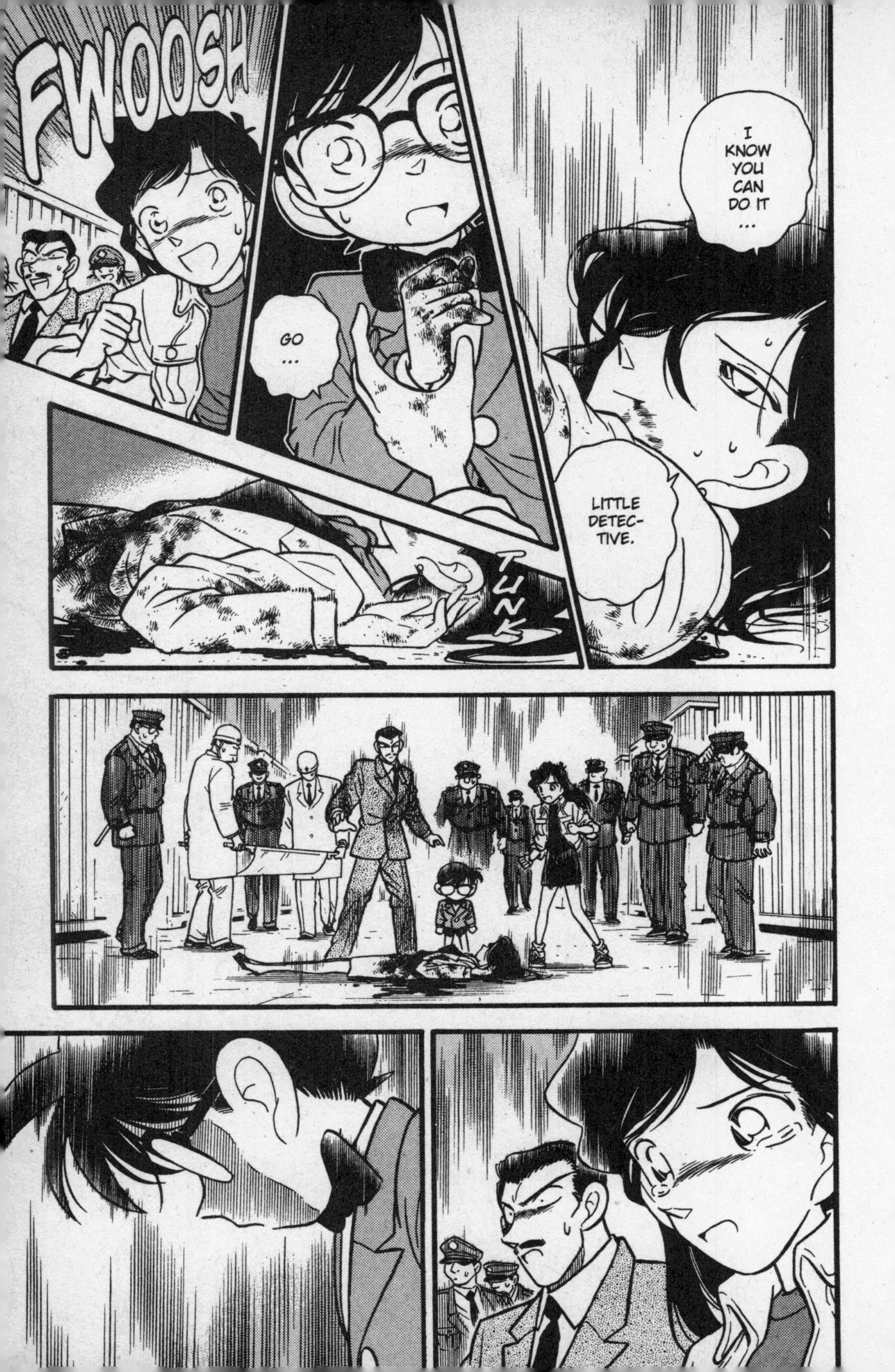
I KNOW YOU CAN DO IT ...
LITTLE DETECTIVE.
GO ...
FWOOSH
TUNK

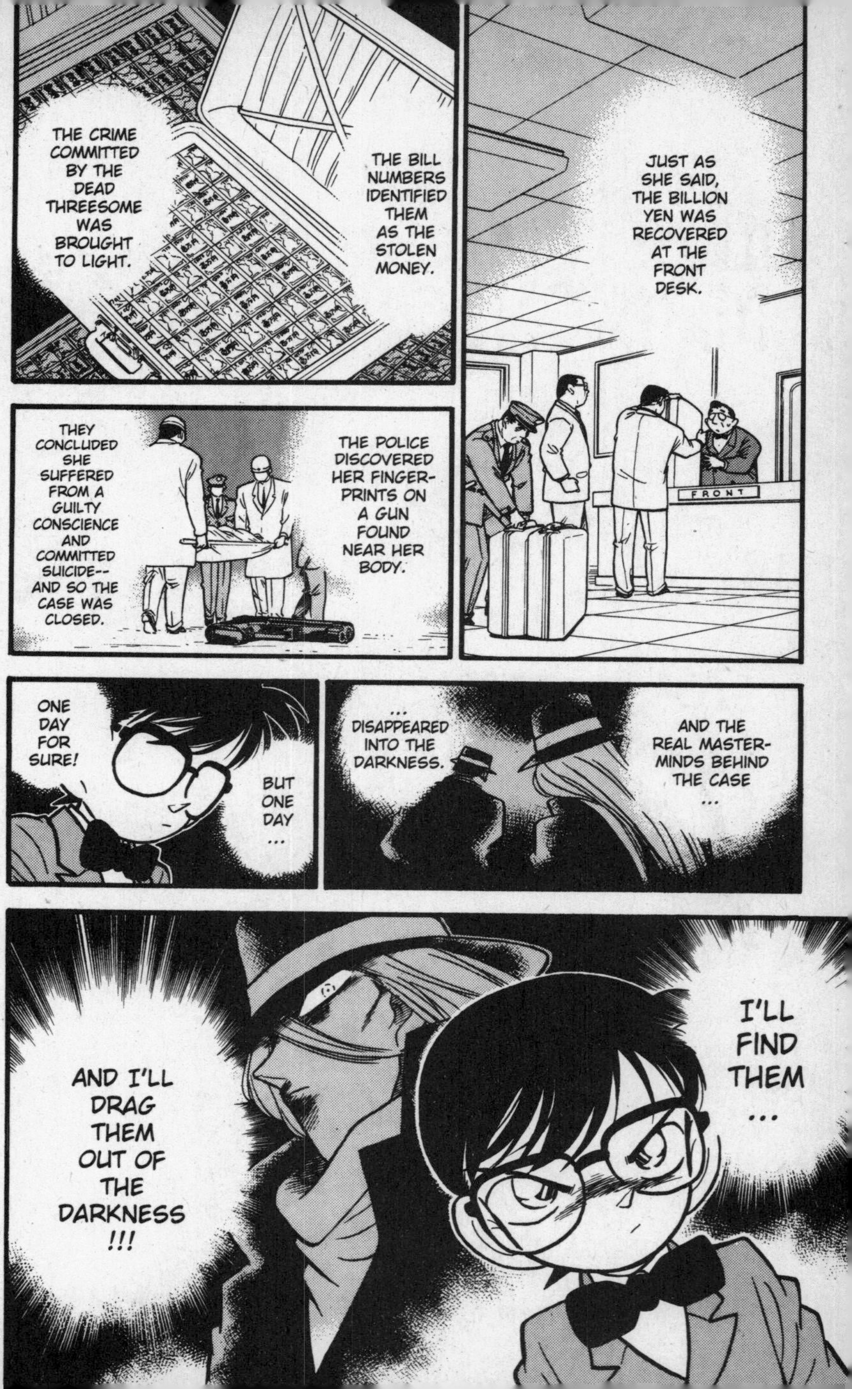
JUST AS SHE SAID, THE BILLION YEN WAS RECOVERED AT THE FRONT DESK.
FRONT
THE BILL NUMBERS IDENTIFIED THEM AS THE STOLEN MONEY.
THE CRIME COMMITTED BY THE DEAD THREESOME WAS BROUGHT TO LIGHT.
THE POLICE DISCOVERED HER FINGER-PRINTS ON A GUN FOUND NEAR HER BODY.
THEY CONCLUDED SHE SUFFERED FROM A GUILTY CONSCIENCE AND COMMITTED SUICIDE-- AND SO THE CASE WAS CLOSED.
AND THE REAL MASTER-MINDS BEHIND THE CASE ...
... DISAPPEARED INTO THE DARKNESS.
BUT ONE DAY ...
ONE DAY FOR SURE!
I'LL FIND THEM ...
AND I'LL DRAG THEM OUT OF THE DARKNESS !!!

FILE 8:
MANSION OF HORROR

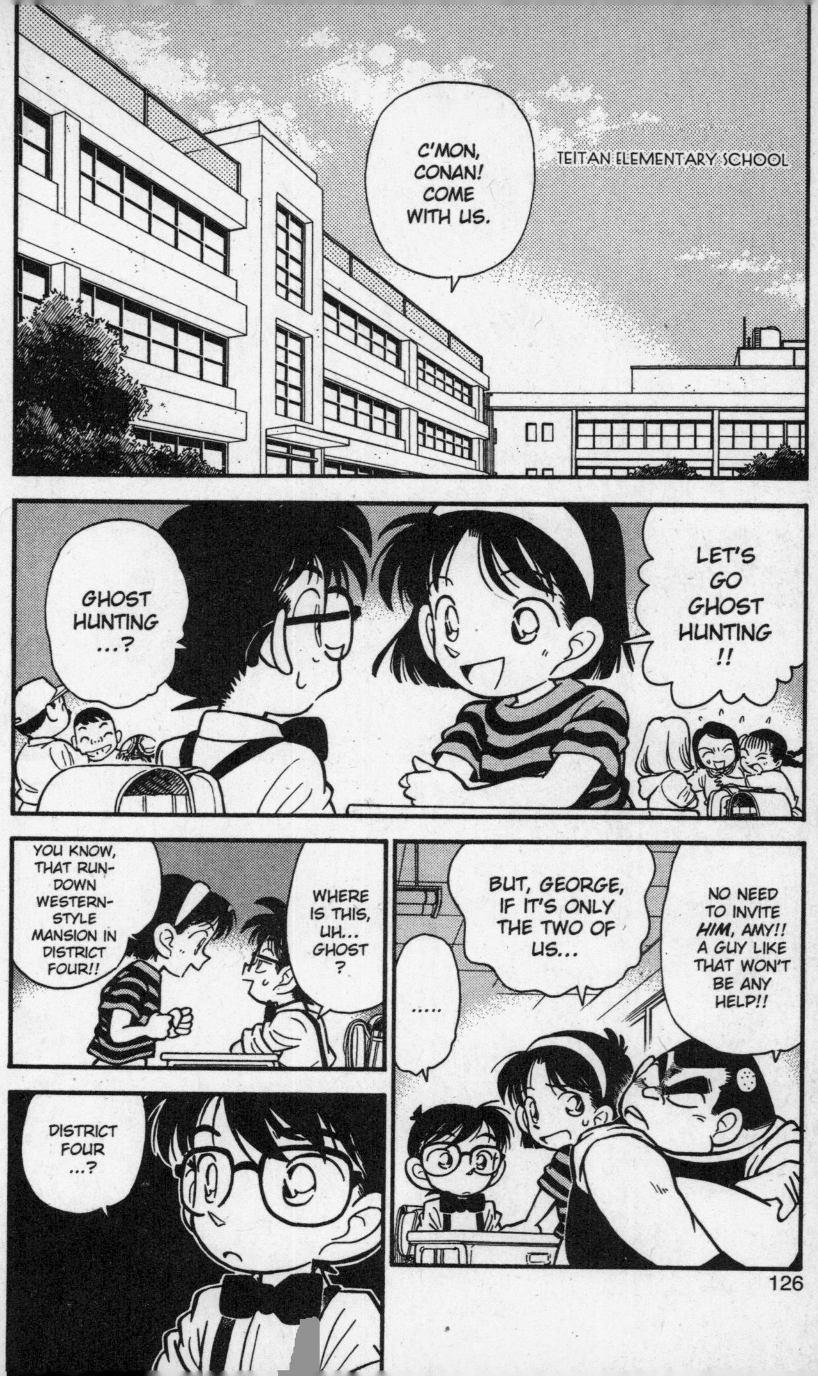
TEITAN ELEMENTARY SCHOOL
C'MON, CONAN! COME WITH US.
LET'S GO GHOST HUNTING!!
GHOST HUNTING ...?
NO NEED TO INVITE *HIM*, AMY!! A GUY LIKE THAT WON'T BE ANY HELP!!
BUT, GEORGE, IF IT'S ONLY THE TWO OF US...
.....
WHERE IS THIS, UH... GHOST?
YOU KNOW, THAT RUN-DOWN WESTERN-STYLE MANSION IN DISTRICT FOUR!!
DISTRICT FOUR ...?

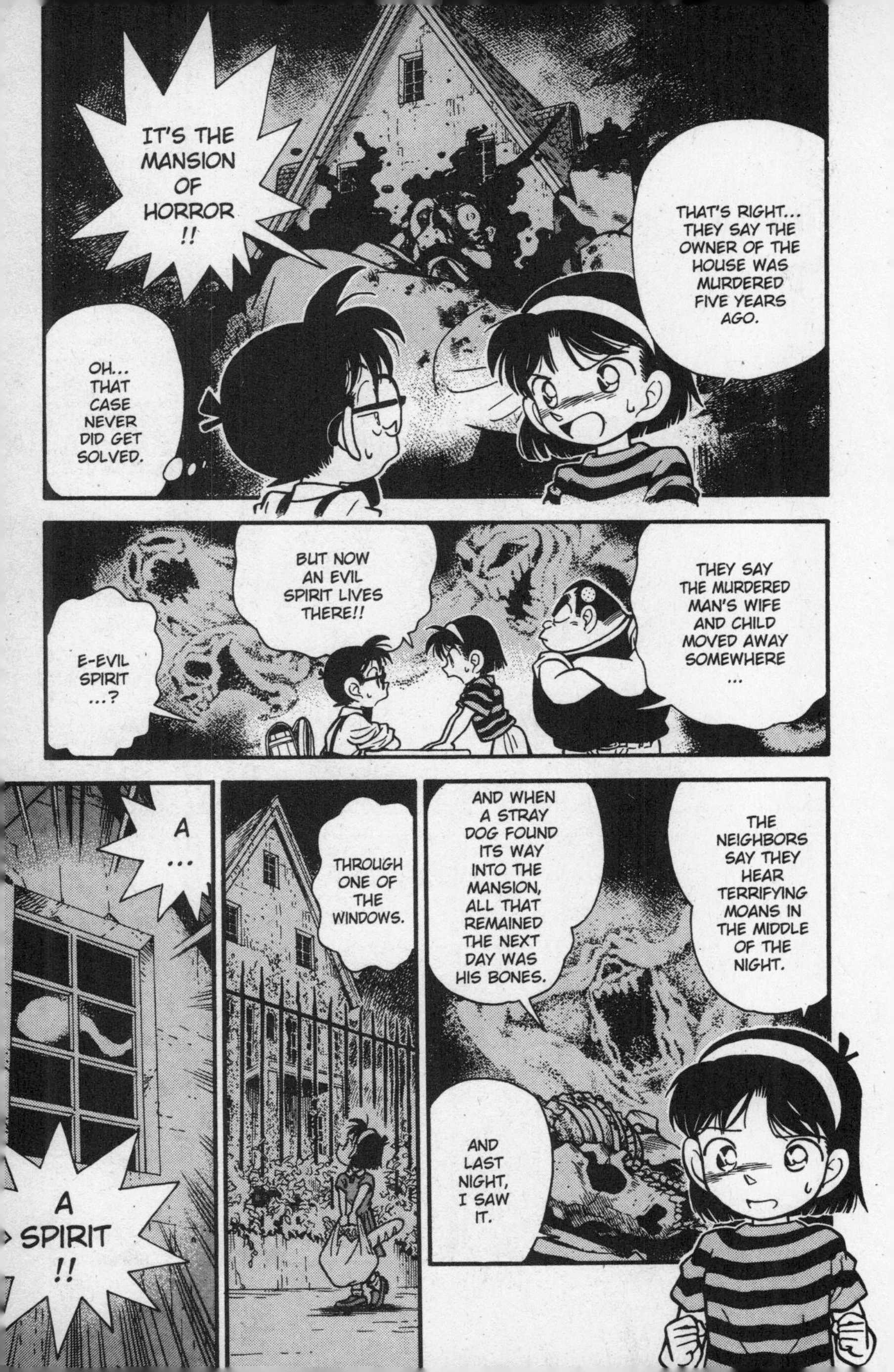
IT'S THE MANSION OF HORROR !!
THAT'S RIGHT... THEY SAY THE OWNER OF THE HOUSE WAS MURDERED FIVE YEARS AGO.
OH... THAT CASE NEVER DID GET SOLVED.
THEY SAY THE MURDERED MAN'S WIFE AND CHILD MOVED AWAY SOMEWHERE ...
BUT NOW AN EVIL SPIRIT LIVES THERE!!
E-EVIL SPIRIT ...?
THE NEIGHBORS SAY THEY HEAR TERRIFYING MOANS IN THE MIDDLE OF THE NIGHT.
AND WHEN A STRAY DOG FOUND ITS WAY INTO THE MANSION, ALL THAT REMAINED THE NEXT DAY WAS HIS BONES.
AND LAST NIGHT, I SAW IT.
THROUGH ONE OF THE WINDOWS.
A ...
A SPIRIT !!

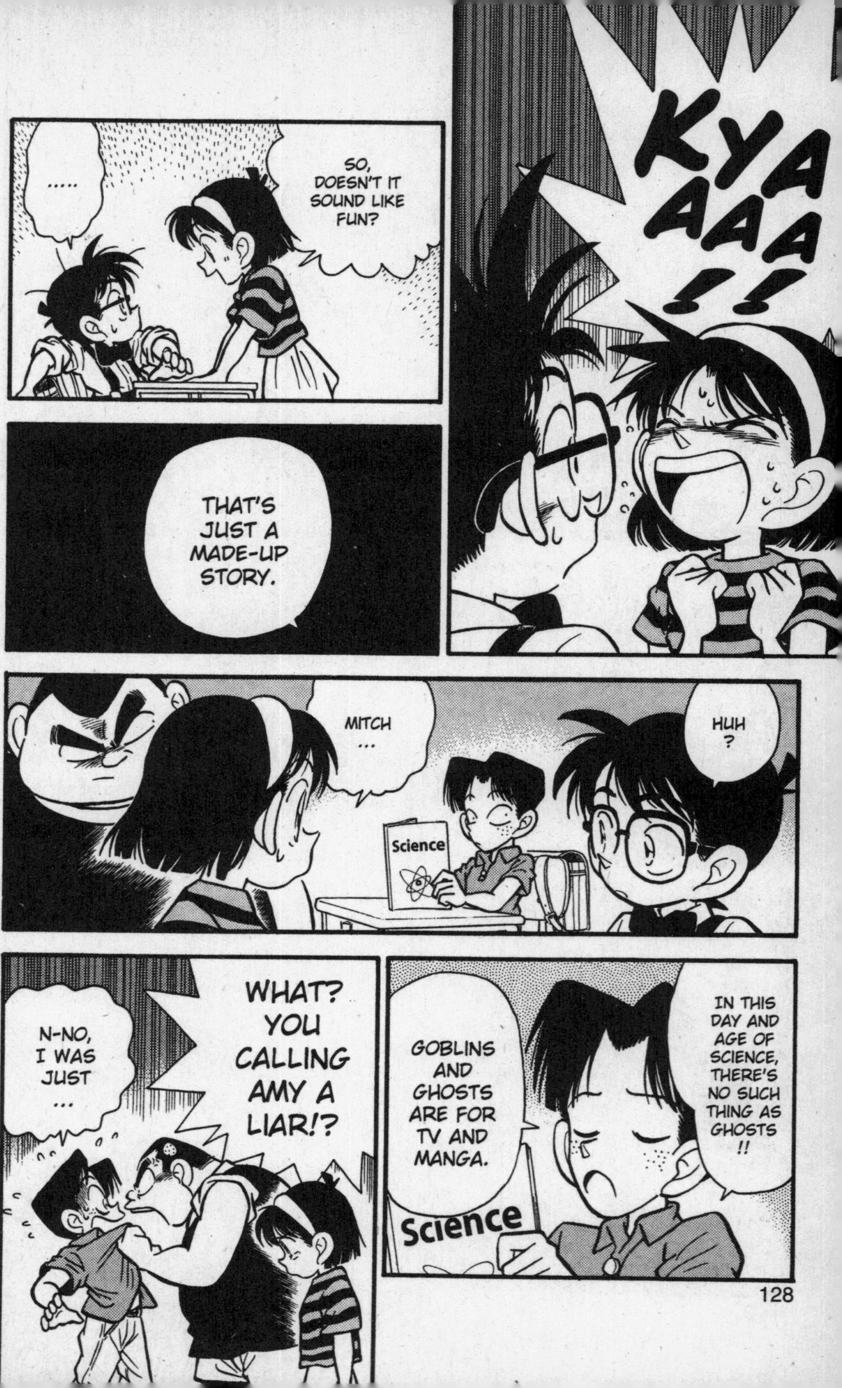
KYAAAA!!
SO, DOESN'T IT SOUND LIKE FUN?
.....
THAT'S JUST A MADE-UP STORY.
HUH?
Science
MITCH ...
IN THIS DAY AND AGE OF SCIENCE, THERE'S NO SUCH THING AS GHOSTS!!
GOBLINS AND GHOSTS ARE FOR TV AND MANGA.
Science
WHAT? YOU CALLING AMY A LIAR!?
N-NO, I WAS JUST ...

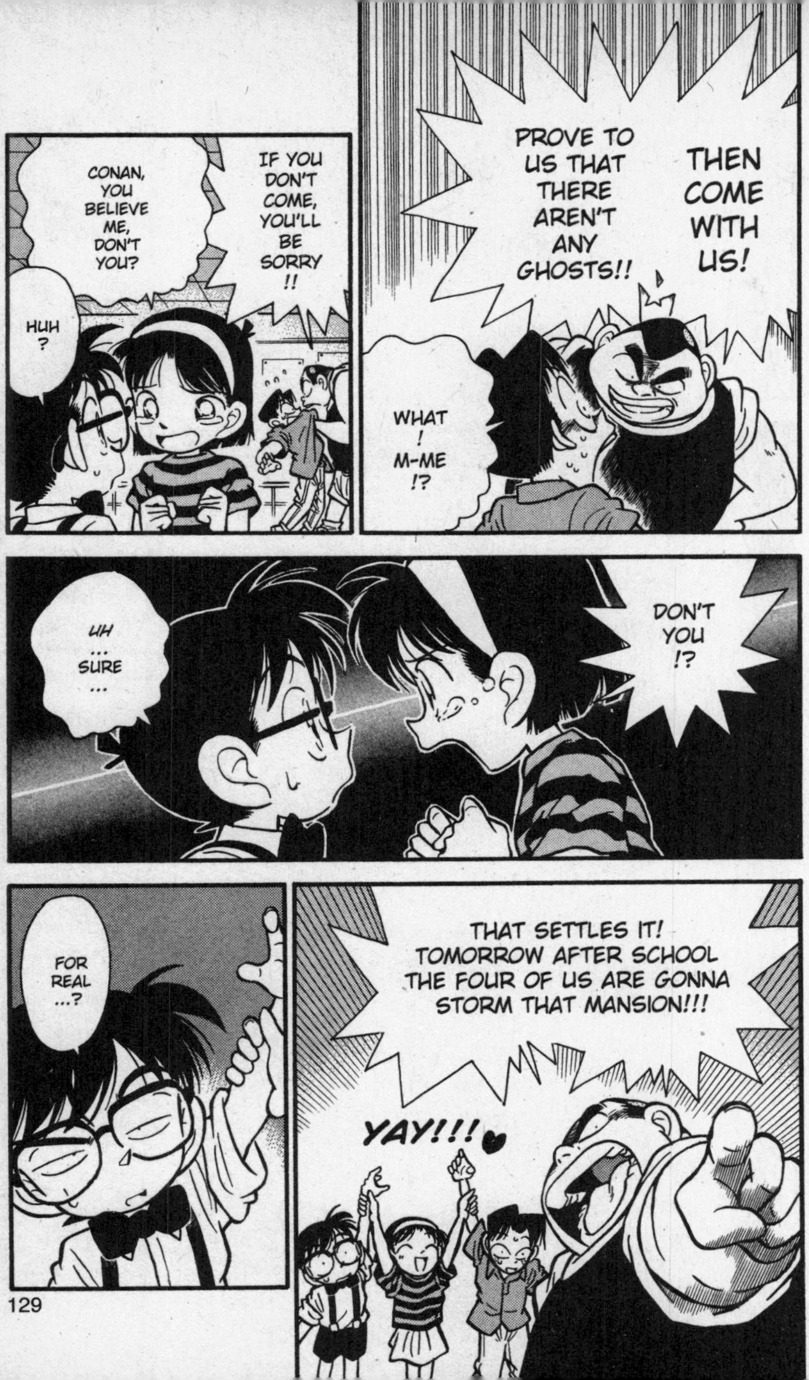
THEN COME WITH US!
PROVE TO US THAT THERE AREN'T ANY GHOSTS!!
WHAT ! M-ME !?
IF YOU DON'T COME, YOU'LL BE SORRY !!
CONAN, YOU BELIEVE ME, DON'T YOU?
HUH ?
DON'T YOU !?
UH ... SURE ...
THAT SETTLES IT! TOMORROW AFTER SCHOOL THE FOUR OF US ARE GONNA STORM THAT MANSION!!!
YAY!!!
FOR REAL ...?

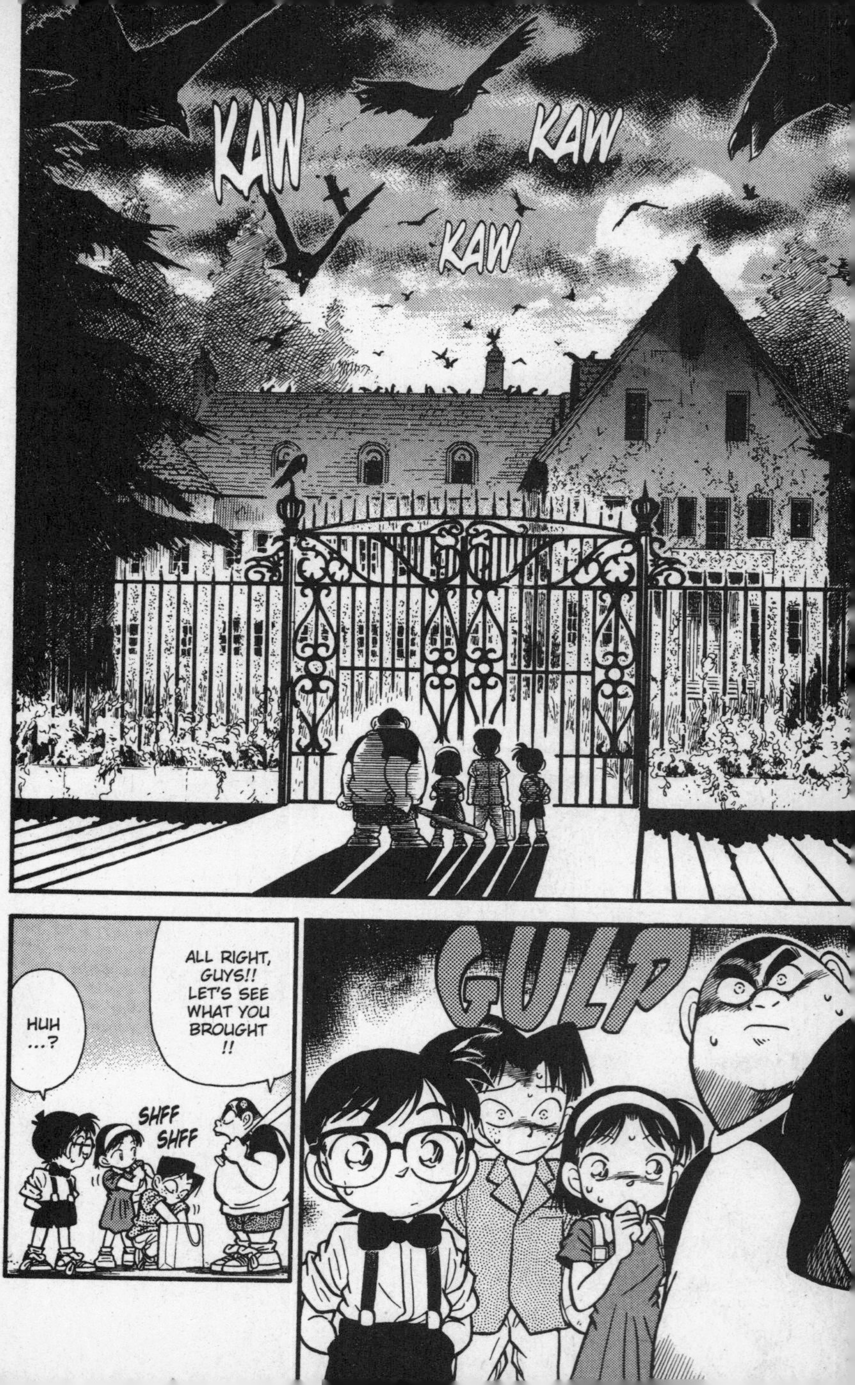
KAW
KAW
KAW
GULP
ALL RIGHT, GUYS!! LET'S SEE WHAT YOU BROUGHT !!
HUH ...?
SHFF SHFF

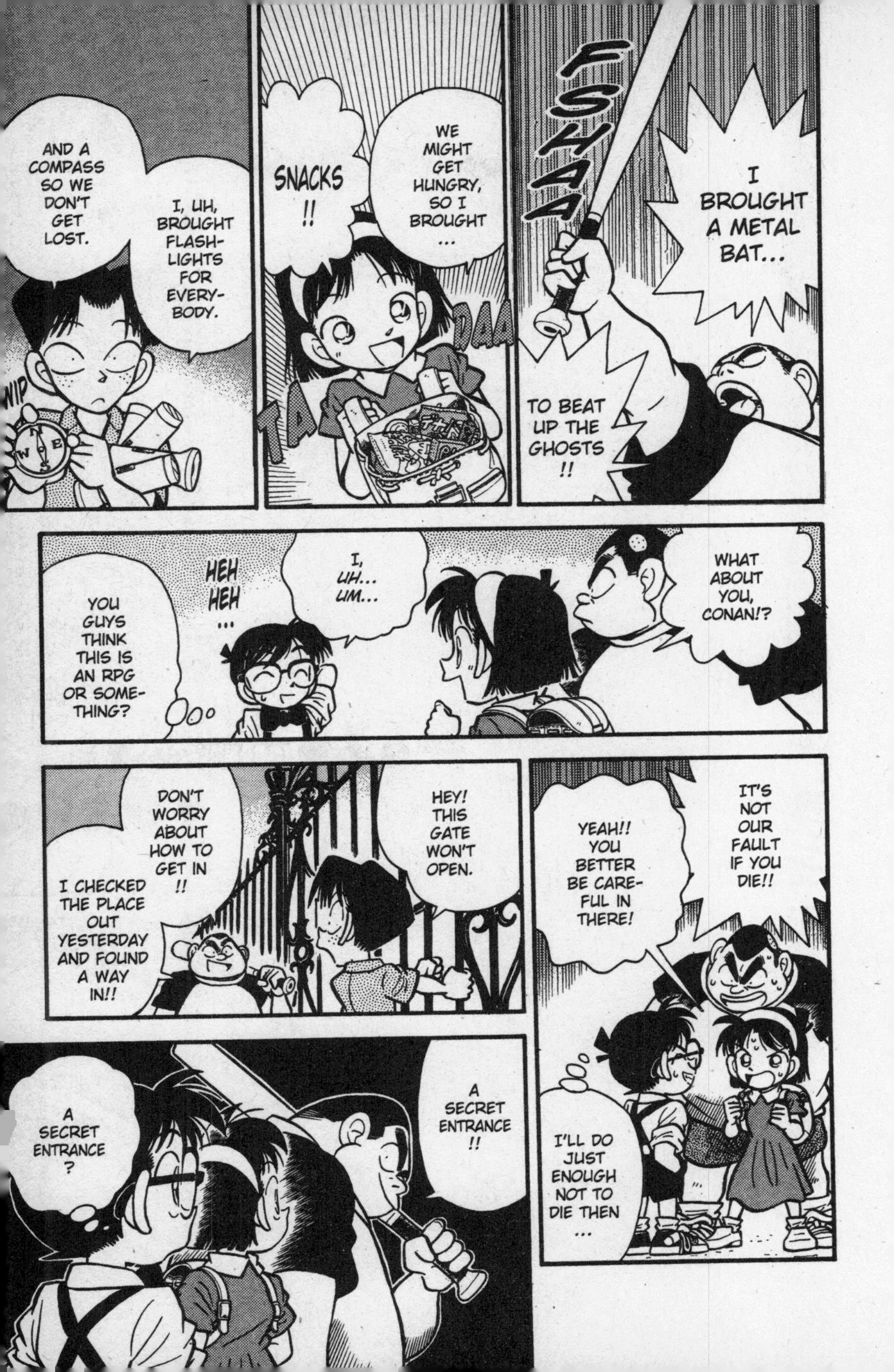
FSHAA
I BROUGHT A METAL BAT...
TO BEAT UP THE GHOSTS!!
WE MIGHT GET HUNGRY, SO I BROUGHT...
SNACKS!!
DAA
TA
I, UH, BROUGHT FLASH-LIGHTS FOR EVERY-BODY.
AND A COMPASS SO WE DON'T GET LOST.
WIP
WHAT ABOUT YOU, CONAN!?
I, UH... UM...
HEH HEH...
YOU GUYS THINK THIS IS AN RPG OR SOME-THING?
IT'S NOT OUR FAULT IF YOU DIE!!
YEAH!! YOU BETTER BE CARE-FUL IN THERE!
I'LL DO JUST ENOUGH NOT TO DIE THEN...
HEY! THIS GATE WON'T OPEN.
DON'T WORRY ABOUT HOW TO GET IN!!
I CHECKED THE PLACE OUT YESTERDAY AND FOUND A WAY IN!!
A SECRET ENTRANCE!!
A SECRET ENTRANCE?

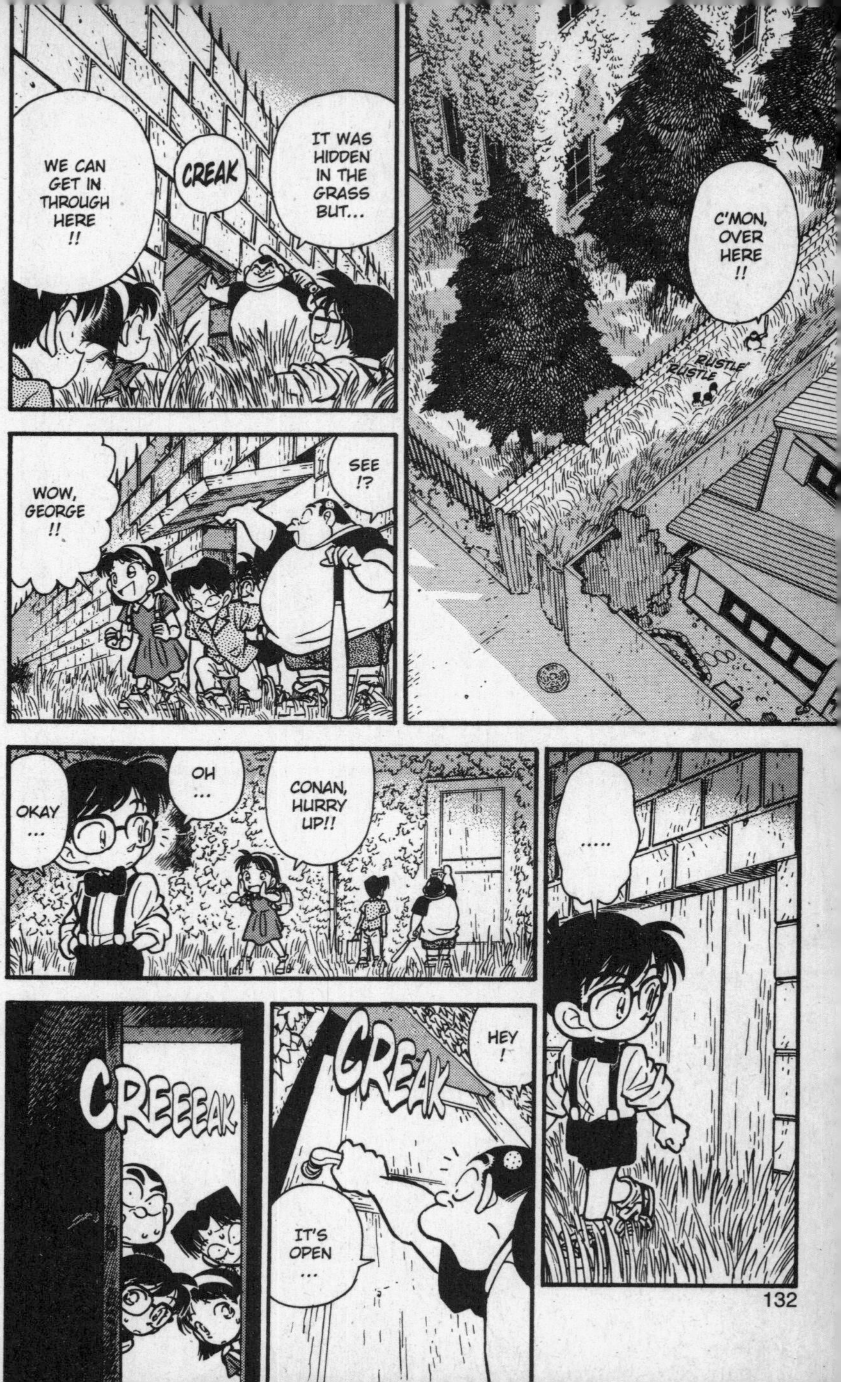
C'MON, OVER HERE !!
RUSTLE RUSTLE
IT WAS HIDDEN IN THE GRASS BUT...
CREAK
WE CAN GET IN THROUGH HERE !!
SEE !?
WOW, GEORGE !!
.....
CONAN, HURRY UP!!
OH ...
OKAY ...
CREAK
HEY !
IT'S OPEN ...
CREEEAK

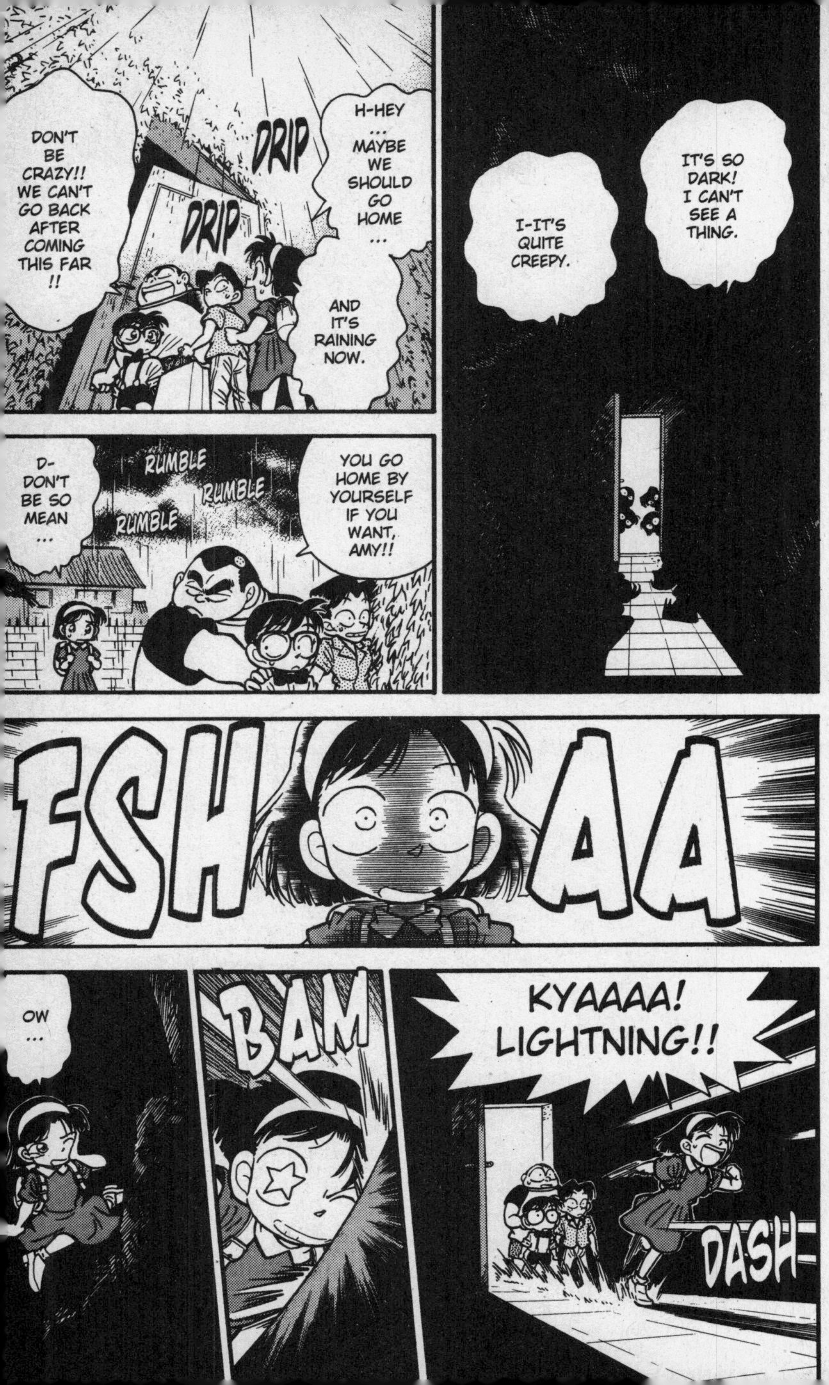
IT'S SO DARK! I CAN'T SEE A THING.
I-IT'S QUITE CREEPY.
H-HEY ... MAYBE WE SHOULD GO HOME ...
DRIP
DRIP
DON'T BE CRAZY!! WE CAN'T GO BACK AFTER COMING THIS FAR !!
AND IT'S RAINING NOW.
YOU GO HOME BY YOURSELF IF YOU WANT, AMY!!
RUMBLE
RUMBLE
RUMBLE
D-DON'T BE SO MEAN ...
FSH
AA
KYAAAA! LIGHTNING!!
DASH
BAM
OW ...

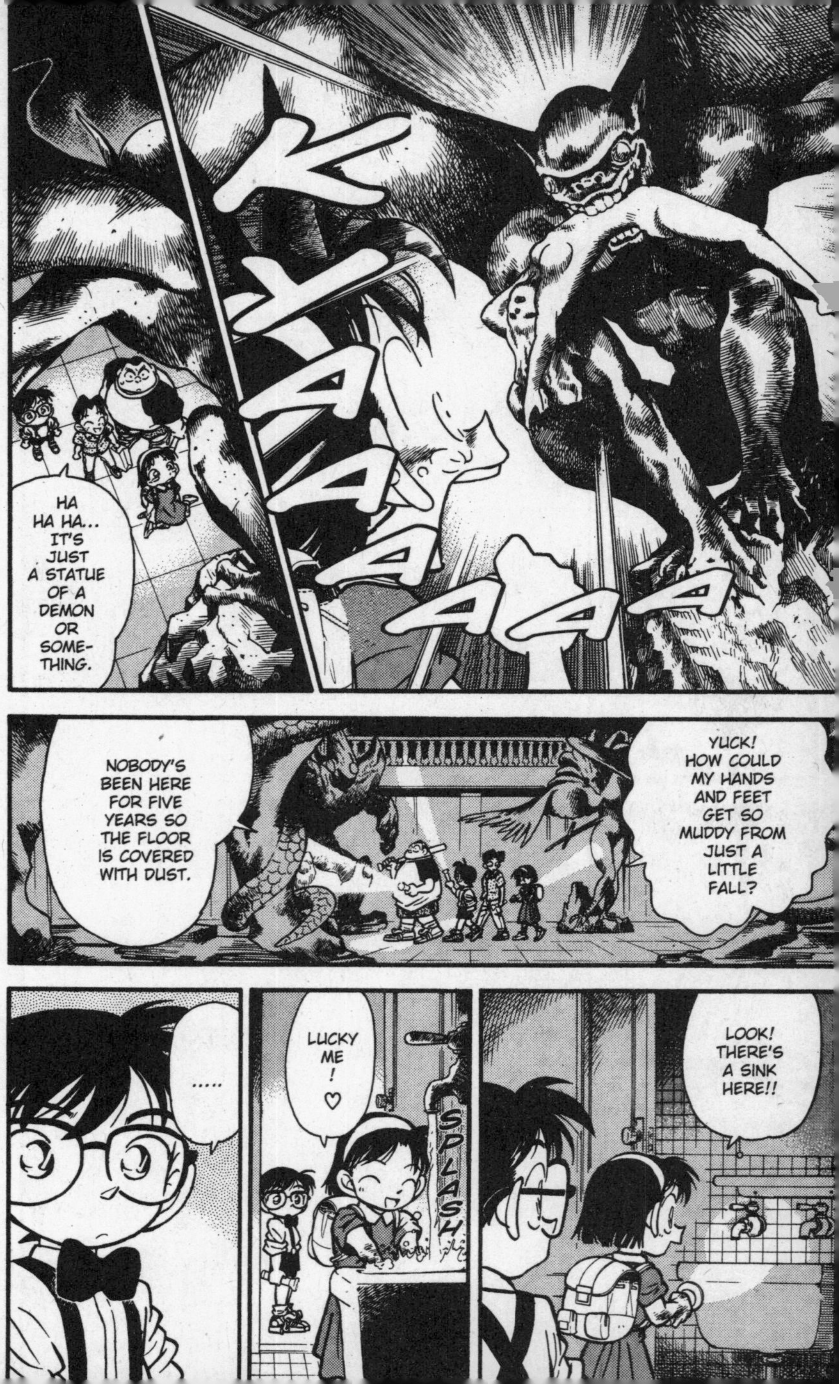
KYAAAAAAA
HA HA HA... IT'S JUST A STATUE OF A DEMON OR SOME-THING.
YUCK! HOW COULD MY HANDS AND FEET GET SO MUDDY FROM JUST A LITTLE FALL?
NOBODY'S BEEN HERE FOR FIVE YEARS SO THE FLOOR IS COVERED WITH DUST.
LOOK! THERE'S A SINK HERE!!
LUCKY ME! ♡
SPLASH
.....

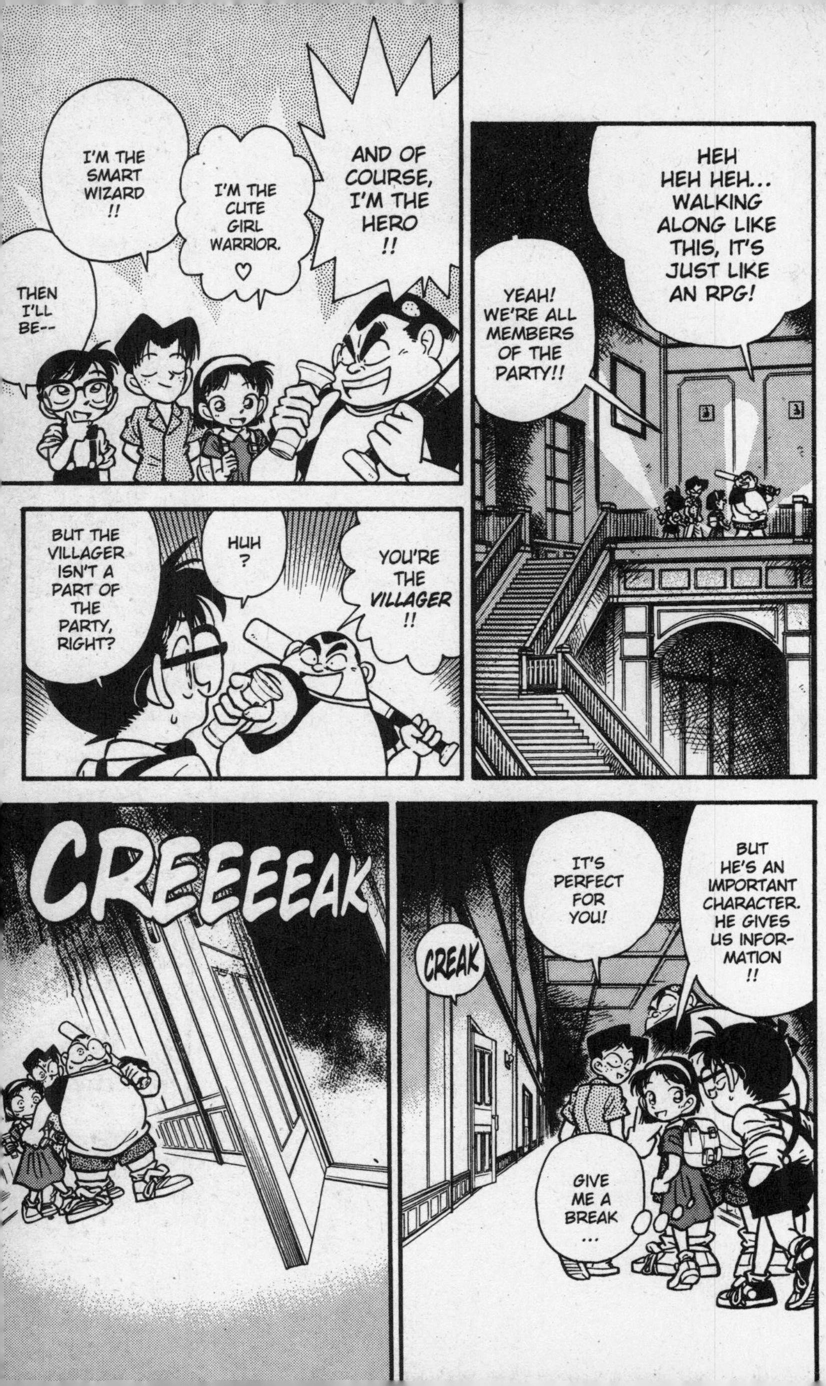
HEH HEH HEH... WALKING ALONG LIKE THIS, IT'S JUST LIKE AN RPG!
YEAH! WE'RE ALL MEMBERS OF THE PARTY!!
AND OF COURSE, I'M THE HERO !!
I'M THE CUTE GIRL WARRIOR. ♡
I'M THE SMART WIZARD !!
THEN I'LL BE--
YOU'RE THE VILLAGER !!
HUH ?
BUT THE VILLAGER ISN'T A PART OF THE PARTY, RIGHT?
BUT HE'S AN IMPORTANT CHARACTER. HE GIVES US INFORMATION !!
IT'S PERFECT FOR YOU!
CREAK
GIVE ME A BREAK ...
CREEEEAK

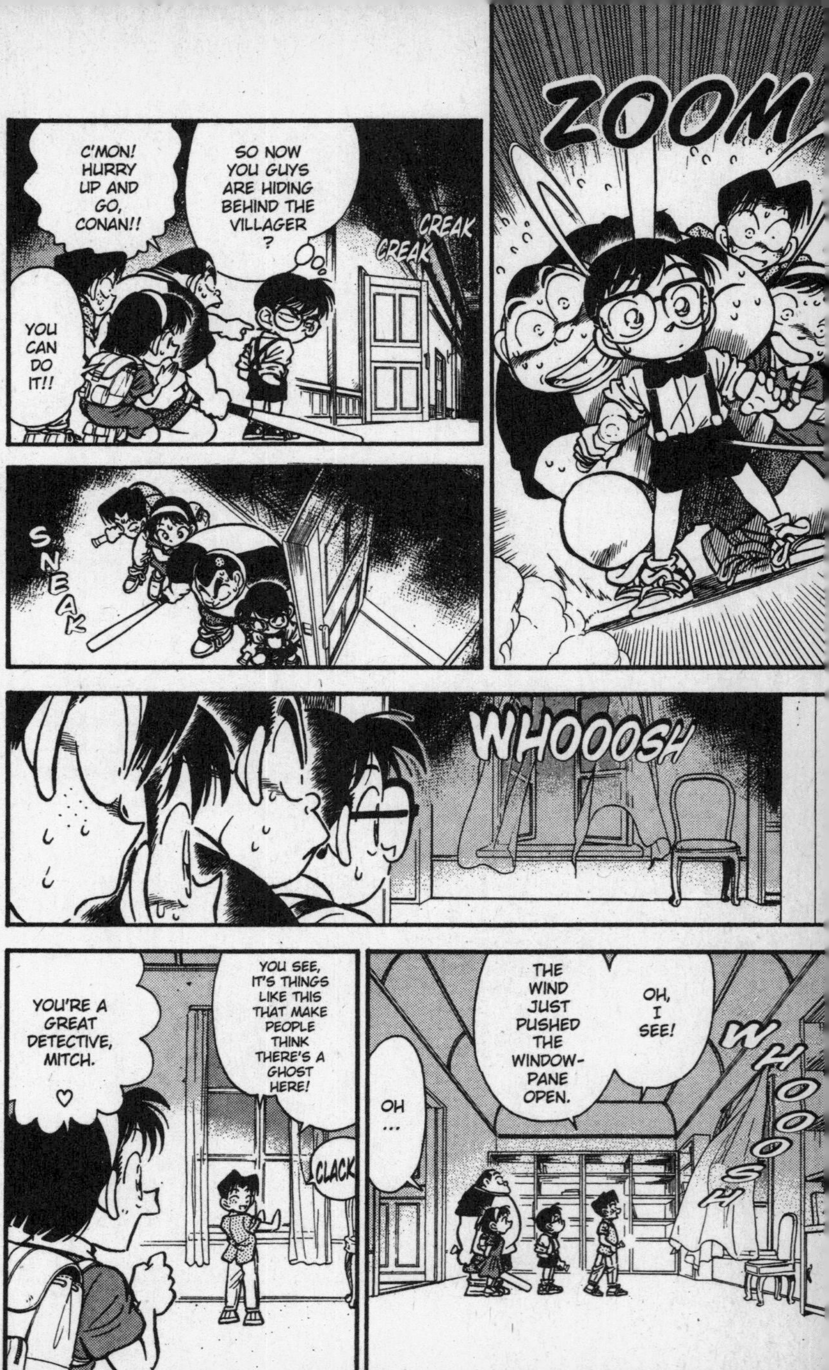
ZOOM
CREAK
CREAK
SO NOW YOU GUYS ARE HIDING BEHIND THE VILLAGER ?
C'MON! HURRY UP AND GO, CONAN!!
YOU CAN DO IT!!
SNEAK
WHOOOSH
WHOOOSH
OH, I SEE!
THE WIND JUST PUSHED THE WINDOW-PANE OPEN.
OH ...
CLACK
YOU SEE, IT'S THINGS LIKE THIS THAT MAKE PEOPLE THINK THERE'S A GHOST HERE!
YOU'RE A GREAT DETECTIVE, MITCH. ♡

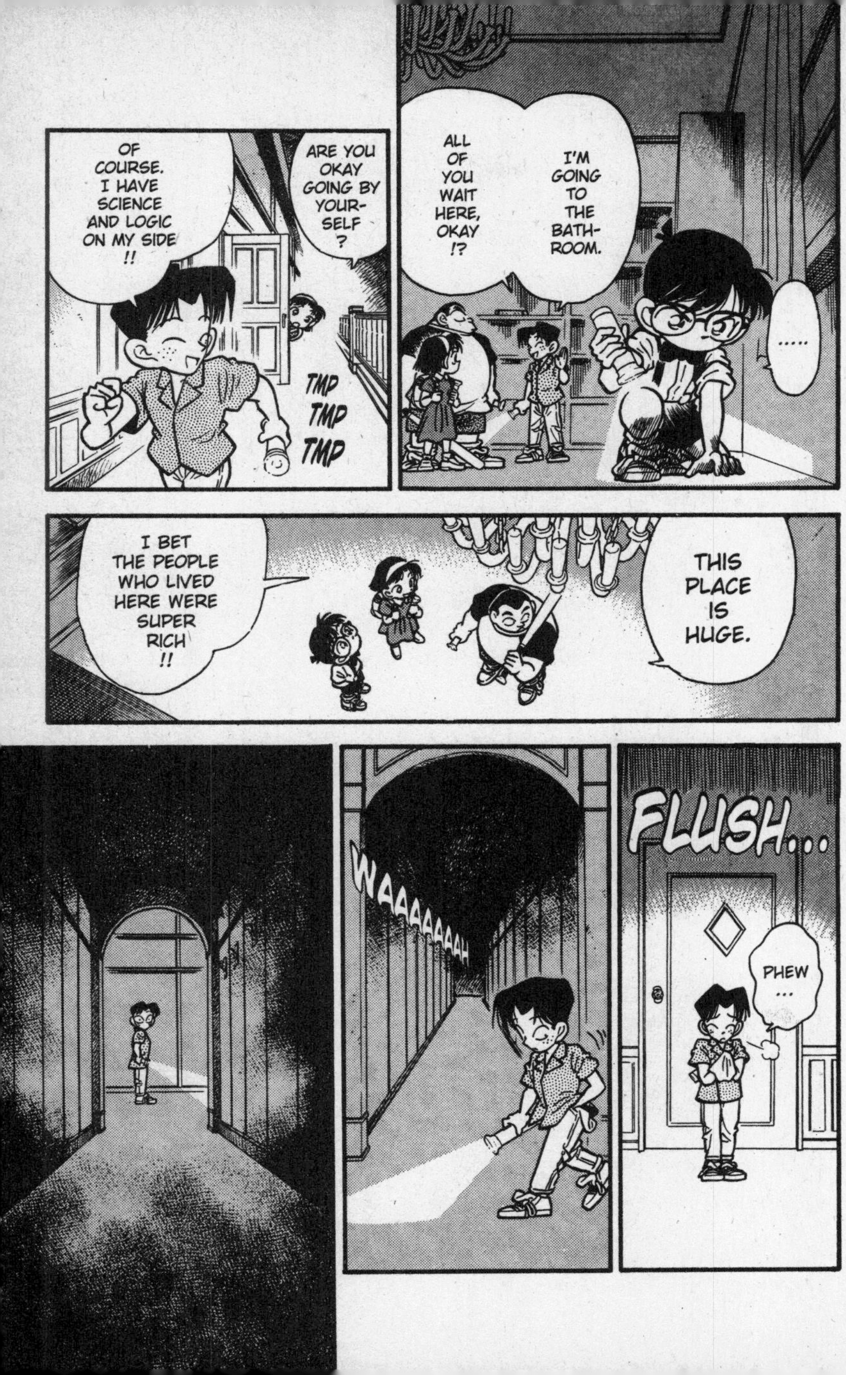
I'M GOING TO THE BATH-ROOM.
ALL OF YOU WAIT HERE, OKAY !?
.....
ARE YOU OKAY GOING BY YOUR-SELF ?
OF COURSE. I HAVE SCIENCE AND LOGIC ON MY SIDE !!
TMP TMP TMP
THIS PLACE IS HUGE.
I BET THE PEOPLE WHO LIVED HERE WERE SUPER RICH !!
FLUSH...
PHEW ...
WAAAAAAAAH

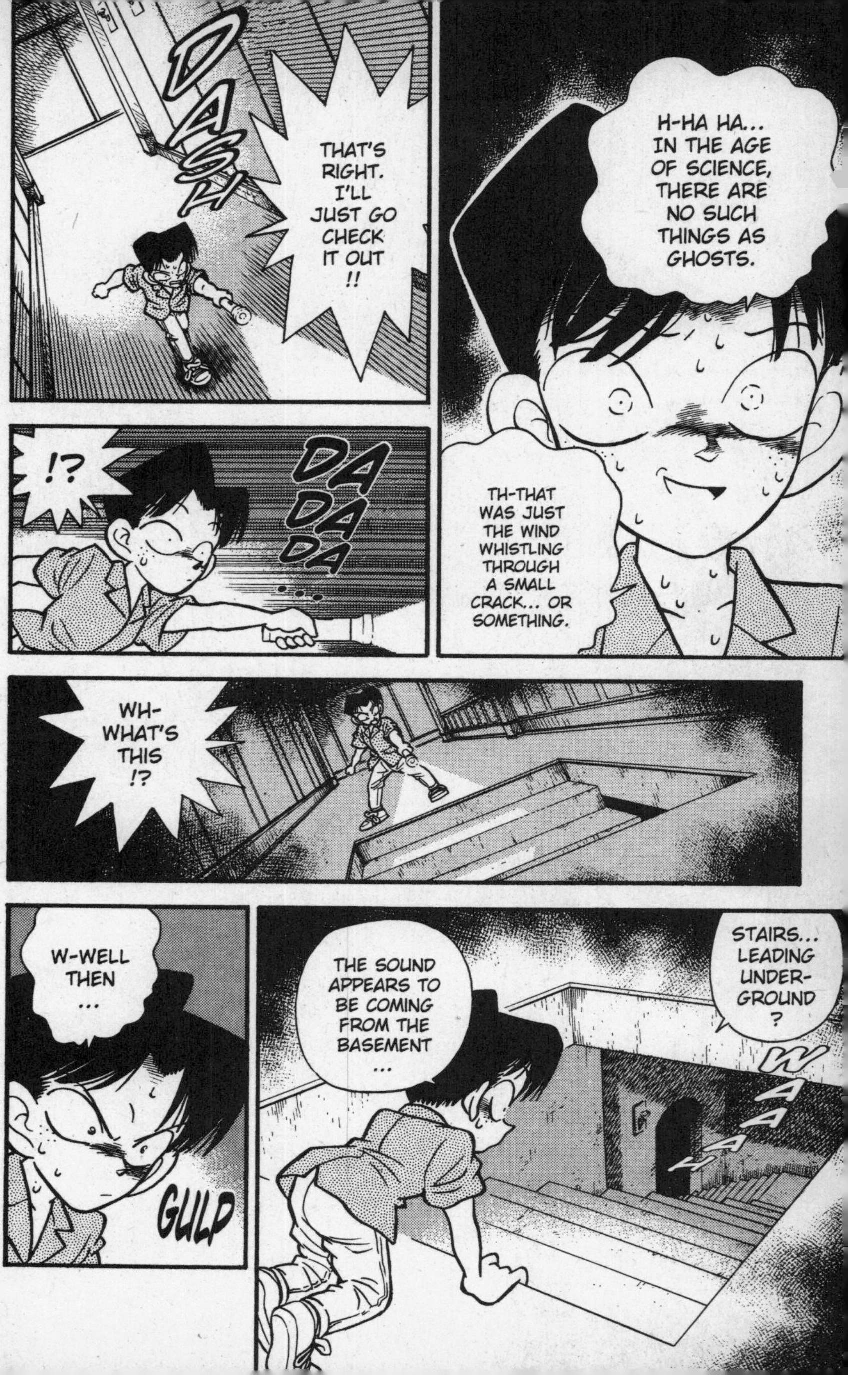
H-HA HA... IN THE AGE OF SCIENCE, THERE ARE NO SUCH THINGS AS GHOSTS.
TH-THAT WAS JUST THE WIND WHISTLING THROUGH A SMALL CRACK... OR SOMETHING.
DASH
THAT'S RIGHT. I'LL JUST GO CHECK IT OUT!!
DADADADA
!?
WH-WHAT'S THIS!?
STAIRS... LEADING UNDER-GROUND?
THE SOUND APPEARS TO BE COMING FROM THE BASEMENT...
WAAAAH
W-WELL THEN...
GULP

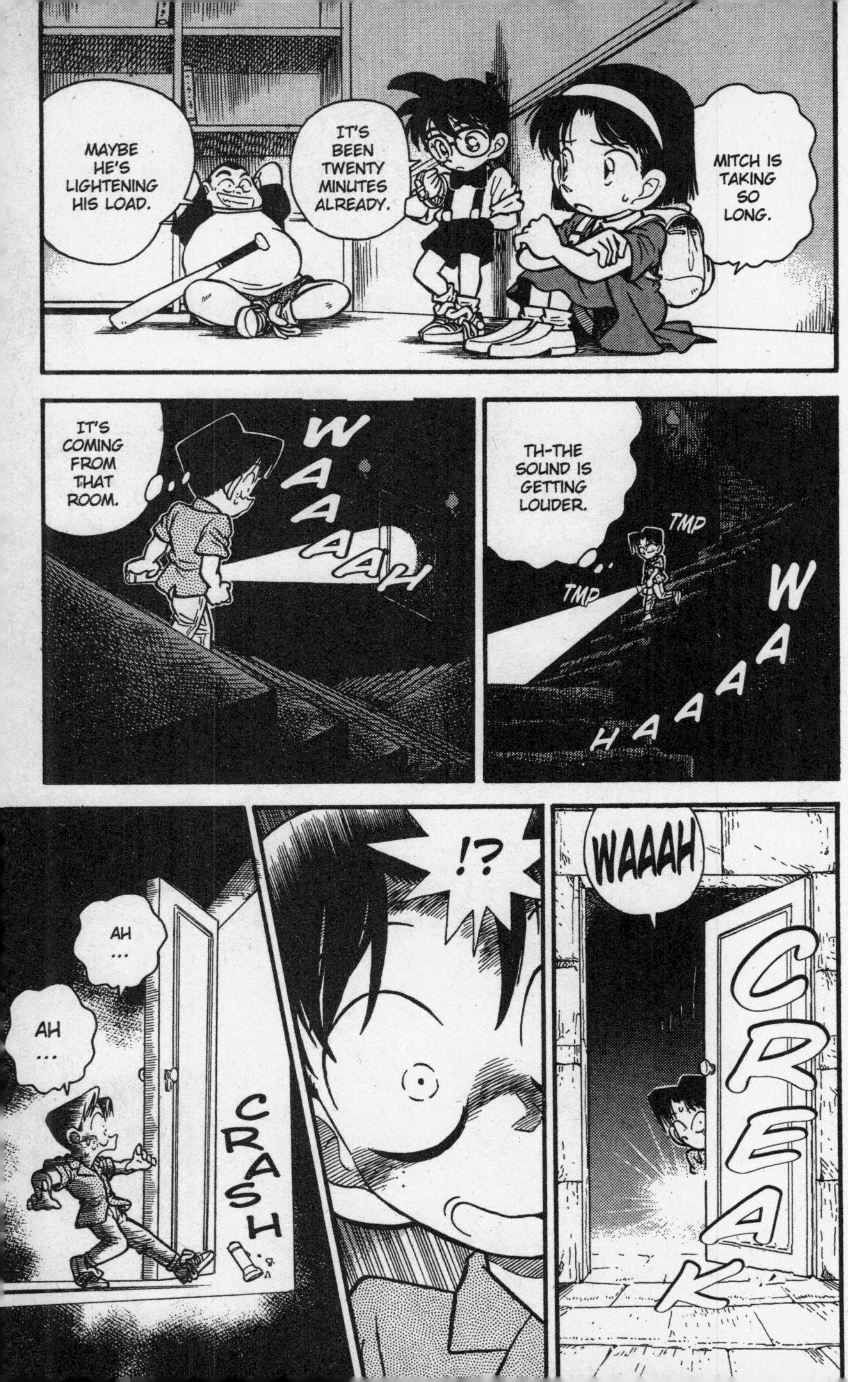
MITCH IS TAKING SO LONG.
IT'S BEEN TWENTY MINUTES ALREADY.
MAYBE HE'S LIGHTENING HIS LOAD.
TH-THE SOUND IS GETTING LOUDER.
TMP
TMP
WAAAAAH
IT'S COMING FROM THAT ROOM.
WAAAAAH
WAAAH
CREAK
!?
AH ...
AH ...
CRASH

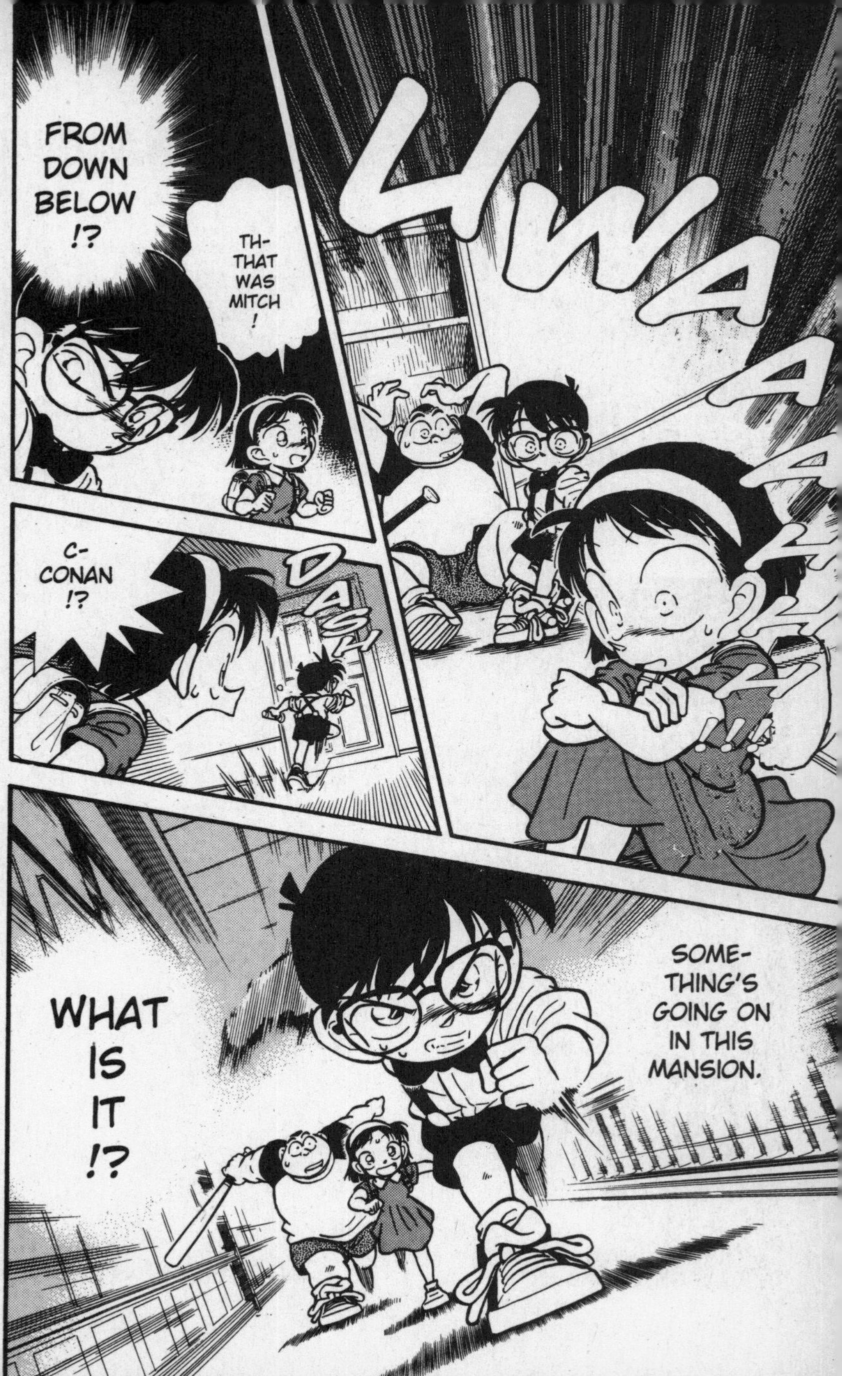
UWAAA!!!
FROM DOWN BELOW!?
TH-THAT WAS MITCH!
C-CONAN!?
DASH
SOME-THING'S GOING ON IN THIS MANSION.
WHAT IS IT!?

FILE 9: DISAPPEARING CHILDREN

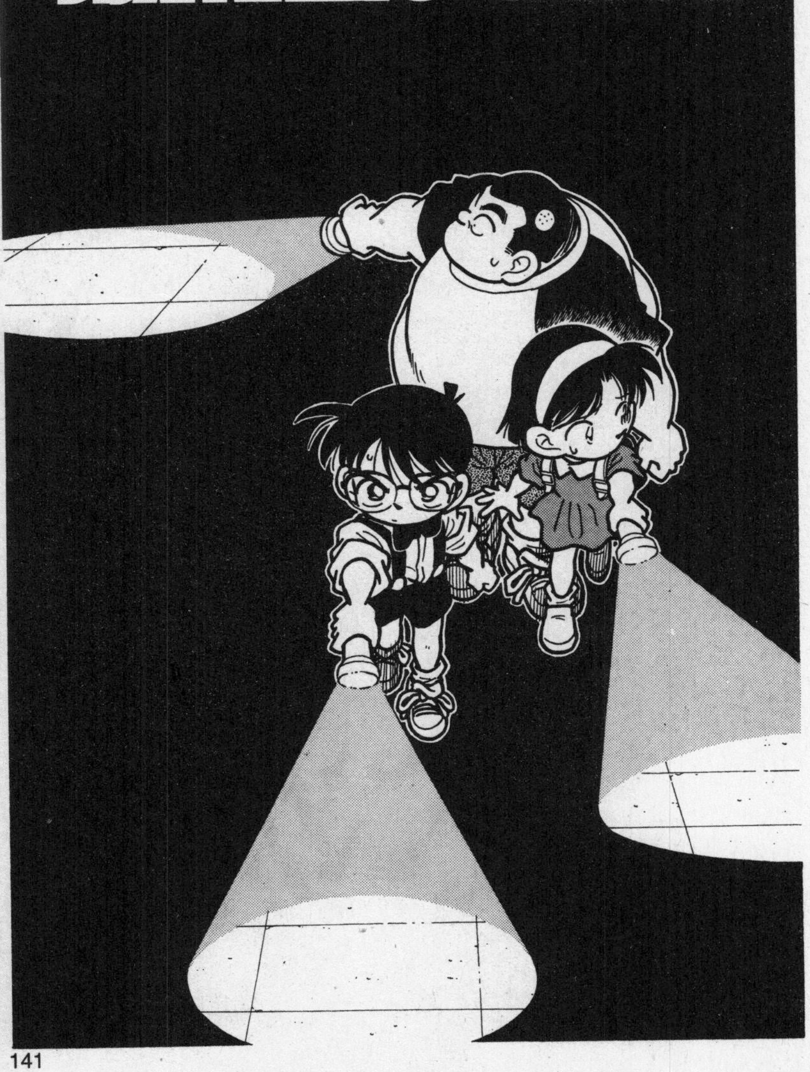

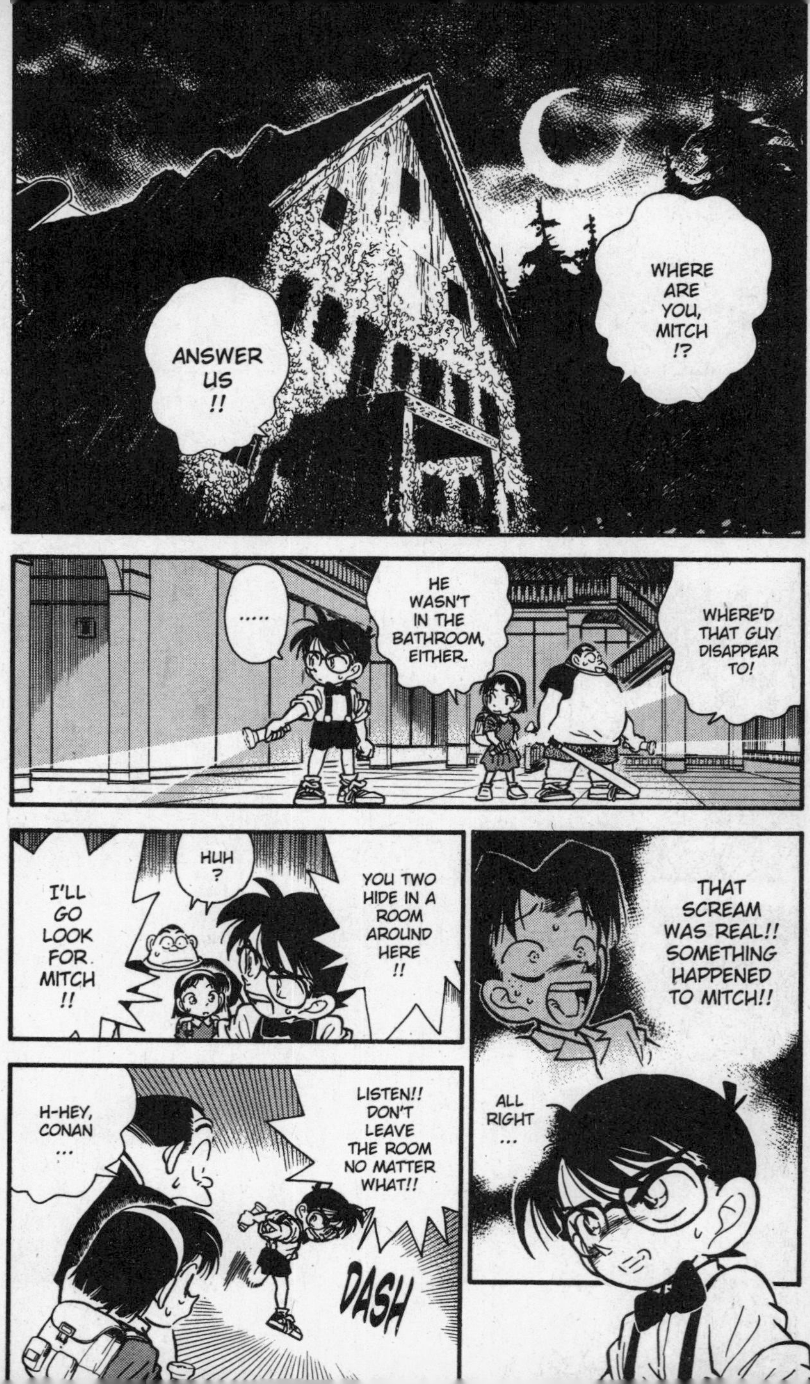
WHERE ARE YOU, MITCH !?
ANSWER US !!
WHERE'D THAT GUY DISAPPEAR TO!
HE WASN'T IN THE BATHROOM, EITHER.
.....
THAT SCREAM WAS REAL!! SOMETHING HAPPENED TO MITCH!!
ALL RIGHT ...
YOU TWO HIDE IN A ROOM AROUND HERE !!
HUH ?
I'LL GO LOOK FOR MITCH !!
LISTEN!! DON'T LEAVE THE ROOM NO MATTER WHAT!!
DASH
H-HEY, CONAN ...

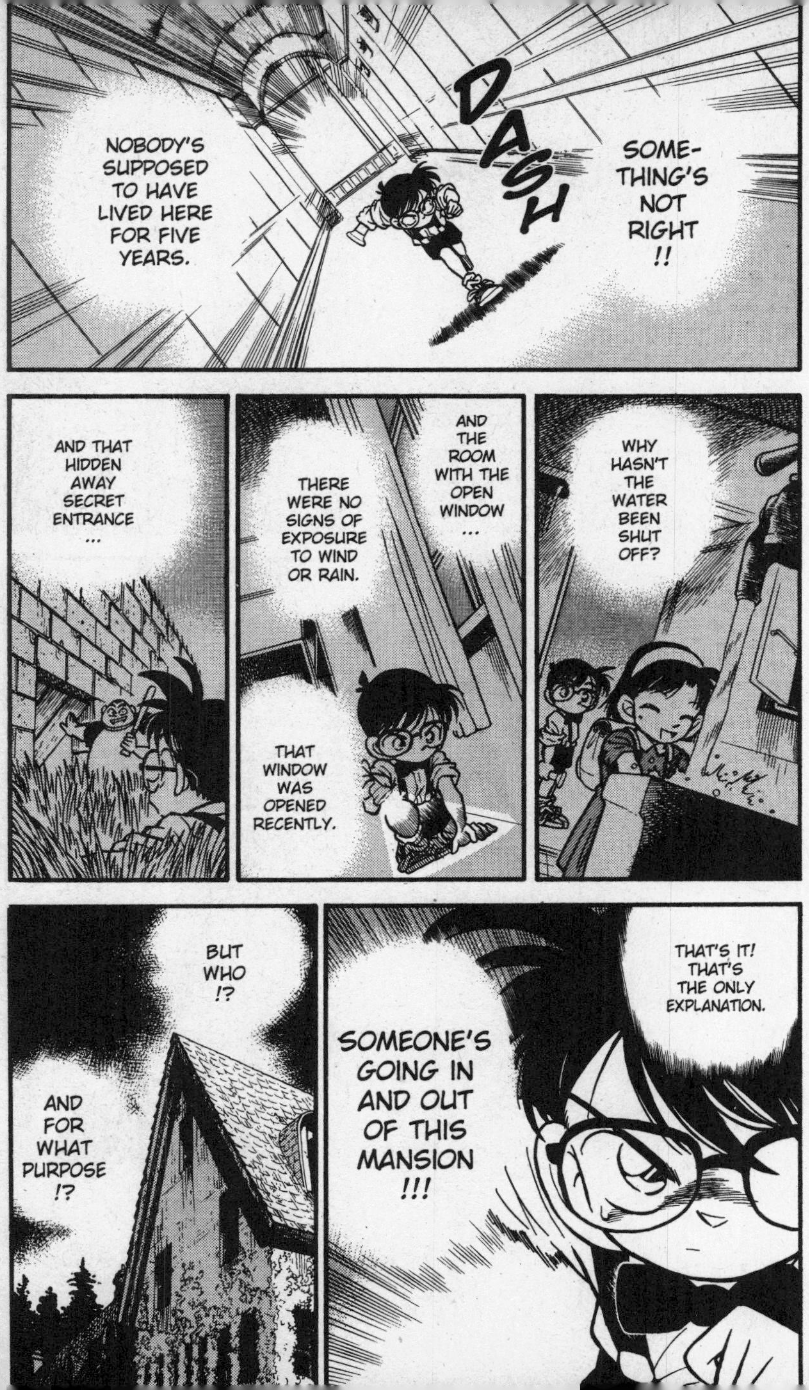
SOMETHING'S NOT RIGHT !!
DASH
NOBODY'S SUPPOSED TO HAVE LIVED HERE FOR FIVE YEARS.
WHY HASN'T THE WATER BEEN SHUT OFF?
AND THE ROOM WITH THE OPEN WINDOW ...
THERE WERE NO SIGNS OF EXPOSURE TO WIND OR RAIN.
THAT WINDOW WAS OPENED RECENTLY.
AND THAT HIDDEN AWAY SECRET ENTRANCE ...
THAT'S IT! THAT'S THE ONLY EXPLANATION.
SOMEONE'S GOING IN AND OUT OF THIS MANSION !!!
BUT WHO !?
AND FOR WHAT PURPOSE !?

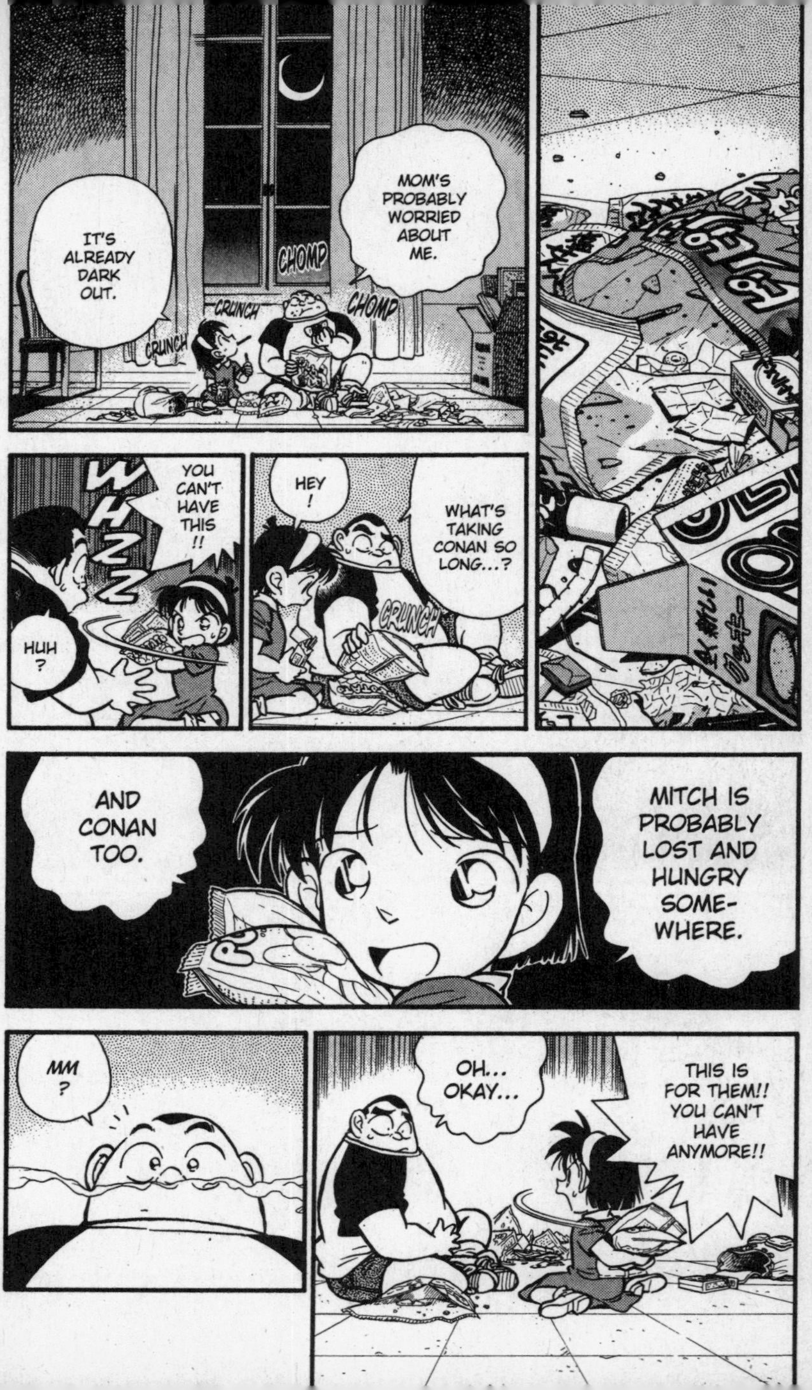
MOM'S PROBABLY WORRIED ABOUT ME.
CHOMP
CHOMP
IT'S ALREADY DARK OUT.
CRUNCH
CRUNCH
WHAT'S TAKING CONAN SO LONG...?
HEY!
CRUNCH
YOU CAN'T HAVE THIS!!
WHZZ
HUH?
MITCH IS PROBABLY LOST AND HUNGRY SOME-WHERE.
AND CONAN TOO.
THIS IS FOR THEM!! YOU CAN'T HAVE ANYMORE!!
OH... OKAY...
MM?

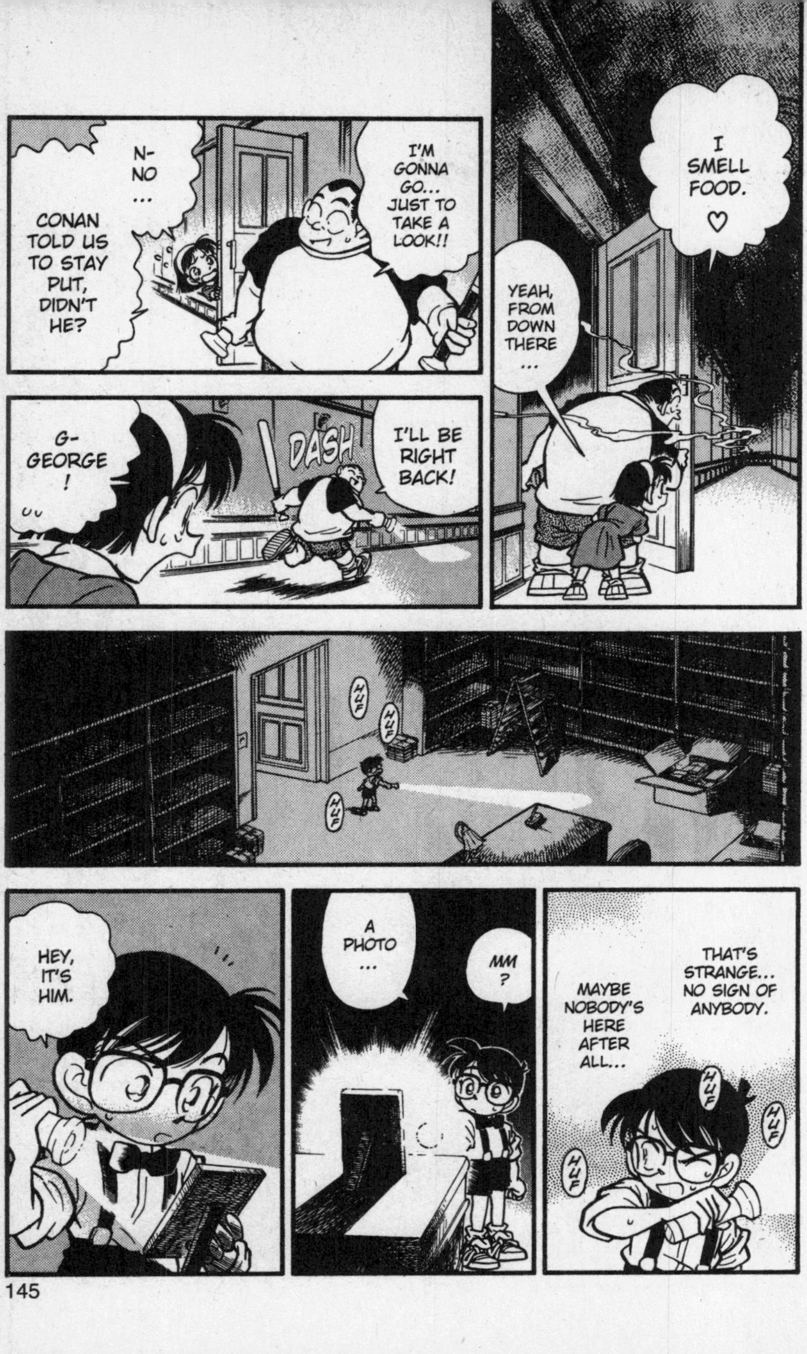
I SMELL FOOD. ♡
YEAH, FROM DOWN THERE ...
I'M GONNA GO... JUST TO TAKE A LOOK!!
N-NO ...
CONAN TOLD US TO STAY PUT, DIDN'T HE?
I'LL BE RIGHT BACK!
DASH
G-GEORGE !
HUF
HUF
HUF
THAT'S STRANGE... NO SIGN OF ANYBODY.
MAYBE NOBODY'S HERE AFTER ALL...
HUF
HUF
HUF
MM ?
A PHOTO ...
HEY, IT'S HIM.

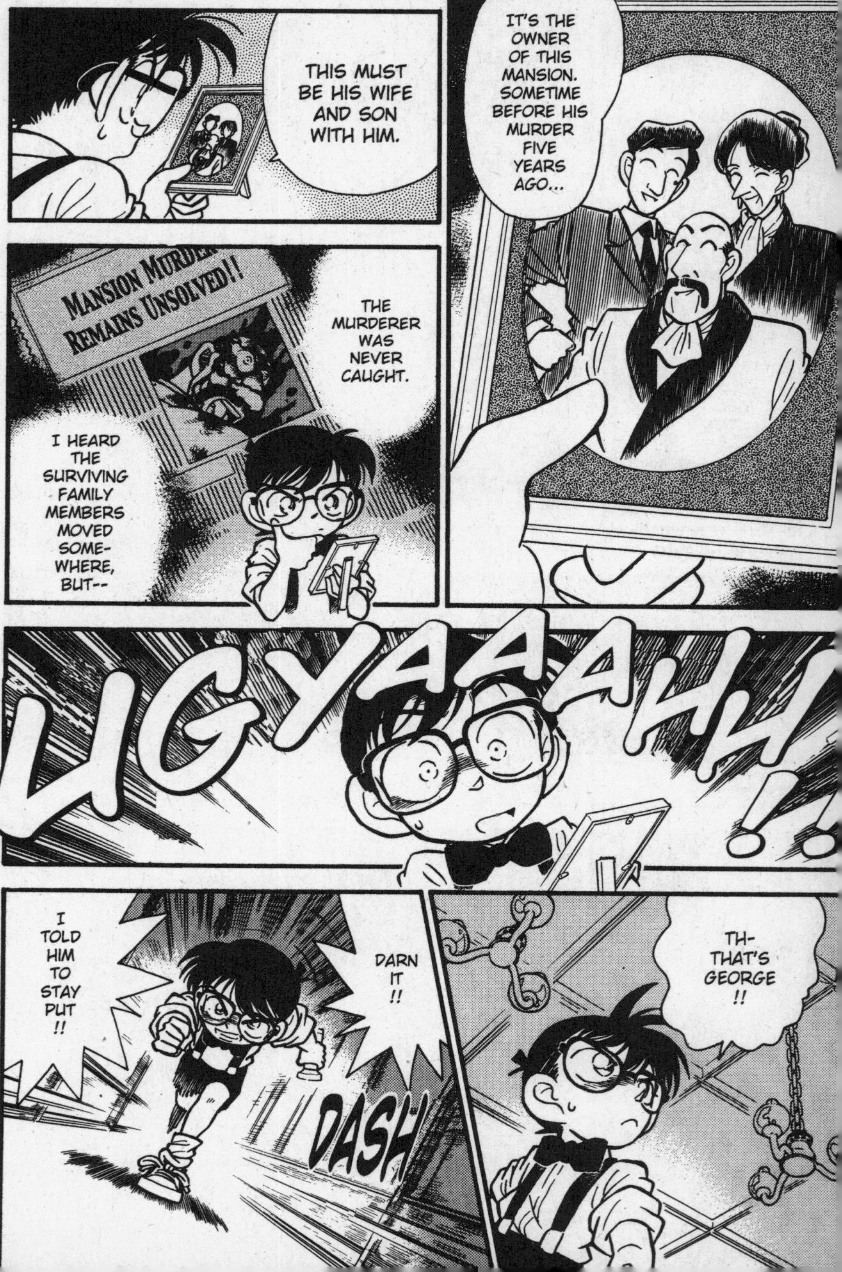
IT'S THE OWNER OF THIS MANSION. SOMETIME BEFORE HIS MURDER FIVE YEARS AGO...
THIS MUST BE HIS WIFE AND SON WITH HIM.
MANSION MURDER REMAINS UNSOLVED!!
THE MURDERER WAS NEVER CAUGHT.
I HEARD THE SURVIVING FAMILY MEMBERS MOVED SOME-WHERE, BUT--
UGYAAAHH!!
TH-THAT'S GEORGE!!
I TOLD HIM TO STAY PUT!!
DARN IT!!
DASH

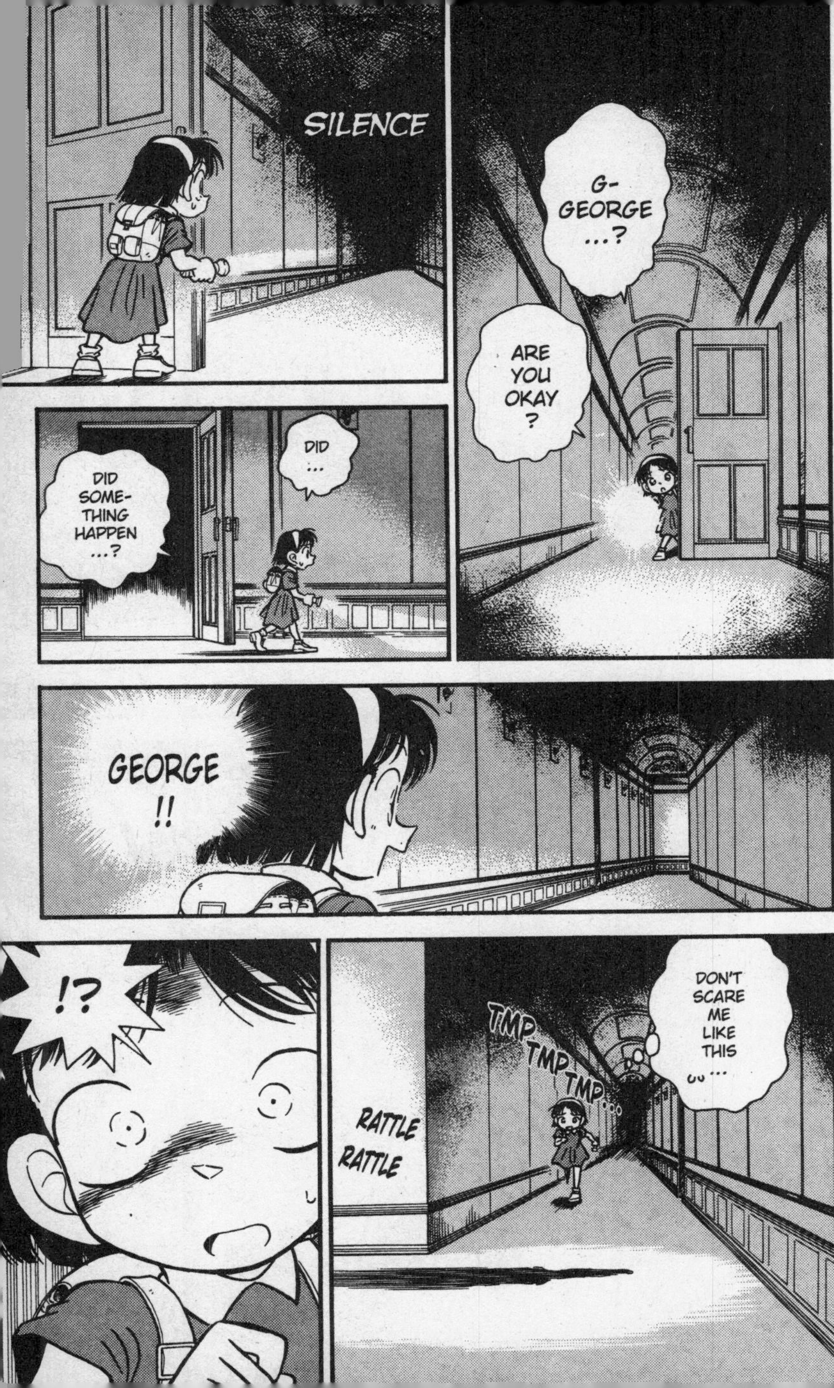
G-GEORGE ...?
ARE YOU OKAY ?
SILENCE
DID ...
DID SOME-THING HAPPEN ...?
GEORGE !!
DON'T SCARE ME LIKE THIS ...
TMP TMP TMP...
RATTLE RATTLE
!?

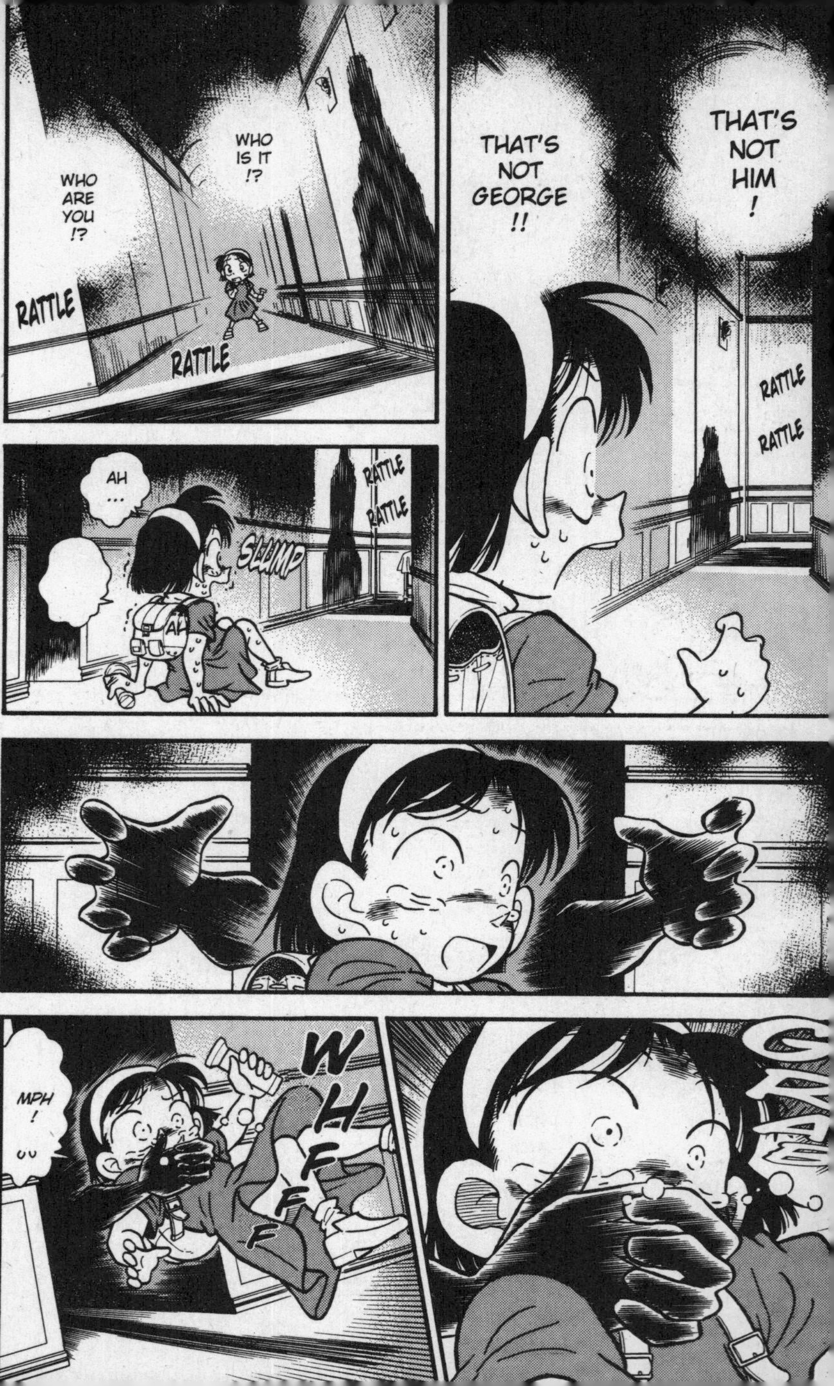
THAT'S NOT HIM!
THAT'S NOT GEORGE!!
RATTLE
RATTLE
WHO IS IT!?
WHO ARE YOU!?
RATTLE
RATTLE
RATTLE
RATTLE
AH...
SLUMP
AH
GRAB
WHFFF
MPH!

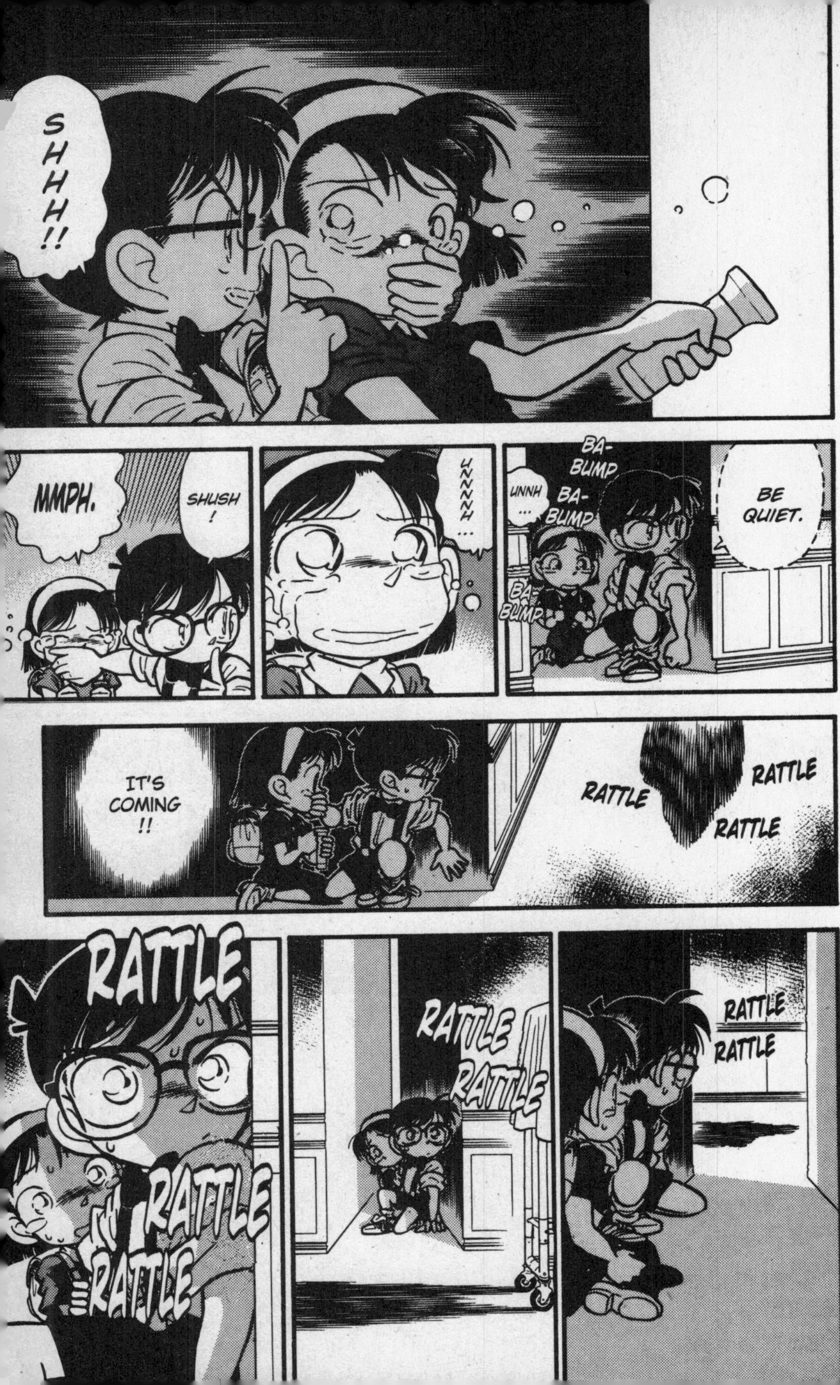
SHHHH!!
BE QUIET.
BA-BUMP
UNNH...
BA-BUMP
BA-BUMP
UNNNNH...
SHUSH!
MMPH.
RATTLE
RATTLE
RATTLE
IT'S COMING!!
RATTLE
RATTLE
RATTLE
RATTLE
RATTLE
RATTLE
RATTLE

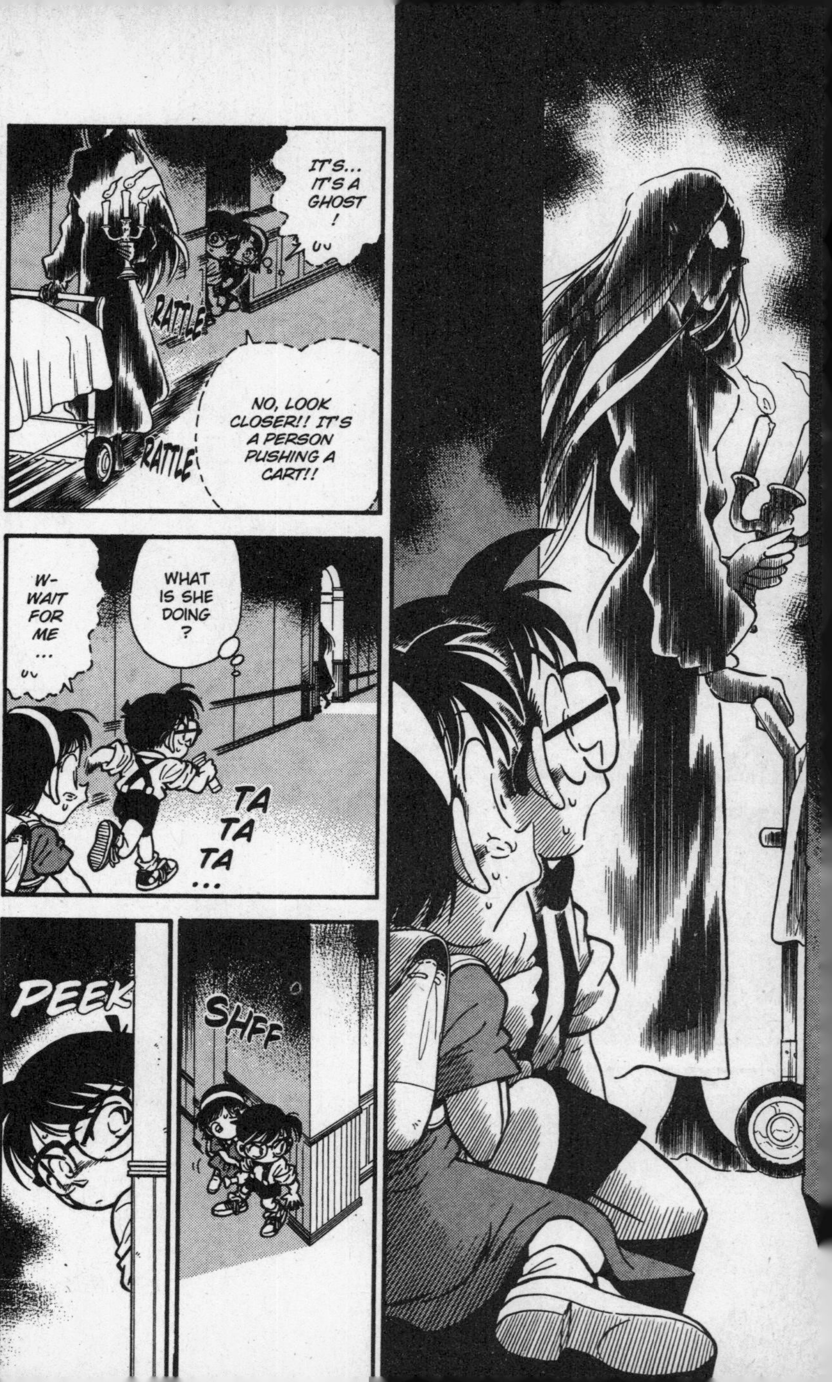
IT'S... IT'S A GHOST!
RATTLE
NO, LOOK CLOSER!! IT'S A PERSON PUSHING A CART!!
RATTLE
WHAT IS SHE DOING?
W-WAIT FOR ME...
TA TA TA...
SHFF
PEEK

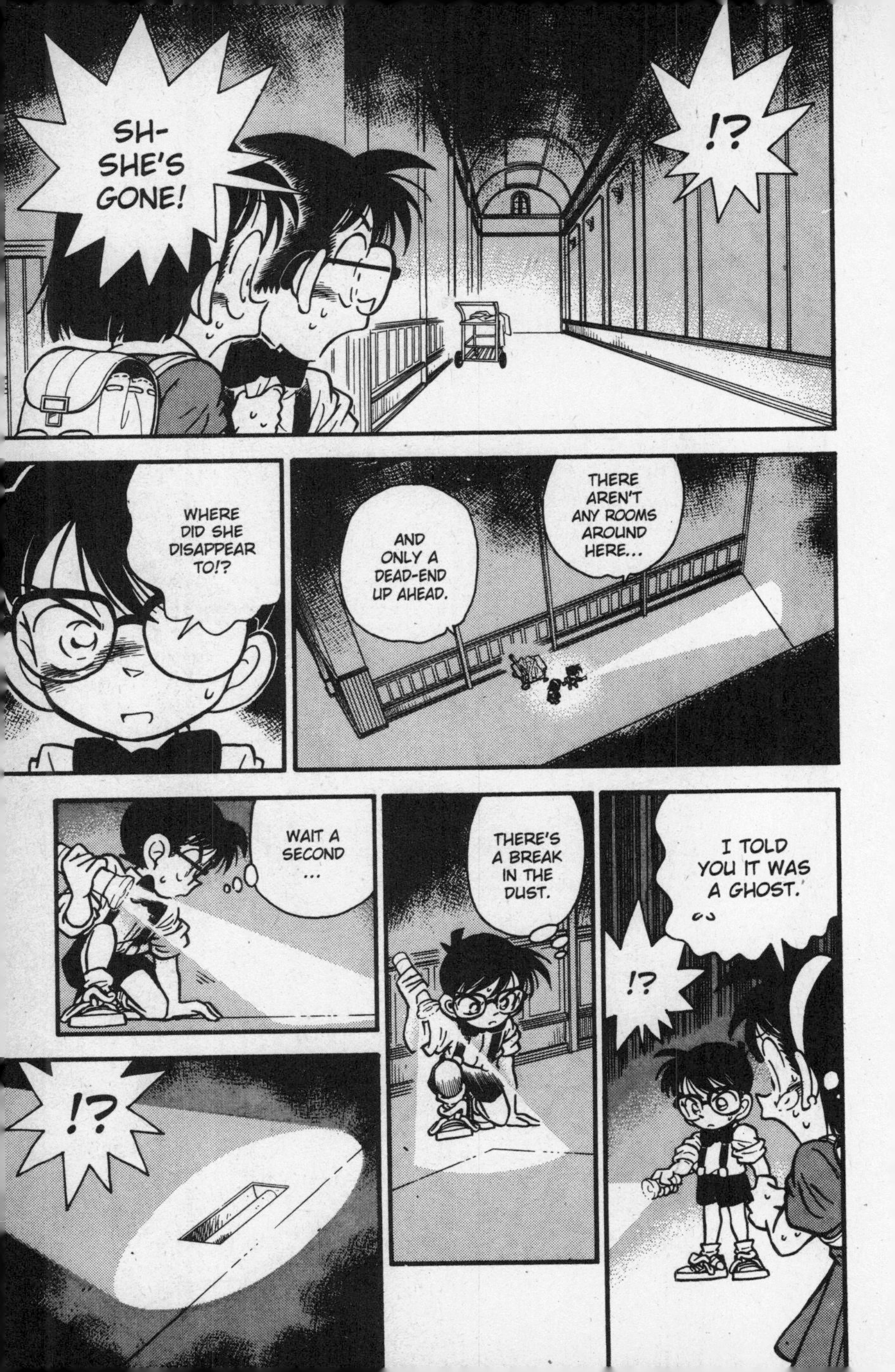
!?
SH- SHE'S GONE!
THERE AREN'T ANY ROOMS AROUND HERE...
AND ONLY A DEAD-END UP AHEAD.
WHERE DID SHE DISAPPEAR TO!?
I TOLD YOU IT WAS A GHOST.
!?
THERE'S A BREAK IN THE DUST.
WAIT A SECOND ...
!?

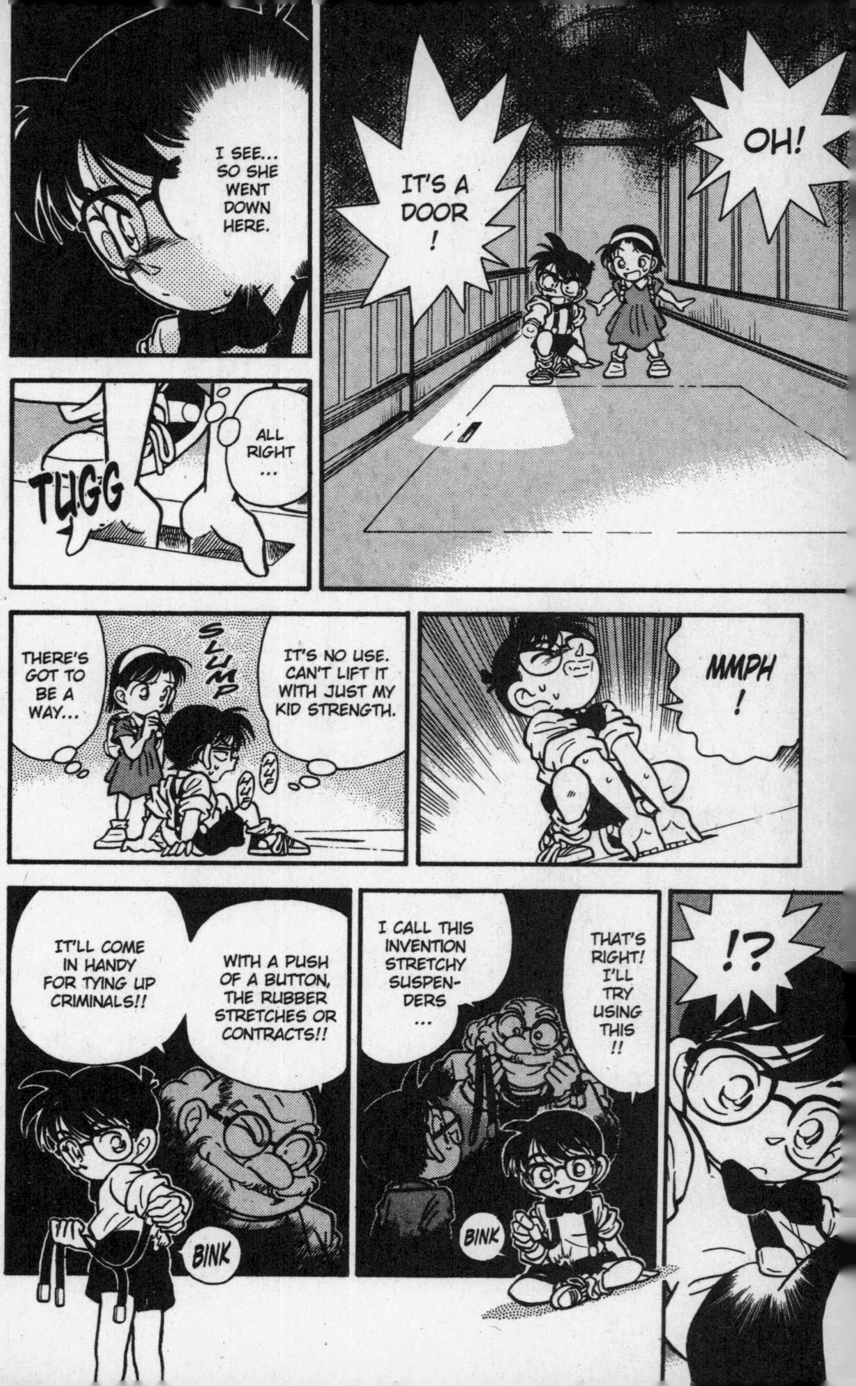
OH!
IT'S A DOOR !
I SEE... SO SHE WENT DOWN HERE.
ALL RIGHT ...
TUGG
MMPH !
IT'S NO USE. CAN'T LIFT IT WITH JUST MY KID STRENGTH.
SLUMP
HUF
HUF
THERE'S GOT TO BE A WAY...
!?
THAT'S RIGHT! I'LL TRY USING THIS !!
I CALL THIS INVENTION STRETCHY SUSPENDERS ...
BINK
WITH A PUSH OF A BUTTON, THE RUBBER STRETCHES OR CONTRACTS!!
IT'LL COME IN HANDY FOR TYING UP CRIMINALS!!
BINK

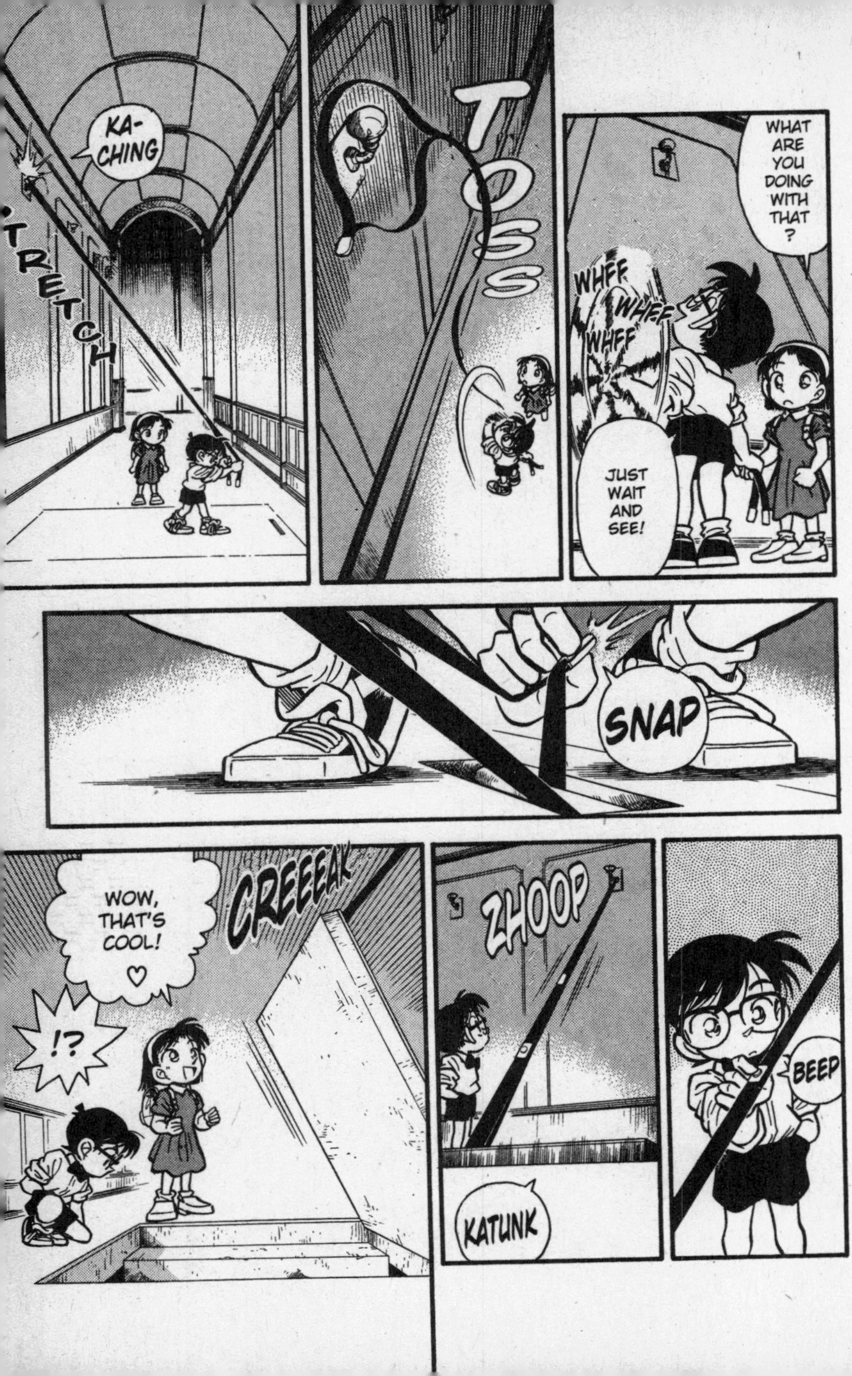
WHAT ARE YOU DOING WITH THAT?
WHFF
WHFF
WHFF
JUST WAIT AND SEE!
TOSS
KA-CHING
STRETCH
SNAP
BEEP
ZHOOP
KATUNK
CREEEAK
WOW, THAT'S COOL! ♡
!?

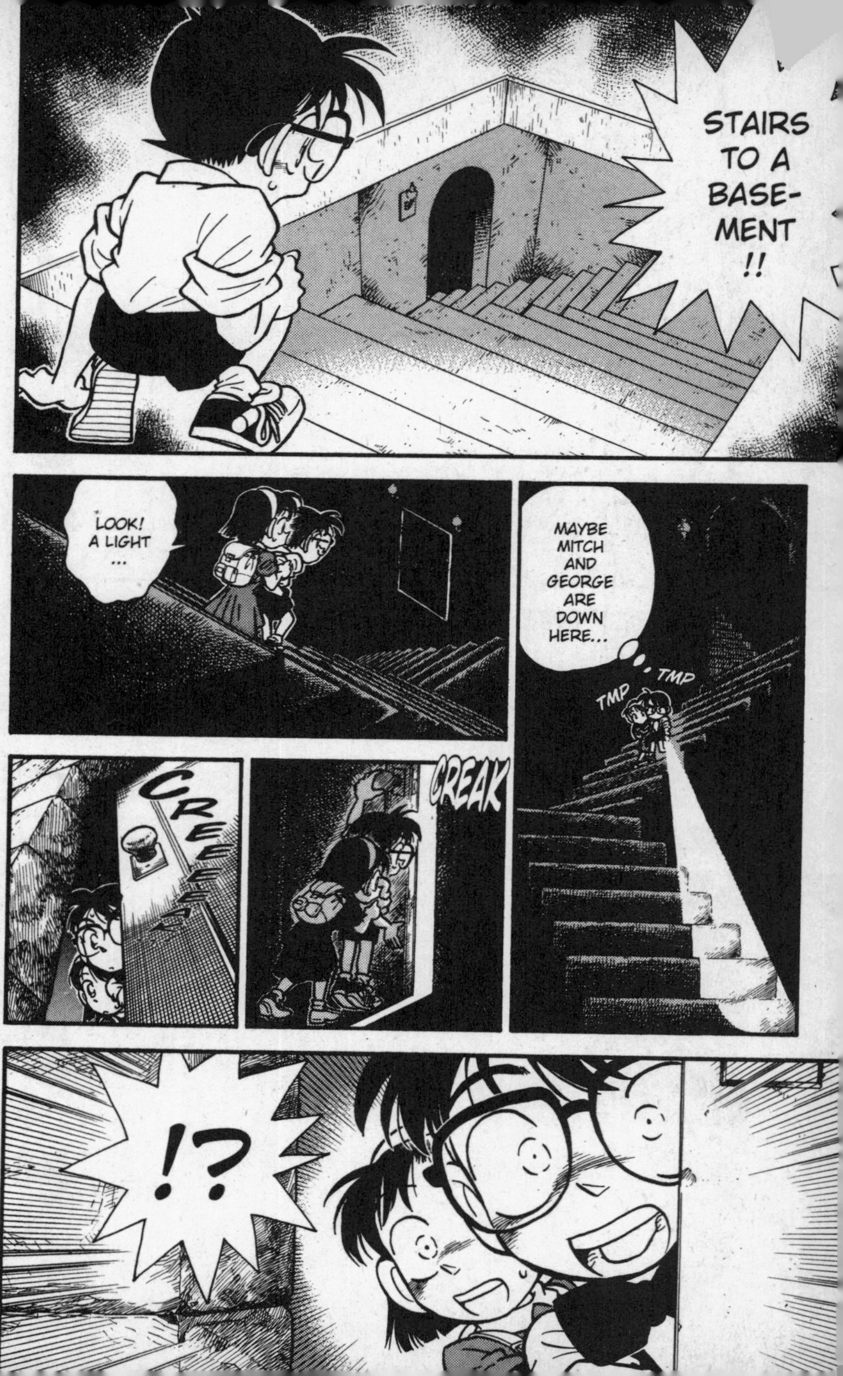
STAIRS TO A BASEMENT!!
MAYBE MITCH AND GEORGE ARE DOWN HERE...
TMP
TMP
LOOK! A LIGHT...
CREAK
CREEEE
!?

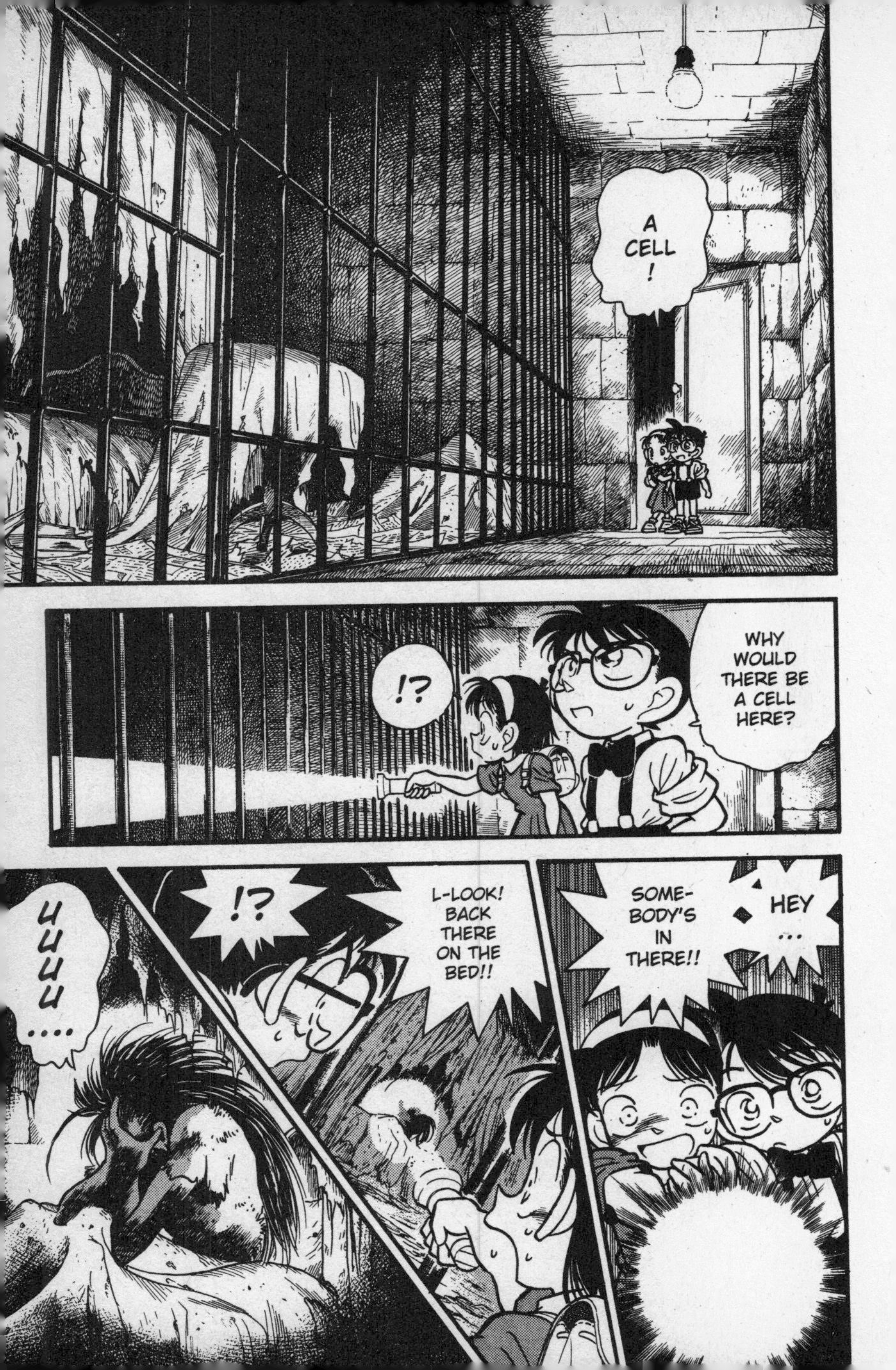
A CELL !
WHY WOULD THERE BE A CELL HERE?
!?
HEY ...
SOME-BODY'S IN THERE!!
L-LOOK! BACK THERE ON THE BED!!
!?
UUUU ....

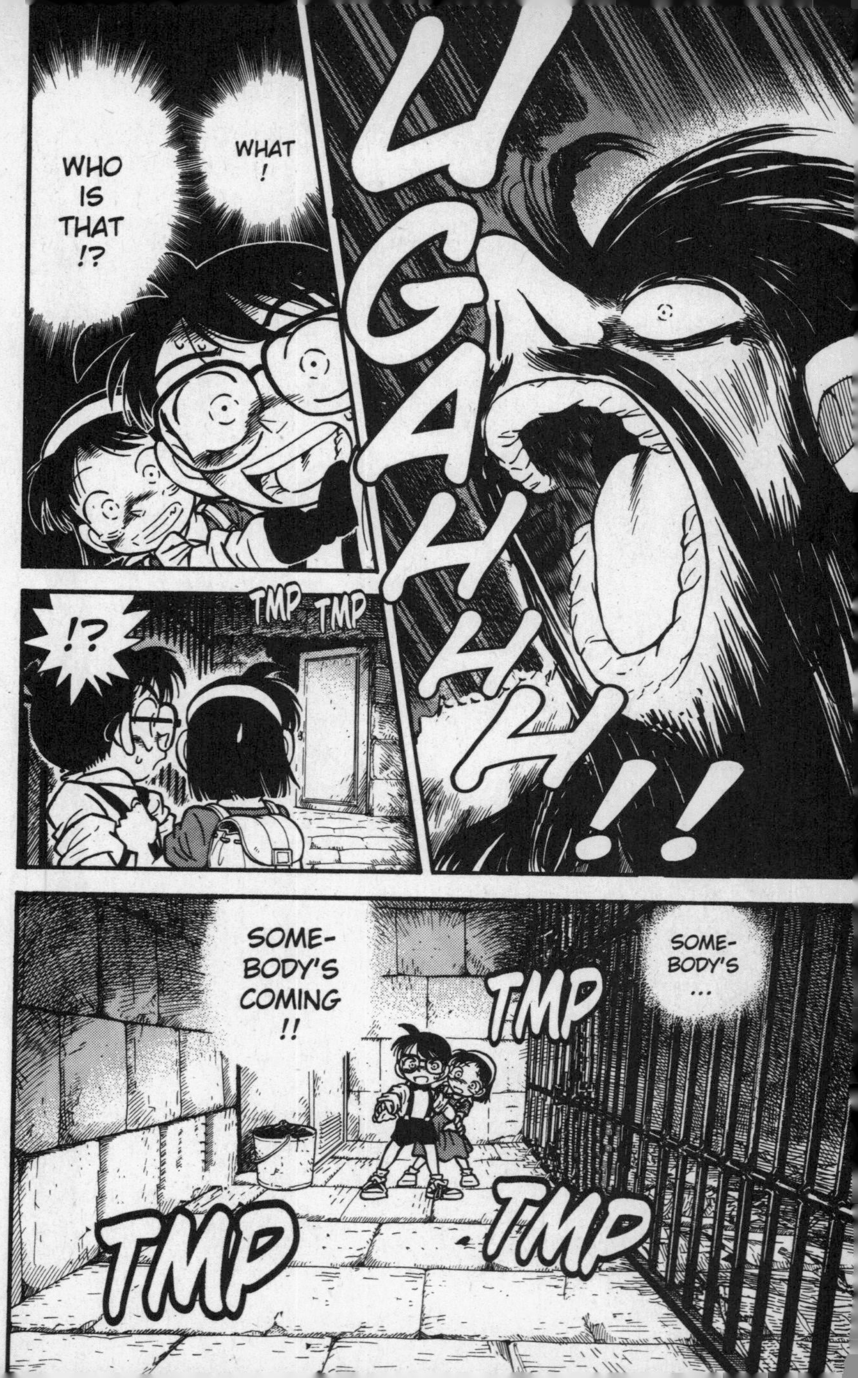
UGAHHHH!!
WHAT!
WHO IS THAT!?
!?
TMP TMP
SOME-BODY'S...
TMP
SOME-BODY'S COMING!!
TMP
TMP

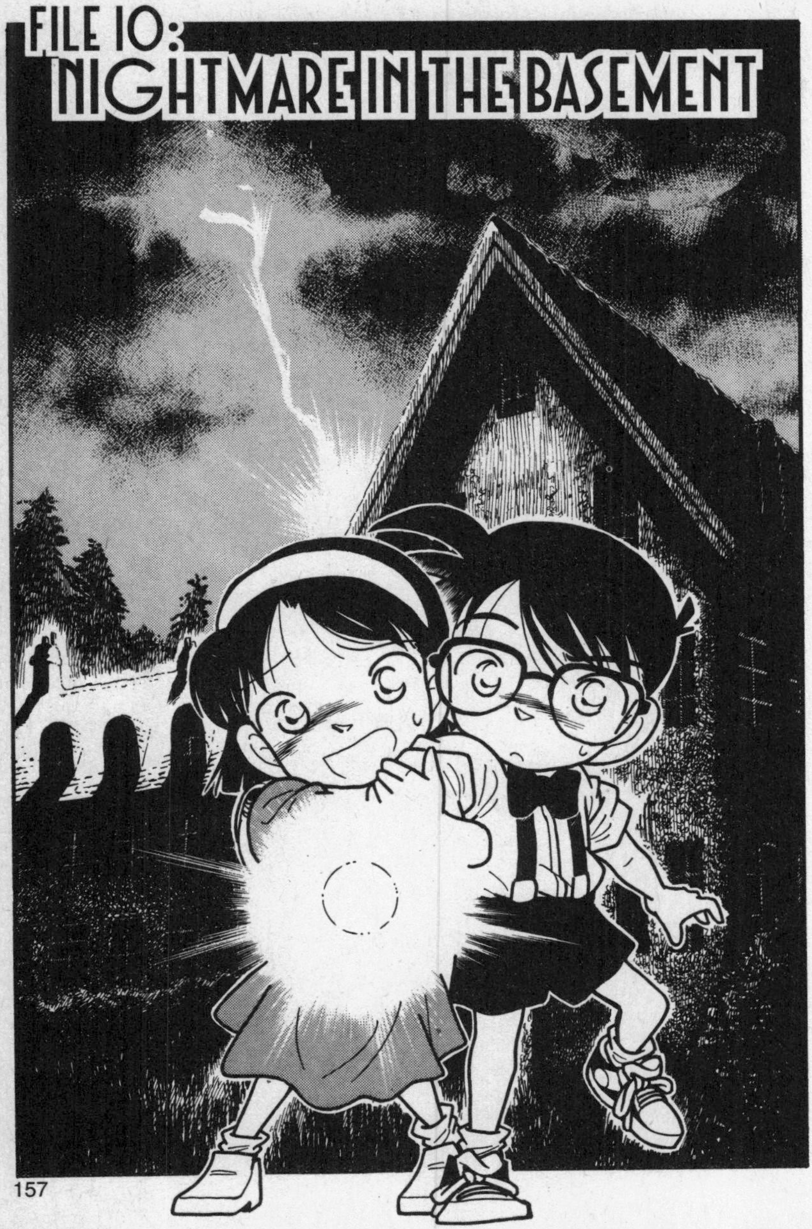
FILE 10:
NIGHTMARE IN THE BASEMENT

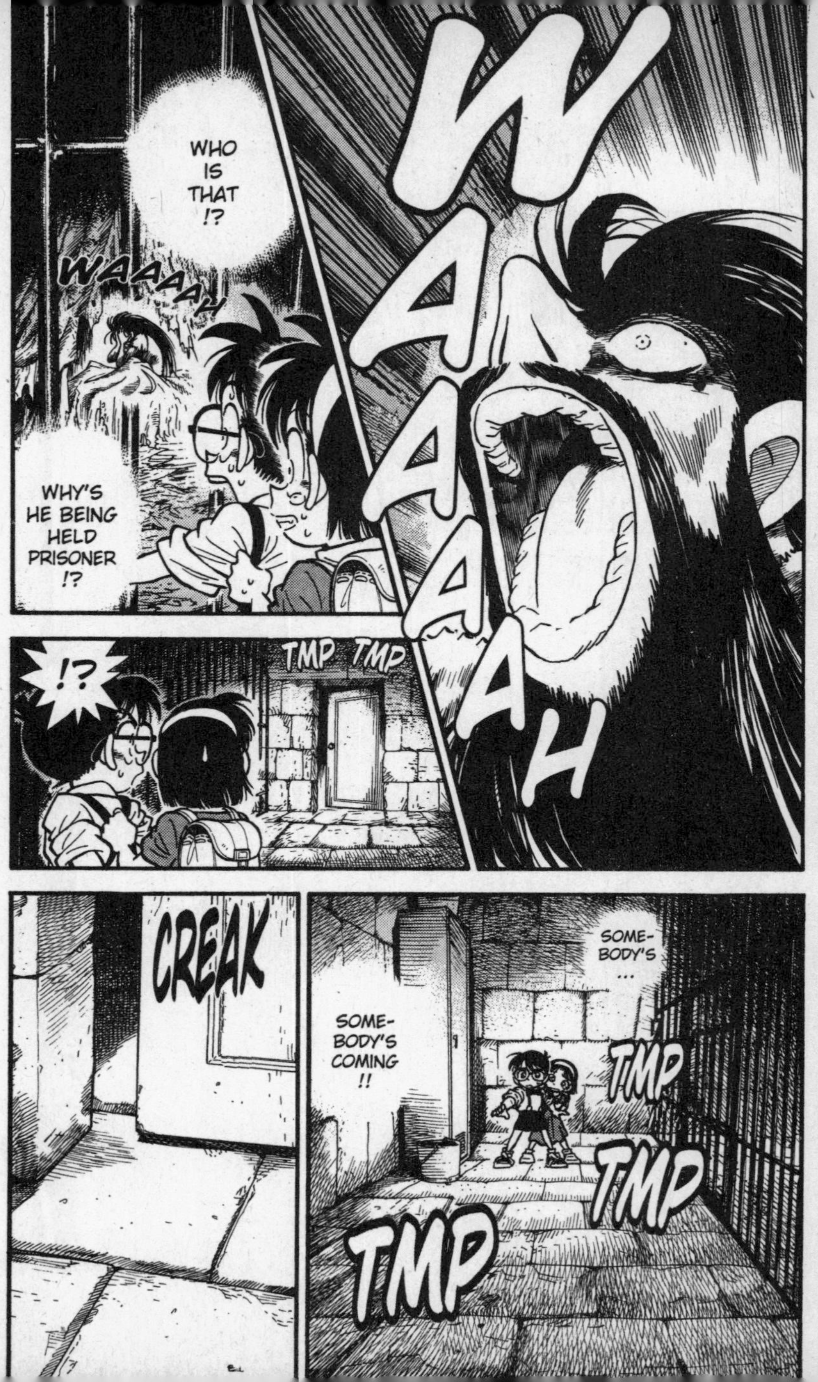
WAAAAH
WHO IS THAT !?
WAAAAH
WHY'S HE BEING HELD PRISONER !?
TMP TMP
!?
SOME-BODY'S ...
SOME-BODY'S COMING !!
TMP
TMP
TMP
CREAK

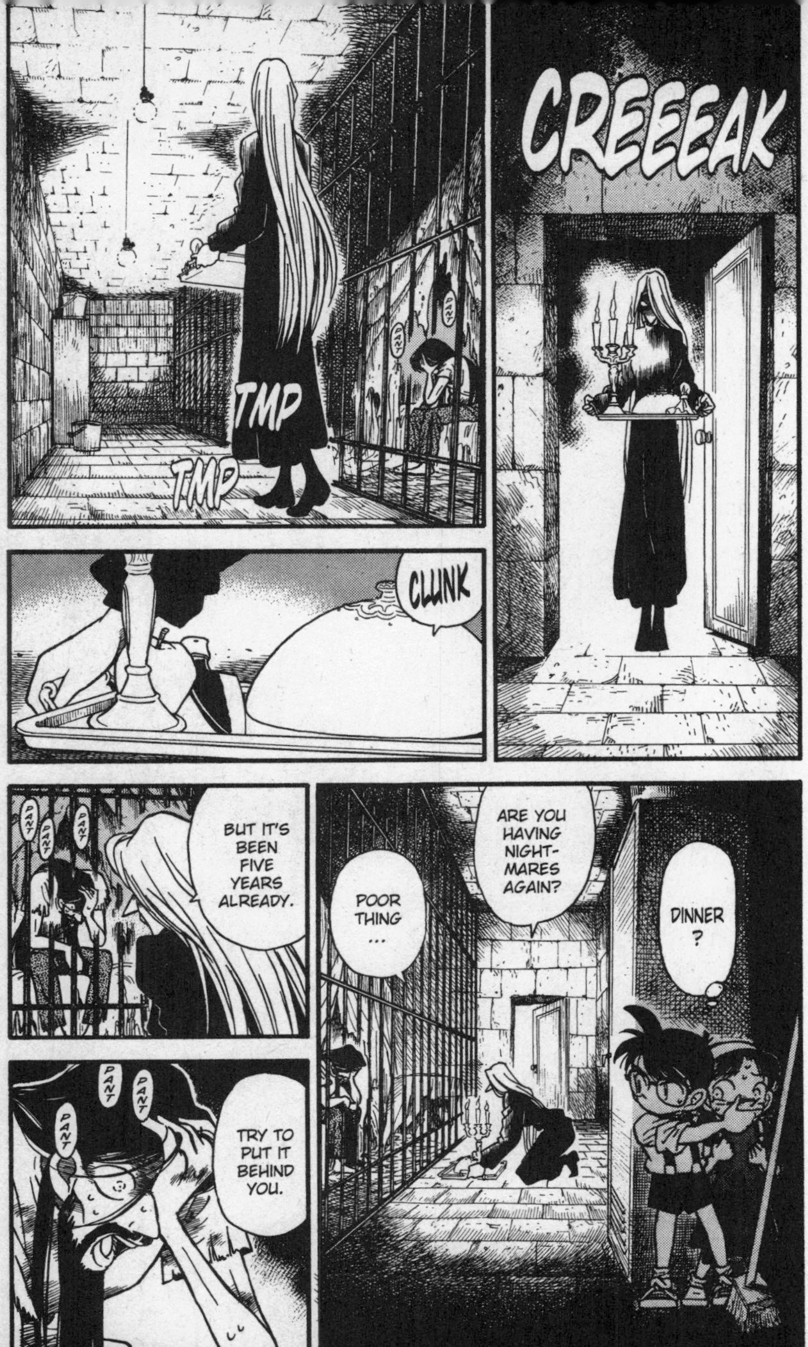
CREEEAK
TMP
TMP
PANT
PANT
CLUNK
ARE YOU HAVING NIGHT-MARES AGAIN?
POOR THING ...
DINNER ?
BUT IT'S BEEN FIVE YEARS ALREADY.
PANT
PANT
PANT
TRY TO PUT IT BEHIND YOU.
PANT
PANT
PANT

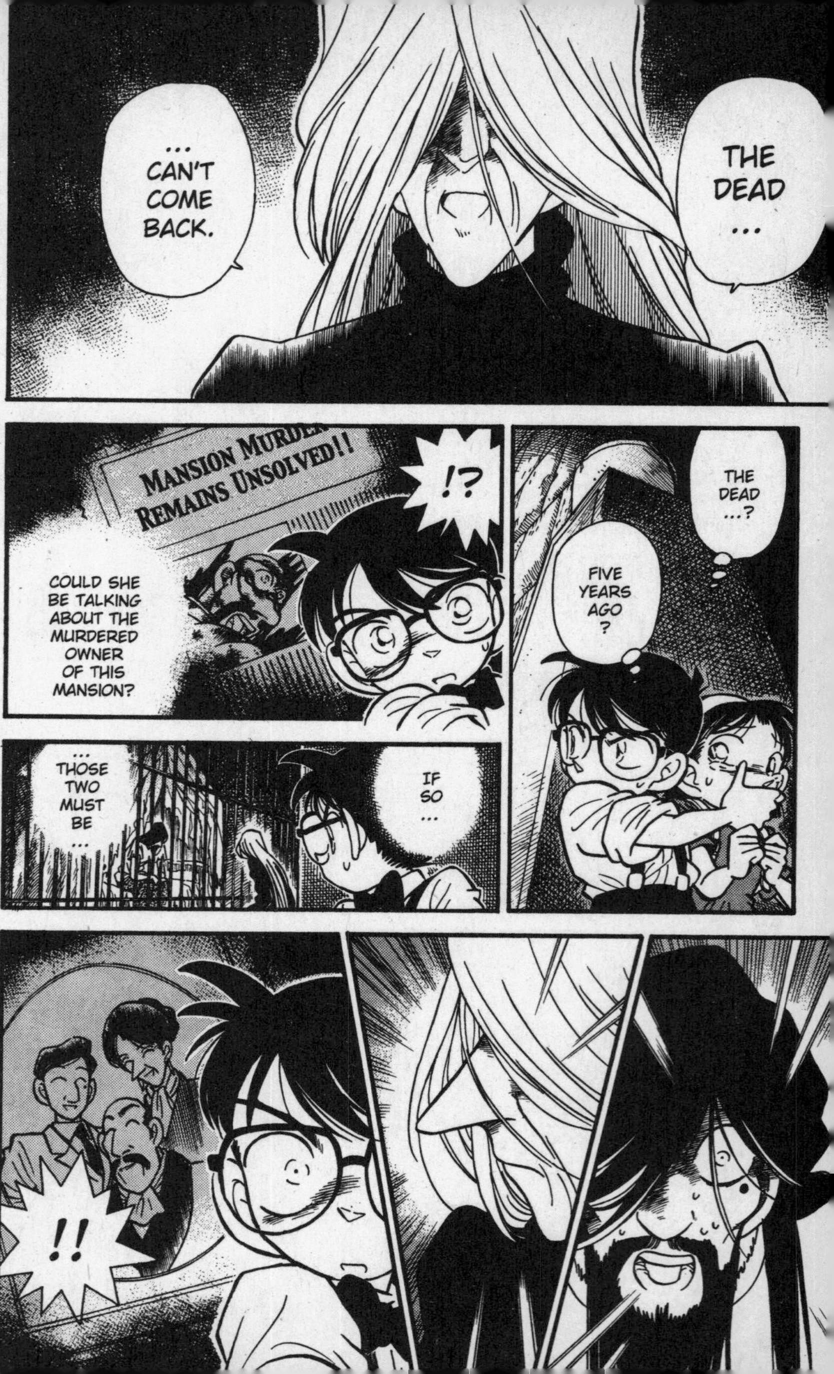
THE DEAD ...
... CAN'T COME BACK.
THE DEAD ...?
FIVE YEARS AGO ?
!?
MANSION MURDE
REMAINS UNSOLVED!!
COULD SHE BE TALKING ABOUT THE MURDERED OWNER OF THIS MANSION?
IF SO ...
... THOSE TWO MUST BE ...
!!

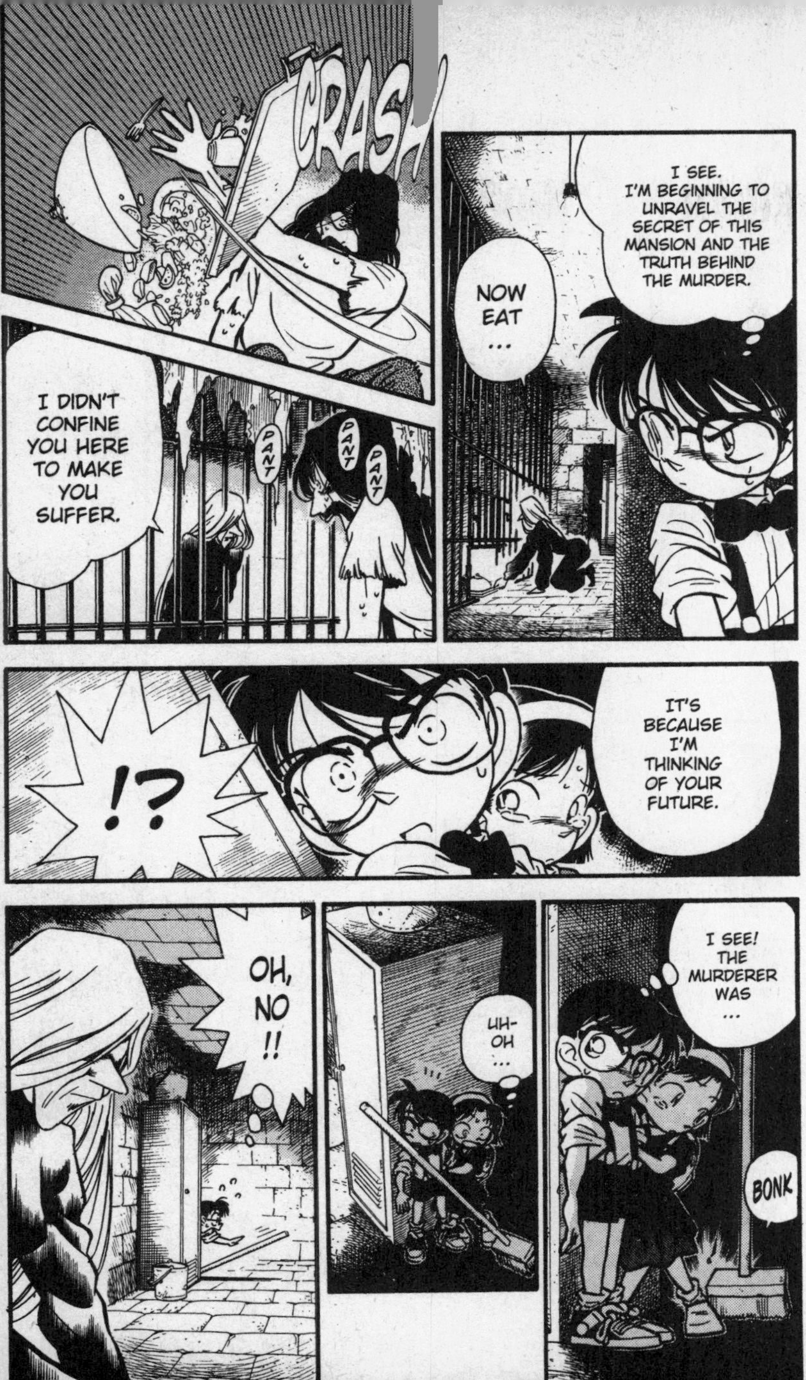
I SEE. I'M BEGINNING TO UNRAVEL THE SECRET OF THIS MANSION AND THE TRUTH BEHIND THE MURDER.
NOW EAT ...
CRASH
I DIDN'T CONFINE YOU HERE TO MAKE YOU SUFFER.
PANT
PANT
PANT
IT'S BECAUSE I'M THINKING OF YOUR FUTURE.
!?
I SEE! THE MURDERER WAS ...
BONK
UH-OH ...
OH, NO !!

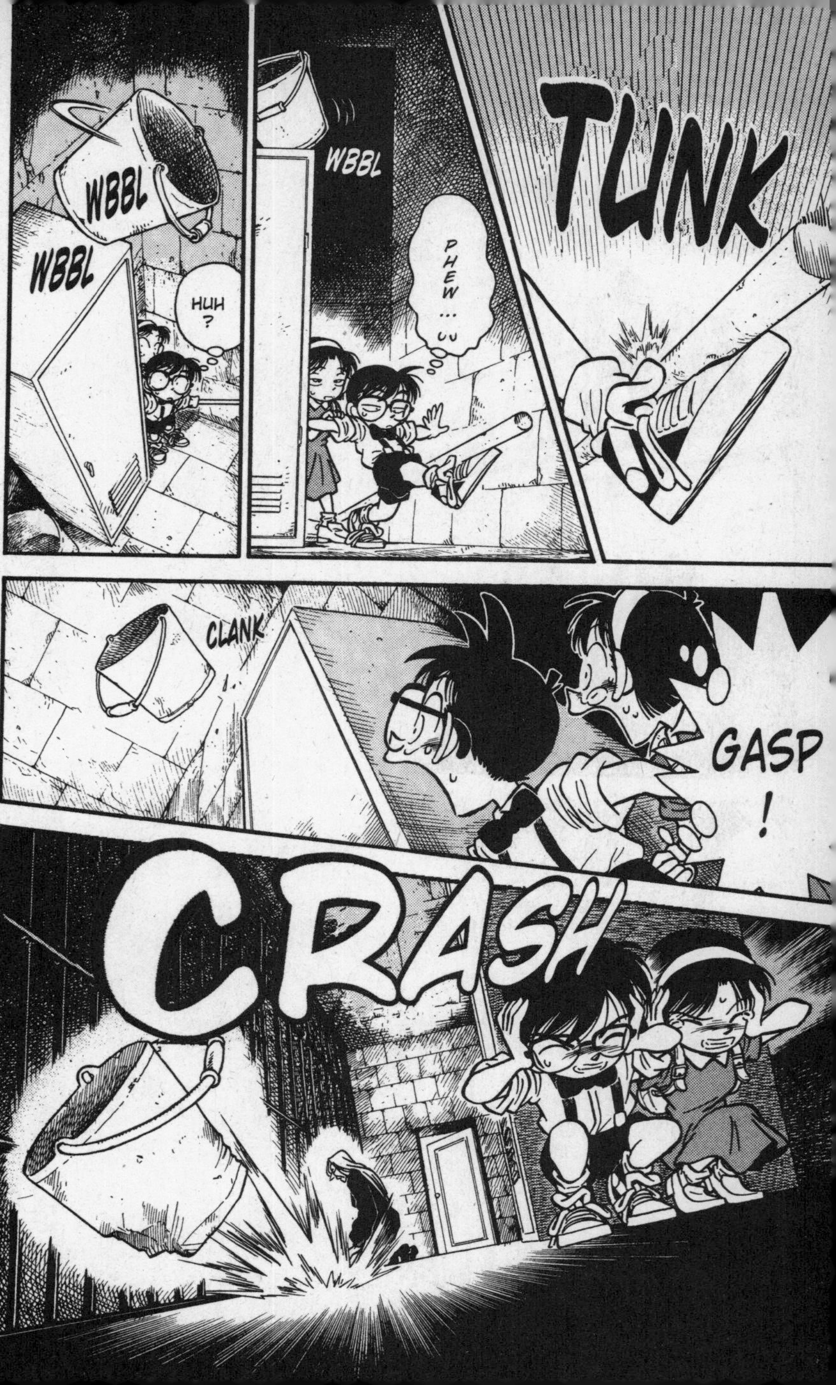
TUNK
WBBL
PHEW...
WBBL
WBBL
HUH?
GASP!
CLANK
CRASH

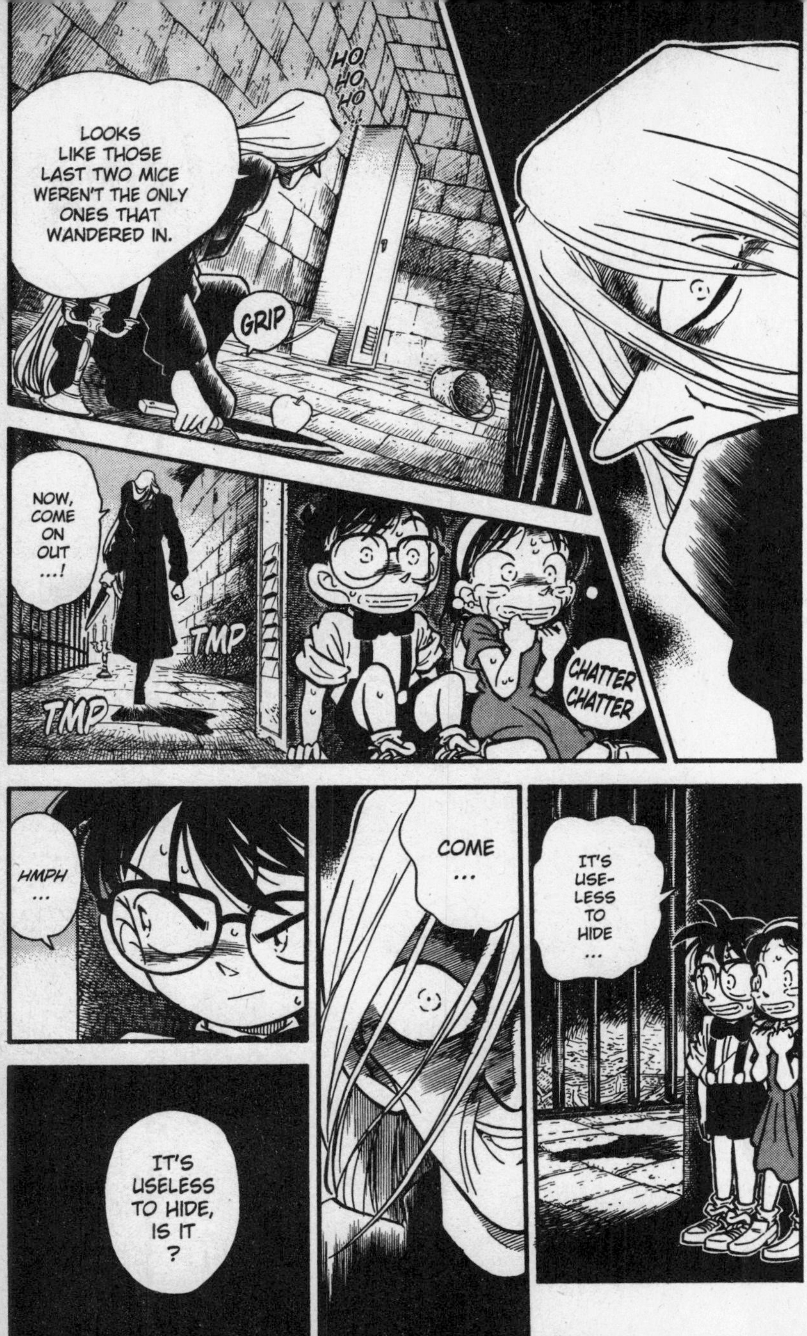
HO HO HO
LOOKS LIKE THOSE LAST TWO MICE WEREN'T THE ONLY ONES THAT WANDERED IN.
GRIP
NOW, COME ON OUT ...!
TMP
TMP
CHATTER CHATTER
IT'S USELESS TO HIDE ...
COME ...
HMPH ...
IT'S USELESS TO HIDE, IS IT ?

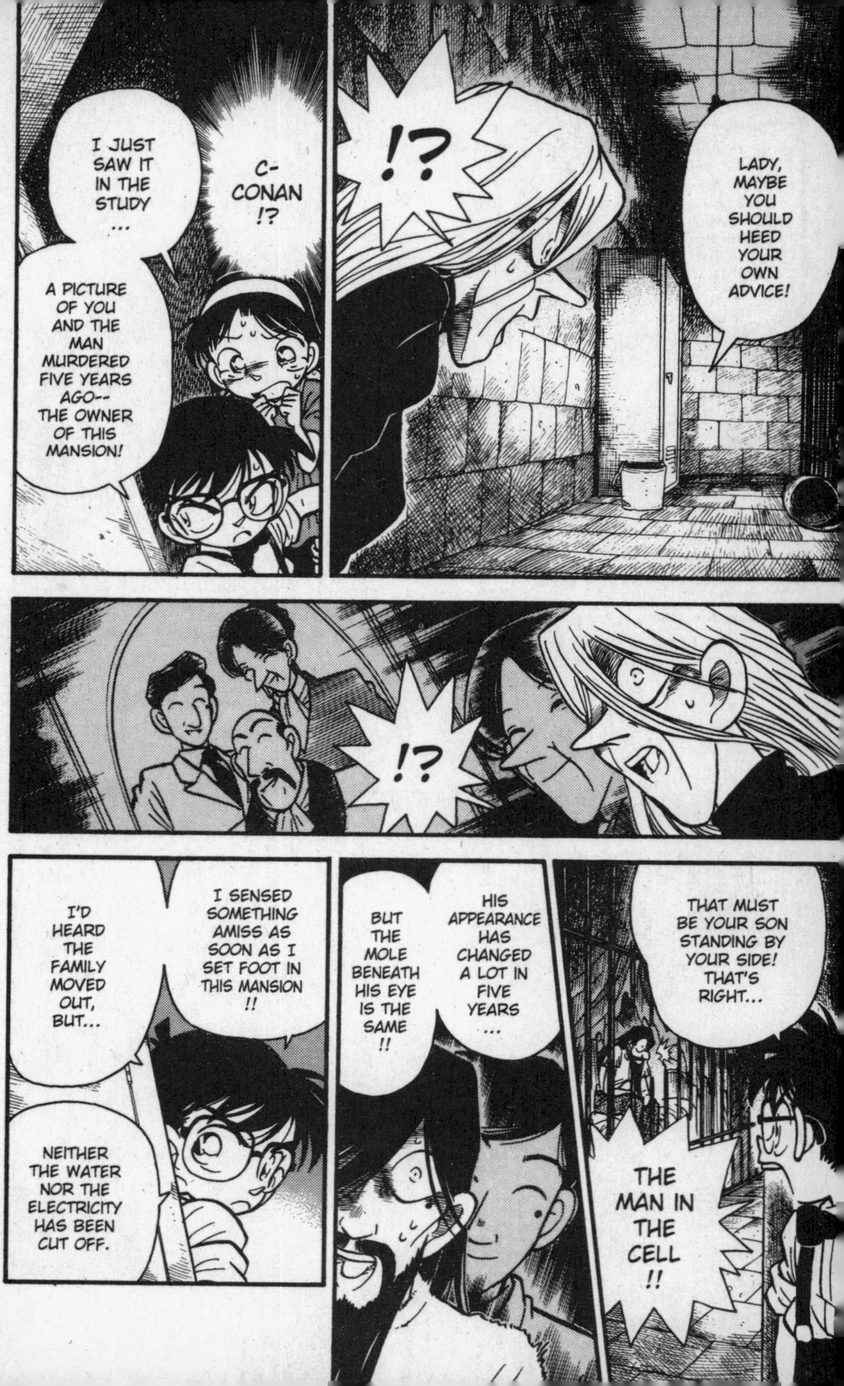
LADY, MAYBE YOU SHOULD HEED YOUR OWN ADVICE!
!?
C-CONAN!?
I JUST SAW IT IN THE STUDY...
A PICTURE OF YOU AND THE MAN MURDERED FIVE YEARS AGO-- THE OWNER OF THIS MANSION!
!?
THAT MUST BE YOUR SON STANDING BY YOUR SIDE! THAT'S RIGHT...
THE MAN IN THE CELL!!
HIS APPEARANCE HAS CHANGED A LOT IN FIVE YEARS...
BUT THE MOLE BENEATH HIS EYE IS THE SAME!!
I SENSED SOMETHING AMISS AS SOON AS I SET FOOT IN THIS MANSION!!
I'D HEARD THE FAMILY MOVED OUT, BUT...
NEITHER THE WATER NOR THE ELECTRICITY HAS BEEN CUT OFF.

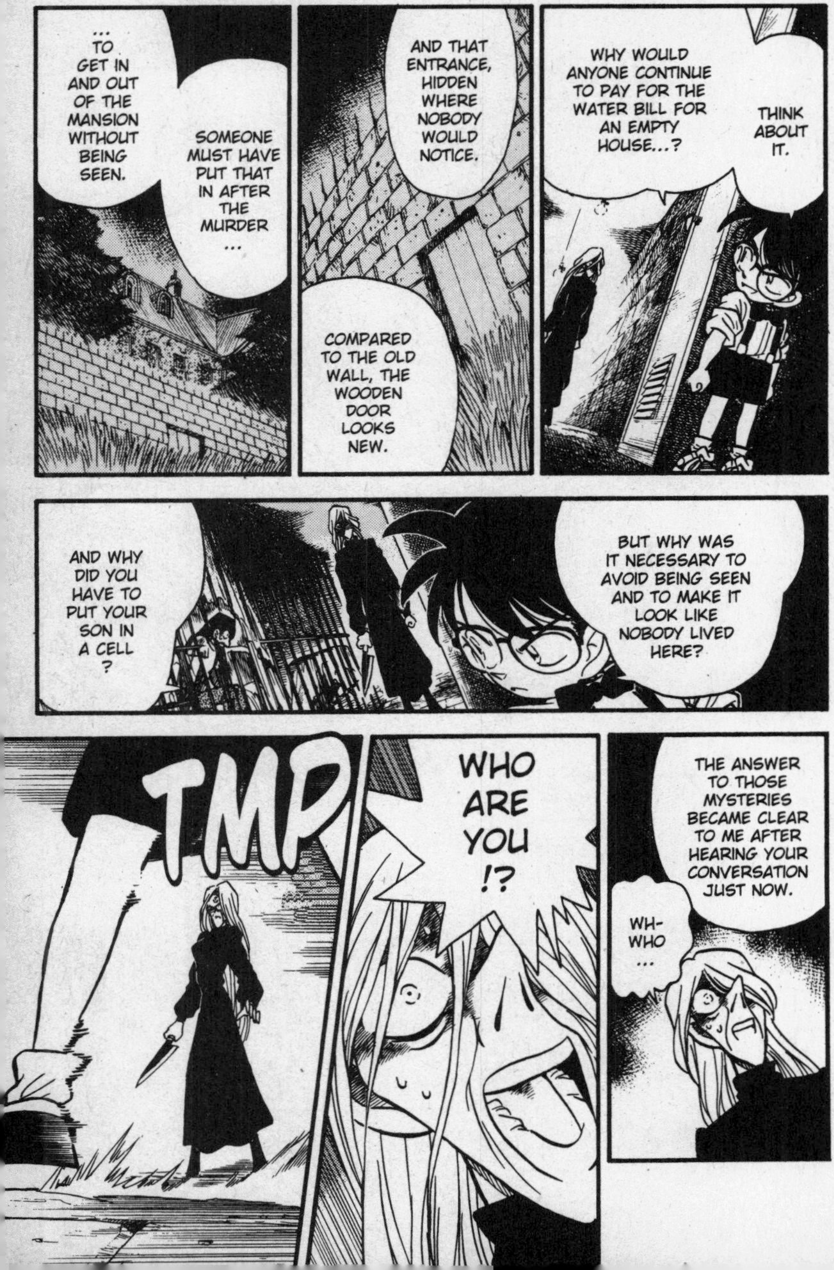
THINK ABOUT IT.
WHY WOULD ANYONE CONTINUE TO PAY FOR THE WATER BILL FOR AN EMPTY HOUSE...?
AND THAT ENTRANCE, HIDDEN WHERE NOBODY WOULD NOTICE.
COMPARED TO THE OLD WALL, THE WOODEN DOOR LOOKS NEW.
SOMEONE MUST HAVE PUT THAT IN AFTER THE MURDER...
...TO GET IN AND OUT OF THE MANSION WITHOUT BEING SEEN.
BUT WHY WAS IT NECESSARY TO AVOID BEING SEEN AND TO MAKE IT LOOK LIKE NOBODY LIVED HERE?
AND WHY DID YOU HAVE TO PUT YOUR SON IN A CELL?
THE ANSWER TO THOSE MYSTERIES BECAME CLEAR TO ME AFTER HEARING YOUR CONVERSATION JUST NOW.
WH-WHO...
WHO ARE YOU!?
TMP

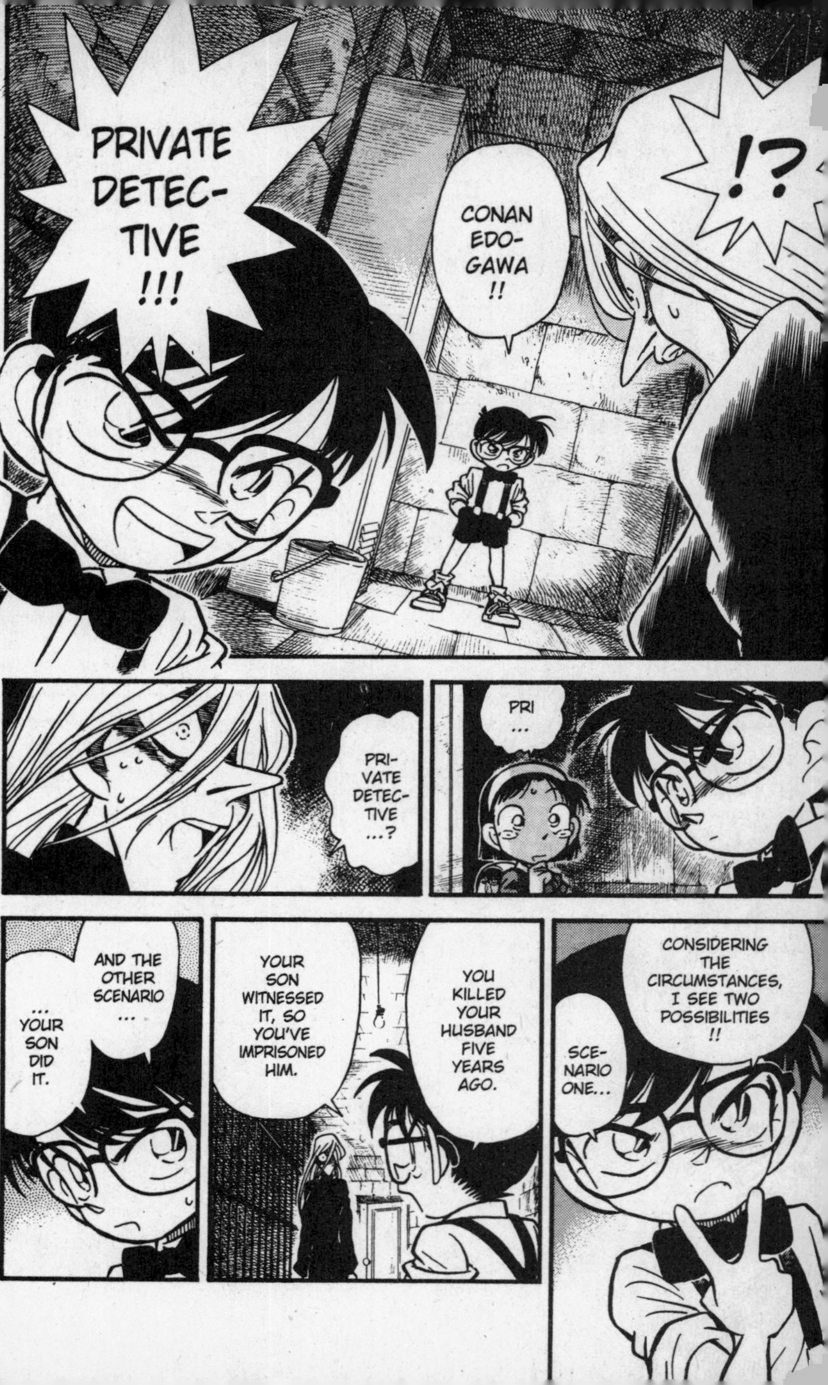
!?
CONAN EDOGAWA !!
PRIVATE DETECTIVE !!!
PRI ...
PRIVATE DETECTIVE ...?
CONSIDERING THE CIRCUMSTANCES, I SEE TWO POSSIBILITIES !!
SCENARIO ONE...
YOU KILLED YOUR HUSBAND FIVE YEARS AGO.
YOUR SON WITNESSED IT, SO YOU'VE IMPRISONED HIM.
AND THE OTHER SCENARIO ...
... YOUR SON DID IT.

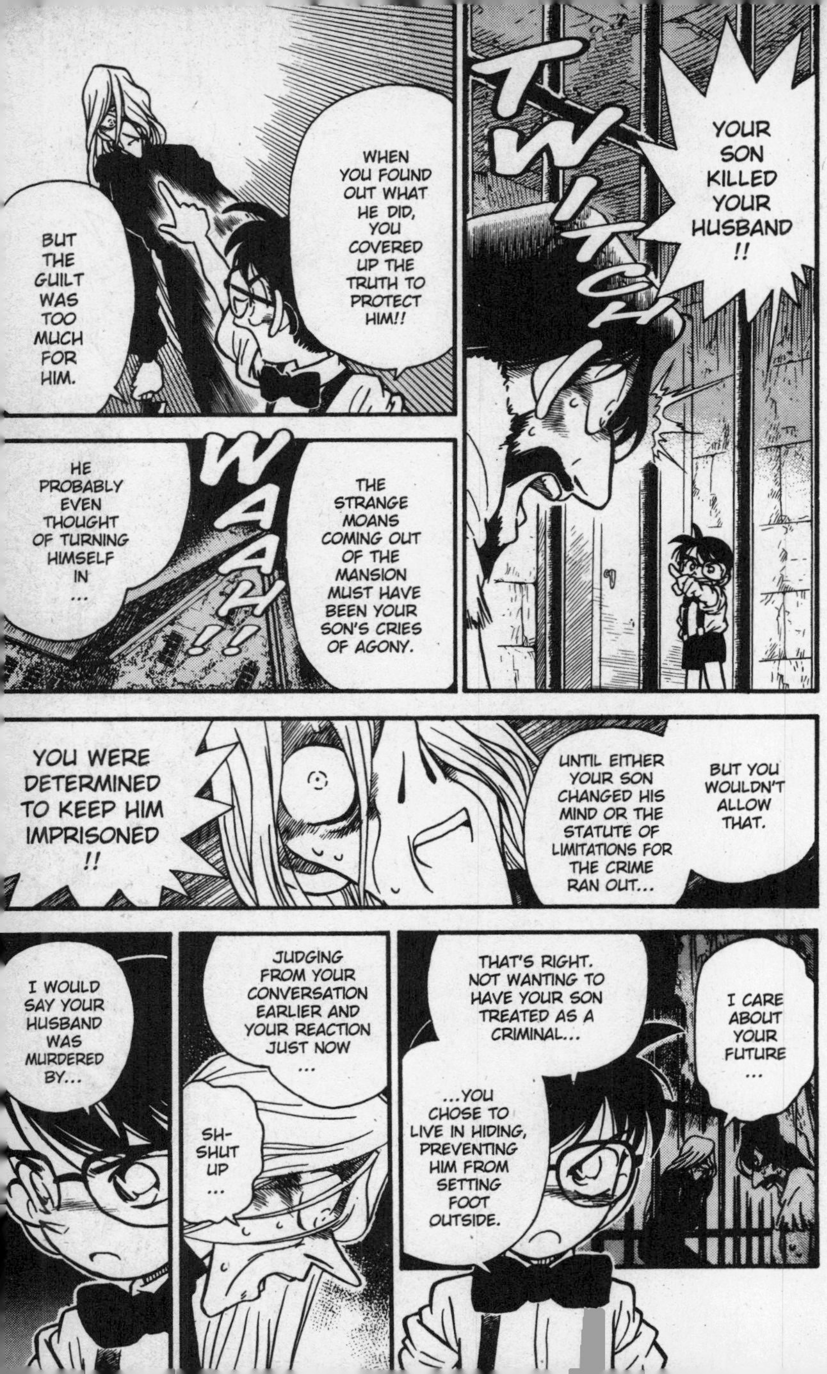
YOUR SON KILLED YOUR HUSBAND!!
TWITCH
WHEN YOU FOUND OUT WHAT HE DID, YOU COVERED UP THE TRUTH TO PROTECT HIM!!
BUT THE GUILT WAS TOO MUCH FOR HIM.
THE STRANGE MOANS COMING OUT OF THE MANSION MUST HAVE BEEN YOUR SON'S CRIES OF AGONY.
WAAH!!
HE PROBABLY EVEN THOUGHT OF TURNING HIMSELF IN...
BUT YOU WOULDN'T ALLOW THAT.
UNTIL EITHER YOUR SON CHANGED HIS MIND OR THE STATUTE OF LIMITATIONS FOR THE CRIME RAN OUT...
YOU WERE DETERMINED TO KEEP HIM IMPRISONED!!
I CARE ABOUT YOUR FUTURE...
THAT'S RIGHT. NOT WANTING TO HAVE YOUR SON TREATED AS A CRIMINAL...
...YOU CHOSE TO LIVE IN HIDING, PREVENTING HIM FROM SETTING FOOT OUTSIDE.
JUDGING FROM YOUR CONVERSATION EARLIER AND YOUR REACTION JUST NOW...
SH-SHUT UP...
I WOULD SAY YOUR HUSBAND WAS MURDERED BY...

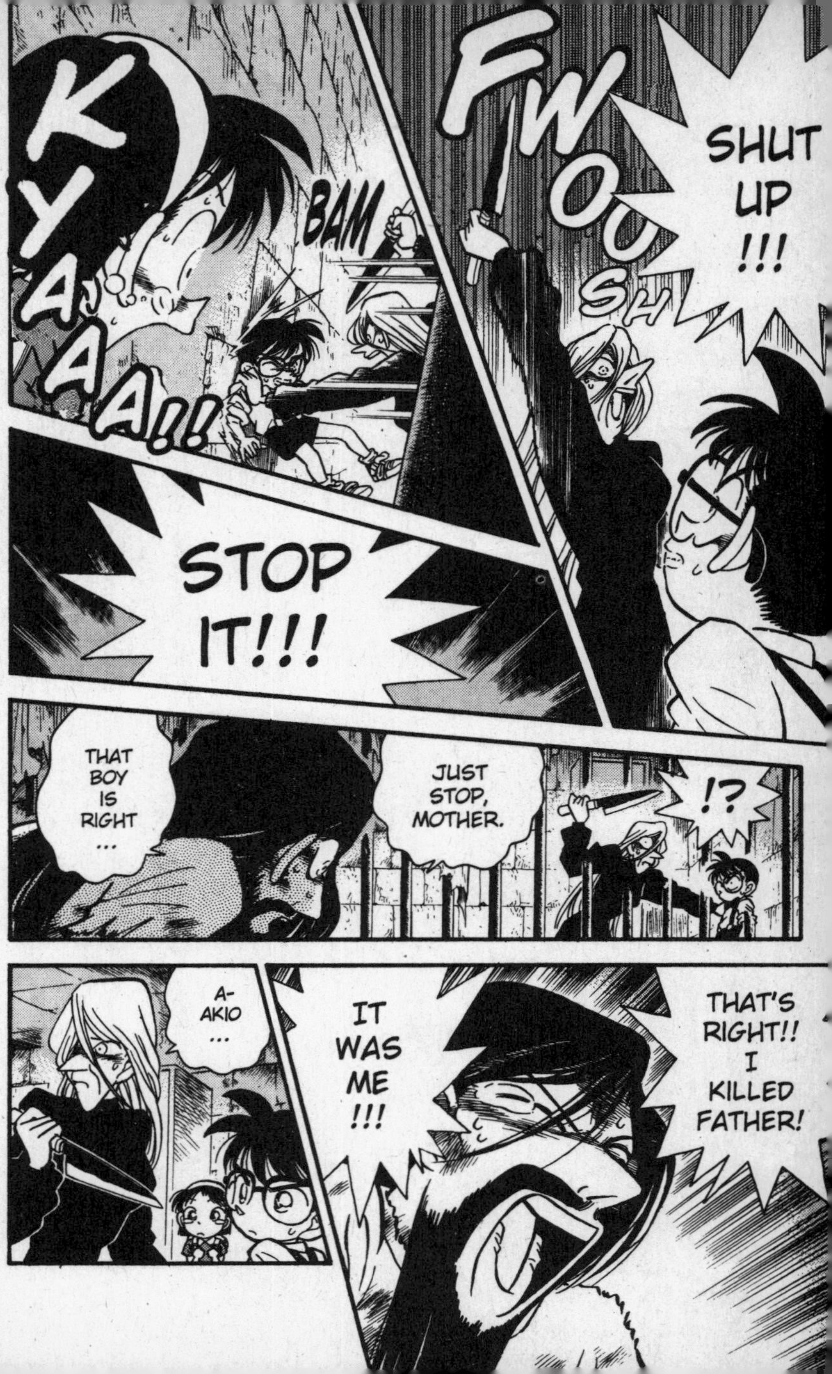

SHUT UP!!!
FWOUSH
BAM
KYAAAA!!
STOP IT!!!
!?
JUST STOP, MOTHER.
THAT BOY IS RIGHT ...
THAT'S RIGHT!! I KILLED FATHER!
IT WAS ME!!!
A-AKIO ...

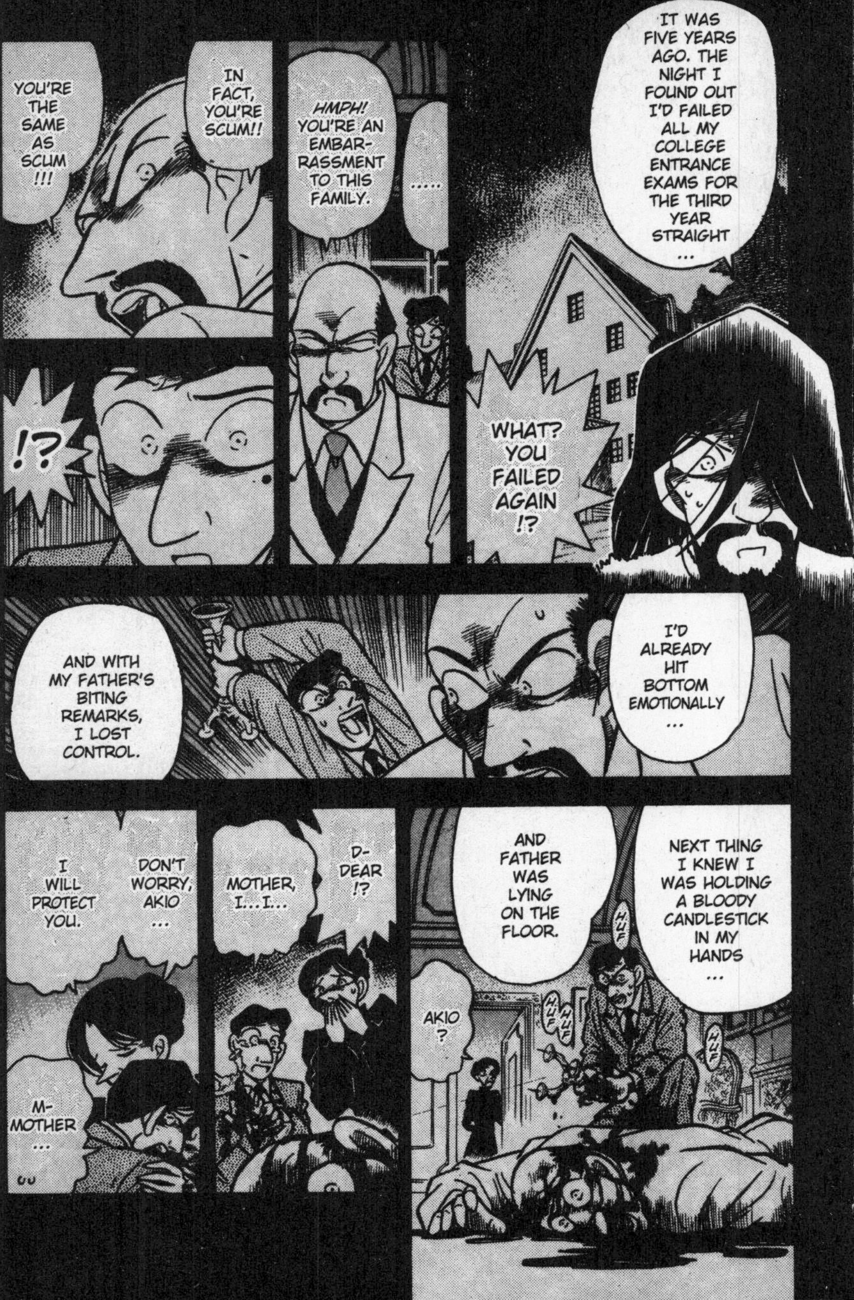
IT WAS FIVE YEARS AGO. THE NIGHT I FOUND OUT I'D FAILED ALL MY COLLEGE ENTRANCE EXAMS FOR THE THIRD YEAR STRAIGHT ...
WHAT? YOU FAILED AGAIN !?
.....
HMPH! YOU'RE AN EMBAR- RASSMENT TO THIS FAMILY.
IN FACT, YOU'RE SCUM!!
YOU'RE THE SAME AS SCUM !!!
!?
I'D ALREADY HIT BOTTOM EMOTIONALLY ...
AND WITH MY FATHER'S BITING REMARKS, I LOST CONTROL.
NEXT THING I KNEW I WAS HOLDING A BLOODY CANDLESTICK IN MY HANDS ...
AND FATHER WAS LYING ON THE FLOOR.
HUF
HUF HUF
HUF
AKIO ?
D- DEAR !?
MOTHER, I... I...
DON'T WORRY, AKIO ...
I WILL PROTECT YOU.
M- MOTHER ...

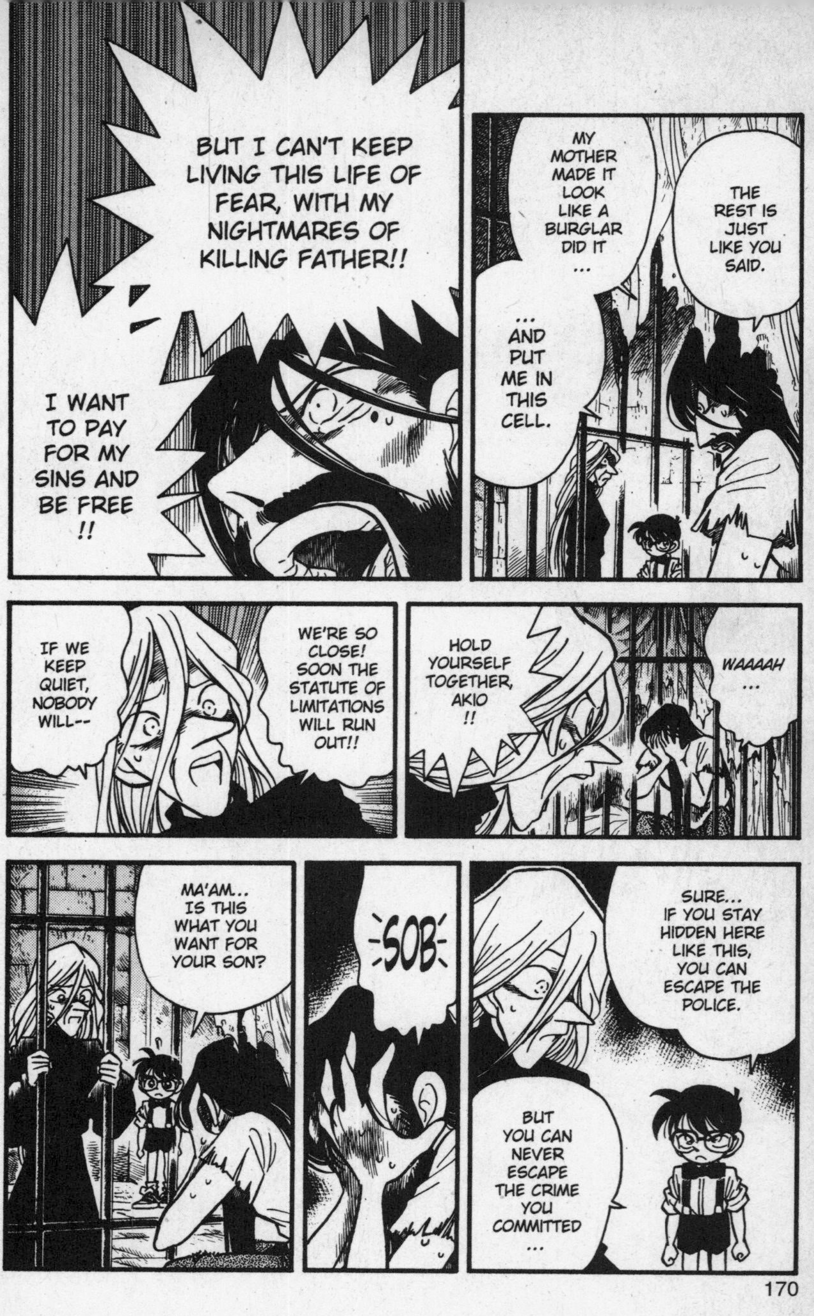
MY MOTHER MADE IT LOOK LIKE A BURGLAR DID IT ...
... AND PUT ME IN THIS CELL.
THE REST IS JUST LIKE YOU SAID.
BUT I CAN'T KEEP LIVING THIS LIFE OF FEAR, WITH MY NIGHTMARES OF KILLING FATHER!!
I WANT TO PAY FOR MY SINS AND BE FREE !!
WAAAAH ...
HOLD YOURSELF TOGETHER, AKIO !!
WE'RE SO CLOSE! SOON THE STATUTE OF LIMITATIONS WILL RUN OUT!!
IF WE KEEP QUIET, NOBODY WILL--
SURE... IF YOU STAY HIDDEN HERE LIKE THIS, YOU CAN ESCAPE THE POLICE.
BUT YOU CAN NEVER ESCAPE THE CRIME YOU COMMITTED ...
SOB
MA'AM... IS THIS WHAT YOU WANT FOR YOUR SON?

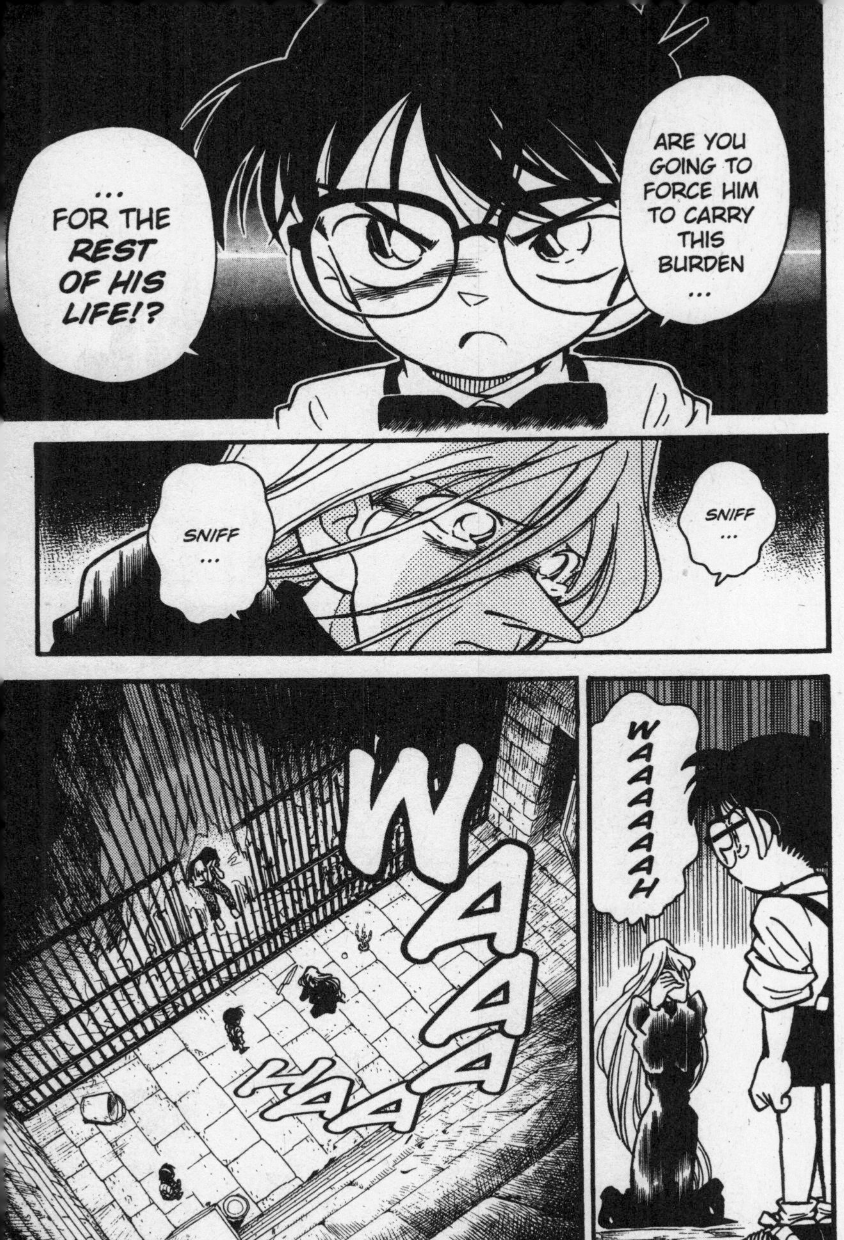
ARE YOU GOING TO FORCE HIM TO CARRY THIS BURDEN ...
... FOR THE *REST OF HIS LIFE!?*
SNIFF ...
SNIFF ...
WAAAAAAAH
WAAAA
HAAA

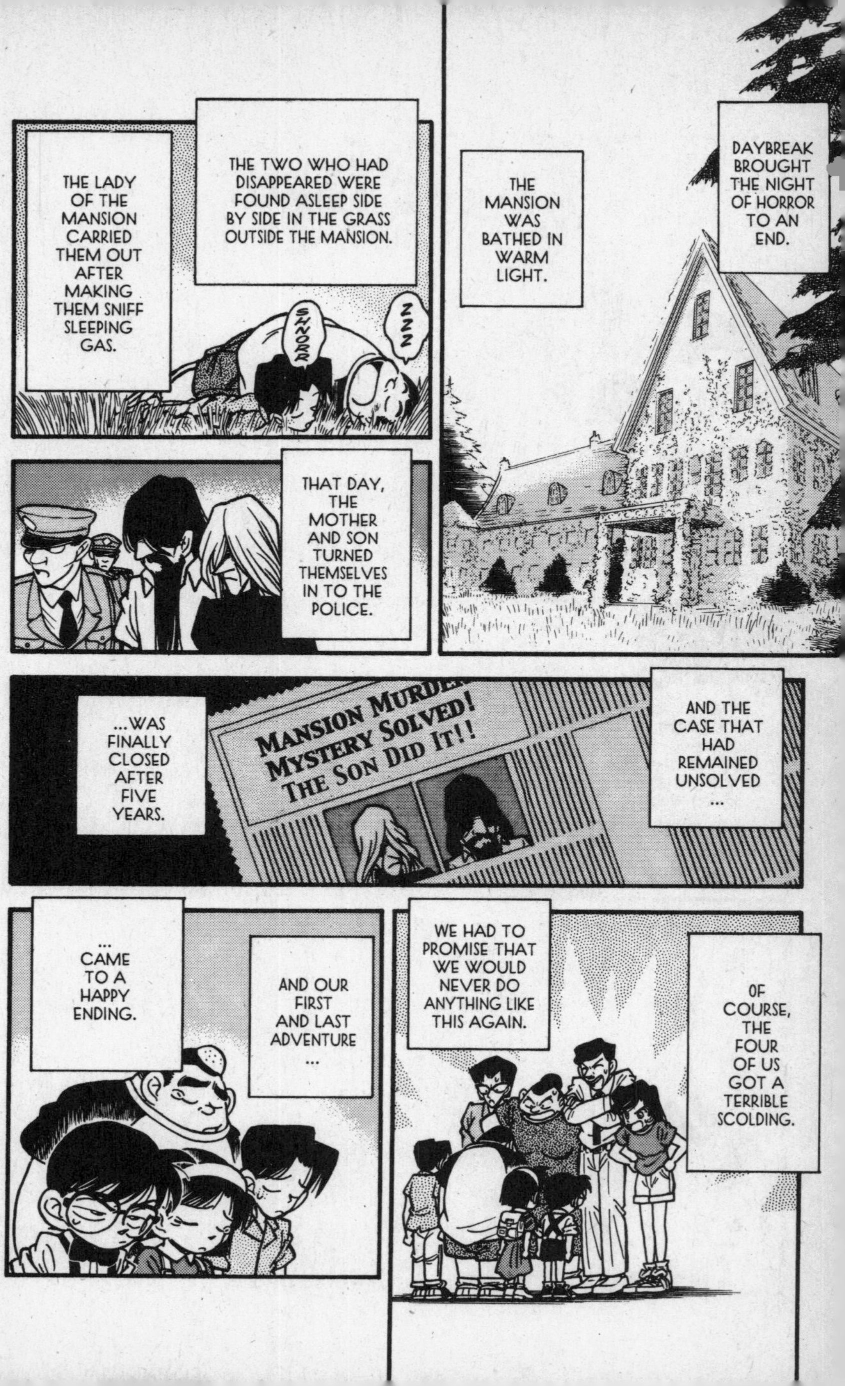
DAYBREAK BROUGHT THE NIGHT OF HORROR TO AN END.
THE MANSION WAS BATHED IN WARM LIGHT.
THE TWO WHO HAD DISAPPEARED WERE FOUND ASLEEP SIDE BY SIDE IN THE GRASS OUTSIDE THE MANSION.
THE LADY OF THE MANSION CARRIED THEM OUT AFTER MAKING THEM SNIFF SLEEPING GAS.
ZZZ
SHNORR
THAT DAY, THE MOTHER AND SON TURNED THEMSELVES IN TO THE POLICE.
AND THE CASE THAT HAD REMAINED UNSOLVED ...
MANSION MURDE
MYSTERY SOLVED!
THE SON DID IT!!
...WAS FINALLY CLOSED AFTER FIVE YEARS.
OF COURSE, THE FOUR OF US GOT A TERRIBLE SCOLDING.
WE HAD TO PROMISE THAT WE WOULD NEVER DO ANYTHING LIKE THIS AGAIN.
AND OUR FIRST AND LAST ADVENTURE ...
... CAME TO A HAPPY ENDING.

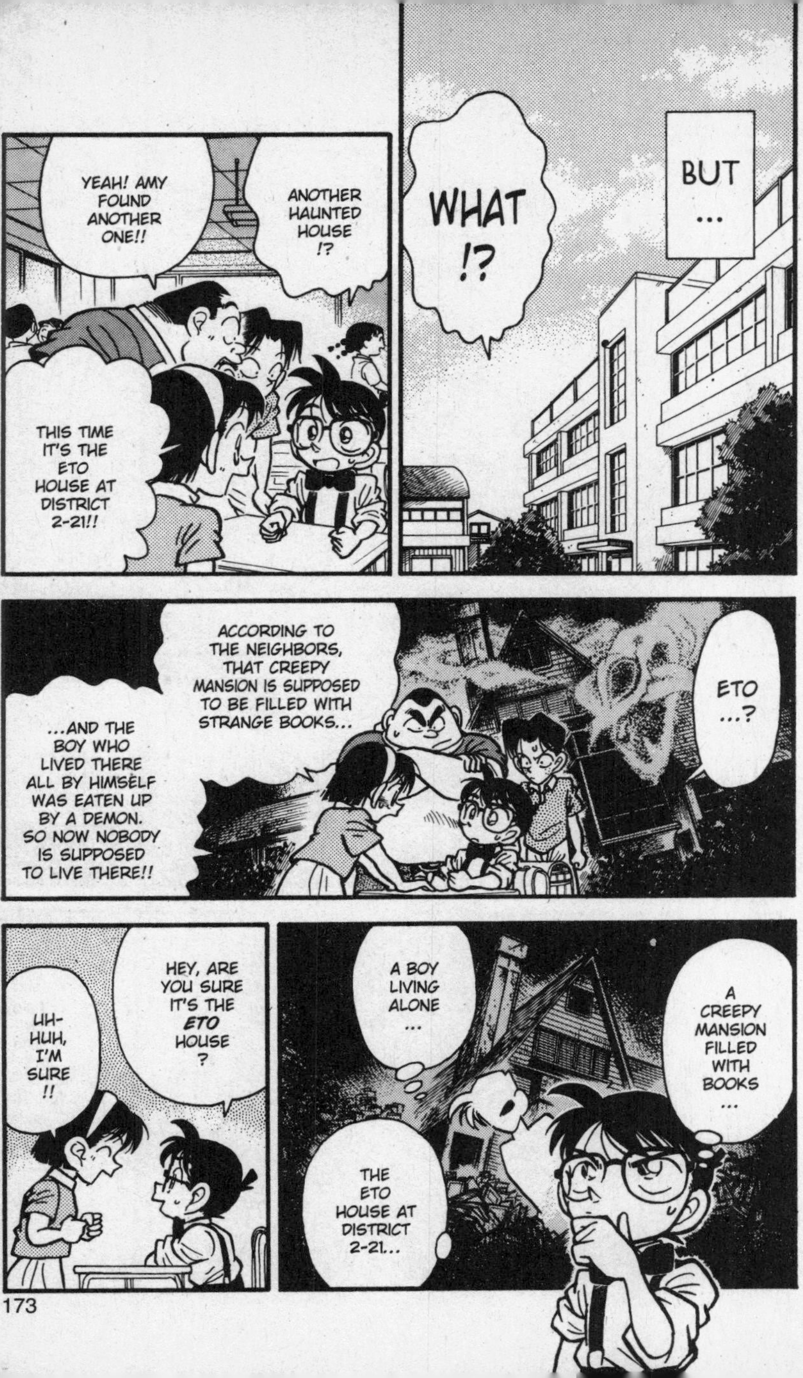
BUT ...
WHAT !?
ANOTHER HAUNTED HOUSE !?
YEAH! AMY FOUND ANOTHER ONE!!
THIS TIME IT'S THE ETO HOUSE AT DISTRICT 2-21!!
ETO ...?
ACCORDING TO THE NEIGHBORS, THAT CREEPY MANSION IS SUPPOSED TO BE FILLED WITH STRANGE BOOKS...
...AND THE BOY WHO LIVED THERE ALL BY HIMSELF WAS EATEN UP BY A DEMON. SO NOW NOBODY IS SUPPOSED TO LIVE THERE!!
A CREEPY MANSION FILLED WITH BOOKS ...
A BOY LIVING ALONE ...
THE ETO HOUSE AT DISTRICT 2-21...
HEY, ARE YOU SURE IT'S THE *ETO* HOUSE ?
UH-HUH, I'M SURE !!

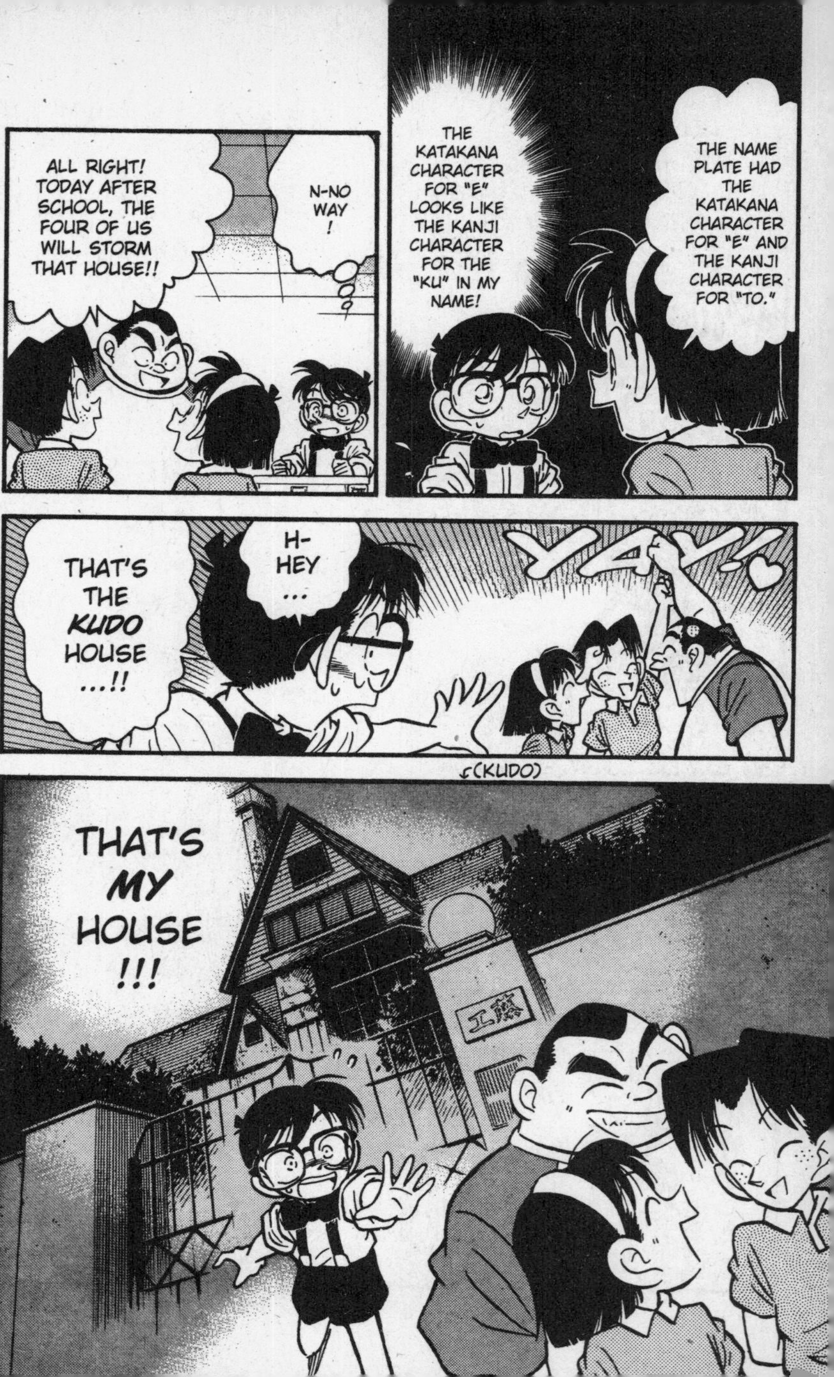
THE NAME PLATE HAD THE KATAKANA CHARACTER FOR "E" AND THE KANJI CHARACTER FOR "TO."
THE KATAKANA CHARACTER FOR "E" LOOKS LIKE THE KANJI CHARACTER FOR THE "KU" IN MY NAME!
N-NO WAY!
ALL RIGHT! TODAY AFTER SCHOOL, THE FOUR OF US WILL STORM THAT HOUSE!!
YAY!♥
H-HEY...
THAT'S THE *KUDO* HOUSE...!!
(KUDO)
THAT'S *MY* HOUSE!!!

END OF VOLUME BONUS PAGES

The Great Private Detective Gosho Aoyama and The Young Men's Detective Club

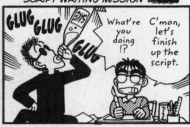

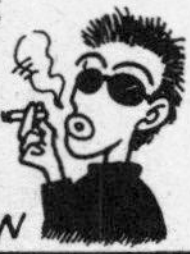

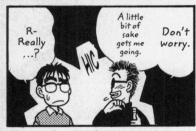

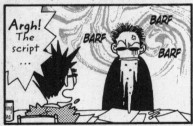

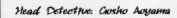

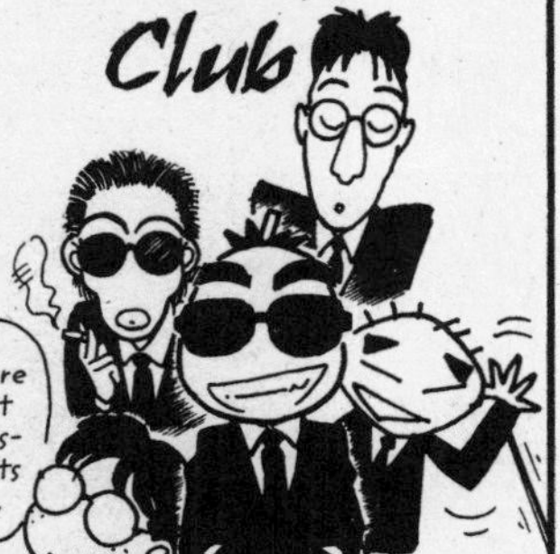

We're just assis-tants ...

Head Detective: Gosho Aoyama

Yutaka Tani Keiji Aso
Eiichi Yamagishi Masaki Negishi

LEAVE IT TO ME!! BY ALCOHOLIC DETECTIVE YUTAKA TANI

FILE 256 THE GREAT SCRIPT WRITING MISSION

C'mon, let's finish up the script.
What're you doing !?
SAKE
GLUG GLUG GLUG
Don't worry.
A little bit of sake gets me going.
HIC
R-Really ...?
BARF
BARF
BARF
Argh! The script ...
Oolong tea
ZZZ
SNAP
Wake up !
Oolong tea

We Are All Friends
BY PUPPET PLAY DETECTIVE YAMA-CHAN

La la la ... Gosho Sensei's desk is a magical desk
Things always disappear from it
Where's my ruler !?
Where's my pencil !?
Why is it gone ?
Tani, find it !!
Again ...
Keep your desk clean!
Look yourself before you ask others!
I'm busy ...
Where !?
It's gotta be around here ...
My pencil disappears on its own!
La dee daa... Want me to pull your tongue out?

Gosho is a Baby
by Frail Detective Keiji Aso

Can you open this?
I've no finger strength left after drawing so much.
Sure.
INK
PLIK
Open this too.
You know, I lack finger strength!
Yeah, yeah.
POP
This too.
All this work makes my fingers ...
P-PUSHUUU...
Fine, okay ...
烏龍茶
(Oolong tea)
Open it. I don't have the strength !!
This "Case" is going to be put to a close right here and now!
CLICK CLICK

Common Occurrence
by Chubby Detective
Masaki Negishi

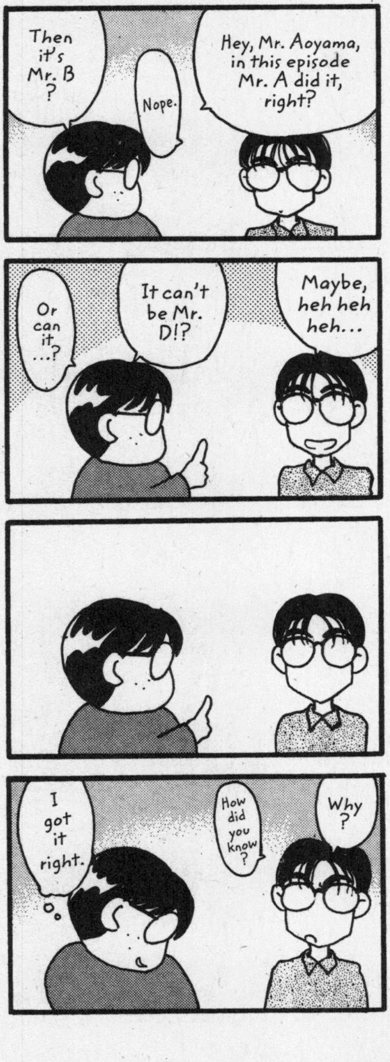
Hey, Mr. Aoyama, in this episode Mr. A did it, right?
Nope.
Then it's Mr. B?
Maybe, heh heh heh...
It can't be Mr. D!?
Or can it...?
Why?
How did you know?
I got it right.

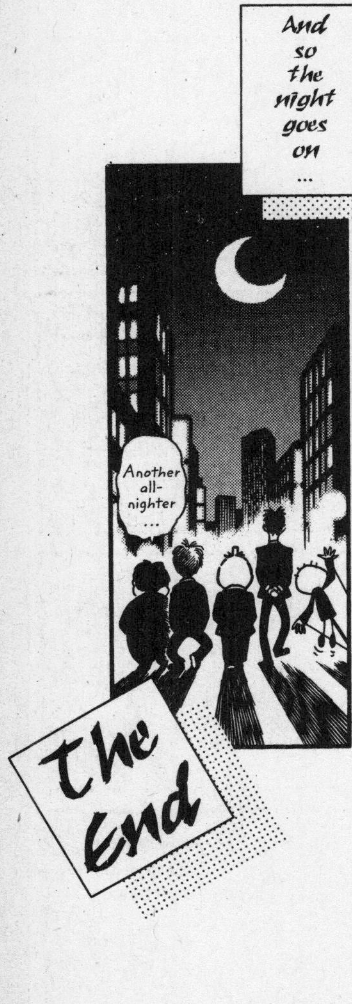
And so the night goes on ...
Another all-nighter ...
The End

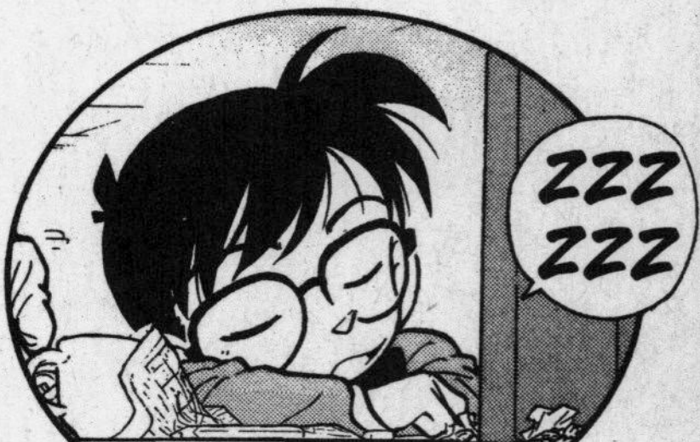
ZZZ
ZZZ

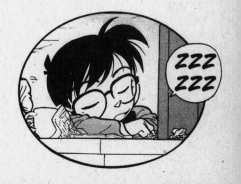

Hello, Aoyama here.

Recently, I've been watching a lot of mysteries on TV and at the movies. Maybe it's because I'm working on this series. When I'm watching these mysteries, I enjoy them... The only thing is that I suffer from nightmares every night... And I'm already low on sleep because of my busy schedule. Woe is me! (sob sob...)

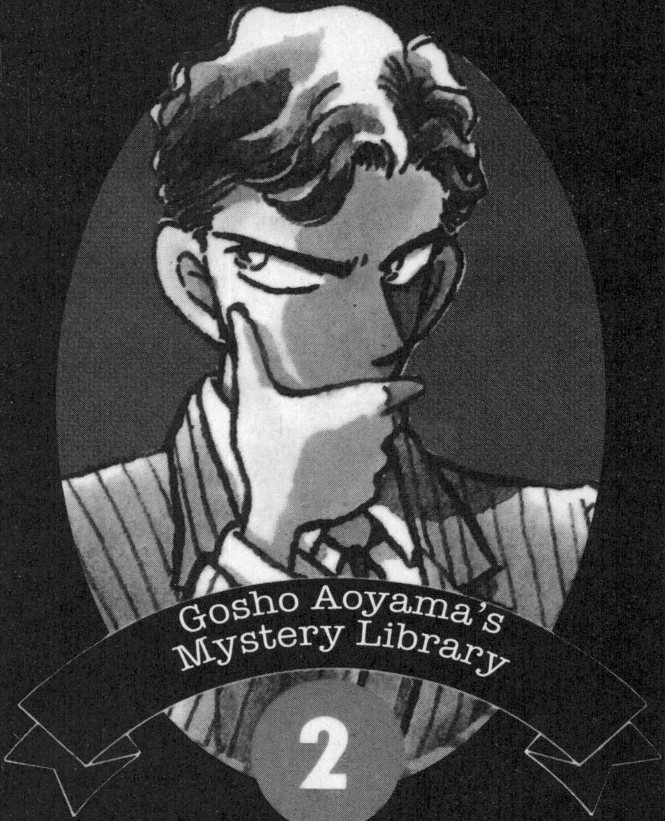
Gosho Aoyama's
Mystery Library
2

KOGORO AKECHI

Richard Moore's name in the original Japanese version of Detective Conan is Kogoro Mori. This name is inspired by the famous Japanese detective, Kogoro Akechi, a character created by author Edogawa Rampo. Most people picture Akechi as a dandy young gentleman, however, he was first introduced with unkempt hair wearing dirty Japanese style clothes. He lived surrounded by books in a four and a half mat room (approximately 4' x 5') on the second floor of a tobacco shop. Emphasizing the human psyche over hard evidence, Akechi uses psychology in his criminal investigations. Readers beware: Akechi is a master of disguise! The cases he handles are usually shrouded in the bizarre and surreal. For those who are faint of heart such as myself, it would be wise not to read these stories alone late at night. I recommend **Ogon Kamen** ("Golden Mask").

COMPLETE OUR SURVEY AND LET
US KNOW WHAT YOU THINK!

☐ Please do NOT send me information about VIZ products, news and events, special offers, or other information.

☐ Please do NOT send me information from VIZ's trusted business partners.

Name: _____

Address: _____

City: _____ **State:** _____ **Zip:** _____

E-mail: _____

☐ Male ☐ Female **Date of Birth** (mm/dd/yyyy): ___/___/_____ (Under 13? Parental consent required)

What race/ethnicity do you consider yourself? (please check one)

☐ Asian/Pacific Islander ☐ Black/African American ☐ Hispanic/Latino

☐ Native American/Alaskan Native ☐ White/Caucasian ☐ Other: _____

What VIZ product did you purchase? (check all that apply and indicate title purchased)

☐ DVD/VHS _____

☐ Graphic Novel _____

☐ Magazines _____

☐ Merchandise _____

Reason for purchase: (check all that apply)

☐ Special offer ☐ Favorite title ☐ Gift

☐ Recommendation ☐ Other _____

Where did you make your purchase? (please check one)

☐ Comic store ☐ Bookstore ☐ Mass/Grocery Store

☐ Newsstand ☐ Video/Video Game Store ☐ Other: _____

☐ Online (site: _____)

What other VIZ properties have you purchased/own? _____

_____

How many anime and/or manga titles have you purchased in the last year? How many were VIZ titles? **(please check one from each column)**

ANIME	MANGA	VIZ
☐ None	☐ None	☐ None
☐ 1-4	☐ 1-4	☐ 1-4
☐ 5-10	☐ 5-10	☐ 5-10
☐ 11+	☐ 11+	☐ 11+

I find the pricing of VIZ products to be: (please check one)

☐ Cheap ☐ Reasonable ☐ Expensive

What genre of manga and anime would you like to see from VIZ? (please check two)

☐ Adventure ☐ Comic Strip ☐ Science Fiction ☐ Fighting

☐ Horror ☐ Romance ☐ Fantasy ☐ Sports

What do you think of VIZ's new look?

☐ Love It ☐ It's OK ☐ Hate It ☐ Didn't Notice ☐ No Opinion

Which do you prefer? (please check one)

☐ Reading right-to-left

☐ Reading left-to-right

Which do you prefer? (please check one)

☐ Sound effects in English

☐ Sound effects in Japanese with English captions

☐ Sound effects in Japanese only with a glossary at the back

THANK YOU! Please send the completed form to:

VIZ Survey
42 Catharine St.
Poughkeepsie, NY 12601

All information provided will be used for internal purposes only. We promise not to sell or otherwise divulge your information.